Resisting Protectionism

HELEN V. MILNER

Resisting Protectionism

Global Industries and the Politics of International Trade

PRINCETON UNIVERSITY PRESS

PRINCETON, NEW JERSEY

Published by Princeton University Press, 41 William Street,
Princeton, New Jersey 08540
In the United Kingdom: Princeton University Press, Guildford, Surrey

Publication of this book has been aided by the Whitney Darrow Fund
of Princeton University Press

This book has been composed in Linotron Baskerville

Clothbound editions of Princeton University Press books
are printed on acid-free paper, and binding materials are
chosen for strength and durability. Paperbacks, although
satisfactory for personal collections, are not usually
suitable for library rebinding

Printed in the United States of America by
Princeton University Press, Princeton, New Jersey

Library of Congress Cataloging-in-Publication Data

Milner, Helen V., 1958–
Resisting protectionism : global industries and the politics
of international trade / Helen V. Milner.
    p. cm.   Bibliography: p.   Includes Index.
ISBN 0-691-05670-6 (alk. paper)
1. Free trade and protection. 2. International business
enterprises. 3. International trade. 4. Tariff—
United States—Case Studies. 5. Tariff—France—
Case studies. I. Title.
HF1713.M56 1988   382.7—dc19   88-9945

To my Mom and Dad

CONTENTS

viii   Contents

LIST OF TABLES

THIS BOOK began as the result of a lengthy argument with one of my dissertation advisors about *American Business and Public Policy*, by Raymond Bauer, Ithiel de Sola Pool, and Lewis Dexter. Long a standard work in the field, it did not seem to me to capture the flavor of trade politics today, especially in its discussion of firms and their role in the process. The book was, however, one of the few I knew that actually looked at the question of how firms developed political preferences. I wondered whether firms' preferences were as ill-defined and as unrelated to self-interest as the book suggested they often were. Moreover, I questioned whether Congress, and the U.S. government in general, was as unconstrained in trade politics as these authors described.

My interest in firms' preferences also led me to ask whether antiprotectionist groups existed in the domestic political economy. Most previous studies of trade politics had focused on pressures *for* protection. Indeed, theoretical work on collective goods implied that antiprotectionist groups were unlikely to voice their preference, let alone oppose the protectionists. Bauer, Pool, and Dexter's work was to some extent the exception to this. Although they too concluded that protectionists were much more likely to act politically, they did find growing free trade sentiment among American businesses in the early 1950s. I wanted to determine whether antiprotectionist preferences were evident among firms and whether they were strong enough to motivate firms to fight protectionist influences. I found that firms may develop both protectionist and antiprotectionist preferences and act on both.

In addition, Bauer, Pool, and Dexter's argument about the autonomy of Congress from societal actors foreshadowed the current debate over the relative autonomy of the state and the question of state "structure." Bauer, Pool, and Dexter attributed the autonomy of Congress more to its overall structure and less to the particular policy-making process in trade issues. Their conclusion was similar to current arguments about the relative autonomy of "strong" states, but it contradicted various state-structure arguments which concluded that the U.S. government in fact lacked freedom from industry pressure, especially in the trade area. This contradiction perplexed me. Why does the state appear differentially constrained by domestic societal forces?

Though I have not directly answered that question here, it has motivated my thinking about the relationship between states and firms.

One way to explore this issue further was to compare two states whose relations with domestic societal groups supposedly differed. France was an obvious choice, because unlike the United States, it was seen by many as having a "strong" state. The U.S.–France comparison also served to test my arguments about firms' trade policy preferences. Did the same types of factors drive firms' preferences in the two countries? And could antiprotectionist preferences develop among French firms, which had historically tended to be ardent protectionists? The answers to these two questions reached below may surprise those who assume that the two countries are very different, especially in their governments' relationships with industry.

PORTIONS of the argument made here have appeared before. A condensed analysis of the comparison of American and French trade politics appeared in my article, "Resisting the Protectionist Temptation: Industry and the Making of Trade Policy in France and the U.S. in the 1970s," *International Organization* 41 (Autumn 1987). Elements of the comparison of the United States in the 1920s and the United States in the 1970s appear in another article, "Trading Places: Industries for Free Trade," *World Politics* 40 (April 1988).

I owe thanks to many people for their help in making this book possible. My parents supported all of my work, as well as me, for the longest of times. I can never thank them enough. I only wish I had finished earlier so that my father could have seen the book. Other than my family, the one to whom I owe the deepest debt is Robert O. Keohane. Not only did he initially spark my interest in international political economy and graduate work, but he also guided me through graduate school. In listening to complaints, reading endless versions of the dissertation and book, encouraging me, and sharing his own work and thoughts, he made the difference. My other Ph.D. advisors, Robert Putnam, Stephan Haggard, and Peter Hall, have also been most generous with their time and helpful in their comments. I also wish to thank David Baldwin, Peter Cowhey, Jeffry Frieden, Peter Gourevitch, Joanne Gowa, Peter Katzenstein, Charles Lipson, Mary Musca, John Odell, John Ruggie, Duncan Snidal, Jack Snyder, and Ezra Suleiman, who read all or part of the book and offered helpful criticisms. I am also indebted to Sanford G. Thatcher and Elizabeth Gretz of Princeton University Press for their close scrutiny of the manuscript and wise editorial advice. The Brookings Institution, the Atlantic Institute, Columbia University, and Columbia's Council on Research in the Humanities and Social Sciences helped make this book possible by providing office space and other essential resources.

New York City
October 1987

Resisting Protectionism

CHAPTER 1

Introduction

HOW CAN STATES resist the temptation to protect their markets in times of economic distress and mounting foreign competition? If closure of their domestic markets is a natural response by states to serious economic difficulties, as has been the case historically, how can we explain the maintenance of open markets in times of widespread economic recession and instability? A broad understanding of international trade policy formation—one that goes beyond the usual focus on the sources of protectionism—is necessary to answer these questions. As a response to economic difficulties, protectionism not only has strong intuitive appeal but also has been much examined. But states' decisions *not* to protect their markets need more attention.

Choices about the degree of openness of a state's markets are quintessentially political ones. They entail decisions about the societal allocation of the costs and benefits of economic change. Moreover, these policy choices have undeniable political significance. For example, a key issue of the late 1980s is whether, in response to economic distress, the United States will close its markets to foreign products. Should it do so, it would completely alter the postwar international trading system and reshape the domestic political economy.

In addition to being politically relevant, exploring how trade policy is developed is interesting theoretically. The formulation of a nation's trade policy involves a struggle among domestic groups, the national government, and foreign governments. The complex interactions of these groups provide insights into the relationship between domestic and international politics. Furthermore, this struggle brings to light connections between politics and economics. It shows how the existing distribution of power among actors influences their ability to obtain the economic policies they desire and thereby affects the distribution of wealth. It also may reveal how the current distribution of wealth affects the influence these groups can wield. By illuminating relationships not only between domestic and international forces but also between political and economic ones, the analysis of trade policy making can advance our knowledge of the dynamics of the political economy.

THE PUZZLE

This study examines trade policy formulation in two periods—the 1920s (1921-31) and the 1970s (1971-81)—when certain pressures for protectionism were quite intense. According to several well-accepted explanations of trade policy, two conditions ignite protectionist sentiment. The first involves economic downturns; in this view, economic depressions, instability, and rising foreign competition contribute to the growth of protectionist pressures.[1] Second, the decline of the international economy's dominant state—the hegemon—has been seen as a precipitant for protectionist policies.[2] In light of these arguments, the serious economic difficulties and the declining power of the reigning hegemon in both the 1920s and the 1970s might have been expected to produce similar protectionist responses in the two periods.

Indeed the history of the 1920s has been frequently cited as an analogy for the 1970s. Casual observers predicted the coming of a protectionist spiral in the 1970s and 1980s equivalent to that of the 1920s.[3] Moreover, theorists of international political economy drawing parallels between the decline of American dominance since the 1960s and the erosion of British hegemony after the 1910s also anticipated the adoption of trade policies in the 1970s resembling those of the 1920s. Robert Gilpin has claimed that "the dominant economy itself [i.e., the United States] is in relative decline and is being challenged by rising centers of economic power. With the decline of the dominant eco-

---

[1] Timothy McKeown, "Firms and Tariff Regime Change," *World Politics* 36 (January 1984):215-33; Giulio Gallarotti, "Toward a Business Cycle Model of Tariffs," *International Organization* 39 (Winter 1985):155-87; Wendy Takacs, "Pressures for Protection: An Empirical Study," *Economic Inquiry* 19 (1981):687-93; Susan Strange and Roger Tooze, eds., *The International Politics of Surplus Capacity* (London: Butterworths, 1980).

[2] Charles Kindleberger, *The World in Depression, 1929-39,* (Berkeley: University of California Press, 1973), pp. 307-308; David Lake, "Structure and Strategy: The International Sources of American Trade Policy, 1887-1939" (Ph.D. dissertation, Cornell University, 1983); Robert Gilpin, *U.S. Power and the Multinational Corporation* (New York: Basic Books, 1975); Charles Kindleberger, "Dominance and Leadership in the International Economy," *International Studies Quarterly* 25 (June 1981):242-54; Robert Gilpin, *War and Change in World Politics* (Cambridge: Cambridge University Press, 1981). For more skeptical views, see Stephen Krasner, "State Power and the Structure of International Trade," *World Politics* 28 (April 1976):317-47; Robert Keohane, "The Theory of Hegemonic Stability and Changes in International Economic Regimes," in *Change in the International System*, ed. Ole R. Holsti, Randolph M. Siverson, and Alexander L. George (Boulder, Colo.: Westview, 1980), pp. 131-62.

[3] Examples are Harald Malmgren, "Coming Trade Wars?" *Foreign Policy*, no. 1 (Winter 1970):115-43; C. Fred Bergsten, "The Crisis in U.S. Trade Policy," *Foreign Affairs* 49 (July 1971):619-35; June Kronholz, "Trade and Currency Wars Deepen the Depression," *Wall Street Journal*, October 23, 1979, p. 1.

nomic power, the world economy may be following the pattern of the latter part of the nineteenth century and of the 1930s: it may be fragmenting into regional trading centers, exclusive economic alliances, and economic nationalism."[4]

Despite these predictions, substantial differences in trade policy outcomes characterized the two periods. This puzzle can be better appreciated if the similar preconditions yet different policy outcomes in the two periods are examined in more detail.

Serious economic distress and instability have been seen as a key precondition for rising protectionist activity. As one economist has noted:

> It is generally agreed that in a modern industrial economy the cyclical state of the economy and the country's competitive position internationally are the principal determinants of the degree of protectionist pressure. Low levels of economic activity, high unemployment, unused capacity, trade deficits, rapid increases in imports, and increases in import penetration all operate to increase the temptation to protect domestic industries from import competition.[5]

Economic difficulties were strikingly similar in Western Europe and the United States in the 1920s and 1970s, marked in particular by relatively high unemployment rates and sizable agricultural and industrial overcapacity. In the 1920s these economies suffered two major downturns—in 1920-23 and 1929-33. Price fluctuations, labor unrest, and international monetary problems created further economic instability.[6] In the 1970s these economies again experienced serious recessions in 1973-75 and 1978-82. Sparked by the oil price increases, these downturns were aggravated by rapidly shifting trade patterns, price volatility, and a confused international monetary situation. These high levels of economic distress were expected to prompt high levels of protectionism.

Indeed, given the absolute levels of economic difficulty in the two periods, the 1970s might have seen even greater levels of market clo-

---

[4] Gilpin, *U.S. Power*, pp. 258-59.

[5] Takacs, "Pressures for Protection," p. 687.

[6] See Derek Aldcroft, *From Versailles to Wall Street, 1919-1929* (Berkeley: University of California Press, 1981), chs. 3-11; W. Arthur Lewis, *Economic Survey, 1919-1939* (London: Allen, Unwin, 1949); U.S. Dept. of Commerce, *Survey of Current Business*, various issues (Washington, D.C.: GPO, 1919-1930); U.S. Dept. of Commerce, Bureau of the Census, *Historical Statistics of the U.S., Colonial Times to the Present* (Washington, D.C.: GPO, 1975); Kindleberger, *World in Depression*, esp. chs. 5-8; League of Nations, *Economic Fluctuations in the U.S. and U.K., 1918-1942* (Geneva: League of Nations, 1942); Martin Feldstein, ed., *The American Economy in Transition* (Chicago: NBER, 1980), p. 12.

sure than the 1920s.[7] For instance, in the United States the averages for three major economic indicators were all worse in the 1970s than in the 1920s, as table 1.1 indicates. This suggests that if economic difficulty is a precursor to protectionism, the 1970s should have experienced a significant protectionist resurgence.

A second similarity between the 1920s and 1970s linked to protectionist outbreaks is the decline of the world's hegemonic state. In the 1920s, the hegemon of the nineteenth century, Great Britain, was rapidly losing its status. From a peak of 24 percent in 1870, Great Britain's share of world trade fell to 14 percent before World War I.[8] Its share of the world's manufacturing output tumbled from a dominant 32 percent in 1870 to a third-rate level of 14 percent by 1913, as Germany and the United States overtook it in industrial competitiveness in certain critical, advanced sectors.[9] Moreover, Britain's control over the international monetary system was declining. Its problems in returning to and maintaining the gold standard in the 1920s, as well as its final abandonment of that system in 1931, signaled this loss of influence.

A fairly similar situation existed in the 1970s. By the early part of

TABLE 1.1 A Comparison of U.S. Economic Conditions in the 1920s and 1970s (in percent)

	1923-29	1973-79
Average annual growth in real GNP	3.1	2.3
Average mean value of unemployment rate	3.5	6.8
Average value of nonresidential fixed investment to GNP	11.2	10.2

SOURCE: Martin Feldstein, ed., *The American Economy in Transition* (Chicago: NBER, 1980), pp. 104-105.

[7] Sidney Ratner, James Soltow, and Richard Sylla, *The Evolution of the American Economy* (New York: Basic Books, 1979), pp. 482, 502. The worst economic difficulties of the Great Depression, occurring in the early 1930s, followed, rather than preceded, the tariff increases. For instance, unemployment averaged 3 percent in 1930, the year Smoot-Hawley was passed, but rose to 25 percent by 1933, the year before the RTAA.

[8] David Lake, "International Economic Structures and American Foreign Economic Policy," *World Politics* 35 (July 1983):525, table 1.

[9] Ratner, Soltow, and Sylla, *Evolution of American Economy*, p. 385.

the decade, the global dominance the United States had exercised in the 1950s and 1960s had been reduced substantially as it was challenged by other nations. The United States' share of world trade dropped from 18.4 percent in 1950 to 13.4 percent in 1977.[10] More telling, its share of the world's manufactured exports plummeted from a peak of nearly 30 percent in 1953 to about 13 percent by the late 1970s.[11] In addition, from a dominant 62 percent in 1950, its share of the world's manufacturing output had dropped to 44 percent by 1977.[12] Many American industries had lost their comparative advantages and faced bitter competition at home and abroad. The hegemony of the United States in the international monetary system was also somewhat diminished. By 1973, it had scuttled the monetary system it had created and found itself unable to fashion or direct a new, stable one. U.S. hegemony in monetary relations in the 1970s was not as limited as was Britain's in the 1920s.[13] But American hegemony, especially in trade and production, had declined substantially by the 1970s, leaving the international distribution of power in the 1970s more similar to that of the interwar period than to that of the immediate post–World War II period. This eclipse of hegemony was expected to produce greatly increased protectionism, as it had in the 1920s.

Though a situation of declining hegemony existed in both the 1920s and the 1970s, this may be less important for explaining our puzzle than the relative position held by the United States during the two periods. The United States' international economic position relative to other countries was very similar in the late 1920s and late 1970s. Moreover, its position at these two times was very different from the one it held in the 1950s and 1960s. The United States' share of the world's manufacturing output reached 42 percent in 1929; similarly, as noted above, in 1977 it had leveled off at 44 percent.[14] In contrast, the United States absolutely dominated in the 1950s and 1960s, con-

---

[10] Lake, "International Economic Structures," p. 541, table 3; Robert Keohane and Joseph Nye, *Power and Interdependence: World Politics in Transition* (Boston: Little, Brown, 1977), p. 141.

[11] Feldstein, *American Economy*, pp. 193, 196.

[12] Ibid., p. 191.

[13] U.S. hegemony in money was much less diminished than in trade. Its ending of the Bretton Woods system was more an act of power than of weakness, according to many analysts. See Keohane and Nye, *Power and Interdependence*, pp. 141, 165-86; John Odell, *U.S. International Monetary Policy: Markets, Power, and Ideas as Sources of Change* (Princeton: Princeton University Press, 1982), ch. 4, esp. p. 219.

[14] Ratner, Soltow, and Sylla, *Evolution of American Economy*, p. 464; Feldstein, *American Economy*, p. 191.

trolling between two-thirds and one-half of all such output in the 1950s and early 1960s.[15] In trade the U.S. position was similar in the 1920s and the 1970s. Although it had greater control in the 1920s than in the 1970s, it was nowhere near as dominant at either time as it was in the 1950s. In the 1920s it was the world's largest exporter and biggest foreign investor and ranked second only to Britain in its imports.[16] By the late 1970s, the United States was only the world's second largest exporter of manufactures; its 13 percent was topped by West Germany with almost 16 percent and was being challenged by Japan, which held 11 percent.[17] In contrast, the United States reigned supreme in trade in 1953, controlling nearly 30 percent of all manufactured exports.[18]

A similar story is told by changes in other measures of economic strength. In terms of its relative economic size and productivity, the United States' position was almost identical in 1929 and 1977.[19] Again the contrast to its clear predominance in 1950 is striking. Moreover, in both 1929 and 1977 the United States was similarly situated relative to its nearest rivals. In 1929 it led all countries, barely edging out Britain while retaining a substantial lead over France and Germany. In 1977, it was virtually even with West Germany but still outdistanced Japan and France.

Hence, two strong similarities in the international distribution of economic power existed in the 1920s and 1970s. In both a hegemon was in decline; and in both the United States' relative economic position was slightly superior to all others but was gravely challenged by several nations. These conditions in the international economic structure have been linked to rising protectionism and thus might have been expected to engender similar protectionist responses in the two periods.[20]

The argument here is not that in all respects the 1920s and the 1970s were alike. Two important differences existed that may attenuate the comparison. First, the United States was a rising hegemon in the 1920s and a declining one in the 1970s. Though hegemonic stability arguments offer no theoretical reason to expect this difference

---

[15] Feldstein, *American Economy*, p. 191.

[16] Ratner, Soltow, and Sylla, *Evolution of American Economy*, p. 464.

[17] Feldstein, *American Economy*, pp. 196-97.

[18] Ibid.

[19] David Lake, "Beneath the Commerce of Nations," *International Studies Quarterly* 28 (June 1984):143-70, figures 5, 6.

[20] See ibid. I differ with Lake's interpretation of these two structures and their differences.

to affect the hegemon's trade policy, some scholars have argued for the notion of a lag. They suggest that a rising hegemon may fail to appreciate its own significance and that a declining one may not understand its weakness and need for closure. This difference may account for dissimilarities between the two periods. But such a lag has been attributed to entrenched domestic interests, about which the theory has little to say.[21]

Second, the monetary systems operating at the two times differed. In the 1920s there was a shift from a managed, flexible exchange rate system before 1925 to a fixed, gold standard system until 1931. In the 1970s the opposite movement occurred: from a fixed, dollar-gold standard to a managed, flexible rate system by 1973. The consequences of these two different systems for trade policy are unclear, however. The effects of different exchange rate systems on trade are not well understood. Some have claimed that flexible rates should hinder protectionism because such barriers are nullified by exchange rate changes.[22] Others maintain that flexible rates augment protectionist pressures by increasing risk and that fixed rates are best for ensuring free trade.[23] It seems fair to say that the exchange rate systems operating in these two periods did little to provide a stable environment for international trade.[24]

Despite these differences, the 1920s and the 1970s were similar in

---

[21] Krasner, "State Power," argues that the lag during the interwar period and since the 1960s is due to entrenched domestic interests. The argument here can thus be seen as complementary to his, because it suggests which domestic interests were resisting protection in the later period.

[22] Herbert Grubel, *International Economics* (Homewood, Ill.: Irwin, 1977), ch. 22; Charles Kindleberger and Peter Lindert, *International Economics*, 6th ed. (Homewood, Ill.: Irwin, 1978), ch. 21; Robert Baldwin and J. David Richardson, *International Trade and Finance*, 3rd ed. (Boston: Little, Brown, 1986), ch. 21.

[23] C. Fred Bergsten and William Cline, "Trade Policy in the 1980s: An Overview," in *Trade Policy in the 1980's*, ed. William Cline (Washington, D.C.: Institute for International Economics, 1983), pp. 59-98.

[24] Kindleberger and Lindert, *International Economics*, ch. 21, esp. figure 21.5. A related issue is whether the value of U.S. exchange rates affected trade policy differentially in the two periods. The claim is that the level of exchange rates was driving trade policy, especially in the 1970s. Thus the relative undervaluation of the dollar in the late 1970s weakened protectionist pressures, and its overvaluation in the early 1980s led to new pressures for barriers. The problem with this argument is that the 1920s look very similar. The U.S. dollar appears undervalued in general after World War I, once again supposedly mitigating protectionist pressures. But by the late 1920s the dollar seems overvalued relative to the mark, lira, franc, and gold, although undervalued relative to sterling. Differences in exchange rate levels, then, do not seem to differentiate the two periods a great deal. For evidence, see ibid., ch. 21, figure 21.3. Note how all other currencies rise in value against the dollar after the 1931 change.

terms of their economic difficulties and the relative economic position of the United States. According to other theories, these conditions should have led to similar trade policy outcomes in the two periods. The 1970s, however, were not marked by the extensive closure of the U.S. market that occurred in the 1920s. Throughout the 1920s Western Europe and the United States responded to their economic difficulties by adopting successively more protectionist trade policies. In the United States, protectionist sentiment reignited after World War I. Industries, fearing renewed European competition, and agriculture, stunned by rapid price deflation, demanded that the government protect them.[25] As a result, in 1921 the Emergency Tariff Bill was enacted; in 1922, this interim act was institutionalized in the Fordney-McCumber Tariff, which raised import duties to an average of 38 percent, much above those of the 1913 Underwood Tariff.[26] Finally, in 1930 the Smoot-Hawley Tariff Bill was enacted. This bill represented the zenith of American protectionism; it elevated tariff rates to an average of 45 percent, with duties over 50 percent on some important items.[27]

Western Europe experienced a similar trend in the 1920s. Political chaos and recession after World War I led to the erection of new trade barriers throughout Europe.[28] For example, in 1921 Britain abandoned its long-standing commitment to open markets and raised import duties through the Safeguarding of Industries Act. France acted similarly, elevating specific duties through government fiat.[29] Trade barriers in these countries and in Germany were increased further in the late 1920s. After 1926, monetary instability, agricultural price deflation, and social unrest ignited more protectionist pressure, eventually prompting new tariff and quota legislation.[30] The Smoot-Hawley

[25] Sidney Ratner, *The Tariff in American History* (New York: Van Nostrand, 1972), pp. 47-48; Frank Taussig, *The Tariff History of the U.S.*, 8th ed. (New York: Putnam & Sons, 1931), pp. 449-54; William Kelly, ed., *Studies in U.S. Commercial Policy* (Chapel Hill: University of North Carolina Press, 1963), pp. 6-8.

[26] U.S. Tariff Commission (USTC), *Trade Barriers: An Overview*, pub. no. 665 (Washington, D.C.: GPO, 1974), 1:80.

[27] Ibid., 1:80; Ratner, *Tariff in American History*, p. 51.

[28] H. Liepmann, *Tariff Levels and the Economic Unity of Europe* (New York: Macmillan, 1938), pp. 111-33; Arthur Isaacs, *International Trade: Tariff and Commercial Policies* (Chicago: Irwin, 1948), pp. 352-79.

[29] For Britain, see the National Institute of Economic and Social Research (NIESR), *Trade Regulations and Commercial Policy in the U.K.* (Cambridge: Cambridge University Press, 1943), pp. 13-20. For France, see Frank Haight, *The History of French Commercial Policies* (New York: Macmillan, 1941), pp. 108-112.

[30] NIESR, *Trade Regulations*, pp. 20-29; Haight, *French Commercial Policies*, p. 18; Liepmann, *Tariff Levels*, pp. 341-45.

Tariff provoked European retaliation, leading to new trade restrictions matching, if not surpassing, those of the United States. This spiraling protectionism culminated in the early 1930s when, in conjunction with the global depression, it helped depress the volume of world trade by over 60 percent.[31]

In the 1970s the advanced industrial countries maintained relatively open markets for industrial goods. In fact, tariff barriers affecting industrial goods were reduced substantially, as the Kennedy Round Agreements of the General Agreement on Tariffs and Trade (GATT) were phased in and the Tokyo Round negotiations were completed. By 1971, average tariff rates for the industrial countries were approximately 10 percent; by 1979 these rates were cut to less than 5 percent.[32] For the United States, these reductions meant that between 1933 and 1974 average tariff duties on manufactured products had been slashed by 72 percent.[33]

On the other hand, nontariff barriers (NTBs) to trade grew in importance. Although these barriers remain difficult to measure and were not measured while tariffs remained high, their relative importance increased in the late 1970s. By that time, nearly 30 percent of all categories (not values) of American manufactured imports were affected by them, and similar proportions of traded goods were sheltered in Japan and Western Europe.[34] These barriers have not been that restrictive, however. They have had a limited effect on the volume of trade, unlike in the 1930s, as global and U.S. trade has continued to grow throughout the 1970s and to grow faster than production. One empirical study concludes that these new NTBs have had only limited protectionist effects; the authors point out, "on average over a full range of manufactured products, the protection given by NTBs that may limit or reduce imports . . . is not nearly as large as the protection afforded by tariffs . . . or natural barriers to trade."[35] Further, they project that "if the United States continues on its present policy course, the U.S. economy will be considerably more open in 1985 than it was in 1976."[36] Overall, despite the growth of these new trade bar-

[31] Kindleberger, *World in Depression*, p. 172; see in general, Joseph Jones, *Tariff Retaliation: Repercussions of the Smoot-Hawley Bill* (Philadelphia: University of Pennsylvania, 1934), pp. 1-34.

[32] USTC, *Trade Barriers*, pp. 81-82.

[33] Ibid., p. 9.

[34] Robert Reich, "Beyond Free Trade," *Foreign Affairs* 61 (Spring 1983):786.

[35] Peter Morici and Laura Megna, *U.S. Economic Policies Affecting Industrial Trade: A Quantitative Assessment* (Washington, D.C.: National Planning Association, 1983), p. 11.

[36] Ibid., p. 103.

riers during the 1970s, a protectionist spiral like that of the 1920s was not apparent. A small net increase in protection may have occurred by the early 1980s, but this increase did not approach the levels of the 1920s and early 1930s even though two key preconditions—serious economic distress and declining hegemony—characterized both periods. Given the very fertile ground of the late 1970s, protectionism could have grown like a weed, as it did in the 1920s. For some reason, it did not.

OTHER EXPLANATIONS

The puzzle, then, is why trade policy was markedly different in the 1920s and 1970s when key pressures influencing it were similar. This question has been addressed by a number of other studies; three explanations are particularly important.

One type of explanation examines the international distribution of power. These explanations involve three modifications of the hegemonic stability thesis, which, as has been shown, cannot in its original form explain the different policy outcomes of the 1920s and 1970s.[37] First, some have said that American hegemony has not declined enough to set off the expected protectionist response.[38] It is argued that even though other countries have caught up with the United States, it still remains the strongest, especially when its military might is included. This view depends on the United States' military capabilities being an important factor in its trade policy considerations. The fungibility of these power resources, however, is questionable.[39] A second hegemonic stability argument in fact denies this fungibility. It considers only trade-related power resources, and it also suggests that U.S. hegemony has not declined enough to evoke extensive protectionism.[40] However, relative to its trade position in the 1920s, the United States held a similar, or even less dominant, position in the 1970s. One explanation for this disparity is the lag phenomenon dis-

[37] Krasner, "State Power," casts doubt on the argument.

[38] Bruce Russett, "The Mysterious Case of Vanishing Hegemony," *International Organization* 39 (Spring 1985):207-231; Susan Strange, "Still an Extraordinary Power," in *Political Economy of International and Domestic Monetary Relations*, ed. Lombra and Witte (Ames: Iowa State University Press, 1982).

[39] David Baldwin, "Power Analysis and World Politics," *World Politics* 31 (January 1979):161-94; Keohane and Nye, *Power and Interdependence*, ch. 2.

[40] Keohane and Nye, *Power and Interdependence*, ch. 3; Robert Keohane, *After Hegemony: Cooperation and Discord in the World Political Economy* (Princeton: Princeton University Press, 1985), chs. 4, 9; Vinod Aggarwal, *Liberal Protectionism: The International Politics of Organized Textile Trade* (Berkeley: University of California Press, 1985), chs. 2, 7.

cussed earlier. But why such a lag occurs is not clear. A third argument that modifies the hegemonic stability thesis proposes that different configurations of states, in terms of their relative economic power, lead to different trade policy outcomes. This argument, however, has trouble explaining the differences between the 1920s and 1970s, since the configuration of states at those two times was very similar.[41]

A second type of explanation focuses on the existence of an international regime in trade. In this view, the GATT system of the postwar period has been partially responsible for the maintenance of a relatively open international economy. In the 1920s, the lack of any such regime helped protectionism spread. The ways GATT is seen to be working against protectionism are numerous. Some claim it operates through the externalization of a norm—e.g., "embedded liberalism"—which promotes trade but also minimizes its domestic costs and hence protectionist demands.[42] Others suggest that the regime and its norms are eventually embodied in domestic policies and practices; that the regime constrains and shapes domestic rules and behavior.[43] Others see the regime as directly encouraging international commerce itself by increasing efficiency.[44] Differences thus exist over exactly how the regime has abated protectionist pressures, but generally it is seen as exerting a brake on domestic pressures for protection in the 1970s.

In these views, however, regimes play only an intermediate role. They are acknowledged as an intervening variable, influencing the preferences, pressures, and practices already established at the domestic and international levels.[45] Examination of these pre-existing factors seems necessary in order to judge exactly what effect the re-

[41] Lake, "Structure and Strategy," esp. ch. 2; Lake, "International Economic Structures," pp. 517-43; Lake, "Commerce of Nations." To overcome this difficulty, Lake makes two arguments. One is that due to the disruption caused by World War I, much greater uncertainty existed in the 1920s, which prompted more protectionist activity. As a second point, he implies that the height of protectionism globally was in the 1930s, not the 1920s, when the structure was somewhat different. Protectionism, however, was rising worldwide throughout the 1920s; it hit its peak in the United States in 1930 and elsewhere by 1933 or 1934. His argument provides a more sophisticated and perhaps more accurate explanation of trade policy outcomes than do other hegemonic stability arguments, but it still has difficulty accounting for the 1920s and 1970s differences.

[42] John Ruggie, "International Regimes, Transactions, and Change," *International Organization* 36 (Spring 1982):379-415.

[43] Charles Lipson, "The Transformation of Trade," *International Organization* 36 (Spring 1982):417-56; Stephanie Lenway, *The Politics of U.S. International Trade* (Boston: Pitman, 1985).

[44] Lipson, "Transformation of Trade."

[45] See Stephen Krasner, ed., "International Regimes," *International Organization* 36 (Spring 1982), esp. the introduction by Krasner.

gime has had. Regime analysis needs to be supplemented by analysis of other domestic and international forces.

A third type of explanation focuses on the structure of the domestic policy-making system. It is argued that though there were pressures for protection in the 1970s, a different policy structure existed that helped defuse them. This structure insulated political actors, especially Congress, from societal demands for protection. The state was therefore able to resist these pressures in the 1970s but not in the 1920s, when the structure was more permeable to societal input. Accounts of how this insulation occurred differ. Most acknowledge the central importance of the shift in tariff-making authority from Congress to the President.[46] Others point to the nature of the relationship between Congress and the executive;[47] some to the way trade policy is made within the executive branch;[48] some to the lessons of the 1930s and the norms and ideology now surrounding those lessons;[49] and others to the way Congress functions and responds to societal pressures.[50]

This proliferation of domestic policy "structures" points out an interesting aspect of the trade policy process. Trade policy is not made within one structure in most countries. Many economic actors are involved in trade matters, and they bring their complaints and pressure to bear on different political actors. No single, coherent national trade policy exists. Policy relating to one sector may differ completely from that concerning another. Trade policy toward automobiles, for example, may differ greatly from that toward wheat, textiles, or telecommunications equipment. Moreover, for each of these industries the influence of different political actors and institutions varies. No one trade policy "structure" exists. Knowing who the relevant domestic ac-

---

[46] Robert Pastor, *Congress and the Politics of U.S. Foreign Economic Policy* (Berkeley: University of California Press, 1980); Judith Goldstein, "The Political Economy of Trade," *American Political Science Review* 80 (March 1986):161-84; I. M. Destler, *American Trade Politics: System under Stress* (Washington, D.C.: Institute for International Economics, 1986).

[47] Pastor, *Politics of U.S. Foreign Economic Policy.*

[48] Roger Porter, *Presidential Decision-Making: The Economic Policy Board* (Cambridge: Cambridge University Press, 1980); Gilbert Winham, "Robert Strauss, the MTN, and the Control of Faction," *Journal of World Trade Law* 14 (September-October 1980):377-97.

[49] Goldstein, "Political Economy of Trade"; Judith Goldstein, "A Reexamination of American Commercial Policy" (Ph.D. dissertation, University of California, Los Angeles, 1983).

[50] E. E. Schattschneider, *Politics, Pressures and the Tariff* (Englewood Cliffs, N.J.: Prentice-Hall, 1935); Raymond Bauer, Ithiel de Sola Pool, and Lewis Dexter, *American Business and Public Policy* (Chicago: Aldine-Atherton, 1972).

tors are and what their trade preferences are is essential for understanding the influence of a sector's policy "structure" on policy outcomes.

THE ARGUMENT IN BRIEF

The argument here differs from the three just outlined. As will be
discussed in detail in chapter 2, I claim that a change in the way domestic and international economies are integrated has affected the
trade preferences of domestic, nonstate actors, and has thus influenced trade policy outcomes. Increased international economic interdependence in the post–World War II period helped prevent the
spread of protectionism in the 1970s and early 1980s. Certain effects
of the greater integration of advanced industrial countries into the international economy altered domestic actors' preferences and thus
worked against recourse to protectionism.

This argument will be examined over time and cross-nationally.
First, firms' trade policy preferences in the 1920s and 1970s are compared. Interdependence should have similar effects in both periods.
Internationally oriented firms in the two periods should have resisted
protectionist urges better than their domestically oriented competitors. Second, this antiprotectionist preference should be evident
among firms in other advanced industrial countries who have experienced these new levels of interdependence. To address this, I examine
the trade policy preferences of firms in two countries, the United
States and France, in the 1970s. My argument predicts that rising international economic integration in the form of exports, multinationality, and global intrafirm trade should have affected firms' preferences *similarly* in the two countries, regardless of other differences.
This finding would be striking, given the frequent characterization of
France and the United States as having distinctly different domestic
political structures.[51]

This study does not provide a complete understanding of all the
factors influencing trade policy. It focuses on corporate trade preferences and does not examine directly the influence of public opinion,
ideology, organized labor, domestic political structure, or other possible factors. But it does control indirectly for these influences. By looking at different industries, at different times, and in different countries, it allows these factors to vary, while showing that the basic

[51] Peter Katzenstein, ed., *Between Power and Plenty: Foreign Economic Policies of Advanced Industrial States* (Madison: University of Wisconsin Press, 1978); John Zysman, *Governments, Markets, and Growth* (Ithaca: Cornell University Press, 1983).

argument still holds: despite variance in these other influences, internationally oriented firms are less protectionist than their domestic colleagues in times of economic adversity.

This study also does not account completely for trade policy outcomes. Its focus is on firms' preferences, not on policy makers' actual decisions. It is asked in the cases below whether these preferences do influence political choices. Chapter 8 explicitly compares the trade policy process in France and the United States and demonstrates how corporate preferences are integrated into the process. I argue that though firms' preferences do not account completely for trade policy outcomes, they play an important and understudied role in shaping them.

This study focuses on the domestic forces responsible for international systemic outcomes—specifically, that the global trading system collapsed into closure in the 1920s and 1930s but remained fairly open in the 1970s. For these outcomes to occur, the major industrial countries in each period had to behave similarly. They had to adopt protection in the 1920s and resist it in the 1970s. Why did this convergent behavior among different states appear? One reason the economic difficulties of the 1920s elicited protectionist responses among most industries in developed countries is that the industries had few international ties; in the 1970s many more industries resisted protectionist urges, despite the economic turmoil, because they were deeply tied to the international economy. Only the responses of industries in France and the United States are surveyed here. That they confirm the argument lends it greater credence but does not confirm that it holds for other countries. Elsewhere other factors may play a more important role either in determining firms' preferences or in shaping trade policy outcomes. Influences such as organized labor, corporatist political structures, and historical tradition, to name a few, may override or attenuate the effects of growing international interdependence on industries. The argument here only suggests an explanation for the different international *systemic* outcomes of the 1920s and 1970s.

This book seeks to contribute to the study of international political economy in three ways. First, it addresses the problem of change in policy over time. Although key questions in international political economy deal with the problem of change, more analyses of policy making at two (or more) points in time are needed to determine how policies are shaped over time. Looking at the 1920s and the 1970s, this work identifies an important force for change—the growing international economic integration of domestic economies. Second, it is hoped that the study's detailed examination of preference formation and policy making among a number of different industries will illuminate how particular factors affect societal actors' determination of their preferences. Under certain conditions societal actors can and do understand the preferences generated by their structural positions within the economy. Comparison across industries also sheds light on the nature of states' trade policies. Developed in myriad ways at any one point in time, the stylized whole called a country's trade policy may really be a collection of often conflicting policies, each designed to address different problems. A third contribution of this work concerns its cross-national aspect. By presenting a detailed and structured comparison of trade policy making among industries in France and the United States, this study identifies and explores the sources of policy across states.

THE PLAN OF THE BOOK

This book has three sections. Chapters 1 and 2 introduce the central question, main argument, and approach. The next section, chapters 3, 4, and 5, presents the case studies, examinations of six U.S. industries in the 1920s, six in the 1970s, and six French industries in the 1970s. The final section, chapters 6, 7, 8, and 9, uses the cases to draw conclusions. Chapter 6 reviews the evidence about firms' trade policy preferences in the three sets of cases and asks whether internationally oriented firms are indeed less protectionist than more domestic ones, even when they face grave economic difficulties. Chapter 7 examines how divisions among firms in an industry affect their ability to realize their preferences. It also looks at other factors influencing firms' capabilities to shape trade policy outcomes. Chapter 8 compares the French and American trade policy processes and considers how even in a "strong state" like France, firms influence trade policy. Chapter 9 places the argument within broader debates in international and comparative political economy.

CHAPTER 2

The Argument

WHY DID American trade policies in the 1970s differ from those in the 1920s, when both periods were characterized by declining hegemony and troubled international economies? I argue that the increased international economic interdependence of the post–World War II period has been a major reason why protectionism did not spread widely in the 1970s and early 1980s. The greater integration of American industries into the international economy altered domestic actors' preferences and thus forestalled recourse to protectionism. Though increased interdependence subjected the economy to new foreign competition, it also greatly augmented international economic ties for some firms. These ties manifested themselves in the form of exports, imports of critical inputs, multinational production, and global intrafirm trade. The growth of these international ties by American firms between the 1920s and 1970s reduced their interest in protectionism and thus contributed to the maintenance of a relatively open market in the 1970s, despite other pressures for closure.

THE VARIABLES

The explanation here focuses on two key variables linking domestic firms and the international economy: (1) export dependence and (2) multinationality. Each of these embodies a different aspect of a firm's integration into the world economy, and hence each gives rise to a distinct set of preferences relating to trade policy. In general, the argument is that firms with more extensive exports and multinationality should be less likely to demand protection, and more likely to resist it actively, even when facing serious import competition.

Some similarities between this argument and other domestic interest group accounts of trade policy should be noted.[1] In this literature, one

---

[1] Most studies focus on trade policy outcomes, but some discuss influences on corporate trade preferences and their impact on these outcomes. See Richard Caves, "Economic Models of Political Choice: Canada's Tariff Structure," *Canadian Journal of Economics* 9 (May 1976):278-300; Robert Baldwin, "The Political Economy of Protectionism," in *Import Competition and Response*, ed. Jagdish Bhagwati (Chicago: University of Chicago Press, 1982), pp. 263-92; William Brock and Stephen Magee, "The Economics of Special Inter-

set of hypotheses about industry trade preferences focuses on the political costs of demands for protection. It points out that the industries likely to lose from such demands are those that are export dependent and multinational. For these industries, demands for protection may spark retaliation abroad that hurts their own foreign operations. The more important foreign operations are for the industry, the less protectionist it will be.

Empirical tests of these hypotheses have produced mixed results. Several aggregate-level studies of U.S. industries have shown that high levels of export dependence reduce industries' preferences for protection and lead to lower trade barriers for these industries.[2] Other nonquantitative studies also reveal that in the 1920s the growth of an export sector contributed to attempts to open the American and foreign markets.[3] Some studies show that producer groups tied to the international economy have in the past been opponents of high tariffs.[4] Some have also linked the 1934 adoption of the Reciprocal Trade Agreements Act (RTAA), with its antiprotectionist bent, to the influence

---

est Politics: Case of the Tariff," *American Economic Review Papers and Proceedings* 68 (May 1978):246-50; Gerald K. Helleiner, "The Political Economy of Canada's Tariff Structure: An Alternative Model," *Canadian Journal of Economics* 4 (May 1977):318-26; Robert Baldwin, *The Political Economy of U.S. Import Policy* (Cambridge: MIT Press, 1986); Jonathan Pincus, *Pressure Groups and Politics in Antebellum Tariffs* (New York: Columbia University Press, 1977); Edward Ray, "The Determinants of Tariff and Nontariff Trade Restrictions in the U.S.," *Journal of Political Economy* 91 (February 1981):105-121; Edward Ray, "Tariff and Nontariff Barriers to Trade in the United States and Abroad," *Review of Economics and Statistics* 63 (May 1981):161-68; John Cheh, "U.S. Concessions in the Kennedy Round and Short-Run Adjustment Costs," *Journal of International Economics* 4 (1974):323-40; Réal Lavergne, *The Political Economy of U.S. Tariffs: An Empirical Analysis* (Toronto: Academic Press, 1983); James Riedel, "Tariff Concessions in the Kennedy Round and Structure of Protection in West Germany," *Journal of International Economics* 7 (1977):133-43; Robert Baldwin and Kim Anderson, "The Political Market for Protection in Industrial Countries: Empirical Evidence," *World Bank Staff Working Paper*, no. 492 (October 1981); Vinod Aggarwal, Robert Keohane, and David Yoffie, "The Dynamics of Negotiated Protectionism," *American Political Science Review* 81 (June 1987):345-66. An exception to these problems is Thomas Pugel and Ingo Walter, "U.S. Corporate Interests and the Political Economy of Trade Policy," *Review of Economics and Statistics* 67 (1985): 465-73.

[2] Glenn Fong, "Export Dependence and the New Protectionism" (Ph.D. dissertation, Cornell University, 1982); R. Baldwin, *U.S. Import Policy*; Lavergne, *Political Economy of U.S. Tariffs*.

[3] Joan H. Wilson, *American Business and Foreign Policy, 1920-33* (Boston: Beacon, 1971); William Becker, *The Dynamics of Business-Government Relations* (Chicago: University of Chicago Press, 1982).

[4] Peter Gourevitch, "International Trade, Domestic Coalitions, and Liberty," *Journal of Interdisciplinary History* 8 (Autumn 1977):281-313; Peter Gourevitch, *Politics in Hard Times* (Ithaca: Cornell University Press, 1986).

of American exporters and multinationals.[5] These studies have lent credence to the idea that export-dependent industries may not prefer protection and may even advocate the dismantling of trade barriers.

Other studies have examined how multinationality and its related intrafirm trade affect trade policy. The idea that the spread of multinational firms would reduce trade barriers has been discounted to some extent, because these firms often enter a market to circumvent such barriers and thus come to see them as a way to keep out other foreign competitors. Instead, the growth of global intrafirm trading has led to the view that firms with such trade would be against protection of their markets.[6] Analysis at the aggregate industry level has produced mixed evidence for both the multinational and the intrafirm trade variables.[7]

Overall, these empirical tests are plagued by two problems. First, these tests look only at the industry and not at the firms within them. Firms are central, because they develop international ties, anticipate the costs of protection, and formulate trade preferences, yet most of these studies examine international ties at the industry level. In addition, since these ties are usually unevenly distributed among the firms in an industry, the influence of these ties on preferences is often obscured in industry-level analysis. Examination of both international ties and preferences at the firm level is thus likely to yield better results about what conditions corporate preferences. Second, these theories about industry preferences are embedded in models that explain actual trade outcomes. The intermediate step of explaining industry demands is rarely taken. Empirical tests of these theories thus suffer because they are only indirect tests of theories of demand. In other words, factors influencing demand may be obscured when examining outcomes, since certain variables may prompt trade policy demands that are not satisfied in the policy process. Looking at demands by firms is essential. The analysis here avoids both of these problems by focusing on firms and on their actual demands.

[5] Thomas Ferguson, "From Normalcy to New Deal," *International Organization* 38 (Winter 1984):40-94. For a contrasting view, see Stephan Haggard, "The Institutional Foundations of Hegemony: Explaining the RTAA of 1934," *International Organization* 42 (Winter 1988):91-120.

[6] Gerald K. Helleiner, "Transnational Enterprise and the New Political Economy of U.S. Trade Policy," *Oxford Economic Papers* 29 (March 1977):102-116; Gerald K. Helleiner, "Transnational Corporations and Trade Structure," in *On the Economics of Intra-firm Trade*, ed. Herbert Giersch (Tubingen: Mohr, 1979), pp. 159-84; Susan Strange, "Protectionism and World Politics," *International Organization* 39 (Spring 1985):233-60; Lipson, "Transformation of Trade."

[7] R. Baldwin, *U.S. Import Policy*; Lavergne, *Political Economy of U.S. Tariffs.*

This work also emphasizes the international dimension, because the distinction to be made among domestic groups rests on the extent of their integration into the international economy. The first variable, export dependence, expresses the firm's ties to the international economy that arise from its trade relations. In this context, export dependence refers to the net balance of exports to imports as well as to the relative importance of these exports vis-à-vis domestic production. Thus, the level of a firm's export dependence expresses its vulnerability to reductions in these foreign sales.

The second variable involves the character of a firm's multinationality. It reveals the significance of a firm's production capacity and profits in foreign markets relative to those in its home market and thus captures a firm's vulnerability to changes affecting these foreign operations. Furthermore, it examines the nature of that foreign investment. In general, production operations abroad can be either highly integrated into a firm's worldwide trade and production network or self-contained and not dependent on other operations of the firm. In the former case, intrafirm trade flows will be very significant; in the latter each production unit will be autonomous. High levels of intrafirm trade then also indicate a significant attachment to the international economy.

The logic linking a firm's degree of export dependence and multinationality to its trade policy preferences is based on the balance of costs and benefits that would accrue to a firm from the further opening or closing of its home market, given the extent of its linkages to the international economy. These costs and benefits have three sources. First, they may be the consequence of reactions by foreign governments to such a policy change. These *policy* reactions by foreign governments are likely to entail disruption of the firm's international trade flows and/or of its foreign investments. Second, the opening or closing of markets has *economic* (price and supply) effects that will redound upon the firm and are likely to be felt in both its home and its foreign markets. Third, the firm will be concerned about the effects of a trade policy change upon its *domestic market position*. The differential impact of such a policy change upon the firms in an industry may alter the competitive position of firms within the domestic market.

These three general sources of costs and benefits generate hypotheses linking firms' international positions to their trade policy preferences. In terms of export dependence, the argument is that the higher a firm's export dependence, the less likely is it to prefer protection of its home market, even in the face of severe import competition.

Three particular factors make protection of its home market costly for an export-dependent firm. First, closing the home market may prompt retaliation by foreign governments. This retaliation may include protecting their own markets, which thus threatens the firm's exports and ultimately its profitability.

Second, even if retaliation is not forthcoming, the exporter is likely to face economic costs—as opposed to politically induced ones—that diminish its ability to export.[8] In particular, because it reduces available supplies, closure of the home market will tend to drive up the price of a firm's product and make it less competitive abroad. Protection of one market is also likely to increase competition in other markets. This supply effect means that the firm will face more competition in its foreign markets as other suppliers redirect their sales away from the closed market. The result of this shift can entail price cutting in these foreign markets and/or the loss of export sales, both of which (*ceteris paribus*) will tend to reduce the firm's profits. In addition, the closure of one country's market may diminish the foreign-exchange earnings available in other countries and make them less able to buy exports. All of these economic costs of protection will raise the export-dependent firm's resistance to protective trade practices.

A third set of costs associated with protection for these firms concerns the consequences for their domestic markets. Closure of the home market will provide differential benefits to firms within an industry. Those firms that are less export dependent and less competitive will benefit more than others. Protection will thus shift competitive conditions at home and place the export-dependent firm at further disadvantage. By strengthening some of its rivals at home, protection will be costly to the firm with strong international trade ties. All of these costs—those associated with foreign retaliation, economic changes, and domestic competition—may dissuade an export-dependent firm from seeking protection even when it faces severe import competition at home.

In terms of multinationality, the argument is that the more sizable and the more integrated a firm's direct foreign investments are, the more likely it is to resist protection and to prefer open markets, even if it is confronting intense competition from imports. For a highly integrated multinational—that is, one with substantial global intrafirm

---

[8] Fong, "Export Dependence," esp. ch. 1. For a theoretical discussion, see W. M. Corden, *The Theory of Protection* (Oxford: Oxford University Press, 1971); W. M. Corden, "The Costs and Consequences of Protection: A Survey of Empirical Work," in *International Trade and Finance: Frontiers in Research*, ed. Peter Kenen (Cambridge: Cambridge University Press, 1975).

trade—the costs of protecting its home market may outweigh any benefits from doing so.

Similar to export-dependent firms, the costs of protection for a multinational firm arise from three sources: foreign-government retaliation, general economic effects, and the effects on its domestic market position. First, the multinational may fear that protection at home will prompt protection abroad, which may close markets for vital inputs or for its own exports. This retaliatory protection is likely to disrupt the multinationals' integrated world trade flows and thus make foreign production more costly. In addition, retaliation may be targeted more directly against the foreign investment itself. The foreign government, in response to the closure of the multinational's home market, may impose new rules upon the firm—e.g., that it must export a certain percentage of its production. In the extreme, expropriation of the firm's foreign property may be threatened. The multinational's vulnerability to retaliation is probably greater than that of the export-dependent firm. Thus the multinational's temptation to protect the home market should be even less.

Second, a highly integrated multinational might find protection too costly because it may affect its own intrafirm trade. If the firm itself exports to its home market, then closing this market would curtail its own exports and defeat its own purpose. A firm with such internal trading networks is unlikely to see protection as the answer to its problems. Rather, the firm is likely to be an ardent advocate of open markets.

Third, as in the case of an export-dependent firm, closure of the multinational's home market will alter competitive conditions within the industry. Costs and benefits of protection will be distributed unequally among the firms, and those that are less competitive and less internationally oriented will gain relatively more overall. Protection may then strengthen the multinational's domestic rivals. Furthermore, it may induce foreign firms to locate in the multinational's home market, thus creating powerful new rivals domestically. The problems that protection causes the multinational in its home market may add to the expected costs of such a policy and, along with the costs of retaliation and intrafirm trade disruption, may prevent even a multinational in a distressed and highly import-penetrated industry from preferring such a policy.

I argue that, assuming that other solutions to their problems—such as diversification or exit—are about equally costly to all firms, internationally oriented ones should be less likely to demand protection, given its higher relative cost to them.[9] Protection will be more costly for internationally oriented firms in two ways. It will be more costly relative to other options and as a result, other ways of resolving their problems will be more attractive for these firms. In addition, protection will benefit these firms less than domestically oriented ones. For domestically centered firms under import pressure, protection will be a less costly option since they do not have international ties. Thus, serious foreign competition will be more likely to elicit preferences for protection by domestically oriented firms than by internationally oriented ones, because it is so much more costly for this latter group relative to other possible solutions.

PREFERENCES FOR PROTECTION: HYPOTHESES

Preferences for or against protection, arising out of the expected costs and benefits of such a policy, can be linked to the nature and extent of firms' ties to the international economy. Four hypotheses, presented in table 2.1, are posited. First, firms with minimal export dependence and multinationality (Type I) will view protectionism as very desirable when faced with severe import competition. Protectionism will have no major international repercussions for them, while its sizable domestic benefits will be an inducement. In contrast, firms that are significantly export dependent (Type II) will be likely to resist protection, despite import competition at home. The costs of closing the home market, largely in terms of diminished exports, will outweigh the possible benefits. However, the interest of these firms will be primarily the opening of markets abroad and only secondarily the opening of the home market.

Third, firms with both substantial export dependence and integrated multinationality (Type III) will resist protection most fiercely and will be the most likely to view further opening of markets world-

---

[9] The assumption that the costs of other options are about equal for all firms is debatable. It is unclear whether any systematic difference in costs exists for internationally oriented versus domestically oriented firms. It could be argued that domestically centered firms, being generally smaller and more flexible, will find adjusting to foreign competition less costly, as Michael Piore and Charles Sabel do in *The Second Industrial Divide: Prospects for Prosperity* (New York: Basic Books, 1984). On the other hand, large multinationals may have advantages—e.g., in obtaining capital or buying into new ventures—that will make adjustment less costly for them. Whether it will be more costly for one group over the other probably depends on the particular firms and industry. For an interesting discussion of how other options affect demands for protection, see Aggarwal, Keohane, and Yoffie, "Negotiated Protectionism." Their argument focuses on industries instead of firms, though.

TABLE 2.1 The Four Hypotheses

	Low	High
High	TYPE IV Mixed interests; less protectionist than Type I; selective protectionist	TYPE III Least protectionist; most free trade
Low	TYPE I Most protectionist; for global protection; intensity of demand varies with economic difficulty	TYPE II Less protectionist than Type I; most favored is open markets abroad

MULTINATIONALITY (left axis)

Low   High

EXPORT DEPENDENCE

wide as the best response to import competition at home. Finally, multinational firms that lack substantial export dependence and intrafirm trade (Type IV) but face strong competition at home from imports will find themselves in a difficult, cross-pressured situation. Their multinational interests will raise the costs of protection, but the loss of their home market and the lack of trade ties will push toward a policy of selectively closing their home market. In particular, the less its foreign and home operations are linked together in a worldwide trading network and the more its foreign rivals are already producing in its home market, the more likely the firm will be to seek selective protection—i.e., closing the market only to its strongest competitors—since two of the key factors making protection costly for a multinational will have been removed.

A final group's interests in trade require examination; these are the foreign multinationals operating in the host market. Trade preferences of these foreign subsidiaries are likely to be of two types. Foreign subsidiaries, depending on their role in the local market, are in general expected to behave like Type III or Type IV multinationals. If the subsidiary's operations in the host market service only the domestic market and were intended originally to circumvent trade barriers to that market, the subsidiary will have little interest in reducing those barriers. The foreign enterprise will desire at least the maintenance of those barriers and perhaps even their elevation in times of rising import penetration.[10] If the operation is part of the parent's global production and trade network, however, then further protection will be undesirable, and reduction of existing barriers may even appear desirable.

Generally, the behavior of these foreign subsidiaries fits the arguments about Type III and IV firms. When foreign subsidiaries are a part of Type IV firms—i.e., those lacking an integrated worldwide intrafirm trade network—their preferences are likely to reflect those of their parents and be selectively protectionist. In other words, the more like a purely domestic firm they are, the more protectionist they are likely to be. When part of a globally integrated multinational, these subsidiaries will be more free-trade oriented, as will their parent firms.

THE GROWTH OF INTERNATIONAL TIES

The character of firms' ties to the international economy indicates one reason why trade policy differed between the 1920s and 1970s: different ties existed between the domestic economy and the world economy in the two periods. Different levels of dependence on the international economy generated different preferences for openness or closure among firms. The greater integration of the domestic and international economies in the 1970s—i.e., the greater proportion of export-dependent and multinational firms—helped forestall the adoption of widespread protectionism, despite the significant inroads made by imports in the period.

Evidence of the growth of these international ties is abundant. In general, the magnitude of American trade grew phenomenally over these fifty years; more goods and more different types of goods were traded.[11] More specifically, America's trade dependence grew substantially. U.S. industrial exports rose from about 2 percent of total domestic production in 1923 to 9 percent in 1960 and to about 20 percent by the late 1970s.[12] Likewise, its industrial imports climbed from 2.5 percent in 1921 to 5 percent in 1960 and to over 20 percent of total domestic consumption in 1980.[13] The multinationality of Ameri-

[10] C. Fred Bergsten, Thomas Horst, and Theodore Moran, *American Multinationals and American Interests* (Washington, D.C.: Brookings Institution, 1978), pp. 297-300.

[11] Ratner, Soltow, and Sylla, *Evolution of American Economy*, pp. 463-66.

[12] For measures of export dependence in the 1920s, see Robert Lipsey, *Price and Quantity Trends in the Foreign Trade of the United States* (Princeton: Princeton University Press, 1963), pp. 434-35; for the postwar period, see Report of the President's Commission on Industrial Competitiveness, *Global Competition: The New Reality* (Washington, D.C.: GPO, 1985), 1:36, chart 15.

[13] For measures of import penetration, see ibid.

can firms also rose over these five decades. The total of American direct foreign investment abroad grew from about $5.5 billion in 1923 to $11.8 billion in 1950 and to over $86 billion in 1970.[14] The internationalization of American industry also grew in relative terms. Foreign assets of United States industry accounted for only 2.6 percent of total industrial assets in 1922, but over 20 percent by the 1970s.[15] In addition, the global operations of these firms intensified, which led to the creation of webs of international trade flows within firms. In particular, exports by American multinationals from foreign production sites back to the United States have grown immensely. An almost unknown practice before the 1940s, these types of transfers now account for somewhere between 15 and 50 percent of all U.S. industrial imports.[16] In sum, the United States' integration into the international economy through both trade and multinationality has deepened considerably since the 1920s (see table 2.2).

The argument here applies on two levels. In the aggregate, the different composition of the economies, in terms of export-dependent and multinational firms, accounts partially for the overall differences in trade policy during the two periods. On a microeconomic level, differences in firms' international linkages, regardless of which economy they are embedded in, are responsible for the firms' different preferences regarding trade policy. Two highly multinational firms, one in the 1920s and one in the 1970s, may thus be expected to have similar preferences. These preferences should at least be closer to one another's than to those of other *non*multinational firms operating in the same time period. In other words, the trade preferences of a 1920s and a 1970s large, integrated multinational should appear more simi-

---

[14] Robert Dunn, *American Foreign Investments* (New York: Viking Press, 1926), p. 182; Kent Hughes, *Trade, Taxes, and Transnationals* (New York: Praeger, 1979), p. 94. Ratner, Soltow, and Sylla, in *Evolution of American Economy*, p. 464, show it grew in the 1920s to $17.2 billion and then retreated to $11.5 billion by end of the 1930s. Robert Pollard, *Economic Security and the Origins of the Cold War* (New York: Columbia University Press, 1985), p. 205, shows U.S. DFI dropped to its lowest point in the century so far in 1946.

[15] For the 1920s, data on the value of direct foreign investment for industry are from U.S. Senate, *American Branch Factories Abroad*, 71st Cong., 3rd sess., 1931, S. Doc. 258, p. 27; for the value of U.S. industrial GNP in the 1920s, see Lipsey, *Price and Quantity Trends*, p. 424. For the 1970s, see U.S. Dept. of Commerce, *1977 Enterprise Statistics* (Washington, D.C.: GPO, 1981), p. 375, column Q over column R.

[16] Figures for this vary widely. See Joseph Grunwald and Kenneth Flamm, *The Global Factory: Foreign Assembly in International Trade* (Washington, D.C.: Brookings Institution, 1985), p. 7; Gerald K. Helleiner and Réal Lavergne, "Intra-firm Trade and Industrial Exports to the U.S.," *Oxford Bulletin of Economics and Statistics* 41 (November 1979):297-312; Helleiner, "Transnational Corporations and Trade Structure," pp. 159-84.

TABLE 2.2 Average U.S. International Economic Ties, 1920s and 1970s

---

U.S. Industrial Export Dependence

1920s	2.1% (1925)
1970s	20% (1975)

U.S. Manufacturing Multinationality

1920s	2.5% (1929)
1970s	20% (1977)

SOURCES: For average U.S. industrial export dependence (the value of industrial exports as a percentage of total industrial GNP): data for 1920s from Robert Lipsey, *Price and Quantity Trends in the Foreign Trade of the United States* (Princeton: Princeton University Press, 1963), pp. 434-35; data on the 1970s from 1985 *Economic Report of the President* (Washington, D.C.: GPO, 1986), tables B-10, B-101. For average multinationality of U.S. industry: 1920s data on value of direct foreign investment by industry from U.S. Senate, *American Branch Factories Abroad*, 71st Cong., 3rd sess., 1931, S. Doc. 258, p. 27; data on the value of industrial GNP from Lipsey, *Price and Quantity Trends*, p. 424. Data on the 1970s from U.S. Dept. of Commerce, *1977 Enterprise Statistics* (Washington, DC: GPO, 1981), for value of all foreign assets of U.S. manufacturing as a percent of total manufacturing assets (column Q over column R).

lar to one another than do the preferences of a 1920s multinational and a 1920s nonmultinational.

This cross-sectional, microlevel hypothesis about the similarity among firms in the two periods may appear problematic. The different contexts of the 1920s and 1970s should affect firms' behavior. Some of the main differences in the two economic contexts—that is, the differences in U.S. industries' competitive position, the industries' domestic market structure, and their multinational status—may enrich, rather than vitiate, the central argument, however.

Context does shape the way a firm determines its preferences. But these preferences may still be more directly influenced by the firm's own calculation of the costs and benefits of different policies given its dependence on foreign markets. Moreover, contextual factors may enhance the role that international linkages play in the firm's calculations of its interests. The existence of more widespread and well-developed multinational ties throughout the economy in the 1970s and the contextual influence this may exercise on all industries may bolster the general argument. That more firms are tied more deeply to the international economy affects all areas of the domestic economy. In particular, it increases the political allies and ideological underpinning upon which firms hoping to resist protectionist temptations can rely.

THE CROSS-NATIONAL COMPARISON

The issue of context also relates to the national setting in which firms operate. This study's primary argument concerns changes in trade policy pressures over time. For this, analyses of American trade policy making in the 1920s and 1970s are undertaken. But the cross-sectional argument that firms with extensive ties to the international economy are less likely to demand protection of their home markets calls for examination cross-nationally. Do firms behave similarly in different countries? More specifically, do the ties of export dependence and multinationality have the same impact on firms' calculations of their trade preferences when they are located in different countries? Conversely, does the overall national context in which a firm is located have effects that override the importance of the firm's economic interdependence in the calculations of its preferences?

To address this question, a cross-national comparison is undertaken. In addition to looking at six industries in the United States in the 1920s and six in the 1970s, a set of six French industries in the 1970s is also examined. In general, finding similarities in the behavior of firms in these two countries would strengthen confidence in this study's argument. If firms based in different countries react similarly to rising interdependence, then the forces influencing firms' calculations of their trade preferences cannot be overwhelmingly dependent on their national contexts.

France was chosen because it both shares important similarities with the United States and exhibits strong differences. France has experienced growing international economic interdependence, as has the United States (see table 2.3). Thus it too should show greater resistance to protectionism as a result of changes in its firms' preferences. But France was principally chosen because of its differences from the United States. These differences make it a difficult test of the argument. Our theory suggests that French firms should react similarly to American ones to their increased interdependence, but the very different national contexts in which these firms operate make finding such similar behavior unlikely.

Among advanced industrial democracies, the United States and France are viewed as opposites in many respects. Their dissimilarity has at least five important dimensions. First, the two countries occupy different positions and roles in the international system. Although de-

Table 2.3 Rising U.S. and French International Economic Ties since 1950 (in percent)

	1958	1968	1981
FRANCE			
Export Dependence[a]	12	21	33
Import Penetration[b]	15	23	30
Multinationality[c]	low		10

	1960	Late 1970s	
UNITED STATES			
Export Dependence[d]	9	20	
Import Penetration[e]	5	20	
Multinationality[f]	—	20	

[a] Export dependence measures industrial exports as a percentage of total domestic industrial production. See CEREM, *Crise, Concurrence Internationale, et Stratégies Multinationales* (Paris: CEREM, 1981), p. 27, table 3; Ministère de l'Economie et de Finances, La DREE, *Une Décennie du Commerce Extérieur Français* (Paris: Documentation Française, November 1983), p. xiv.

[b] Import dependence measures industrial imports as a percentage of total domestic consumption. CEREM, *Crise, Concurrence Internationale, et Stratégies Multinationales*, p. 27, table 3; Ministère de l'Economie et de Finances, la DREE, *Une Décennie du Commerce Extérieur Français*, p. xiv.

[c] Foreign production by French firms as a percentage of total French industrial production was very low before the 1960s; it grew greatly after that. See Julien Savary, *Les Multinationales Françaises* (Paris: Presses de l'Universitaires Françaises, 1981), pp. 19-29, 110-12; John Ardagh, *France in the 1980s* (New York: Penguin, 1982), pp. 45-47; Julien Savary, "Les Multinationales Françaises," *Economie et Humanisme* 257 (January-February 1981), p. 75.

[d] Export dependence measures industrial exports as a percentage of total domestic industrial production. See Report of the President's Commission on Industrial Competitiveness, *Global Competition: The New Reality*, vol. 1 (Washington, D.C.: GPO, 1985), p. 36.

[e] Import dependence measures industrial imports as a percentage of total domestic consumption. Report of the President's Commission on Industrial Competitiveness, *Global Competition*, 1:36.

[f] Comparable data are not available before the 1970s. Data from 1977 is from U.S. Dept. of Commerce, *1977 Enterprise Statistics* (Washington, D.C.: GPO, 1981).

clining, the United States is a more dominant global actor, less able to lead perhaps but still crucial. France, on the other hand, is a mid-sized power; it is considered an "ordinary" country, not a superpower.[17] This difference in international position should influence both political actors' definitions of their nations' interests as well as economic actors' views of their positions within the international economy. Second, the two differ in terms of their size and resources. The United States has a much bigger domestic market and a larger domestic supply of raw materials than does France.[18] This difference means that the United States has greater autonomy to direct its economy. In general, then, American firms have less need for and dependence on foreign markets.

Third, the role of the state in the two societies is seen as being dramatically different. France is pictured as the quintessential mercantilist state, one imbued with a powerful sense of its national interest and deeply involved in many aspects of social, economic, and political life.[19] On the other hand, the American state is characterized as the embodiment of the laissez-faire ideal, reluctant to intervene (if not incapable of it), lacking a single vision of the national interest, and highly penetrated and divided by competing societal interests.[20] Two states with such different roles and ideologies are likely to establish political contexts that vary in the incentives and costs they impose on different economic activities and hence on firms' calculations of their political preferences.

A fourth key difference between the two countries lies in the distribution of power within their political systems. While the Fifth Republic in France is viewed as a system led by a president, as is the United States, the significance of other political institutions varies. In France,

[17] Kindleberger, *World in Depression*, ch. 14; Lake, "International Economic Structures"; William Andrews and Stanley Hoffmann, eds., *The Fifth Republic at Twenty* (Albany: SUNY Press, 1981), esp. pts. 3, 5; John Ardagh, *France in the 1980s* (New York: Penguin, 1982), esp. ch. 2.

[18] Raymond Vernon, ed., *Big Business and the State* (Cambridge: Harvard University Press, 1974), esp. chs. 1, 6; Lionel Stoleru, *L'Impératif Industriel* (Paris: Seuil, 1969).

[19] Stanley Hoffmann, ed., *In Search of France* (Cambridge: Harvard University Press, 1963), esp. chs. 1, 2; Andrew Shonfield, *Modern Capitalism* (New York: Oxford University Press, 1965), esp. chs. 5, 7, 8; Stephen S. Cohen, *Modern Capitalist Planning* (Berkeley: University of California Press, 1977); John Zysman, "The French State in the International Economy," in *Power and Plenty*, ed. Katzenstein, pp. 255-94; Zysman, *Governments, Markets, and Growth*, esp. chs. 3, 6; Richard Kuisel, *Capitalism and the State in Modern France* (Cambridge: Cambridge University Press, 1981), esp. chs. 1, 8-10.

[20] Shonfield, *Modern Capitalism*, chs. 13-15, pt. 4; Katzenstein, ed., *Power and Plenty*, esp. chs. 3, 8, 9.

the ministries and their bureaucracies are seen as the central focus of policy making, implementation, and oversight. In contrast, in the United States much of this activity occurs in Congress rather than in the executive departments. Moreover, the capacity of the U.S. Congress to act as a check on executive dominance has no analogue in France, where the parliament today plays a minor role.[21] Different political actors and institutions are responsible for trade policy making in the two countries, which shapes in different ways how societal actors make demands.

Finally, the organization of political and social life in the two countries is usually depicted as being different. For the United States, organization outside of state-controlled institutions is prevalent and critically important. The desire, capacity, and need to organize into groups prevail in American life, while such behavior is less common among the French.[22] This cross-national disparity should affect how industries organize in the two countries and suggests that the aggregation of firms' interests along industry lines may be accomplished differently. These five differences in the contexts of French and American firms would make the finding of similarities in firms' calculations of their preferences and in their behavior remarkable indeed, thereby adding further validity to the argument about differences in trade policy over time.

THE CASE STUDIES AND METHODOLOGY

The industries examined were selected by establishing "hard cases" for the argument. In studies of protectionism, one of the most well established hypotheses is that high and rising levels of import penetration lead to demands for, as well as high levels of, protectionism. This empirical finding suggests that industries most severely affected by foreign competition should be a priori likely to want protection. This finding was used as the main criteria in selecting the industries: those

[21] Katzenstein, ed., *Power and Plenty*, chs. 3, 8, 9; Andrews and Hoffmann, eds., *Fifth Republic at Twenty*, esp. ch. 4; William Andrews, *Presidential Government in Gaullist France* (Albany: SUNY Press, 1982), esp. chs. 5, 6; Patrick Messerlin, "Bureaucracies and the Political Economy of Protection: Reflections of a Continental European," *World Bank Staff Working Paper*, no. 568, 1983. For the United States, see Pastor, *Politics of U.S. Foreign Economic Policy*; Stephen D. Cohen, *The Making of U.S. International Economic Policy* (New York: Praeger, 1977), esp. chs. 4, 6.

[22] Alexis de Tocqueville, *Democracy in America*, trans. J. P. Mayer (New York: Doubleday, 1969), esp. pt. 2, ch. 4; Michel Crozier, *The Bureaucratic Phenomenon* (Chicago: University of Chicago Press, 1964); Stanley Hoffmann, "Paradoxes of the French Political Community," in *In Search of France*, ed. Hoffmann.

facing the greatest increases in import penetration in each period were chosen. In addition, the industries had to have high absolute levels of import penetration and had to show other signs of economic distress, such as rising unemployment, unused capacity, and falling profit rates.

These criteria imply that each of the industries selected had at least a presumptive interest in increasing protection of its home market. The key questions thus are whether they all demonstrated this preference and, if not, whether the difference between those that did and those that did not related to the extent of their ties to the international economy. If the cases demonstrate that, despite severe economic pressures, especially import competition, industries with extensive ties to the international economy withstood the temptation to demand protection better than did industries without such international ties, the argument will be strongly validated.

Tables 2.4, 2.5, and 2.6 present the cases chosen. Many previous studies of trade policy have focused on policy trends in the national

TABLE 2.4 U.S. Industries Selected for the 1920s (1919-23)

Industry	Level of Import Penetration[a]		Increase in Import Penetration[b]
	A[c]	B[d]	
Newsprint	7.5	13.9	85.4
Woolen Goods	4.1	12.9	215
Clocks and Watches (1919-21)	0.6	5.9	880
Fertilizer	4.3	34.9	712
Photographic Equipment	1.9	7.5	294
Textile Machinery	0.9	4.7	420

SOURCES: Data on the value of imports from U.S. Dept. of Commerce, *Foreign Commerce and Navigation of the U.S.* (Washington, D.C.: GPO, various issues in the 1920s); data on the value of domestic production from U.S. Dept. of Commerce, *Census of Manufactures, 1929* (Washington, D.C.: GPO, 1930).

[a] Value of imports as a percentage of the value of total domestic production.
[b] Percentage change between column A and column B.
[c] The lowest value.
[d] The highest value after the lowest.

economy or on broad economic sectors. In this study, however, the unit of analysis adopted is initially the industry, and then within the industry, the firm. The firm as it operates within the context of an industry—that is, within the structure set by the competing producers of similar goods—is the central actor, the one calculating and voicing its preferences. The industry provides the analytic framework in which this behavior makes sense and thus is used as the initial focus. This layered analysis, relying on both the industry and the firm, is useful for several reasons.[23]

First, the industry, rather than some broader economic aggregate,

TABLE 2.5 U.S. Industries Selected for the 1970s (1970-77)

Industry (SIC Code)	Level of Import Penetration[a]		Increase in Import Penetration[b]
	A[c]	B[d]	
Footwear (non-rubber)			
3143	11	19	70
3144	15	27	80
3149	22	67	210
Semiconductors			
3674	9	22	144
Tires and Inner Tubes			
3011	5	12	140
Machine Tools			
3541	7	14	100
Watches and Clocks			
3873	18	36	100
Radios and TVs			
3651	30	43	50

SOURCES: Data from U.S. Dept. of Commerce, *U.S. Commodity Exports and Imports as Related to Output, 1977/76* (Washington, D.C.: GPO, 1982).
[a] Value of imports as a percentage of total domestic consumption.
[b] Percentage change between column A and column B.
[c] The lowest value.
[d] The highest value after the lowest.

[23] R. Baldwin, *U.S. Import Policy*; Lavergne, *Political Economy of U.S. Tariffs*; Takacs, "Pressures for Protection."

TABLE 2.6 French Industries Selected for the 1970s (1971-79)

Industry (NAP 600)	Level of Import Penetration[a]		Increase in Import Penetration[b]
	A[c]	B[d]	
Glass			
1601	18	28	56.8
1602	7	15	112
Pharmaceuticals			
1901	0.7	2.2	214
1902	17	25	51
Watches & Clocks			
3401	31	59	91.3
Radio & Television			
2921	17	39	133
Footwear			
4601	12	30	163
Rubber Tires			
5201	10	20.4	108

SOURCES: Data from INSEE, unpublished computer printout, 1985.
[a] Value of imports as a percentage of the value of total domestic consumption.
[b] Percentage change between column A and column B.
[c] The lowest value.
[d] The highest value after the lowest.

must be considered because it shapes how firms experience growing economic interdependence. An examination of categories broader than the industry obscures the nature of firms' international ties, since their effects are felt most profoundly in the competition with other firms within their market. For example, a firm's export activity is influenced by the behavior of other producers of equivalent or closely substitutable products—i.e., its industry.

A second reason that the industry is central to the argument involves the logic connecting firms' interdependence to their trade preferences. This logic depends on three factors already discussed: (1) the costs of foreign retaliation, (2) the effects on profitability caused by price and supply shifts due to trade diversion, and (3) the impact of protectionism on domestic competitive position. The weight of these factors for any firm can only be evaluated within the context of its industry. For instance, the influence of the second factor—the price and supply effects for a firm—depends upon the behavior of its competitors at home and abroad—i.e., on its industry context. In addition, the impact of various trade policies on a firm's domestic competitive situation, the third factor, is obviously conditioned by its industrial structure. If it is a monopolist or if direct foreign investment is not a likely response, then this factor will not weigh heavily in the calculation of its trade preferences. Hence, the net costs of demanding protection are conditioned by a firm's situation within the industry because this context affects how it experiences its international interdependence.

A third reason for focusing initially on the industry involves how demands concerning trade policy are made. Both firms and industry associations make trade policy demands. Firms are the actors who calculate their interests, but bargaining and conflict over the voicing of these preferences occur frequently at the industry level, since firms often seek the support of their competitors when pursuing political initiatives. Thus not only firms but also industry associations can be expected to express policy preferences. The extent to which, and the reasons why, these industry preferences diverge from those of the individual firms need exploration.

Looking at the industry, then, provides a broader view of how interests are aggregated. Overall, an initial focus on the industry is necessary for three reasons: it sets the context for understanding a firm's behavior; it conditions how a firm's international ties affect how it calculates its preferences; and it influences the way these preferences are voiced.

Though industry-level analysis is crucial for the argument made here, it is not sufficient. Viewing the industry as some unified whole leads one to overlook crucial differences within the industry and thus to misunderstand the politics of international trade. The concept of industry should not be reified. The firms within an industry are the real actors. They are the ones developing links to the international economy, calculating their preferences, pursuing strategies, and voicing demands. In this sense, the industry does not really exist. It is composed of various firms competing over the production and sale of similar products. Operating at the industry level obfuscates crucial differences among the firms. Most important for the argument here, these differences concern the character of firms' ties to the international economy, the intra-industry struggles over competitive position, and the definition of "industry" preferences. As will be shown, divisions among firms within an industry are crucial both in the definition of the industry's preferences and in their realization.

The methodology used for analyzing the cases is that of "structured, focused comparison," which requires asking the same questions of each case.[24] Two key questions are asked. The first relates to the study's independent variable, i.e., to the degree of the industry's ties to the international economy. The question is to what extent, and how, the industry is linked to the international economy. This independent variable has two components: the extent of export dependence, and the nature and degree of multinationality.[25]

The Independent Variable

The first component, the extent of export dependence, is captured by two measures: an industry's net trade position and its percentage of exports to production.[26] These indicate the direction of an industry's involvement in world trade flows as well as its vulnerability to reductions in its exports. The relative importance of different trade flows is shown partially in its net trade position: the value of its exports minus that of its imports. A positive balance suggests that exports are a more important component of its operations than are imports. A second indicator of the significance of an industry's foreign sales involves its proportion of exports relative to domestic production. This measure indicates the importance of its exports relative to its total output. The larger it is, the more costly protectionist actions will be for the industry.

Export dependence is one element used in constructing the four categories of cases. Although export dependence is continuous, it is used here in a dichotomous fashion. Industries can show either high or low export dependence. A highly export-dependent industry is one that has *both* a net trade surplus *and* a high proportion of exports to domestic production. An industry with low export dependence possesses a net trade deficit and a proportion of exports relative to do-

[24] Alexander L. George, "Case Studies and Theory Development: The Method of Structured, Focused Comparison," in *Diplomacy: New Approaches in History, Theory, and Policy*, ed. Paul G. Gordon (New York: Free Press, 1979).

[25] For a detailed discussion of the sources and problems with this independent variable, see Helen Milner, "Resisting the Protectionist Temptation: Industry and Trade Politics in the U.S. and France in the 1920s and the 1970s" (Ph.D. dissertation, Harvard University, 1986), ch. 3.

[26] For a discussion of this variable's first systematic use in explaining trade policy, see Fong, "Export Dependence," esp. chs. 1, 2. These are the ones most commonly used, and they reflect the elements of export dependence crucial to the argument here.

mestic production that is low.[27] Table 2.7 reports export dependence
for the industries, showing the cutoff between high and low values.

The second component of the independent variable focuses on the
extent and nature of its multinational operations. Five elements of this
component can be identified: (1) the level of direct foreign investment, (2) the direction of change in this level over time, (3) the profitability of the foreign operations, (4) the extent of intrafirm trade,
and (5) the direction of this trade.[28] These elements capture the basic
features of multinationality. They demonstrate its importance to the
firm and thus its role in the firm's calculation of its preferences.

The first three elements of multinationality reveal its value for the
firm. Relative to its domestic operations, the higher its level of direct
foreign investment, the more this level is increasing, and the more
profitable this investment is, the more valuable these foreign operations are for the firm. The last two elements suggest the nature of
these foreign operations. Whether it involves a self-contained series of
national operations or a globally integrated network of production activities can in part be established by examining the degree and direction of intrafirm trade. The more extensive this trade is in both volume and geographic spread, the more integrated a firm is
internationally. Overall, it is hypothesized that the more important
multinationality is for the firm and the more integrated its operations,
the more costly protectionist actions will be.

Like export dependence, this second component of the independent variable, multinationality, is used to classify the industries into different categories. Although it is continuous, multinationality is used
dichotomously here. A highly multinational industry is one with both
a high and growing proportion of foreign assets relative to domestic
ones and an integrated set of foreign operations. Although comparable figures for multinationality among the three sets of cases are difficult to generate, table 2.8 lists the industries and their values for this
component of the independent variable.[29]

[27] The cutoffs between high and low industries are comparable across periods and
countries. In other words, a high industry in the 1920s would be so classified in the 1970s
in France or the United States. Also, in the case studies, industry-level data has been
supplemented and differentiated by firm-level data. Aggregate figures are presented
first, and then key firms' positions within these aggregates are discussed. A similar technique was used in selecting the cases. Interlacing analysis of the industry and firm levels
facilitates examination of the intra-industry struggles over trade policy.

[28] For a detailed discussion of this variable's sources and problems, see Milner, "Resisting the Protectionist Temptation," ch. 3.

[29] This table should be treated cautiously, because the most accurate data available usually is for *firms* and not industries.

TABLE 2.7 Industry Export Dependence (value of exports as a percentage of total production)

LOW

U.S. Footwear, 1970s[2]	.05 (1970s ave.)		
U.S. Woolens, 1920s[1]	2.1 (1923)	1.3 (1927)	1.8 (1929)
U.S. Watches and Clocks, 1920s[1]	4% (1920s ave.)		
U.S. Newsprint, 1920s[1]	4.5 (1921)		1.7 (1929)
U.S. Tires, 1970s[2]	3.5 (1970s ave.)		6 (1981)
U.S. Watches and Clocks, 1970s[2]	2 (1970)	13%[a] (1977)	10%[a] (1981)
U.S. Radios and TVs, 1970s[2]	5 (1970)	10 (1977)	17 (1981)
French Radio and TVs, 1970s[3]	3.7 (1972)		
French Footwear, 1970s[3]	21[b] (1970)		18[b] (1981)

HIGH

U.S. Textile Machinery, 1920s[1,c]	15 (1921)		11 (1929)
U.S. Machine Tools, 1970s[2]	17 (1970)	12 (1977)	18 (1981)
French Watches and Clocks, 1970s[3,d]	44 (1971)	68 (1977)	63 (1982)
U.S. Photo Equipment, 1920s[1]	23 (1919)	21 (1923)	31 (1929)
U.S. Fertilizer, 1920s[1]	9%[c] (1920s ave.)		
U.S. Semiconductors, 1970s[2]	22 (1970)	17 (1979)	27 (1981)
French Tires, 1970s[3]	40 (1970)	50 (1979)	—

TABLE 2.7 (*cont.*)

French Pharmaceuticals, 1970s[3]	13 (1970)	20 (1980)	—
French Glass, 1970s[3]	30 (1970)	42 (1979)	—

[a] Mainly parts.

[b] Highly concentrated among largest firms.

[c] For cotton machinery, over 25 percent.

[d] For electronic watches, 0 percent in late 1970s.

[e] Average for 1920s; some products, like phosphates, with much higher percentage.

[1] Data on the value of exports from U.S. Dept. of Commerce, *Foreign Commerce and Navigation of the U.S.* (Washington, D.C.: GPO, various issues in the 1920s); data on the value of domestic production from U.S. Dept. of Commerce, *Census of Manufactures, 1929* (Washington, D.C.: GPO, 1930).

[2] Data from U.S. Dept. of Commerce, *US Commodity Exports and Imports as Related to Output, 1977/76* (Washington, D.C.: GPO, 1982).

[3] Sources for export dependence for each industry vary from case to case; for the individual citations, see the notes in ch. 5.

Using both of these indicators, four general categories of firms can be constructed, as shown in table 2.9. Type I firms have little of either kind of international linkage. Type II firms have extensive export dependence but little multinationality. In Type III, firms possess both extensive export and extensive multinational ties. Finally, those in Type IV have significant multinational operations but little export dependence.

The Dependent Variable

The second key question focuses on the dependent variable. What are the firms' trade policy preferences? The degree of firms' export dependence and multinationality explains the nature and intensity of their demand for trade policies. Assessing the demand for such policies requires understanding what is meant by protectionism. In this study a broad definition of protection is used: any policy that increases the price of a country's imports or decreases that of its exports is considered protectionist. This definition necessitates examining a wide range of political arenas, beginning with the traditional trade policy-making ones, to determine an industry's trade preferences.

To understand industries' preferences, I surveyed their activities in a number of arenas. In the 1920s, the main arenas were (1) the U.S.

TABLE 2.8 Industry Multinationality (in percent)

Industry	Multinationality	Multinational Trade
LOW		
U.S Footwear, 1970s	4[1]	2[4]
U.S. Machine Tools, 1970s	16[1, a]	9[4]
French Footwear, 1970s	2[2]	low[5]
French Watches and Clocks, 1970s	2[2]	low[5]
U.S. Woolens, 1920s	.05[3, b]	low[5]
U.S. Watches and Clocks, 1920s	.09[3]	low[5]
U.S. Textile Machinery, 1920s	.5[3, c]	low[5]
HIGH		
U.S. Tires	19[1]	19[4]
U.S. Radios and TVs, 1970s	9[1, d]	14[4]
U.S. Watches and Clocks, 1970s	19[1]	10[4]
U.S. Semiconductors, 1970s	24[1]	87[4]
French Glass, 1970s	28[2]	high[5]
French Pharmaceuticals, 1970s	8[2]	high[5]
French Radios and TVs, 1970	4[2, e]	low[5]
U.S. Fertilizer, 1920s	1.5[3, f]	high[5]
U.S. Photo Equipment, 1920s	2[3]	high[5]
U.S. Newsprint, 1920s	15[3]	very high[5]
French Tires, 1970s	15[2]	very high[5]

[a] Overstated; category is all machine tools.

[b] Category is "textile yarns and knits."

[c] Category is "other machinery."

[d] Understated; includes communications equipment, which includes the large but completely domestic firm of AT&T.

[e] Understated; sector moving from low to high in 1970s.

[f] Understated; category is "other chemicals," larger than fertilizer.

[1] Figures from U.S. Dept. of Commerce, *1977 Enterprise Statistics* (Washington, D.C.: GPO, 1981), pp. 374-78; they show foreign assets as a percentage of total assets for 1977.

[2] Figures from Julien Savary, *Les Multinationales Françaises* (Paris: Presses de l'Universitaires Françaises, 1981), p. 21; they show foreign production as a percentage of total production for 1974.

[3] U.S. Senate, *American Branch Factories Abroad*, 71st Cong., 3rd Sess., 1933, S. Doc. 120, p. 31. These data are difficult to compare to the others because they show the sector's DFI as a percentage of total U.S. manufacturing DFI in 1929.

[4] Réal Lavergne, unpublished paper for the United Nations Transnational Corporations study, July 1981.

[5] See the text of the case studies for a fuller explanation.

TABLE 2.9 The Cases by Type

Type I: Low Export Dependence, Low Multinationality
  U.S. Woolen Goods, 1920s
  U.S. Watches and Clocks, 1920s
  U.S. Footwear, 1970s
  French Footwear, 1970s

Type II: High Export Dependence, Low Multinationality
  U.S. Textile Machinery, 1920s
  U.S. Machine Tools, 1970s
  French Watches and Clocks, 1970s

Type III: High Export Dependence, High Multinationality
  U.S. Fertilizer, 1920s
  U.S. Photo Equipment, 1920s
  U.S. Semiconductors, 1970s
  French Tires, 1970s
  French Glass, 1970s
  French Pharmaceuticals, 1970s

Type IV: Low Export Dependence, High Multinationality
  U.S. Newsprint, 1920s
  U.S. Tires, 1970s
  U.S. Radios and Televisions, 1970s
  U.S. Watches and Clocks, 1970s
  French Radios and Televisions, 1970s

Congress, which handled most issues related to tariff levels; (2) the U.S. Tariff Commission (USTC), which investigated industry complaints about trade matters; and (3) industry trade associations, whose internal deliberations over trade issues were reported in various newspapers and industry trade journals. For the 1970s, four slightly different arenas in the United States were surveyed: (1) the U.S. Congress, which both authorizes tariff level changes for the GATT negotiations and introduces bills to help industries; (2) the U.S. International Trade Commission (ITC), which investigates industries' trade complaints; (3) the U.S. Special Trade Representative (STR) and other executive agencies, which decide industry complaints and handle the GATT negotiations; and (4) the industry trade associations, which develop and articulate industry-wide trade positions.

In France, an even larger number of actors is involved in the process. Most traditional trade policy is under the auspices of the European Community (EC) and not the French. The EC's Commission develops GATT trade negotiation positions and investigates industry complaints, although these activities require the input and agreement of national authorities. Domestically, concern for trade and industrial policy is centered primarily within the bureaucracy but is spread among a number of ministries. The Ministry of Industry, the Direction for External Economic Relations (DREE), the Ministry of Finance, the Ministry of Foreign Trade, the Ministry of Foreign Affairs, and other ministries responsible for particular industries are involved. Firm and industry activities in trade and industrial policy issues in all of these arenas, as well as in the industry trade associations, were surveyed.

From these sources, a detailed description of the U.S. and French industries' trade policy preferences and activities was constructed.[30] Several problems in the measurement of the dependent variable, however, merit discussion. In general, the true preferences of social actors are notoriously difficult to determine, given the advantages of posturing and obfuscation and the intrusion of hindsight. In the case studies, gauging the nature of firms' preferences is difficult for two specific reasons. First, trade policy preferences do not fall along a single, simple continuum. Although the desires for open markets and/or protection from foreign competition mark two clear extremes, demands for "fair trade," complaints of unfair trade practices, and requests for temporary aid or subsidies to ease adjustment burdens do not fall easily within these two extremes. On the one hand, these types of demands may be equivalent to calls for protectionism in a new, more acceptable guise; on the other hand, firms voicing these demands may prefer open markets in general but believe that some temporary restraint is necessary to "correct" the market or to coerce others into competing more fairly. These types of demands are not always aimed at curbing foreign competition. The degree to which they actually reflect protectionist preferences depends much upon the situation.

A second difficulty inherent in determining trade policy preferences involves assessing the intensity of such preferences. The question of how much a firm wants protection or open markets is related directly to the question of what it really prefers. For instance, claiming you prefer open markets but being completely unwilling to devote any attention or resources to realizing this preference clearly calls into question the extent to which this should be termed a preference. Con-

---

[30] For a full discussion of the sources and problems of the dependent variable, see Milner, "Resisting the Protectionist Temptation," ch. 3.

versely, maintaining you prefer free but fair trade, while doing everything in your power to heighten uncertainty over the future of trade in your market, may reveal a stronger protectionist bent than would otherwise be apparent.

The intensity of firms' preferences must be assessed not only to gauge the actual nature of their preferences but also to compare preferences among firms. Whether a firm prefers open markets is a first question, but whether it prefers them as much as another firm is important for the argument as well. This cross-firm (and cross-industry) ranking of preferences requires evaluating the effort that firms put into realizing their trade policy preferences. For example, in the American cases the number and type of petitions for trade relief filed under U.S. trade laws, the frequency and duration of court cases regarding foreign competition, the nature and amount of congressional lobbying, and the extent of internal political discussion and organization related to trade issues can all be employed to measure the relative intensities of different firms' preferences. Not only what a firm says it prefers but how often it states this preference and what it does to realize it are important elements in understanding its preferences.

One further aspect of this argument should be noted before examining the cases. The firms chosen were likely to act on their preferences. These firms were all in serious economic distress. It is reasonable to expect that their precarious position would prompt them to act even if that action were costly, because inactivity might mean their demise. Both rational actor and satisficing models of firms would expect these endangered firms to try to improve their situations.

Moreover, the argument is not that firms in an industry will always be able to act in a unified way to promote some industry-wide position. By focusing on the firm, the argument anticipates that firms may have very different preferences and may not be able to agree on a unified position. However, the firms in an industry may all have a similar international orientation and may develop a common position. In this case collective action problems should be minor. All will face strong economic pressure to act, and in very few instances will the number of relevant firms be large enough to pose collective action dilemmas. Because of the cases chosen, therefore, individual and collective action problems should be minimal: these distressed firms will be impelled to act, and industry-wide political activity should be impeded mostly by differences in preferences among firms.

CHAPTER 3

The 1920s U.S. Case Studies

THIS CHAPTER presents detailed analyses of six American industries in the 1920s. In each case, the industry's presumptive interest in protection is established by reviewing its high levels of economic distress, and then the nature and extent of the industry's export dependence and multinationality are elaborated. Next, the industry's trade policy preferences over the 1920s are the center of attention. The main instrument for protecting industries during this period was the tariff, and thus the industry's position on its tariff rate was the most important indicator of its trade preferences. The discussion focuses primarily on the industry's testimony to Congress during the two tariff revisions of the decade. The industry's complaints to the U.S. Tariff Commission (USTC) and the political controversies surrounding trade issues among the industry's firms are also examined. The central concern, in the analysis of each case, is to determine whether the extent of the industries' international ties affects the nature of their trade policy preferences in the predicted fashion.

CASE 1: WOOLEN GOODS

American wool manufacturers and growers in the early twentieth century were important political actors, especially in the area of trade, where they had waged fierce battles for protection throughout much of the nineteenth century.[1] Around the turn of the century, developments occurred that changed the industry: wool growers moved west, wool manufacturers were largely unable to move out of New England to lower-cost areas, and new substitute fabrics like cotton, rayon, and silk displaced wool.[2] Because of these conditions, this domestically oriented industry experienced serious economic difficulties and in the 1920s resorted once again to vigorous demands for more protection from foreign competition.

U.S. wool manufacturers' problems were continuous during the

[1] Chester Wright, *Wool-Growing and the Tariff* (Cambridge: Harvard University Press, 1910), pp. 213-27; Victor Clark, *History of the Manufactures of the United States, 1893-1928*, vol. 3 (New York: McGraw-Hill, 1929), pp. 191-210.

[2] Wright, *Wool-Growing*, chs. 7-9; Clark, *History of the Manufactures*, pp. 204-210.

decade. Their secular decline had two primary sources: one was foreign competition and the other was related to shifts in consumer preferences from woolens to cotton and rayon fabrics. Foreign competition had been a constant problem. Great Britain, and to a lesser extent Germany, had dominated the wool manufactures industry worldwide for most of its industrial history.[3] The U.S. industry had always been pressed by imports, but these surged in the 1920s. The value of woolen goods imports increased steadily throughout the decade; in 1921, their value was $35 million, and by 1929 it was $65 million.[4] Moreover, the level of import penetration rose substantially over the period; in 1919 the ratio stood at 4 percent, in 1921 it had moved to 16.4 percent, and by 1929 it was at 22.3 percent.[5] The rate of increase in import penetration was extremely high, approximating 300 percent in the beginning of the decade.

In addition, there was widespread evidence of the wool manufacturers' economic difficulties in other areas. The prices of their goods, their profits, the number of firms and workers engaged in the industry, and their capacity utilization levels all declined in the 1920s.[6] Such serious problems suggest why they had an a priori strong interest in increased tariffs.

American manufacturers of woolen goods not only possessed good reasons for their protectionist preferences but also were not constrained in pursuing them by any significant ties to the international economy. These manufacturers displayed little export dependence or multinationality at either the industry or firm level in the 1920s, and thus were typical of a Type I industry.

The export dependence of U.S. wool manufacturers was limited in the 1920s. After 1919, this industry registered an increasingly negative trade balance over the next decade.[7] In addition, the industry's value of exports relative to the value of its domestic production remained low. In 1923, the wool manufacturers' ratio of exports to domestic production was about 2.1 percent, and it declined further over

[3] National Industrial Conference Board (hereafter NICB), *Trends in the Foreign Trade of the United States* (New York: NICB, 1930), pp. 279-83.

[4] U.S. Bureau of Foreign and Domestic Commerce (hereafter U.S. BFDC), *Foreign Commerce and Navigation of the United States* (Washington, D.C.: GPO, 1922, 1927, 1929).

[5] Imports from U.S. BFDC, *Foreign Commerce*; domestic production from U.S. Dept. of Commerce, Bureau of the Census, *Census of Manufactures, 1929* (Washington, D.C.: GPO 1930). Import penetration is measured as the value of imports as a percentage of domestic production.

[6] For extensive data on these, see Milner, "Resisting the Protectionist Temptation."

[7] U.S. BFDC, *Foreign Commerce*, 1922, 1929.

the decade.[8] At the industry level, these manufacturers exported little and thus had few of the ties to the international economy that would have been forged by significant export dependence. Moreover, all firms within the industry, not just a majority, lacked export sales.[9]

American wool manufacturers' lack of ties to the international economy was manifested further by their limited multinational operations. Of the numerous studies made concerning U.S. direct foreign investment in the 1920s, not one mentions woolen manufacturers, or textiles in general, as being among the leading industries in this movement abroad.[10] This lack of multinationality was not surprising, given the attributes cited as conducive to direct investment abroad. As one author notes, five characteristics of firms were strongly associated with extensive multinationality in the 1920s: the newness of an industry, distinctive (trademarked or highly advertised) products, technological leadership, large firm size, and significant export sales.[11] None of these (pre-)conditions for direct foreign investment existed in the woolen manufactures industry, which perhaps explains why it had so few foreign operations.

Foreign investment by the woolen goods industry was limited as well. At its upper limit, the industry's manufacturing investments abroad totaled $66 million in 1932, or about 4.0 percent of total U.S. manufacturing direct foreign investment. At its lower limit, the value of its foreign operation in 1932 was $0.7 million, or merely .05 percent of total U.S. manufacturing direct foreign investment.[12]

[8] U.S. BFDC, *Foreign Commerce*, for exports in 1922, 1927, 1929, and U.S. Dept. of Commerce, *Census, 1929*, for domestic production. Average U.S. export dependence for manufactures was 3.3 percent at the time.

[9] The available sources rarely mention exports for this industry, and when they do it is often as an afterthought. See Moody's *Moody's Manual of Industrial Securities: 1927* (New York: Moody's, 1927); National Archives, U.S. Tariff Commission (hereafter N.A. USTC) files, "Tariff Information Surveys," surveys on wool and yarns, wool cloths, and wool wearing apparel, RG 81, 1920.

[10] See, e.g., Cleona Lewis, *America's Stake in International Investments* (Washington, D.C.: Brookings Institution, 1938); Mira Wilkins, *The Emergence of Multinational Enterprise* (Cambridge: Harvard University Press, 1970); Mira Wilkins, *The Maturing of Multinational Enterprise* (Cambridge: Harvard University Press, 1974); Dunn, *American Foreign Investments*; Frank Southard, *American Industry in Europe* (Boston: Houghton Mifflin, 1931); U.S. BFDC, *Foreign Commerce*, 1930; Senate, *American Branch Factories Abroad*, 1931, Doc. 258; Senate, *American Branch Factories Abroad*, 73rd Cong., 2nd sess., 1933, S. Doc. 120.

[11] Wilkins, *Maturing of Multinational Enterprise*, p. 89.

[12] Senate, *American Branch Factories* , Doc. 120, 1933, p. 31. Total U.S. DFI in manufacturing was $1.5 billion in 1932; the value for the "other textile" group was $66 million. This "other textile" group figure greatly overstates the amount for just the woolen goods

Multinationality at the firm level was also scarce for the industry. In studies listing the key U.S. firms operating abroad in the 1920s, no woolen manufacturers are ever mentioned.[13] In addition, examinations of U.S. foreign investments by the country or region in which they are located rarely mention textile manufacturing of any sort.[14] Finally, the U.S. wool manufacturers themselves testified in 1921 that they had no production facilities in Europe and that they did not manufacture abroad for re-export to the United States.[15] This testimony supports the aggregate statistics, which imply that these manufacturers had few if any multinational production operations in the 1920s.

The woolen manufactures industry's limited export dependence and multinationality make it a Type I industry. Three other features, however, also warrant discussion. First, the industry had a weak international competitive position. During the nineteenth century, the U.S. wool manufacturers were nurtured by exceedingly high tariff levels. The industry grew up behind these tariff walls and never learned to compete without them.[16] The American firms were not and probably would never be able to compete with the British and the Germans, who dominated the industry globally.[17]

Second, the U.S. wool manufacturing industry had limited industrial concentration. In 1928 the leading six firms in the industry controlled only 35 percent of total U.S. production.[18] In addition to this

sector. The lower limit cited in the text is for the smaller category of textile yarns and knits, which underestimates the woolen goods sector. In any case, these are estimates for 1932; values for the 1920s are not available and would probably be much less, since the expansion of U.S. DFI occurred mostly in the late 1920s. See U.S. BFDC, *American Direct Investments in Foreign Countries*, Trade Info. Bulletin 731 (Washington, D.C.: GPO, 1930), pp. 37-41, esp. p. 40.

[13] See citations in note 10 in general; and Wilkins, *Maturing of Multinational Enterprise*, pp. 208-216, in particular.

[14] For Europe, see Southard, *American Industry*; C. Lewis, *America's Stake*; Wilkins, *Emergence of Multinational Enterprise*; and Wilkins, *Maturing of Multinational Enterprise*. For Latin America, see both works by Wilkins; Max Winkler, *Investments of U.S. Capital in Latin America* (Boston: World Peace Foundation, 1928); and Dudley Phelps, *The Migration of U.S. Industry to South America* (New York: McGraw-Hill, 1936). For Canada, see Herbert Marshall, Frank Southard, and Kenneth Taylor, *Canadian-American Industry* (New Haven: Yale University Press, 1936). Overall, see U.S. BFDC, *American Direct Investments*.

[15] Senate, Finance Committee, *Tariff Act of 1921*, hearings, 67th Cong., 2nd. sess., 1921, sch. K, pp. 3545-47.

[16] Clark, *History of Manufactures*, p. 204; Wright, *Wool-Growing*, pp. 227-29.

[17] NICB, *Trends in Foreign Trade*, pp. 279-83; Dunn, *American Foreign Investments*, pp. 59, 62-85. Multinational data from Moody's, *Manual: 1927*, and N.A. USTC files, "Tariff Information Surveys," woolens, RG 81, 1920.

[18] Senate, Finance Committee, *Tariff Act of 1929*, hearings, 71st Cong., 1st sess., 1929, sch. 11, p. 2.

lack of market dominance by a few firms, a large number of small firms entered and exited the industry with frequency.[19] This plethora of woolens firms, large and small, contributed to the economic turbulence experienced by the manufacturers and prompted them to organize politically in a single group, the National Association of Wool Manufacturers.[20] This was the industry's primary vehicle for political action. Given the firms' similar situations—their lack of international ties and weak international competitive positions—and their relatively small size, the need for and development of such an organization was hardly surprising.

Third, the U.S. wool manufacturing industry had a peculiar relationship with wool growers. The wool growing industry (sheep raising) provided the primary input for the wool manufacturers. But during the 1920s the American raw wool supply was not sufficient to meet the manufacturers' demand for it; therefore, about 50 percent of the manufacturers' raw wool needs came from imports.[21] This placed the manufacturers in an awkward position: though they wanted lower-priced wool imports, they feared opposing tariffs on raw wool since this was likely to prompt wool growers to oppose tariffs on wool manufactures.[22] This situation induced the two groups to cooperate. Throughout the 1920s the growers and manufacturers not only refrained from opposing each other in public but also developed a coalition consisting of western wool growers and eastern wool manufacturers in order to press for higher tariffs.[23] This coalition was powerful because it combined industrial and agricultural interests and united western Republicans and New England Democrats in Congress.[24]

In summary, U.S. wool manufacturers faced serious economic difficulties in the 1920s. The industry was beset by rising imports and declining domestic demand. These manufacturers were Type I producers with few economic ties to the international economy.

The Dependent Variable

The trade policy preferences of American wool manufacturers were consistently protectionist in the 1920s. These manufacturers lobbied

[19] N.A. USTC files, "Tariff Information Surveys," woolens, RG 81, 1920.

[20] House, Ways and Means Committee, *General Tariff Revision of 1921*, hearings, 67th Cong., 1st sess., 1921, sch. K, pp. 2551-64.

[21] *New York Times* (hereafter *NYT*), August 6, 1922, pt. 3, p. 1:5-8.

[22] Wright, *Wool-Growing*, pp. 213-27.

[23] *NYT*, November 22, 1922, p. 20:1; *NYT*, January 8, 1921, p. 19:1.

[24] *NYT*, March 22, 1921, p. 1:6; *NYT*, April 14, 1921, p. 17:3; *NYT*, November 23, 1929, p. 1:8.

as a group for higher rates of duties on imports. The main reason for this preference was simply survival; as one observer noted, "it was generally felt among wool manufacturers in this country that the industry could not exist without a protective tariff that was reasonably high."[25] Their trade preferences were enunciated primarily in Congress during the major tariff revisions of the 1920s. Their complaints to the U.S. Tariff Commission (USTC) and their intra-industry debates, however, are also of interest.

During the 1920s the U.S. wool manufacturers lobbied Congress for enhanced protection at every opportunity. There were three: the 1921 Emergency Tariff hearings, the 1921-22 Fordney-McCumber Tariff hearings, and the 1929-30 Smoot-Hawley Tariff hearings. In each, the wool manufacturers pressed for higher duties and/or for changes in the methods of import valuation that would further reduce the sale of these foreign goods. Moreover, in each case the industry lobbied as a unit through the National Association of Wool Manufacturers and acted in coalition, usually a tacit one, with the U.S. wool growers.

During 1920 and 1921, Congress supervised an emergency revision of the tariff. One of the main proponents of this revision was the wool-growing industry. In the 1913 tariff revision, all raw wool had been placed on the free list and the tariff on wool goods had been reduced. These changes were not noticeable until after 1920, because the war in Europe had halted trade in wool products.[26] The postwar revival of world trade, however, sent the American growers and manufacturers into a panic. By 1920, with their prices and profits falling and imports rising, they both began pressing for increased protection. In the 1921 congressional hearings on the Emergency Tariff, the wool manufacturers supported new duties on raw wool and asked for a return to the highest duties ever on woolen goods, i.e., the compensatory duties of the 1867 tariff bill.[27] The manufacturers got involved in the 1921 bill largely because of the very stiff duties proposed on raw wool. Their search for protection was galvanized by the pending success of the wool growers. The spokesman for the National Association of Wool Manufacturers stressed,

The [emergency] measure [as passed by the House] does not include any provision for the protection of the industry of wool man-

[25] Herman T. Warshow, ed., *Representative Industries in the U.S.* (New York: Holt & Co., 1928), p. 637.

[26] *NYT*, March 22, 1921, p. 1:6.

[27] Senate, Finance Committee, *Emergency Tariff*, hearings, 66th Cong., 3rd sess., 1921, pt. 2, pp. 67-70.

ufacturing, which at the present time is in as desperate a situation
and menaced by as serious a foreign competition as any [industry].
. . . [W]e are unwilling to oppose or delay immediate relief for those
industries which are covered by the pending bill *provided that* it is so
amended that no additional disadvantage to those now existing is
imposed upon the various branches of wool manufacture.[28]

But the wool manufacturers did not receive any protection in the
Emergency Bill.[29] Hence, in addition to their desire to reduce import
pressures and raise prices, the manufacturers possessed the additional
incentive to seek greater protection provided by their failure and the
growers' success.

In the general tariff revision conducted by Congress in 1921-22, the
wool manufacturers played a more visible role than they had earlier.
Their association spent much time and energy pressing Congress to
elevate the duties on woolen goods. Citing lower labor costs abroad
and the unstable international exchange situation, the manufacturers
called for an upward revision of their duties, in effect advocating an
increase of some 130 percent.[30] In addition, the industry demanded
new ratios between the duties on raw and manufactured wool, which
would enhance the effective protection on the final goods, and the
maintenance of specific duties in place of ad valorem ones, a move
intended to allow continued differential discrimination against lower-
priced wool goods in which the U.S. firms were least competitive.[31]
The wool manufacturers lobbied successfully for all of these preferences. Their tariffs were significantly increased and the duties were
kept specific and in a graduated ratio to those on raw wool.[32]

The wool manufacturers in 1921-22 showed their protectionist bent
in other ways. For example, when the issue of foreign versus U.S. valuation arose, they favored U.S. valuation.[33] This method of valuation
effectively elevated tariff rates by basing the duty on the equivalent
U.S. price of the import rather than on its actual foreign price. In
addition, the National Association of Wool Manufacturers opposed

[28] Ibid., p. 67. Emphasis added.

[29] *NYT*, January 8, 1921, p. 19:1; Senate, Finance, *Tariff Act of 1921*, sch. 11, p. 3537.

[30] House, Ways and Means, *General Tariff Revision of 1921*, sch. K, pp. 2552-70; *NYT*,
August 20, 1922, p 1:8.

[31] House, Ways and Means, *General Tariff Revision of 1921*, sch. K, pp. 2551-83, and
Senate, Finance, *Tariff Act of 1921*, sch. 11, pp. 3525-70.

[32] N.A. USTC files, "Applications and Investigations," investigation of wool goods, RG 81,
1923; *NYT*, October 15, 1922, pt. 9, p. 3:1-4. Tariffs were increased from an ad valorem
of 35 percent in 1913 to 71 percent in 1922.

[33] Senate, Finance, *Tariff Act of 1921*, sch. 11, p. 3536.

any attempts to introduce a flexible tariff provision into the bill.[34] Such a provision was intended to allow the President to alter tariff duties upward or downward by 50 percent without Congress's approval if economic circumstances warranted such action. The wool manufacturers opposed such flexibility, ostensibly because it would be "unsettling to business, due to the liability to sudden and frequent [rate] changes," but actually because the industry feared the executive would be less susceptible to its pressure for high tariff duties.[35] On both of these issues, the wool manufacturers lost their case; a system of foreign valuation and the flexible tariff provision were written into the final bill.[36]

The wool manufacturers' later approaches to Congress for help were as protectionist as these earlier ones. During the 1929-30 general tariff revision, the industry again requested higher tariff rates. This time, however, the desired increase was rather small, only 10 percent in certain grades of woolens.[37] The manufacturers also retained their support for the U.S. valuation scheme and their opposition to the flexible tariff provision.[38] Two events reduced their willingness to seek protection. First, the industry had a hard time developing an argument for enhanced protection. In its testimony to Congress, its arguments appeared half-hearted and unconvincing, in part because the level of tariffs was already so high it was difficult to ask for further increases and in part because the primary source of its economic problems was clearly not imports but competition from other fabrics, especially cotton and rayon.

A second pressure mitigating the wool manufacturers' preferences for protection was the active opposition by importers and U.S. clothing manufacturers and retailers. The high tariffs on woolens enacted in 1921 had stimulated their opposition, and they began organizing and publicly denouncing the rates and any attempt to increase them.[39] The wool manufacturers thus remained protectionist in 1929, but their desire for higher tariff rates was dampened by their fear of the opposition this would prompt.

[34] *NYT*, December 15, 1921, p. 26:2.

[35] *NYT*, December 15, 1921, p. 26:2; Senate, Finance, *Tariff Act of 1921*, sch. 11, p. 3542.

[36] *NYT*, September 13, 1922, p. 1:3.

[37] House, Ways and Means Committee, *Tariff Readjustment—1929*, hearings, 70th Cong., 2nd sess., 1929, sch. K, pp. 6069-71.

[38] Ibid., pp. 6101-6405; Senate, Finance, *Tariff Act of 1929*, sch. K, pp. 193-224.

[39] House, Ways and Means, *Tariff Readjustment—1929*, sch. K, pp. 6405-6422, the testimony of the importers; Senate, Finance, *Tariff Act of 1929*, sch. K, pp. 242-58; *NYT*, February 8, 1929, p. 24:2; *NYT*, February 9, 1929, p. 8:2.

Another political arena in which the wool manufacturers could have pressed their case was the U.S. Tariff Commission. Under the trade laws of the Fordney-McCumber Act, firms could petition for tariff rate changes under different pretexts. These petitions were directed to the USTC, which would decide whether to investigate the case and subsequently recommend duty changes to the President. The wool manufacturers rarely employed this approach in the 1920s. The focus for their demands was Congress; moreover, since their petitions there tended to be successful, they had little need to bother with the USTC.

Intra-industry debates about trade policy for the industry were limited in the 1920s. Most wool manufacturers shared a similar sentiment about woolens imports: they viewed them as a threat and preferred their strict limitation.[40] The fact that the U.S. manufacturers were represented by a single association throughout the congressional hearings of the decade also suggests this unanimity of interest. No individual firm testified to Congress, and public statements regarding the tariff were made only by the association.[41] The high degree of unity on this issue is not surprising, given the U.S. firms' very similar lack of international ties and strong domestic orientation.

Cases in which one would expect deviance from the domestic industry's position are those involving importers, retailers, and foreign multinationals in the U.S. market. In the early 1920s, neither the importers nor the retailers played a role in the congressional tariff revision. Two reasons for this quiescence are plausible. First, neither group was very large or well organized in 1921-22. By 1929, however, they had become a significant and vocal force against further tariff increases. Second, because the tariff level on woolens was relatively low (in historical perspective), importers and retailers felt that its elevation was not that objectionable. By 1929, however, the duties on woolens were very high, and the two groups increased their opposition to further increases in them. But the large majority of American wool manufacturers were neither importers nor retailers, so this opposition came from outside the group of main producers and never threatened the manufacturers' unity of interest.

The foreign firms operating in the United States were the one force

---

[40] This sentiment is made evident in the industry's testimony to Congress throughout the 1920s and in various issues of the industry's main trade journal, *Bulletin of the National Association of Wool Manufacturers*.

[41] House, Ways and Means, *General Tariff Revision of 1921*, sch. K; House, Ways and Means, *Tariff Readjustment—1929*, sch. 11; Senate, Finance, *Tariff Act of 1921*, sch. K; Senate, Finance, *Tariff Act of 1929*; various issues of the *Bulletin of the National Association of Wool Manufacturers* for the 1920s.

that might have engendered serious divisions among the producers. In the woolen goods industry, only one sizable multinational existed. The Botany Consolidated Mills, the third largest firm in the United States, was affiliated with a large German woolens combination.[42] This firm, however, was in German hands only between 1924 and 1929 and did not generate much debate over the issues during this brief period.

Overall, the wool manufacturing industry supports the argument about Type I industries. U.S. wool manufacturers, when faced with serious economic distress combined with rising imports, sought relief in the form of increased protection of the home market. Their uniform lack of exports or multinational production ensured that their pursuit of protection would be vigorous and industry-wide. Firms in the industry had few qualms about advocating protectionism, because they had no foreign markets to lose and only the domestic market to gain. The thoroughly protectionist sentiment among wool manufacturers in the 1920s can thus be understood as a consequence of its limited international ties.

CASE 2: WATCHES AND CLOCKS

Though small, the watch and clock industry occupied a critical position in the U.S. economy as the twentieth century began. It was "a leader in the introduction of the system of interchangeable parts production and in the mass marketing of 'luxury' consumer goods."[43] The industry's technological and marketing leadership persisted in the early years of the century, as its firms developed precision timing devices for military-related activities. By the end of World War I, however, the industry was losing its dynamism; it had reached "an advanced stage of development [in which] the end of the rapid expansion of the market and a further increase in the intensity of competition" were most likely.[44]

Between 1919 and 1923 and again between 1929 and 1934, U.S. watch and clock manufacturers faced serious economic recessions, induced by domestic problems and exacerbated by foreign competition.[45] Over the decade, imports rose substantially, and their penetration of the domestic market surged intermittently. The value of watch

[42] Moody's *Manual: 1927*, p. 2351; it was the third largest in terms of capitalization.

[43] John Murphy, "Entrepreneurship in the Establishment of the American Clock Industry," *Journal of Economic History* 26 (June 1966):169.

[44] Charles Moore, *Timing a Century: History of the Waltham Watch Company* (Cambridge: Harvard University Press, 1945), pp. 134-35.

[45] Ibid., pp. 134-35, 209-212.

and clock imports grew from $10 million in 1921 to $17 million in 1929, while imports as a percentage of domestic production increased from 16.7 percent in 1919 to 18.6 percent in 1929.[46] Although the average rate of increase in import penetration over the decade was not that large (12 percent or so), strong surges in this rate occurred in 1919-21 (80 percent) and in 1925-27 (70 percent). These imports derived mainly from a single source, Switzerland, which claimed about 90 percent of total U.S. imports. Furthermore, the surges in imports occurred directly before the decade's major tariff revisions and thus contributed to the perceived threat posed by this foreign competition.[47]

The industry's economic distress was widespread. Profitability, the number of firms and employees, and capacity utilization rates all suffered, especially in 1919-23 and after 1929. Profitability declined over the decade, and in its early and late years individual firms were unable to generate sufficient income.[48] In 1921 and 1923, for instance, one of the two largest firms in the business, the Waltham Watch Company, was unable to pay its debts and had to be reorganized by its creditors.[49] By and large the early 1920s were an economic disaster for the U.S. watch and clock industry.

After 1923 the industry's economic problems were confined more to the watch segment. Clock manufacturers, though suffering in the 1919-22 period, operated at a stable level for the rest of the decade; their small increases in production did not keep up with the rest of the economy, but at least they were not declining.[50] The watch manufacturers, on the other hand, experienced difficulty throughout the decade.[51] This was most disturbing, because watches, in particular the new products known as wristwatches, and not clocks, were the dynamic segment of the sector.[52] These troubles and high import penetration in the watch segment meant that the United States was losing

[46] Import figures from U.S. BFDC, *Foreign Commerce*, 1922, 1927, 1929; figures on domestic production from U.S. Dept. of Commerce, *Census, 1929*.

[47] Senate, Finance, *Tariff Act of 1921*, sch. C, p. 2003.

[48] House, Ways and Means, *General Tariff Revision of 1921*, sch. C, p. 1031; Moore, *Timing a Century*, pp. 134-37; Moody's, *Manual: 1927*, entries for Waltham Watch Co.; Moore, *Timing a Century*, pp. 112, 137.

[49] Moore, *Timing a Century*, pp. 112, 118, 127, for the story.

[50] Dept. of Commerce, *Census, 1929*, pp. 1031-33.

[51] Ibid., pp. 1031-33; House, Ways and Means, *Tariff Readjustment—1929*, sch. C, pp. 2348-49; Moore, *Timing a Century*, pp. 209-212.

[52] Moore, *Timing a Century*, pp. 134-35, 217-18; U.S. BFDC, *Foreign Commerce*, 1928, pp. 2-4.

the battle in the most technologically advanced and fastest growing portion of the market.

The serious economic distress felt by American watch and clock manufacturers was likely to induce them to seek greater protection of the home market, especially since their worst problems immediately preceded the general tariff revisions of the 1920s. That these manufacturers also had weak ties to the international economy further increased the likelihood of their preference for protection. In the 1920s the U.S. watch- and clockmakers possessed fairly low levels of export dependence and only incipient multinational operations. They were Type I producers.

In terms of export dependence, the industry was gradually, but not very successfully, developing foreign markets. Exports grew over the decade, but they were directed away from America's primary competitors, the Europeans.[53] In these non-European markets, the U.S. firms met stiff competition from their European counterparts, but it was nothing like what they faced in the Europeans' own markets.

The industry's international trade ties were limited in the 1920s. Its net trade balance became increasingly negative.[54] Export dependence, as measured by the ratio of exports to domestic production, was also low. Over the decade, it averaged 4 percent.[55] The watch and clock manufacturers were thus small exporters. They did have some export ties, but these were minor and directed away from their main competitors.

At the firm level, export dependence was unequally distributed. Only the eight largest firms exported, and only three of these exported beyond Canada.[56] The ratio of exports to domestic sales even for these three firms ranged between 6 and 8 percent in the 1920s, a low figure historically.[57] Thus, export dependence was concentrated among the few largest manufacturers and, even for them, was low.

One aspect of their trading relations was growing during the decade, however. This involved the increasing use of imported parts by U.S. firms in their manufacturing of watches and, to a lesser extent, clocks. Imports of clock parts doubled between 1922 and 1926, while the value of watch parts' imports tripled in the same period.[58] Ameri-

[53] U.S. BFDC, *Foreign Commerce*, 1922, 1927, 1928 (pp. 3-4), 1929.

[54] Ibid.

[55] U.S. BFDC, *Foreign Commerce*, 1928, p. 2; House, Ways and Means, *General Tariff Revision of 1921*, sch. N, pp. 3340-41.

[56] House, Ways and Means, *General Tariff Revision of 1921*, sch. N, pp. 3340-41.

[57] Ibid.; Moore, *Timing a Century*, pp. 252-55.

[58] U.S. BFDC, *Foreign Commerce*, 1928, pp. 3-4.

can watch and clock manufacturers realized that one way to reduce their costs was to use parts produced abroad. Import-assembly operations attained a prominent place over the decade in the production of many U.S. firms. These operations were most widely adopted by the smallest firms in the industry, and not by the leaders.[59] This diluted their political impact and limited the constraining effect they might have had on the industry's protectionist preferences.

Low export dependence was combined with a small-scale, nascent multinationality. At the industry level, direct foreign investment by American watch and clock manufacturers was very small in the 1920s. The total capital invested abroad as of 1932 was $1.4 million,[60] and it was geographically concentrated. Nearly half ($0.7 million) was located in Canada, and the rest was in Great Britain and Europe.[61]

This limited direct foreign investment was new and undeveloped. Several of the foreign subsidiaries had been bought or established only in the 1920s. Moreover, they were usually begun as adjuncts to the firms' export operations. The foreign company was mainly a selling operation at first, but in time it tended to develop its own assembly and production operations. In fact, of the three European watch and clock subsidiaries of the American industry, only one was a factory with complete production.[62] The foreign operations of U.S. watch and clock manufacturers were primarily sales or distribution agencies throughout the 1920s; they were not developed into a worldwide chain of production.

Among the firms, foreign investment, like export activity, was concentrated. Foreign investment was carried out by only five of the largest firms in the industry and was not very important even for these firms.[63] Thus, the foreign operations of individual American watch and clock manufacturers supports the industry-level data: their multinational operations in the 1920s were small and undeveloped. They could hardly be expected to play a critical role in the firms' calculations of their trade policy preferences.

Foreign firms operating in the United States were one group in

[59] Moore, *Timing a Century*, p. 214. This distribution is not unexpected, since larger firms were likely to have had a much easier time fabricating all the different parts used in the completed good.

[60] Senate, *American Branch Factories*, Doc. 120, 1933, p. 11.

[61] Ibid., pp. 11-19.

[62] Dunn, *American Foreign Investments*, pp. 150, 159; Moody's, *Manual: 1927*; Moore, *Timing a Century*, pp. 252-55; Southard, *American Industry*, p. 111; U.S. BFDC, *Foreign Commerce*, 1928, p. 31.

[63] Senate, *American Branch Factories*, Doc. 120, 1933, pp. 11-19; Moody's, *Manual: 1927*; Moore, *Timing a Century*, pp. 252-55.

which such a key role might be exerted by their foreign operations (i.e., by their U.S. subsidiaries). Although the European watch and clock manufacturers tended to be large and export-oriented, they did not have many direct foreign investments in the United States.[64] Only two foreign firms had U.S. manufacturing subsidiaries. One was the Bulova Watch Company, which had its main operations in Switzerland but also had two U.S. plants. Bulova was the largest seller of wristwatches in the United States in the 1920s and thus represented an enormous threat to U.S. manufacturers.[65] In addition to Bulova, a foreign "threat" was seen in the operations of the Gruen Watch Company.[66] The behavior of these two foreign firms on trade issues should have been different than that of the domestic manufacturers. The significant international ties of Bulova and Gruen should have affected their trade policy preferences and steered them away from protectionism.

Overall, the serious economic distress and import competition felt by the U.S. watch and clock manufacturers in the 1920s, combined with their relatively weak export dependence and multinationality, should have resulted in demands for protection. As Type I producers without significant international ties, the domestic firms had little to restrain them from demanding protection. The only firms likely to experience sizable costs from such policies were, first, the foreign multinationals and, second, the few U.S. firms that had large exports. This latter group, however, was only likely to resist protection if it felt that retaliation would endanger its exports. Since these exports were concentrated in markets away from their main foreign competitors, the threat of retaliation was weakened. Though greater protection of the U.S. market might intensify competition in these exporters' foreign markets, it would not inevitably mean losing them. For these U.S. exporters, the costs of advocating protection were still low in the 1920s.

The Dependent Variable

The trade policy preferences of the U.S. watch and clock industry in the 1920s were expressed in three main arenas. Most important was the U.S. Congress, where manufacturers spent much of their effort lobbying for changes in the tariff. The industry focused less pressure

[64] The list of European firms exporting to the United States is given in Senate, Finance, *Tariff Act of 1921*, sch. C, pp. 2003-2004. All of these firms operated through distributors in the United States, not through their own branches.

[65] Senate, Finance, *Tariff Act of 1929*, sch. N, pp. 706-709.

[66] Ibid.; Senate, Finance, *Tariff Act of 1921*, sch. C, pp. 2000-2004; Moody's, *Manual: 1927*, p. 1039.

on the U.S. Tariff Commission; however, it did try several times to use U.S. trade laws and the USTC to institute changes in trade policy. Intra-industry debate was the final arena in which the industry's preferences were aired. These debates revolved around the particular concerns of the domestic firms and around the battle between the importers, allied with the foreign multinationals, and the domestic firms. In all three arenas, the domestic firms' interest in greater protection was evident. This interest became more nuanced over the course of the decade. Increasing use of imported watch and clock parts and the mounting resistance of importers and foreign firms led the domestic manufacturers away from their most strident protectionist positions by the late 1920s.

The watch and clock manufacturers testified extensively to Congress during its two major tariff revisions of the 1920s. In the 1921 debates over the Fordney-McCumber Bill, the domestic manufacturers asked Congress for substantial increases in the tariff on watches and clocks. In general, these producers wanted the tariff to be raised from its "low" level of 30 percent ad valorem to a higher rate, similar to that adopted in the Payne-Aldrich Tariff of 1909 (40 percent).[67]

Even prior to the 1921 tariff revision, the watch and clock manufacturers had begun to lobby for increased tariffs. In preparation for the general tariff revision in 1921 by Congress, the USTC had been directed to report on the condition of all U.S. industries. For its survey on watches and clocks, the USTC received information and "advice" from the domestic firms. The watch manufacturers communicated the same general demands that they would later make to Congress. They wanted a change in their tariff classification, higher tariff duties on completed watch movements, and a shift to specific rates from ad valorem ones.[68] The information and demands contained in the firms' letters were clearly designed to influence the USTC's report to Congress and thus pave the way for the domestic firms' lobbying.

During the 1921 revision, the firms turned to Congress for help. The U.S. *clock* manufacturers sought to have the duties increased to a minimum of 50 percent ad valorem, with a specific duty added according to the number of jewels in the watch. They cited the vigorous German competition in clocks as the cause of all their problems at home and thus the reason for the duty increase.[69] The clock firms lobbying

[67] House, Ways and Means, *General Tariff Revision of 1921*, sch. C, pp. 1023-40, and sch. N, pp. 3335-51; Senate, Finance, *Tariff Act of 1921*, sch. N, pp. 2005-2021.

[68] N.A. USTC files, "Tariff Information Survey," survey of watches and clocks, RG 81, 1920.

[69] House, Ways and Means, *General Tariff Revision of 1921*, sch. C, pp. 1023-35.

Congress did so without the use of a central political association, and were unified in their desire to elevate the tariff, although often at odds over the exact level desired.

The U.S. *watch* manufacturers also lobbied for higher tariffs. Although they too had no industry association, they were united in their desire for a return to the old tariff level of 1909. Their main argument was that the heavy foreign imports from Switzerland and Germany should be curtailed because they were wreaking havoc in the U.S. industry and because they were unfairly promoted by the foreign governments.[70] The watch manufacturers also wanted specific duties to be added to the ad valorem ones, the effect of which would be to discriminate against the goods in which foreigners were most competitive.[71]

In addition, the U.S. watch manufacturers lobbied to change the tariff classification on watches. They wanted watches to be moved from the "metals and manufactures" schedule (Schedule C) to the "sundries" schedule (Schedule N).[72] This was to ensure that their duties would not be reduced. In the 1920s, many of the industries involved in metals and their manufacturing—e.g., the auto industry and makers of farm equipment and machine tools—were highly competitive, international firms that were increasingly disenchanted with the high U.S. tariff policy.[73] The watchmakers feared their whole tariff schedule would be influenced by the antiprotectionist sentiment of these powerful industries and thus wished to retain their protection by being considered in the context of another schedule.

During the Fordney-McCumber hearings, the only opposition to the elevation of duties requested by the U.S. manufacturers came from a group of importers and retailers. This opposition was meager, however. The group testified only once and its objections were limited.

By the 1929 Smoot-Hawley Tariff deliberations, the intensity of both the domestic watch and clock manufacturers' preferences for and the importers-retailers' opposition to protection had changed. The domestic producers were less protectionist in 1929 than they had been in 1921. Though still desiring protection, they no longer wanted it

[70] Ibid., sch. N, pp. 3343-47.

[71] Ibid., pp. 3335-43.

[72] Ibid.

[73] See their testimony in House, Ways and Means, *General Tariff Revision of 1921*, sch. C; Senate, Finance, *Tariff Act of 1921*, sch. C. See also *NYT*, January 15, 1921, p. 7:3; *NYT*, January 17, 1921, p. 23:3. For their foreign ties, see Wilkins, *Maturing of Multinational Enterprise*, chs. 3-6 on the 1920s. See also U.S. Tariff Commission (USTC), *5th Annual Report of the U.S. Tariff Commission* (Washington, D.C.: GPO, 1921), p. 22.

increased on all watch and clock items, largely because of their own international trade in these items. The domestic producers who testified argued that their main problem was not imports per se but imports that "evaded" the tariff, namely smuggled goods and subassemblies.[74] To reduce these imports, the domestic firms claimed it was necessary to make the tariff specific, to increase duties on small, cheap models (wristwatches), and to elevate the duties on nearly completed subassemblies. The increases they desired were circumscribed, but were still directed against their main foreign competition.

The firms also proposed reductions in certain rates. In particular, the domestic manufacturers pressed for decreases in duties on larger, more expensive watches and clocks and on certain parts, the two categories in which the firms traded heavily. The U.S. firms wanted duty reductions on large, expensive watches because they were the firms' main export product.[75] Similarly, they desired a reduction on certain parts' duties because they had to import these goods to produce the finished items.[76] The industry's growing trading links to the international economy thus helped reduce their protectionist bent by the late 1920s.

The domestic firms' preferences may also have been affected by the rising vocal opposition to protection among importers, retailers, foreign firms in the United States, and foreign governments. In the 1929 tariff deliberations, each of these groups spoke out against increasing protection. Unlike in 1921, these groups testified extensively to Congress in 1929 and vehemently opposed protection. The importer-retailer group lobbied against any further increases in protection for the domestic firms. Its detailed testimony stressed the good performance of the domestic industry, the huge costs of protection, and the costly effects of retaliation against the growing U.S. exports of watches and clocks.[77]

The foreign multinationals also testified on their own against the domestic firms. The Bulova Watch Company claimed that the U.S. manufacturers were in good economic shape and thus deserved no further protection.[78] The Gruen Watch Company also voiced its concerns over further protection, but Gruen apparently had negotiated a

[74] House, Ways and Means, *Tariff Readjustment—1929*, sch. C, pp. 2348-49, 2357-59, 2403-2409; Senate, Finance, *Tariff Act of 1929*, sch. C, pp. 687-701.

[75] Senate, Finance, *Tariff Act of 1929*, sch. C, pp. 687-701; U.S. BFDC, *Foreign Commerce*, 1928, pp. 1-6.

[76] Ibid.; Moore, *Timing a Century*, pp. 213-14.

[77] House, Ways and Means, *Tariff Readjustment—1929*, sch. C, pp. 2367-75.

[78] Senate, Finance, *Tariff Act of 1929*, sch. C, pp. 729-43.

deal with the domestic manufacturers in which it agreed not to oppose the specific tariff increases they proposed in return for their promise not to request as stiff an increase.[79] The Swiss government was also involved in the tariff revision. The Swiss protested the high duties written into the House version of the bill and threatened retaliation if these were not altered. This protest apparently was effective, because the rates to which the Swiss objected were reduced in the course of the conference committee's deliberations.[80]

Mounting opposition to further increases in the tariff on watches and clocks in 1929 arose not only from these foreign sources but also from various domestic groups. As the U.S. firms began to import more parts, their interest in excluding these imports was undercut, and they refused to testify in favor of the tariff.[81] This behavior became more widespread in the industry as time progressed; by the early 1930s, increasing dependence on imports of parts had shifted the preferences of numerous domestic firms.[82]

The impact of this new production procedure was felt in the political arena. In addition to reducing the number and unity of the domestic firms favoring protection, the growth of import-assembly operations among the firms split the long-standing New England congressional alliance developed by the domestic manufacturers. By 1929, the New England representatives of the watch industry were divided. Senators Jesse Metcalf and Felix Hebert of Rhode Island began voting against further protection for watches, because their state now contained "a large company which imports foreign watch movements for use in its American-made cases."[83] On the other hand, the Senators from Massachusetts voted for all of the watch and clock tariff increases because their state contained a significant concentration of the largest domestic watchmaking interests.[84] These new production and trading relations transformed the politics of trade policy by the end of the 1920s.

Parts of the industry lobbied the USTC for tariff changes in 1930 after the Smoot-Hawley Bill was enacted. In this case, several major

---

[79] Ibid., pp. 716-26.

[80] *NYT*, April 18, 1930, p. 3:2; *NYT*, April 19, 1930, p. 8:3.

[81] Senate, Finance, *Tariff Act of 1929*, sch. C, pp. 687-701. An example of this was the defection of the South Bend Watch Company from the side of the domestic manufacturers. As the firm shifted more and more to assembly of imported parts in its production, it refused to keep advocating higher tariffs.

[82] Moore, *Timing a Century*, pp. 213-14.

[83] *NYT*, November 14, 1929, p. 12:3-5.

[84] Ibid.

watch producers wanted higher duties on certain watch parts and stricter administration of tariff laws. These producers pushed Congress into requiring the USTC to undertake a section 336 investigation of the watch industry. This investigation led to tariff increases on certain watch parts in 1932.[85] Overall, the industry's pressure on the USTC in the 1920s was secondary in importance to its pressure on Congress, though the concerns voiced at the USTC—i.e., the initial demands for thorough-going protectionism and the later concern over imports of parts—mirrored those that preoccupied the domestic firms during the tariff revisions.

In the 1920s intra-industry divisions over the tariff were limited for this industry. The domestic manufacturers were unified in their preferences, especially in the early part of the decade. Without an industry association, the firms developed a consensus against imports. Their long-standing oligopolistic practices helped achieve this; in fact, the firms' unified stance against imports was the most successful part of their efforts.[86] Even at the end of the decade, consensus—now against imports of subassemblies and wristwatches—among the major firms remained intact. The major opposition to the domestic manufacturers arose from the importers, retailers, foreign multinationals, and foreign governments.

Overall, economic distress in the industry combined with its limited ties to the international economy produced strong and persistent demands for greater protection, as in the case of woolen goods. Nevertheless, the development of greater international trading links through exports and import assembly operations undermined some support for further protectionism by the late 1920s. Furthermore, the foreign multinationals in the United States, which were involved in intricate global trading relationships, proved a major source of opposition to the domestic firms' demands.

CASE 3: THE TEXTILE MACHINERY INDUSTRY

The U.S. textile machinery industry developed slowly and with difficulty in the nineteenth century.[87] Only by closing the domestic market

---

[85] USTC, *14th Annual Report of the U.S. Tariff Commission* (Washington, D.C.: GPO, 1930); Moore, *Timing a Century*, p. 212.

[86] For evidence of their long-standing and often unsuccessful monopolistic practices, see Moore, *Timing a Century*, ch. 5, and *NYT*, September 24, 1927, p. 2:6.

[87] The industry includes all firms producing machines used to transform fibers (cotton, wool, and others) into fabrics (e.g., picking, combing, carding, and spinning machines) and to transform these fabrics into completed goods (e.g., weaving looms, knitting and

and imitating foreign designs could firms in this industry initially survive and develop.[88] The successful manufacture of textile machinery in the United States, though critical for the development of various complementary industries, was not easy to engineer, largely because of the very significant advantages possessed by the British and Germans.

U.S. textile machinery builders, nevertheless, as a result of innovations and strong domestic demand, established a prosperous industry between 1899 and 1921, especially in cotton manufacturing, where the U.S. machines became worldwide leaders.[89] This had two salubrious effects. Firms were propelled into their first long period of prosperity, which lasted from 1899 to 1912 and fostered great growth in the size of the firms.[90] These product innovations also induced the industry's first sizable exports around 1913.[91] The favorable conditions were not long lasting, however; by 1923, the industry was again in a depressed condition and faced serious foreign competition at home and in its new export markets.

The industry entered a long period of economic depression in 1921. In particular, it was hit by rising import competition after World War I. The value of U.S. imports of textile machinery rose continuously over the 1920s. Their value in 1921 was $5.3 million; by 1929, it reached $8.5 million.[92] In addition, levels of import penetration climbed over the decade. The ratio of imports to total domestic production was a mere 0.9 percent in 1919; this rose to 4.1 percent by 1921 and ended the decade at 7 percent.[93] Not only did the import penetration level grow, but its rate of increase surged dramatically at times. Between 1919 and 1921 it rose over 300 percent, for instance, and between 1926 and 1929 it increased some 75 percent.[94] The postwar reconstruction of the European industry thus clearly hurt the U.S.

---

braiding machines, embroidery and lace-making machines). It excludes, most notably, sewing machines.

[88] David Jeremy, "Innovation in American Textile Technology during the Early Nineteenth Century," *Technology and Culture* 14 (January 1973):40-41; Thomas Navin, *The Whitin Machine Works since 1931* (New York: Russell & Russell, 1950), pp. 402, 488-91; House, Ways and Means Committee, *Tariff Readjustment—1929*, sch. 3, pp. 2483-84.

[89] Navin, *Whitin Machine Works*, pp. 307-309; Jeremy, "American Textile Technology," pp. 63, 76.

[90] Navin, *Whitin Machine Works*, pp. 307-309; George Gibb, *The Saco-Lowell Shops* (New York: Russell & Russell, 1950), pp. 412-13, 431-32 (profit data).

[91] Gibb, *Saco-Lowell Shops*, pp. 478-81.

[92] U.S. BFDC, *Foreign Commerce*, 1922, 1927, 1929.

[93] Ibid.; U.S. Dept. of Commerce, *Census, 1929*, pp. 1177-79.

[94] Ibid.

industry, as European exports of textile machinery to the United States soared and increased the problems of already weak domestic firms.

This distress was apparent in the decline of the U.S. firms' profitability, numbers, and employees.[95] Every firm but one was in deficit throughout much of the 1920s.[96] The largest firm in the industry, the Saco-Lowell Shops, lost $0.5 million a year on average between 1923 and 1927. In fact, in 1926 it had to be rescued from its creditors by several banks, who then reorganized the entire firm and closed half of its plants.[97] Saco-Lowell's situation was typical for the industry in the period. In addition, it was plagued by serious overcapacity problems as shifts in the preferences and location of the key textile manufacturers who bought these machines reshaped the machine-building industry.[98]

The textile machinery industry's ties to the international economy in the 1920s were mixed and unstable. The industry demonstrated high levels of export dependence that rose and fell over the decade, but it possessed little multinationality. Overall, the industry was a weak Type II.

In terms of export dependence, the U.S. textile machinery manufacturers had high but unstable links to the international trading system. The value of exports in the 1920s vacillated substantially: in 1921, it reached a peak of $20 million; it then declined to a trough of $9 million in 1924, but rose again to $14 million in 1929.[99] The industry's net trade position was positive throughout the decade, though like its exports, it varied. The surplus of exports over imports peaked in 1921 at $14.7 million, fell to its nadir in 1923 at $2.4 million, and then rose again.[100] The ratio of exports to total production in the industry was substantial, about 9 to 10 percent over the decade. This also rose and fell. It reached a peak in 1921 at 15.5 percent, dropped to 6.4 percent in 1923, and only rose gradually after 1925 to 11.2 percent in 1929.[101]

[95] U.S. Dept. of Commerce, *Census, 1929*, p. 1177; Navin, *Whitin Machine Works*, pp. 348-51. These sources provide extensive data on the industry. See also Milner, "Resisting the Protectionist Temptation," pp. 191-93.

[96] Navin, *Whitin Machine Works*, pp. 336-37; Gibb, *Saco-Lowell Shops*, pp. 461, 492-93; Moody's, *Manual: 1927*.

[97] Navin, *Whitin Machine Works*, pp. 337, 340-41, 353-57; Gibb, *Saco-Lowell Shops*, pp. 461, 492-93, 501.

[98] Navin, *Whitin Machine Works*, pp. 335, 343-48.

[99] U.S. BFDC, *Foreign Commerce*, 1922, 1927, 1929.

[100] Ibid.

[101] Ibid.; U.S. Dept. of Commerce, *Census, 1929*, p. 1177.

Several features of this export dependence are notable. First, export sales were unequally distributed among firms. This distribution was determined less by firm size than by product line. In general, manufacturers of cotton preparatory and finishing machinery were the largest exporters, while those fabricating machinery for the woolens industry did not export much.[102] Among the cotton machinery manufacturers, exports were significant and widespread; they averaged close to 25 percent of total sales for many firms.[103]

Second, the American exports were geographically concentrated. They were sent mainly to the Far East (China and Japan), and then to South America, Canada, and Europe from 1913 to the late 1920s.[104] The industry's key foreign markets were not those of its major foreign competitors, and this reduced the constraining effects of its export dependence. Retaliation by its major competitors abroad in response to rising U.S. protectionism would not directly hurt the U.S. exporters in any significant way, since their foreign markets were not their competitors' home markets.

Third, the export dependence of the 1920s was a new phenomenon. The U.S. industry had not begun exporting in any magnitude until 1913.[105] In fact, the largest firm in the industry (also the largest exporter), the Saco-Lowell Shops, received its first sizable export order only in 1915.[106] Export sales grew rapidly for the industry after this, but the novelty of these sales was slow to wear off. Even at the peak of U.S. exports in 1921, the chairman of the second largest firm in the industry, the Whitin Machine Works, refused to be optimistic about the industry's long-run prospects in the export business, claiming that the British still "monopolize[d] the world's textile machinery business outside of the U.S."[107] This view weakened the industry's perception of the value of its exports. The U.S. firms were not willing to accord their foreign markets the same prospective worth as their domestic markets, thus minimizing the constraining effect these ties exerted on their trade policy preferences.

Combined with their important but limited export dependence, the U.S. textile machinery manufacturers had low levels of multinational-

[102] U.S. BFDC, *Foreign Commerce*, 1922, 1927, 1929; N.A. USTC files, "Applications and Investigations," investigation of woolen cards, no. 388, RG 81, 1924; Gibb, *Saco-Lowell Shops*, pp. 461, 481.

[103] Ibid.

[104] Ibid.

[105] Gibb, *Saco-Lowell Shops*, p. 481.

[106] Ibid., pp. 478–81.

[107] Navin, *Whitin Machine Works*, p. 326.

ity. Few, if any, firms had production facilities abroad. In part, this resulted from the domestic firms' relatively small size and their difficulties in competing internationally. The highest estimate on direct foreign investment for the industry shows it to be small. In 1932, this "other machinery" category was estimated to have $6.9 million invested abroad.[108]

Firm-level data and foreign country studies of direct foreign investment in the 1920s also demonstrate the limited significance of multinationality for this industry. The distribution of this aggregate U.S. foreign investment for "other machinery" was skewed; half of it was located in Europe and the United Kingdom, while another third was in Canada and the remainder was in Latin America.[109] But even country-level studies of American investment abroad in these areas never mention the textile machinery sector or various firms within it.[110] At the firm level as well, neither the country studies, *Moody's Manual*, nor the U.S. Tariff Commission's surveys of the textile machinery builders in the 1920s reveal any account of these manufacturers' foreign operations.[111] The firms' small size, combined with the newness of their export activities, limited their ability to become multinational. In any case, the industry's multinational production activities were not significant in the 1920s and were not a critical consideration for any firm in it.

Although U.S. foreign investment in textile machinery business was insignificant, foreign investment in the U.S. industry was not. In the 1920s both British and German firms had strong ties to, or actual operations in, the United States. As world leaders, the British firms had developed early ties to the U.S. market. By the 1920s they controlled

---

[108] Senate, *American Branch Factories*, Doc. 120, 1933, p. 10. This figure is for the very aggregated level termed "other machinery of metal"; it significantly overestimates the value for just textile machinery but does suggest a maximum level for the industry. This figure accounted for merely 0.46 percent of all U.S. manufacturing direct foreign investment. Even as a maximum, this figure indicates that multinationality was not significant for the industry.

[109] Ibid., pp. 10-19.

[110] See C. Lewis, *America's Stake*; Wilkins, *Emergence of Multinational Enterprise*; Wilkins, *Maturing of Multinational Enterprise*; Dunn, *American Foreign Investments*; John Dunning, *American Investments in British Manufacturing Industry* (London: Allen, Unwin, 1958); Southard, *American Industry*; Winkler, *Investments of U.S. Capital*; Phelps, *Migration of U.S. Industry*; Marshall, Southard, and Taylor, *Canadian-American Industry*; U.S. BFDC, *American Direct Investments*; Senate, *American Branch Factories*, Doc. 258, 1931.

[111] See Moody's, *Manual: 1927*, various entries for the industry; N.A. USTC files, "Tariff Information Surveys," survey of knitting machinery, RG 81, 1920; N.A. USTC files, "Applications and Investigations," woolen cards, no. 388, RG 81, 1924.

two major firms there.[112] The Germans also developed U.S. subsidiaries, but only during the 1920s.[113] Overall, British and German firms' ties to the U.S. market through both imports and foreign investment were significant.

Although the most salient features of the U.S. textile machinery industry are its high but unsteady export dependence and its insignificant multinationality, two other features merit attention. First, despite its successful innovations and growing exports, the U.S. industry in the 1920s was not, and did not think itself, a first-rate world competitor. The industry globally had long been dominated by the British and more recently by the Germans. The U.S. manufacturers, as noted, possessed little confidence in the durability of their new hold on foreign markets.[114]

Second, the textile machinery industry had a close relationship with the textile manufacturing sector, because the textile mills were the machinery builders' primary buyers. These mills sometimes acquired an interest in the textile machinery firms, but more often, through their buying power, they dictated the type, quantity, and price of the machines to be built, as well as the builders' location of production.[115] This relationship extended into the political arena as well. In the late 1800s, the textile machinery builders and textile manufacturers had united in a protectionist alliance that proved successful for both.[116] This was renewed to a lesser extent in the 1920s. The textile machinery builders' close economic relationship brought them into a political alliance with the textile manufacturers. Because the latter group tended to have greater leverage in the relationship, their political preferences, which were solidly protectionist during the 1920s, influenced the machinery builders. However, the machinery manufacturers also used the greater political leverage of the textile manufacturers to realize their preferences. This interindustry relationship was asymmetric but also symbiotic.

The textile machinery industry thus had a substantial but volatile level of export dependence and an insignificant degree of multinationality. It was a weak type II industry. The argument here suggests that despite the high level of economic distress in the industry in the 1920s, its export dependence should have reduced its propensity to demand further protection of its home market. Several features of

---

[112] Navin, *Whitin Machine Works*, pp. 241, 245, 353-55; Gibb, *Saco-Lowell Shops*, p. 432.
[113] Ibid.
[114] Navin, *Whitin Machine Works*, p. 326.
[115] Gibb, *Saco-Lowell Shops*, pp. 418-19; Navin, *Whitin Machine Works*, p. 402.
[116] Navin, *Whitin Machine Works*, pp. 236-38.

this export dependence and of the industry in general, however, mitigated the constraining effects of these exports. That these foreign sales were a new phenomenon, that they were concentrated geographically in areas distant from the main U.S. competitors, and that they were highly unstable all lowered their importance to the industry. The value the firms were willing to attribute to their foreign sales was also undercut by their enduring belief in the superiority of various foreign manufacturers and by the industry's close relationship to the protectionist textile manufacturers. Under these conditions, export dependence was likely to exert only a weak influence on these firms' trade policy preferences.

The Dependent Variable

Evidence on the trade policy preferences of the U.S. textile machinery builders is limited. These manufacturers were not very active on the tariff issue in the 1920s. The available information concerns the industry's lobbying in Congress, certain firms' appeals to the U.S. Tariff Commission for duty changes, and evidence about the intra-industry squabbles over the tariff. Though not detailed, all sources suggest that the machinery builders were divided and ambivalent in their early preferences and later tended to prefer more closure of the domestic market.

In the course of the two general tariff revisions of the 1920s, the domestic textile machinery builders testified little to Congress. During consideration of the 1921-22 Fordney-McCumber Bill, these manufacturers apparently never testified. Two reasons for this lack of interest are likely. First and most important, the industry was unable to take a stand on the issue due to internal divisions, which had two sources. Some firms in the industry in 1921-22 had just experienced new heights in export sales; 1919-21 had been a booming period. At this point, firms may have felt ambivalent about the tariff. Economic difficulties at home encouraged protectionist desires, but hefty foreign sales, which were one of the few positive factors in the firms' balance sheets, engendered concerns about the impact of further closure of the domestic market.[117] Within each firm, then, preferences on the tariff were hard to establish.

Among the leading firms, moreover, the development of a consensus on such preferences was exceedingly difficult to forge. The indus-

---

[117] Gibb, *Saco-Lowell Shops*, ch. 13, suggests some of this ambivalence in Saco-Lowell's decision making. See also N.A. USTC files, "Tariff Information Survey," knitting machinery, RG 81, 1920; N.A. USTC files, "Applications and Investigations," investigation of hosiery machinery, no. 446, RG 81, 1925.

try association, controlled by the top five firms, did not testify most probably because it was unable to establish a unified front. This was due to the fact that among the leading firms were not only the foremost exporters, whose trade policy interests were unclear, but also a major foreign multinational, the H&B Machine Company, which in all likelihood opposed increased protectionism. The lack of activity among the domestic builders on the tariff issue in the early 1920s may thus have stemmed from the complications posed by their ties to the international economy. The difficulties faced by each firm in deciding upon its trade preferences, given its exports, and the divisions among the leading firms over protection undermined consensus on the issue and made silence the best policy.

A second reason for the industry's absence from the congressional hearings is that the domestic firms voiced their preferences elsewhere. In 1920, the machinery builders tried first to have their views on the tariff inserted into the USTC's report to Congress on the industry. The wool-knitting machinery manufacturers, who in particular lacked export ties, pushed the USTC to recommend to Congress that their duties be changed. Their plea for the use of both specific and ad valorem rates did not mention explicit increases in the duties, but these would probably result from such a change.[118] In the tariff information survey concerning this sector, the views of other domestic manufacturers were also evident. Their primary interest was in having textile machinery classified in a new, separate category. Having their duties raised back to the "traditional" (pre-1913) level of 45 percent was only a minor concern.[119] In the early 1920s, the domestic textile machinery builders voiced their preferences on the tariff issue indirectly by influencing Congress's knowledge about the industry and the way it would consider the industry.

While sentiment among the domestic firms for greater protection in 1921-22 was neither widespread nor intensive, sentiment against such protection was more evident. In 1921 the only textile machinery firm to testify to Congress on the tariff issue was the British-controlled importer, Leigh and Butler. This firm opposed any duty increases on textile machinery and preferred the reduction or complete elimination of all duties. In addition, the firm objected to the adoption of the American valuation method and opposed the domestic manufacturers' preferences for a combined specific and ad valorem duty.[120] This

---

[118] N.A. USTC files, "Tariff Information Survey," knitting machinery, RG 81, 1920.
[119] Ibid., pp. 823-26.
[120] Senate, Finance, *Tariff Act of 1921*, sch. 3, pp. 1839-45.

firm's strong opposition to protectionism was expected, given its extensive foreign ties. What was surprising was the domestic manufacturers' lack of activity, given their serious economic distress.

By the tariff revision of 1929, the domestic textile machinery manufacturers were more united and determined to obtain further protection. Mounting economic distress, export losses and instability, and declining foreign investment in the U.S. industry over the 1920s all strengthened protectionist sentiment. But even in 1929, the domestic builders were not demanding the sizable increases in duties that many other industries wanted. In the hearings, the domestic manufacturers lobbied for "a restoration of the traditional rate of 45 percent" on their goods.[121] The firms' central reason for seeking this increase involved the nature of their foreign competitors. The long-standing predominance of the foreign firms and the fear that this engendered in the U.S. builders were the primary motivations in their calculations of interest. The industry's spokesman maintained again and again: "The textile-machinery industry of the U.S. is relatively small and *insecure* as compared with its great English and European competitors. . . . It is true that in size and number of plants, productive capacity, and financial resources the foreign builders are greatly superior to the . . . companies of this [U.S.] country.[122]

The domestic firms' turn to mild protectionism in 1929, therefore, resulted from their insecure international position in terms of both domestic and foreign markets. This insecurity had both historical roots and immediate causes; the legacy of British and German dominance and, most important, the changes in foreign market shares in the 1920s inflamed it. In particular, the great fluctuations in the domestic builders' exports and the decline in their export dependence in the middle of the decade undercut the relative value of their foreign markets in comparison to domestic ones and made protection of the home market more plausible.

In addition to the new impetus to protection in 1929, opposition to it was weakened. By 1929, the primary foreign multinational in the U.S. market, the H&B Machine Company, had been sold to an American company.[123] H&B, its international ties now greatly reduced, became a less vigorous opponent of protection. Unlike the early 1920s,

---

[121] House, Ways and Means, *Tariff Readjustment—1929*, sch. 3, pp. 2483-87; Senate, Finance, *Tariff Act of 1929*, sch. 3, pp. 936-38.

[122] House, Ways and Means, *Tariff Readjustment—1929*, sch. 3, p. 2485.

[123] Navin, *Whitin Machine Works*, pp. 353-55.

by 1929 the internal and external barriers restraining the domestic textile machinery firms' pursuit of protection were lowered.[124]

The intra-industry politics of the textile machinery builders showed the internal divisions prompted by firms' different international ties. The industry revealed little capacity for political cooperation on the tariff. It did develop an industry association and had a lobbyist in Washington, D.C., but neither proved active in the 1920s.[125] Internal disagreement prevented unified action on trade policy. The key divisions were first between the major domestic firms and the importers, allied with foreign multinationals, and second among the domestic firms. The importers and foreign firms took an active stance against attempts to increase protection; the major domestic producers made only feeble, if any, efforts to promote protection. Given the first group's strong international ties, their response was predictable. The domestic firms' lack of pressure for protection despite their severe economic difficulties was a consequence of the new and growing export dependence of some firms and their increasing separation from the other firms who lacked such export ties. The domestic firms' more unified interest in protection by 1929, however, revealed the tenuousness of these ties.

Overall, the textile machinery case lends some support to the argument about Type II industries. In the period when export dependence was most significant—i.e., just before 1921-22—the industry's preferences were most constrained by it. In the early 1920s, severe economic distress at home did not drive the machinery manufacturers into the embrace of protectionism. Rather, the firms' export interests constrained this impulse. The result was a marked lack of preference, apparent in the firms' dearth of testimony to Congress. But these export interests proved fragile, and in the late 1920s these firms' preferences shifted to modest protectionism. This case thus suggests that

[124] Given the actual tariff outcomes, the intensity of the firms' interests in protection may have been less than is suggested here. In 1929, in contrast to 1921, the tariffs on textile machinery were little changed; only the duty on "other textile machines" was increased at all—by 5 percent. And the manufacturers never complained about this. See House, Ways and Means Committee, *Comparison of Tariff Acts of 1913, 1922, 1929* (Washington, D.C.: GPO, 1930), p. 60. In addition, in the 1920s there was only one other case of industry pressure over the tariff. This was an odd case, involving an appeal made to the USTC by a single firm in 1924. The firm requested a tariff increase on its product, after having acquired the design for it rather nefariously from a foreign manufacturer. It hoped to exclude that firm from its market. See Milner, "Resisting the Protectionist Temptation," pp. 207-208, and N.A. USTC "Applications and Investigations," woolen cards, no. 388, RG 81, 1924.

[125] Navin, *Whitin Machine Works*, pp. 236-38.

export ties must be well established, stable, and extensive in order to constrain distressed industries' preferences for closure of the home market.[126]

CASE 4: FERTILIZER

The U.S. fertilizer industry, part of the larger chemical industry, was new in the 1920s, having begun after 1850 in the United States and having experienced its most significant expansion there between 1899 and 1914.[127] The industry involved the chemical combination of three products: nitrogen, phosphates, and potash (potassium).[128] These required inputs from different sources and were manufactured by three separate groups of firms.

Nitrogen came either from Chile in the form of sodium nitrate or from the artificial production of nitrogen in the form of ammonia sulphate.[129] Prior to the 1920s, the U.S. fertilizer industry imported all of its nitrates' supply; in the 1920s, however, one U.S. firm, the American Coal Products Company, acquired the rights to produce ammonia sulphate from its German patent-holders.[130] The second key input, phosphates, was mined in Florida, Tennessee, and parts of the West.[131] Until the 1920s the U.S. mines accounted for much of the world's total output of phosphate. During that decade, however, foreign competition arose, as the French began mining and exporting phosphate from their North African colonies.[132]

The third essential input for the manufacture of fertilizer, potash,

[126] The parallel to the machine tool industry in the 1970s is striking. The novelty and instability of exports seem to reduce greatly their constraining effect on protectionist preferences.

[127] U.S. BFDC, *The American Chemical Industry*, Trade Promotion Series no. 78 (Washington, D.C.: GPO, 1929), pp. 20-21. The development of chemically based fertilizers, rather than the use of natural products as fertilizers, was a new phenomenon at the time.

[128] Senate, *FTC Report on the Fertilizer Industry*, 67th Cong., 4th sess., S. Doc. 347, 1923, pp. 17-33; Warshow, ed., *Representative Industries*, pp. 141-43; William Haynes, *The American Chemical Industry: A History*, vols. 4, 5, 6 (New York: Van Nostrand, 1948, 1949, 1954), 4:311-13.

[129] Senate, *FTC Report*, Doc. 347, pp. 18-24; Joseph Borkin, *The Crime and Punishment of I. G. Farben* (New York: Free Press, 1978), pp. 8-9.

[130] Senate, *FTC Report*, Doc. 347, pp. 18-24; Warshow, ed., *Representative Industries*, pp. 141-43; Haynes, *American Chemical Industry*, 4:312-14; Federal Trade Commission (hereafter FTC), *A Report of the FTC on the Fertilizer Industry* (Washington, D.C.: GPO, 1950), pp. 21-33.

[131] Senate, *FTC Report*, Doc. 347, pp. 24-25; FTC, *Report on Fertilizer Industry*, 1950, pp. 54-60.

[132] FTC, *Report on Fertilizer Industry*, 1950, pp. 65-68.

had to be acquired from a foreign source, Germany.[133] Prior to World War I, Germany supplied virtually all of the world's potash. The war severely reduced Germany's exports of potash and forced other countries to develop their own sources. In the United States a supply of potash was found in the West, mainly in California and Montana. Although not as cheap as German potash, these western sources were developed after 1914 by a group of small firms not primarily in the fertilizer business.[134] When German potash production revived in the 1920s, these small U.S. producers suffered greatly, thereafter never able to gain more than a 10 percent share of the U.S. potash market.[135]

The fertilizer industry was thus divided into three sectors, each of which had significant international components. Nitrogen supplies were derived from Chile and Germany. Both of these foreign sources were nevertheless linked to American firms: the Chileans through U.S. direct investment in the nitrate mines and the Germans through patent agreements with U.S. producers.[136] Phosphates were controlled by the U.S. fertilizer manufacturers, but they faced mounting foreign competition. The third input, potash, was derived primarily from Germany; however, U.S. firms owned some of the German mines and other domestic producers were developing their own sources.

In the 1920s the U.S. fertilizer industry faced a number of severe challenges. Foreign competition increased, and imports became a significant force. In 1919, the value of fertilizer imports was a mere $12 million; in 1921, the value had increased to $30.7 million; and by 1929 it had skyrocketed to $72.3 million.[137] The share of the U.S. market that these foreign goods held grew substantially during the decade as well. Imports as a percentage of total domestic production rose from 4.8 percent in 1919 to 17 percent in 1921 and finally to 31.1 percent in 1929.[138]

The 1920s were also one of the industry's first severe periods of economic distress. Dependent upon the agricultural business, the fer-

[133] Senate, *FTC Report*, Doc. 347, pp. 26-33; FTC, *Report on Fertilizer Industry*, 1950, pp. 85-87.

[134] Senate, *FTC Report*, Doc. 347, pp. 26-33; FTC, *Report on Fertilizer Industry*, 1950, pp. 86-101; U.S. BFDC, *Fertilizers: Some New Factors in Fertilizer Production and Trade*, Trade Info. Bulletin no. 372 (Washington, D.C.: GPO, 1925), pp. 1-3.

[135] Senate, *FTC Report*, Doc. 347, pp. 26-27; FTC, *Report on Fertilizer Industry*, 1950, pp. 86-101.

[136] Senate, *FTC Report*, Doc. 347, pp. 18-24.

[137] U.S. BFDC, *Foreign Commerce*, 1922, 1927, 1929.

[138] Ibid.; U.S. Dept. of Commerce, *Census, 1929*.

tilizer manufacturers followed the U.S. farmers into depression.[139] As agricultural prices declined, farmers were increasingly unable to buy fertilizers; hence, fertilizer demand fell and so did its price. The early and later years of the decade were especially bad for the fertilizer producers, when domestic problems were combined with rising foreign imports.

The industry's economic distress was evident in its declining profitability as well as in reduced numbers of firms and employees. For instance, between 1920 and 1922 the direct losses of the U.S. fertilizer manufacturers were $75 million.[140] Declines in the number of firms reflected not only mergers in the industry but also the closure of some operations. Two of the largest firms had to halt production and be reorganized by their creditors.[141] The industry's problems were further revealed in its declining numbers of workers.[142]

Fertilizer manufacture was a Type III industry. The extent of its ties to the international economy in the 1920s was substantial in terms of both export dependence and multinationality. Export dependence for the industry was significant but somewhat mixed and unstable. Fertilizer exports rose and fell cyclically over the decade, hitting lows in 1920-21, 1924, and 1928.[143] The industry's net international trade balance was consistently and increasingly negative.[144] However, the industry's ratio of exports to domestic production, which averaged about 9 percent during the 1920s, revealed the strength of its exports.[145] The industry's dependence on exports was important but limited.

The different trade positions of the industry's three sectors need examination. Export dependence was very high for the phosphate and superphosphate producers, low but rising for the nitrogenous sector, and low and falling for the potash producers. The United States was a major source worldwide for phosphates. In the 1920s, in fact, these producers were more concerned with foreign markets than with the domestic one; they spent much time and energy developing extensive export associations (Webb-Pomerane) in order to strengthen their for-

[139] House, *Effects of Agricultural Depressions on the Fertilizer Industry*, 67th Cong., 1st sess., 1922, H. Doc. 195, pp. 51-53.

[140] Ibid.

[141] *NYT*, September 4, 1924, p. 27:4; *NYT*, February 17, 1925, p. 36:3; *NYT*, January 8, 1925, p. 26:3; Wilkins, *Maturing of Multinational Enterprise*, pp. 143-45.

[142] U.S. Dept. of Commerce, *Census, 1929*.

[143] U.S. BFDC, *American Chemical Industry*, no. 78, pp. 28-29; U.S. BFDC, *Foreign Commerce*, 1922, 1927, 1929.

[144] U.S. BFDC, *Foreign Commerce*, 1922, 1927, 1929.

[145] Ibid.; U.S. Dept. of Commerce, *Census, 1929*.

eign sales.[146] Export dependence in nitrogen inputs was low because the United States had to import all of its sodium nitrate from Chile, but rising because of a developing U.S. domestic and export capacity in artificial nitrates. Finally, the potash sector was not dependent on exports; in fact, it was fighting primarily to gain a share of the U.S. market. Import penetration was the highest in this sector; the Germans controlled about 90 percent of the U.S. market.[147]

The U.S. fertilizer manufacturers' multinationality was also sectorally differentiated. Each of the sectors had substantial multinational ties except the potash sector, which consisted of small, domestic firms and imports. These ties were created not only through U.S. direct foreign investments but also through various contractual agreements, research and development linkages, and patent licenses. The combination of all of these foreign ties left the industry, save for the potash sector, looking very multinational in the 1920s. The value of U.S. foreign investments in this industry was $17.3 million in 1932.[148] It, however, may have been even higher, perhaps over $70 million, in 1929.[149]

Individual firms also showed substantial multinational ties. Among the ten largest firms in the industry, all but two or three had extensive foreign operations. The Virginia-Carolina Chemical Company, the American Agricultural Chemical Company, the International Agricultural Corporation, and the two meat-packing firms involved heavily in fertilizers, Swift and Armour, all had extensive foreign manufacturing and extractive operations in Europe and Latin America.[150] In addition to these top five producers, two other large U.S. manufacturers had some foreign operations.[151] And, though not a fertilizer producer, one

---

[146] FTC, *Report on Fertilizer Industry*, 1950, pp. 66-69; Jesse Markham, *The Fertilizer Industry: Study of an Imperfect Market* (1958; reprint New York: Greenwood, 1969), pp. 39-43.

[147] U.S. BFDC, *Fertilizers*, no. 372, pp. 1-3; Senate, *FTC Report*, Doc. 347, pp. 26-33; FTC, *Report on Fertilizer Industry*, 1950, pp. 85-98.

[148] Senate, *American Branch Factories*, Doc. 120, 1933, p. 10. Because it is for the much larger "other chemicals" group, this figure overestimates the true level; however, it underestimates the value, since it excludes data for two of the largest fertilizer firms, Armour and Swift, who were primarily meat packers and classified as such.

[149] Winkler, *Investments of U.S. Capital*, pp. 95-107; Dunn, *American Foreign Investments*, pp. 71-74; C. Lewis, *America's Stake*, pp. 257-62.

[150] Haynes, *American Chemical Industry*, 4:xxvii, 6:13-14; Wilkins, *Emergence of Multinational Enterprise*, pp. 98-99, 212-16; Senate, *FTC Report*, Doc. 347, pp. 14-15; Wilkins, *Maturing of Multinational Enterprise*, pp. 107, 143-45; Dunn, *American Foreign Investments*, pp. 62-63, 69, 145-47; Southard, *American Industry*, p. 220, appendix 11.

[151] The Davidson Chemical Company operated in the United Kingdom and in Latin America through its subsidiary, the Rio Tinto Company. In addition, the American Cyanamid Company had substantial fertilizer operations in Canada and possibly elsewhere.

American firm, the Anglo-Chilean Consolidated Nitrate Company, owned by the Guggenheims, controlled about 35 percent of all Chilean nitrate production in 1925 and nearly 50 percent by 1929.[152] This foreign investment gave a U.S. firm nearly complete control over the world's supply of sodium nitrates.

The industry's ties to the international economy were augmented further by extensive patent and R & D agreements and by various collusive measures between U.S. and foreign firms. Patent and R&D licensing, as well as joint production, were common.[153] In addition, the industry attempted to collaborate illegally with the foreign producers. Such arrangements, including price fixing, quotas, and other cartel activities, were not very stable in the 1920s, but they did signal the industry's attempts to organize globally.[154]

Other features of the U.S. fertilizer industry important for understanding its trade policy preferences are its monopoly power at home and abroad and its relations with U.S. agriculture. The U.S. fertilizer industry was economically concentrated. In 1921, the top seven firms accounted for over 65 percent of production, and the top two alone held 33 percent of the market.[155] In the 1920s the fertilizer manufacturers took advantage of their economic power to organize various collusive practices and build a strong political coalition. They solidified their industry organization, the National Fertilizer Association, by bringing all the major firms into it. Rising economic concentration as well as the existence of a critical issue—their long and successful struggle to keep the government out of fertilizer production—unified the producers and focused their attention on the political arena.[156]

Southard, *American Industry*, p. 220, appendix 11; Wilkins, *Emergence of Multinational Enterprise*, pp. 212-16; Wilkins, *Maturing of Multinational Enterprise*, pp. 143-45; *NYT*, July 30, 1925, p. 27:3.

[152] Dunn, *American Foreign Investments*, pp. 71-74; Winkler, *Investments of U.S. Capital*, pp. 95-107; C. Lewis, *America's Stake*, pp. 257-62; Wilkins, *Maturing of Multinational Enterprise*, pp. 104-105. See Harvey O'Connor, *The Guggenheims* (New York: Covici Friede, 1937), chs. 25-29, for the full story.

[153] U.S. firms producing synthetic nitrates were tied to Italian and German firms through these. Moreover, U.S. producers of cyanamid operated through licenses and joint production ventures with the Swiss. U.S. BFDC, *Fertilizers*, no. 372, pp. 10-15; Wilkins, *Maturing of Multinational Enterprise*, pp. 78-84.

[154] *NYT*, May 13, 1930, p. 1 :4; FTC, *Report on Fertilizer Industry*, 1950, pp. 28-36, 43-51; Haynes, *American Chemical Industry*, 4:58; *NYT*, December 17, 1927, p. 13:3.

[155] Senate, *FTC Report*, Doc. 347, pp. 5-6.

[156] John Henahan, *200 Years of American Chemicals* (New York: McGraw-Hill, 1976), pp. 46-48; FTC, *A Report on the Fertilizer Industry* (Washington, D.C.: GPO, 1916), pp. 173-76; *NYT*, March 4, 1923, p. 6:3; Markham, *Fertilizer Industry*, p. 21; Senate, *FTC Report*, Doc. 347, pp. 54-55.

The U.S. fertilizer industry, while oligopolistic, was no match for its foreign rivals in this respect. The German, French, Italian, and British manufacturers were highly cartelized. The German firm I. G. Farbenindustrie controlled not only the country's fertilizers but also its entire chemical industry.[157] In France, Kuhlmann operated the fertilizer cartel; in Britain, the Imperial Chemical Industry controlled chemicals.[158] By the end of the 1920s, these national groups were supplemented by international cartels in synthetic and natural nitrates.[159] This growing web of linkages had in effect created by 1929 a single global fertilizer cartel that confronted the U.S. industry in international markets. The U.S. firms, though economically and politically powerful at home, were dwarfed by these international giants and were only partially involved in the cartel; by and large, they had been excluded from it due to U.S. antitrust laws and the Europeans' opposition.[160]

A second important feature of the U.S. fertilizer industry was its relationship with the agricultural sector. The fortunes of the fertilizer manufacturers depended heavily on those of their major buyers, American farmers.[161] This economic relationship translated into a political one. The farmers, through their organizations, the American Farm Bureau and the National Grange, were involved in the political issues central to the fertilizer industry, especially the tariff. Although their influence did not include defining the manufacturers' position on these issues, the farmers' political clout, in addition to their influence with the fertilizer manufacturers, did give them substantial voice in determining these issues' outcomes.

Overall, the U.S. fertilizer industry in the 1920s had fairly strong ties to the international economy in every sector but potash; it was a Type III industry. Its export dependence was substantial, but varied by sector and was less significant overall than its dependence on imports. Multinationality in every sector but potash was extensive among the largest firms. These international ties were further strengthened by various patent, R&D, and collusive arrangements with foreign firms. The U.S. firms were thus tightly tied to the international fertilizer market. By the end of the 1920s, however, they found themselves

---

[157] FTC, *Report on Fertilizer Industry*, 1950, pp. 28-29; Borkin, *Crime and Punishment*, pp. 8-9; Haynes, *American Chemical Industry*, 4:48-55.

[158] Haynes, *American Chemical Industry*, 4:55-58.

[159] FTC, *Report on Fertilizer Industry*, 1950, pp. 28-36, 43-51, 97-98; *NYT*, December 17, 1927, p. 13:3; *NYT*, August 3, 1930, p. 16:7; *NYT*, August 10, 1930, p. 1:2.

[160] Markham, *Fertilizer Industry*, pp. 21, 65; FTC, *Report on Fertilizer Industry*, 1950, pp. 43-51; *NYT*, March 18, 1923, pt. 8, p. 3:1; *NYT*, August 3, 1930, p. 16:7.

[161] House, *Effects of Agricultural Depressions*, Doc. 195, pp. 51-53.

in a highly cartelized international market and at a disadvantage because they were not members of the cartel.

The Dependent Variable

The U.S. fertilizer industry in the 1920s preferred open markets for
its products. The large multinational manufacturers bucked the decade's trend toward greater protection and remained content with the
duty-free status of their goods. Smaller domestic manufacturers in the
less international sectors did press for increased tariff rates, but these
were vigorously opposed by the larger producers and by the farmers'
organizations. In the late 1920s, however, as world trade in fertilizers
became highly cartelized and as U.S. producers found themselves less
tied to this organized world market, agitation against unfair foreign
competition mounted. This agitation was faint, short-lived, and ineffective; fertilizer and its materials were kept on the free list in 1929.

In the 1921 congressional revision of the tariff, the major U.S. fertilizer producers did not press for increases in the duties on their
products. They wanted the duty-free status of fertilizer and its materials to be retained.[162] As one manufacturer later claimed, it had long
been their "traditional policy" to desire the free entry of their products.[163] It is striking, however, that these producers did not agitate for
any protection at all in 1921. Despite rising levels of imports and other
economic problems at the time, they did not view protection as a viable
solution. Most probably, they felt the costly repercussions that protection would provoke in their international operations outweighed any
potential benefits new barriers could provide.

Further evidence of the major U.S. producers' aversion to protectionism in the 1921-22 tariff revision is provided by their opposition
to the duty increases desired by the domestic U.S. potash producers.
Beginning in 1919 these small producers, who had only gone into
business during the war because of the virtual embargo on German
imports, pressed for removal of potash from the free list.[164] For them,
protection was not only a means of survival but also a measure with
relatively low cost, because they had few ties to the international economy.

[162] The absence of testimony by the industry is striking. See paragraphs 1685, 1740,
1745, 1746, and 1766 in the free-list schedule of House, Ways and Means, *General Tariff
Revision of 1921*, and Senate, Finance, *Tariff Act of 1921*, for the lack of testimony.

[163] For the quote, see House, Ways and Means, *Tariff Readjustment—1929*, free list, pp.
8570-71.

[164] Senate, *FTC Report*, Doc. 347, pp. 26-27; House, Ways and Means, *Tariff Revision of
1921*, sch. N, pp. 3992-4012.

These domestically oriented potash producers lobbied hard for protection in 1921-22. Claiming that the highly cartelized German producers were trying to drive them out of business and that as an "infant industry" they deserved temporary import relief, they urged Congress to provide them with a large duty of 50 cents per 20 pounds of potash.[165] They were initially successful. The House of Representatives removed potash from the free list and put a duty of 2.5 cents per pound on it.[166]

This action provoked immediate opposition from the major fertilizer producers and the farmers. The "big six" fertilizer manufacturers publicly denounced the attempts of the potash producers to secure protection. The largest manufacturer, the Virginia-Carolina Chemical Company, opposed these attempts with great vigor, largely because of its international ties.[167] The others, though lacking such direct investment links to the German supplies, also found protection distasteful because they were linked contractually to the German importers.[168] Protection would disrupt their secure source of potash and raise their costs; in addition, it might prompt retaliation against their foreign operations. The opposition of these major manufacturers,[169] combined with that of the farmers, prompted the Senate to reconsider the proposed duty on potash and return it to the free list.[170] In the end the free trade agitation of the fertilizer producers led the conference committee on the tariff bill to eliminate the proposed duty on potash.[171]

By the end of the decade U.S. fertilizer manufacturers appeared somewhat less enthusiastic about free trade in their products. During the 1929 tariff revision, the National Fertilizer Association, representing the major firms, asked for some protection of complete fertilizers.[172] This request, however, was accompanied by a demand for the elimination of tariff duties on two key fertilizer materials.[173] The call for a duty increase was seen by many as the industry's way of bargaining for these other tariff reductions—i.e., it would be willing to trade the increases away in exchange for reductions elsewhere[174]—and thus

[165] House, Ways and Means, *Tariff Revision of 1921*, sch. N, pp. 4000-4012.
[166] *NYT*, August 9, 1922, p. 19:1-2.
[167] *NYT*, December 30, 1921, p. 12:1; *NYT*, December 31, 1921, p. 12:8.
[168] Ibid.
[169] Ibid.; *NYT*, September 14, 1922, p. 1:5; *NYT*, September 15, 1922, p. 1:4.
[170] *NYT*, August 9, 1922, p. 19:1-2.
[171] *NYT*, September 14, 1922, p. 1:5; *NYT*, September 15, 1922, p. 1:4.
[172] House, Ways and Means, *Tariff Readjustment—1929*, free list, pp. 8570-89, 9068-76.
[173] Senate, Finance, *Tariff Act of 1929*, sch. 16, pp. 729-37.
[174] House, Ways and Means, *Tariff Readjustment—1929*, free list, pp. 8053, 8080, and

cannot be viewed as a preference for protection. It proved in many ways a strategy for opening trade further in fertilizer products. The industry was able to prompt Congress to eliminate duties on two key products, and no duty was ever placed on the completed fertilizers.[175]

The need to resort to a strategic request of this sort had increased due to changes in economic circumstances. First, as already mentioned, the world fertilizer market had become highly cartelized and very unfriendly toward American competition by the late 1920s. The Europeans, led by the Germans, had organized the global market by fixing prices and assigning production and export quotas.[176] These agreements did not include the U.S. firms, who thus remained as potential cartel-breakers and unwelcome participants in international fertilizer markets. This environment was extremely threatening for the U.S. firms, since it shut them out of many markets and determined their product prices in others,[177] and they were prompted to turn their attention back to the home market.

The second change involved reductions in the international ties of the U.S. firms themselves. Over the decade, a number of significant foreign investments by the U.S. firms had been abandoned. In particular, two of the largest U.S. firms had sold off their European operations. The Virginia-Carolina Chemical Company relinquished all of its foreign operations in its 1924 reorganization.[178] And the International Agricultural Corporation sold its large German potash operations, valued at over $4 million in 1926, because of the German government's new regulations on potash, which were intended to aid the cartelization of the industry.[179] These two disinvestments alone significantly reduced the whole industry's multinationality and left the two largest U.S. producers with no foreign investment ties. This consequently lowered the cost of protection for these producers and made a strategy dependent on such protection more feasible.

Though these changes made a request for protection U.S. fertilizer manufacturers more possible, they did not make protection itself

---

sch. 1, p. 15; Senate, Finance, *Tariff Act of 1929*, sch. 1, pp. 44-47, and free list, pp. 243-45.

[175] House, Ways and Means, *Comparison of Tariff Acts of 1913, 1922, 1929*, pp. 163-79.

[176] FTC, *Report on Fertilizer Industry*, 1950, pp. 28-36; Haynes, *American Chemical Industry*, 4:48-58; *NYT*, December 17, 1927, p. 13:3; *NYT*, August 3, 1930, p. 16:7; *NYT*, August 10, 1930, p. 1:2.

[177] FTC, *Report on Fertilizer Industry*, 1950, pp. 43-51; House, Ways and Means, *Tariff Readjustment—1929*, free list, pp. 8570-89.

[178] Wilkins, *Maturing of Multinational Enterprise*, pp. 143-45; *NYT*, September 4, 1924, p. 27:4; *NYT*, February 17, 1925, p. 36:3.

[179] *NYT*, January 28, 1925, p. 26:3.

more preferred. The industry association testified in favor of raising duties on completed fertilizer in the House hearings. But by the time of the Senate hearings, the emphasis of the organization's testimony had switched to reducing duties on other products.[180] Moreover, when the duties were not increased, fertilizer producers did not protest. Though strong opposition by the farmers and importers to any tariff on fertilizer helped prevent any such action, the limited appeal of protection for the producers themselves also meant that pressure in favor of it was not significant. That the fertilizer industry did not pursue protection after failing to obtain it in the Smoot-Hawley Bill indicated further their true lack of interest in it.

The intra-industry division over the tariff on fertilizer followed one clear cleavage in the 1920s, which separated the large, multinational fertilizer manufacturers from the small, domestically oriented potash producers. The large firms, having significant export and foreign operations, were satisfied with the duty-free status of their product. Even their request in 1929 for duties on certain goods appeared less a protectionist demand than a tactic to have duties reduced on other goods. On the other hand, the small, western potash producers, who had no international ties, pursued protection avidly in the 1920s. They lobbied Congress for it in 1921-22 and later petitioned the USTC for import relief.[181] The quarreling between the large and small firms over the potash tariff underlined these two groups' different preferences. Thus, while imports and economic problems affected all firms in the industry in the 1920s, protection was preferred by only the domestically oriented producers in the potash sector.

Overall, the U.S. fertilizer industry fits the argument about Type III producers. Extensive trade and investment ties to the international economy constrained the firms' preferences for protection, even when they were experiencing severe economic distress, in two ways. First, among the large, multinational fertilizer producers sentiment for closure of the domestic market was not apparent. In the early 1920s, these firms wanted the duty-free status of all their products to continue. Later, this easy acceptance disappeared, and a more aggressive

[180] House, Ways and Means, *Tariff Readjustment—1929*, free list, pp. 8570-89; Senate, Finance, *Tariff Act of 1929*, sch. 16, pp. 729-37.

[181] The one appeal for import relief to the USTC by the fertilizer industry was made by a small American potash producer. The larger firms appeared to oppose this effort. For the full story, see Milner, "Resisting the Protectionist Temptation"; also see *NYT*, January 5, 1924, p. 3:2; USTC, *12th Annual Report of the U.S. Tariff Commission, 1928* (Washington, D.C.: GPO, 1928), p. 234; *NYT*, December 30, 1921, p. 12:1; *NYT*, December 31, 1921, p. 12:8.

strategy of demanding protection on some products to obtain freer trade in others materialized, in part as a consequence of the firms' diminished international ties.

Second, intra-industry divisions over the tariff revealed the importance of their foreign connections. The tariff issue split the fertilizer industry in two according to the extent of international ties possessed by the firms. The large, multinational fertilizer manufacturers never favored protectionism; in contrast, the small, domestically oriented potash producers sought import relief continuously. These two groups were the primary opponents in the fertilizer tariff debate in the 1920s. Within a single industry, thus, firms facing similar economic problems do not necessarily react in an identical fashion: their responses, especially in terms of trade policy preferences, are influenced by how integrated into the international economy they are.

CASE 5: PHOTOGRAPHIC EQUIPMENT

The story of the photographic equipment industry revolves around one company, Eastman Kodak, and its strategies to gain and maintain a dominant position. The Eastman Kodak Company came to be a force in the photographic equipment industry in the 1880s, when George Eastman revolutionized it by inventing the kodak, a handheld, consumer-oriented camera, and developing celluloid-based films.[182] Kodak became a market leader after 1900 both at home and abroad. In its home market, its sales of photographic equipment accounted for 43 percent of all U.S. sales in 1909 and over 90 percent in 1919.[183] By the 1920s, only four tiny domestic firms competed with Kodak in the manufacture of cameras and film.[184]

Kodak's dominance extended beyond the U.S. market. Its control of the market for amateur cameras and photographic films was worldwide by the 1920s. In 1920, for instance, it accounted for 94 percent of all cinematic film produced in the world.[185] Its control of the large

[182] Reese Jenkins, *Images and Enterprise* (Baltimore: Johns Hopkins University Press, 1975), pp. 164-69, 188-95, 246-51; Reese Jenkins, "Technology and the Market: Eastman and the Origins of Mass Amateur Photography," *Technology and Culture* 16 (January 1975):14-18. The sectors of the industry considered here are those involved in the manufacture of cameras and unexposed films; other sectors, including motion-picture projectors, dry plates, lenses, and photographic goods, are not discussed.

[183] Jenkins, *Images and Enterprise*, p. 178; *NYT*, April 30, 1923, pp. 1:3, 3:3.

[184] Jenkins, *Images and Enterprise*, pp. 246-51; House, Ways and Means, *General Tariff Revision of 1921*, sch. N, pp. 3466-73; Senate, Finance, *Tariff Act of 1921*, sch. N, pp. 4354-56.

[185] *NYT*, April 30, 1923, pp. 1:3, 3:3.

U.S. market, plus its acquisition of every important patent on photographic products, helped to establish its "business leadership on an international scale."[186] In the international marketplace, however, unlike the domestic market, Kodak did face significant competition after 1920. Its foreign rivals were large firms—Agfa of Germany, Gevaert of Belgium, and Pathé of France—who after 1920 caught up to Kodak and became significant market forces.[187]

Kodak's dominance of the photographic equipment industry did not exempt it, or the industry, from economic distress and instability in the 1920s. This sector encountered serious economic problems from 1920 to 1925 and again in 1929. Difficulties included heightened foreign competition and domestic recession. The U.S. photographic goods industry had faced little foreign competition before the 1920s.[188] In 1919, imports were valued at $1.7 million; in 1921, they surged to $7.5 million; and then they fell back to an average of about $5.3 million between 1923 and 1927, shooting up again to $7.2 million in 1919.[189] The ratio of imports to total domestic production also grew. In 1919, as earlier, it averaged about 2 percent, but in 1921 it hit 11 percent, and it finished the decade at 7 percent.[190]

Economic distress in the industry was evident in its reduced profitability, its declining numbers of firms and workers, and its overcapacity. The whole industry experienced reduced profits in the 1920s.[191] Due to the failure of some firms and the merger of others,[192] numbers of firms and workers also declined. In 1921, for example, two of the five main U.S. film manufacturers closed down, and later in the decade several merged with other larger firms because of their inability to garner decent profits.[193]

The photographic goods industry in the 1920s had extensive and growing ties to the international economy. In terms of both export dependence and multinationality, it ranked high; it was a Type III

[186] Jenkins, "Technology and the Market," p. 18.

[187] House, Ways and Means, *General Tariff Revision of 1921*, sch. N, pp. 3946-50; *NYT*, August 30, 1926, p. 19:2; N.A. BFDC files, "Trade Representatives," memos of BFDC on trade representatives—E. Kodak, RG 151, 1929.

[188] Jenkins, *Images and Enterprise*, p. 296; U.S. BFDC, *Foreign Commerce*, 1922, 1927, 1929.

[189] U.S. BFDC, *Foreign Commerce*, 1922, 1927, 1929.

[190] Ibid.; U.S. Dept. of Commerce, *Census, 1929*.

[191] Moody's, *Manual: 1927*, pp. 1730, 2377-78; Jenkins, *Images and Enterprise*, pp. 330-37; House, Ways and Means, *General Tariff Revision of 1921*, sch. N, pp. 3943-45; Senate, Finance, *Tariff Act of 1921*, sch. N, pp. 4325-27; *NYT*, May 2, 1922, p. 21:6.

[192] U.S. Dept. of Commerce, *Census, 1929*, esp. p. 1345.

[193] Senate, Finance, *Tariff Act of 1921*, sch. N, pp. 4325-26; Jenkins, *Images and Enterprise*, pp. 330-37.

industry. But these international ties were largely possessed by one firm, the Kodak Company.

In the 1920s, the industry's export dependence was high and rising. Its course, however, was not stable, as it registered a sizable decline between 1920 and 1923. Exports of photographic goods were valued at $21 million in 1919 and at $31.6 million in 1929, although they fell between 1921 and 1923 to $15.3 million.[194] The industry's international trade balance was also positive and rose over the decade.[195] Its ratio of exports to total domestic production followed a similar course. In 1919, it reached 23.4 percent, falling to 21.3 percent in 1923 but rebounding to 30.7 percent in 1929.[196]

At the firm level, export dependence was unevenly distributed. Only one firm, Kodak, was responsible for the bulk of the exports.[197] In 1912, for example, Kodak's exports to its English sales organization accounted for over 80 percent of all U.S. exports of photographic goods to England.[198] U.S. exports in this industry were concentrated in the products in which Kodak held its most significant advantages, hand-held cameras and unexposed motion-picture and photographic film.[199]

In the 1920s, the U.S. photographic goods industry also revealed itself to be multinational. By 1932 the industry, including optical goods, had some $31.3 million invested abroad.[200] This ranked it among the top ten U.S. industries in its level of direct foreign investment. Much of this internationalization of the industry, however, occurred after 1926.[201] In general, direct foreign investment in the photographic goods industry was sizable but not widespread in the early 1920s and became increasingly important only in the latter half of the decade.

Like export dependence, this multinationality was concentrated in the hands of Kodak. By 1908, Kodak was operating numerous sales branches throughout the world as well as an independent subsidiary

---

[194] U.S. BFDC, *Foreign Commerce*, 1922, 1927, 1929.

[195] Ibid.

[196] Ibid.; U.S. Dept. of Commerce, *Census, 1929.*

[197] House, Ways and Means, *General Tariff Revision of 1921*, sch. N, pp. 3947-49; Jenkins, *Images and Enterprise*, pp. 177-79.

[198] Jenkins, *Images and Enterprise*, p. 179, note to table 8-2.

[199] U.S. BFDC, *Foreign Commerce*, 1922, 1927, 1929.

[200] Senate, *American Branch Factories*, Doc. 120, 1933, pp. 10-19. This overestimates the true value for just the photographic industry, since it includes the small optical goods sector as well. It is interesting to note that this DFI was concentrated geographically, with over half of it in Canada and the United Kingdom.

[201] Jenkins, *Images and Enterprise*, pp. 240-42.

in England, but it still did not actually manufacture abroad.[202] After 1908 this changed as the company began producing film at its English and Canadian subsidiaries.[203] This foreign expansion abated during World War I, so that by 1920 Kodak was still only manufacturing one product, film, abroad—in the United Kingdom and Canada.[204]

The mid-1920s saw the beginning of Kodak's phenomenal world-wide expansion. In 1927, Kodak acquired production facilities in France and Germany by purchasing two large European firms, the Pathé Cinema Company and the Glanz Film Aktien Gesellschaft.[205] These acquisitions were followed by a rapid expansion of its European operations, which meant that by 1931 Kodak had seven factories in Europe, more than it operated in the United States.[206] All totaled, Kodak operated some 251 factories and sales branches in 53 different countries by 1931.[207] One historian of direct foreign investment noted, "by 1929 [Kodak] had *sales* outlets on every populated continent and manufactured in Europe, Canada, and Australia. Its foreign *manufacturing* had come in the 1920s to include *cameras* as well as film. . . . Kodak ranked *supreme* in its production lines worldwide."[208]

Three features of Kodak's foreign investment story need to be underscored. First, Kodak's foreign manufacturing operations were not well developed until after 1927. Neither Kodak nor the industry had very extensive multinationality in the early 1920s. Second, foreign investment was limited in a product sense. Kodak's foreign production included only motion-picture and photographic film until the mid-1920s; it did not produce cameras abroad until the late 1920s.[209] Third, the nature of these international operations was also limited in the first half of the decade. The manufacturing subsidiaries tended to exist as self-contained units, producing primarily for the market in which they were located. Exports back to the United States were not significant before 1925; after this, however, film exports to the United States, at least from Canada, grew significantly.[210] Kodak's foreign op-

[202] Ibid.

[203] Ibid.

[204] House, Ways and Means, *General Tariff Revision of 1921*, sch. N, pp. 3462-73.

[205] *NYT*, March 17, 1927, p. 32:3; *NYT*, June 18, 1927, p. 25:5.

[206] Eastman Kodak, *29th Annual Report* (New York: Kodak, 1929), pp. 17-19.

[207] Ibid.

[208] Wilkins, *Emergence of Multinational Enterprise*, p. 84. Emphasis added.

[209] Ibid.; Carl Ackerman, *George Eastman* (Boston: Houghton Mifflin, 1930, reissued 1973), pp. 132-33; Jenkins, *Images and Enterprise*, pp. 240-42.

[210] The decentralized, local market–oriented nature of Kodak's DFI is discussed in *NYT*, March 17, 1927, p. 32:3; Ackerman, *George Eastman*, pp. 132-33; and Wilkins, *Maturing of Multinational Enterprise*, pp. 138-46.

erations in the early 1920s were thus not highly integrated; no dense web of intrafirm trading relations bound them together. After this, they expanded greatly in size, products, and trade.

While U.S. foreign investment in the photographic goods industry grew during the 1920s, so did direct U.S. investment by foreign firms. Two key foreign competitors of Kodak began operating in the United States. The French firm Pathé expanded its U.S. sales operations and developed two factories for producing unexposed film in New Jersey.[211] Pathé was a constant threat to Kodak, until Kodak bought it in 1927. In addition, Agfa, controlled by the German chemical trust I. G. Farben, enlarged its U.S. operations with the purchase of the Ansco Company in 1928.[212] This new firm, Agfa-Ansco, was Kodak's most vigorous competitor in the 1930s. These two foreign multinationals represented a significant force in the U.S. market; in fact, they were Kodak's only real competition, in addition to mounting foreign imports.

The fairly extensive international ties and their highly skewed distribution among the U.S. firms in the photographic goods industry were not the only features important for understanding their preferences on trade issues. Kodak's monopoly position was crucial. It controlled 96 percent of the U.S. market for film and about 90 percent of the market for all photographic goods in 1920.[213] This control was challenged both by the U.S. courts and by foreign competition in the course of the decade, and by its end Kodak's market share did recede to less than 80 percent.[214]

What was most important about this market dominance was Kodak's continuing effort to maintain and enhance it. In the 1890s and 1900s, Kodak established its monopoly by gaining control of all important patents related to the industry and by acquiring most of its competitors.[215] Despite having gained a dominant position by 1910, Kodak still tried to enlarge its control by attempting either to drive its rivals out of business or to force them to ally with Kodak. This strategy finally got it into trouble. In 1920 Kodak was convicted of antitrust violations under the Sherman Act and was forced to divest itself of certain acquisitions.[216] In 1923, the Federal Trade Commission filed further

[211] Moody's, *Manual: 1927*, pp. 2070-71; *NYT*, March 17, 1927, p. 32:3; House, Ways and Means, *General Tariff Revision of 1921*, sch. N, pp. 3946-50.

[212] Jenkins, *Images and Enterprise*, pp. 330-37; Moody's, *Manual: 1927*, p. 769.

[213] Jenkins, *Images and Enterprise*, pp. 278, 285-86; *NYT*, April 30, 1923, pp. 1:3, 3:3.

[214] *NYT*, April 30, 1923, pp. 1:3, 3:3.

[215] Jenkins, "Technology and the Market," p. 10.

[216] Jenkins, *Images and Enterprise*, pp. 318-23; *NYT*, October 1, 1922, p. 20:1.

charges against Kodak for attempting to enhance its monopoly position; further divestitures were mandated.[217] Kodak's traditional monopoly strategy was thus having problems in the decade.

Kodak had long been an active monopolist; in the 1920s, with its traditional strategy of acquisitions and patent monopoly challenged and declared illegal, Kodak was left without a strategy but apparently not without the desire to enhance its position. By this time, in any case, its competition no longer really came from it already decimated domestic opponents. Kodak was now threatened by imports and the foreign multinationals, and its key strategy for maintaining its position in the 1920s had to be directed against them. One way to block such rivalry was, of course, to try to close the U.S. market; indeed, in the early 1920s Kodak adopted a strategy for enhancing its market position through promotion of the tariff.

The Dependent Variable

The trade policy preferences of the photographic equipment industry in the 1920s were primarily revealed during the two congressional tariff revisions. In the 1921-22 hearings, the domestic manufacturers proved extremely vocal. But in 1929, reflecting changes in the industry and its preferences, these manufacturers were less active.

During the 1921-22 general tariff revision, the domestic film and camera manufacturers endorsed substantial tariff rate increases on their products. These would raise what were very low initial duty rates; the 1913 Underwood tariff duties on cameras and unexposed film were 15 percent and free, respectively. Although economic distress and rising imports helped ignite these demands, the arguments and motivations for protection varied among the domestic manufacturers. Three distinct positions were apparent.

The three small manufacturers of unexposed film lobbied to end the free status of film and impose a duty of 35 to 50 percent ad valorem.[218] Citing the serious economic problems and rising foreign competition they faced, all three claimed to be operating at a loss and to be unable to match the prices of imported film. These firms also used the argument that they should be protected so that they could survive and thus provide competition to Kodak. They were requesting greater protection of the home market on the grounds that this would enhance domestic competition. The president of one firm declared, "the real question involved in [the Representatives'] decision regarding . . .

[217] *NYT*, April 30, 1923, pp. 1:3, 3:3.
[218] House, Ways and Means, *General Tariff Revision of 1921*, sch. N, pp. 3943-46.

the tariff is whether . . . [they] will permit American labor and American capital to maintain active competition in the domestic market; if [they] leave film on the free list, [they] will inevitably put every American film manufacturer, with one exception [i.e., Kodak], out of business."[219] Having no international economic ties and little chance of competing against imports, these three firms viewed protection as their only means of survival.

The small domestic camera manufacturers held a different position. Speaking on their behalf, the Seneca Camera Manufacturing Company argued for increased duties on cameras but opposed any imposition of duty on unexposed film.[220] This firm wanted the rate on foreign cameras doubled—from 15 percent to 30 percent—and claimed that this was necessary to stay in business against German imports. But the company strongly opposed any duty on film not only because it imported film but also because it viewed the requested duty increase as a ploy by Kodak to drive it out of the camera business. The president of Seneca said:

> This effort on the part of the Eastman Kodak Company to control the industry by asking for 30 percent on films is not a new thing; if a tariff . . . is put on film . . . , Kodak will be the only manufacturer in the country to supply the public with hand cameras . . . , because the independent companies cannot sell cameras unless they are able to supply films, and [they] cannot manufacture the film [themselves].[221]

This manufacturer, then, maintained that free film imports were vital to continued competition in the industry. The firm saw Kodak's motivation in asking for protection as a clear case of its long-running strategy to monopolize the market.

A third view on the tariff was delivered by the Eastman Kodak Company itself. In the 1921 hearings, Kodak appeared in favor of a tariff increase on both unexposed film and cameras. The increases it desired, 30 percent on cameras and 20 percent in films, were lower than those requested by the smaller domestic manufacturers. Kodak, while not ready to oppose even greater increases, was unenthusiastic about such high rates.[222]

The firm's explicit arguments for greater protection had two com-

[219] Senate, Finance, *Tariff Act of 1921*, sch. N, p. 4327.

[220] Ibid., pp. 4354-57.

[221] Ibid., esp. p. 4356.

[222] House, Ways and Means, *General Tariff Revision of 1921*, sch. N, pp. 3465-67, 3472-73; Senate, Finance, *Tariff Act of 1921*, sch. 14, pp. 4323-25.

ponents. Kodak, pointing to cartelization and subsidization of the industry abroad, complained that the mounting foreign competition was due to these unfair trade practices used by the foreign countries. Kodak also felt protection was necessary because every other country imposed high duties on photographic products. The firm believed these duties hurt its exports and would force it to move operations abroad. Kodak's brief stated that "since the war the German manufacturer has captured the market in Italy, when before the war this company had an extensive business . . .[and that] if no duty is imposed [in the U.S.], the tendency will necessarily be to compel American companies to manufacture in Europe instead of in the U.S. in order to successfully compete with foreign manufacturers."[223]

The extent to which these two factors actually prompted the firm's demands for protection is questionable. The "powerful German Chemical Trust," against which Kodak railed, was certainly no more monopolistic than Kodak itself. Furthermore, the company's argument about the effects of other countries' tariffs seemed largely a scare tactic; without a duty increase, the company implied, it would move its operations abroad. The fact that the tariff increase was granted and Kodak still chose to expand abroad suggests that the argument was not completely genuine.

Kodak's preference for the tariff was motivated largely by its desire for greater control of the U.S. market. This was the reason that all of Kodak's competitors cited, whether or not they themselves supported or opposed protection. Pathé, the one foreign multinational in the United States, objected to any increases in the tariff on unexposed film and asserted that such a tariff would merely enhance Kodak's monopoly and that this was the only reason Kodak wanted the duty.[224] U.S. motion picture companies, who were large exporters and multinationals, similarly opposed Kodak's efforts for film duty increases. One U.S. motion picture distributor claimed, Kodak "was seeking through means of a protective tariff to further control and dominate the industry by making it difficult, if not impossible, to procure the product of any concern which attempts to compete."[225] Even domestic manufacturers who favored some protection, like the Seneca Camera Company, saw Kodak's monopoly strategy at work in its tariff proposals. Though Kodak naturally never claimed this as its motive, its pursuit

[223] Senate, Finance, *Tariff Act of 1921*, sch. 14, p. 4324.
[224] Ibid., pp. 4331-37.
[225] House, Ways and Means, *General Tariff Revision of 1921*, sch. N, p. 3946.

of monopolistic control was a more plausible argument for protection than were the two it proffered.

By the 1929 tariff revision, sentiment for protection among the domestic manufacturers of photographic equipment had abated. During the Smoot-Hawley hearings, only Kodak, among domestic manufacturers of cameras or films, testified. And Kodak's preferences were more nuanced. It still asked for some duty increases on cameras, but it also desired reductions of the rate on film.[226] This new preference sprang from its increasing foreign production and export of these films to the United States.[227] Kodak's continued insistence on raising the tariff on cameras probably derived from its continued strategy of maintaining market dominance. Many observers, including a number of Senators, perceived this to be Kodak's primary motivation.[228] In any case, Kodak's preferences in regard to the tariff on unexposed film had changed as its internationalization of production in this product grew. By 1929, the benefits of lower barriers to trade in film outweighed the benefits of enhanced monopoly control in the domestic market for Kodak.

The domestic manufacturers' relative quiescence on the tariff issue in 1929 was paralleled by the foreign multinationals' and importers' vocal opposition. In the 1929 hearings, opposition by these two groups was stronger than any advocacy of the tariff. The large German importer, Zeiss, testified lengthily against further tariff increases on cameras or film. Maintaining that the existing tariff simply enhanced Kodak's monopoly, it pressed for a reduction to 10 percent ad valorem.[229] In addition, the Belgian importer Gevaert appeared numerous times to oppose the tariff.[230] Agfa, the German firm, having recently acquired the American film maker Ansco, lobbied for reducing the duties on photographic dry plates and paper.[231] In sum, opposition to further protection was rising in 1929, while preferences for it were decreasing. These shifts were reflected in the policy outcomes as well.[232]

[226] House, Ways and Means, *Tariff Readjustment—1929*, sch. 14, pp. 7938-40.

[227] Wilkins, *Maturing of Multinational Enterprise*, pp. 138-46; Senate, Finance, *Tariff Act of 1929*, sch. 14, p. 881.

[228] *NYT*, January 21, 1930, p. 16:3-5; *NYT*, March 30, 1930, p. 30:2.

[229] House, Ways and Means, *Tariff Readjustment—1929*, sch. 14, pp. 7940-42.

[230] Ibid., pp. 7943-46; Senate, Finance, *Tariff Act of 1929*, sch. 14, pp. 884-86.

[231] House, Ways and Means, *Tariff Readjustment—1929*, sch. 14, p. 7949; Senate, Finance, *Tariff Act of 1929*, sch. 14, pp. 74-76.

[232] The duty on cameras and on motion-picture film was kept the same; the duty on photo film was reduced. See House, Ways and Means, *Comparison of the Tariff Acts of 1913, 1922, 1929*, pp. 159-60.

The intra-industry debate over the tariff issue in the 1920s revealed serious divisions. Apparently no consensus among the domestic manufacturers of photographic equipment could be fashioned; no single industry association or spokesman ever appeared in the congressional hearings. Given the different concerns of the domestic producers, this lack of unity is not surprising. The small domestic film manufacturers, experiencing serious economic difficulties and having no international ties, were most eager for further closure of the home market; they had little to gain from an open market and much to lose. The small camera manufacturers wanted protection for their product, but because of their need for film imports objected to new duties on film. The industry giant, Eastman Kodak, wanted protection to thwart its main competitors, the foreign importers, and thus enhance its domestic monopoly. Its extensive international ties did not deter it from seeking this strategic use of the tariff, but they did temper the strength of its advocacy, as seen in its preference for a lower tariff in 1921 and for tariff reductions on film in 1929. The importers and foreign multinationals operating in the United States strongly opposed any tariff increases and in 1929 pushed for import duty reductions. These divisions within the U.S. photographic goods industry on the tariff issue reflected the different levels of ties to the international economy possessed by the various firms.

Overall, the photographic goods industry case provides some support for the argument about Type III industries. Given Kodak's fairly extensive export and multinational operations, its preferences might have been expected to be less protectionist than they actually were. In part because Kodak's international ties, especially its direct foreign investments, were relatively new and not extensive in the early 1920s, it could afford to seek protection in the 1921-22 tariff revision. But the growth of these international operations eventually constrained this desire for protection, as was evident in its 1929 testimony.

Kodak's support of the tariff in 1921-22, though, had little to do with international economic considerations. The tariff represented a strategy to fend off any competition with its domestic monopoly. The company was willing to let its small domestic rivals survive under a tariff umbrella in exchange for locking its primary competitors, the foreign importers, out of the market.

Other evidence from this case supports the argument. First, the small domestic manufacturers' ardent advocacy of greatly increased protection in the face of economic distress was understandable, given their complete lack of linkages to the international economy. When one of these firms, Ansco, was acquired by a German firm, it ended its calls for protection and became an advocate of liberalization. The active opposition of the importers and the foreign multinationals based in the United States to tariff increases underscores the argument that international trade and investment ties condition trade preferences. Finally, Kodak's advocacy of a reduction in duties on unexposed film in 1929 in the wake of its growing internationalization and trading in this product strongly supports the argument.

Case 6: Newsprint

The U.S. newsprint industry began growing rapidly in the late 1800s, as the demand for newspapers escalated. By the 1910s this industry, which was already the largest segment of the U.S. paper sector, had developed into one of the nation's ten largest.[233] At this time, however, pressures for change in the industry became intense. As the United States depleted its supply of wood and the Canadians developed their own industry, the U.S. newsprint manufacturers gradually moved their operations north of the border. By the 1920s, the American newsprint industry was losing its national basis and becoming instead a highly multinational and trade-dependent sector.

The 1920s were difficult years for this U.S. industry. Imports began capturing a large part of the U.S. market in the early part of the decade. In 1913, imports were valued at $5.7 million; in 1921 they rose to $79 million; and by 1929 they eclipsed domestic production as they reached $144.5 million.[234] Import penetration (imports as a percent of domestic production) also skyrocketed, growing from 10.7 percent in 1913 to nearly 70 percent in 1921, to 179 percent in 1929.[235] The U.S. industry peaked in 1926; after that, imports overtook domestic production, which began declining. Foreign competition thus became a major concern.

Economic difficulties among newsprint manufacturers were apparent in the 1920s, as they experienced a reversal of the growth trend that had marked the industry since the 1880s. They were hit by profitability problems, overcapacity, and declining numbers of firms and employees. The beginning and end of the decade were the most difficult. In 1921 the industry's losses approached $70 million, and in the late 1920s firm closures and mergers indicated further profit difficul-

[233] U.S. Dept. of Commerce, *Census of Manufactures* (Washington, D.C.: GPO, 1919).
[234] U.S. BFDC, *Commerce Yearbook* (Washington, D.C.: GPO, 1922), pp. 260-66; 1926, p. 554; 1930, vol. 1, p. 540.
[235] Ibid.

ties.[236] The number of firms dropped from 710 in 1927 to 685 in 1929, although the number of employees remained nearly constant.[237] Most important, U.S. production levels for the industry were declining, and capacity utilization levels were extremely low.[238]

Newsprint manufacture was a Type IV industry, with limited exports but extensive multinationality and intrafirm trade relations. In its trade, the U.S. industry was dependent on imports; exports were minor. Its export dependence was low and decreasing, and its value of exports fell over the decade.[239] Key world markets were supplied by exports from Canada, not from the United States.[240] The industry's trade balance was also increasingly negative in this period, reaching a whopping $143 million by 1929.[241] The ratio of exports to domestic production was also low and declining. In 1913, the ratio was 4.5 percent; in 1921 it fell to 1.9 percent and by 1929 to 1.7 percent.[242] The U.S. newsprint industry was not dependent on its exports; they played only a minor role in its performance.

Although their export dependence was insignificant, the U.S. newsprint manufacturers' multinationality was well developed in the 1920s. The major U.S. firms had extensive foreign production operations and intrafirm international trade. The newsprint sector, in fact, had the highest amount of capital invested abroad of any U.S. industry in 1932. Its direct foreign investments were estimated at $224.6 million at the time.[243] Notable also was the fact that this investment was located completely in Canada.[244] The U.S. firms dominated the growing Canadian industry and controlled over 50 percent of the capital invested in it and about 30 percent of total Canadian newsprint-making capacity by the late 1920s.[245]

---

[236] *NYT*, April 16, 1922, pt. 2, p. 15:1; Senate, Finance, *Tariff Act of 1921*, sch. 13, p. 3872; House, Judiciary Committee, *Study of Monopoly Power: Newsprint Paper Industry*, 82nd Cong., 1st sess., 1951, H. Rept. 505, pt. 1, pp. 34-38. The largest firm, the International Paper Co., alone lost $5 million in 1928, according to the *NYT*, May 1, 1928, pp. 1:8, 2:1-6.

[237] U.S. Dept. of Commerce, *Census, 1929*.

[238] *NYT*, April 8, 1927, p. 3:2.

[239] U.S. BFDC, *Commerce Yearbook*, 1922, pp. 260-66; 1926, vol. 1, p. 554; 1930, vol. 1, p. 540.

[240] House, Judiciary, *Study of Monopoly Power*, 1951, Rept. 505, pt. 1, pp. 94-98.

[241] U.S. BFDC, *Commerce Yearbook*, 1922, pp. 260-66; 1926, vol. 1, p. 554; 1930, vol. 1, p. 540.

[242] Ibid.

[243] Senate, *American Branch Factories*, Doc. 120, 1933, p. 11.

[244] Ibid., pp. 11-19.

[245] House, Judiciary, *Study of Monopoly Power*, 1951, Rept. 505, pt. 1, p. 56. Because it

This multinationality was concentrated among four of the largest U.S. newsprint manufacturers.[246] Of these, the largest—the International Paper Company—began significant manufacturing operations outside the United States in the early 1920s. By the end of the decade, International Paper was one of the three largest newsprint producers in Canada, accounting for 14 percent of total Canadian production and 12 percent of total U.S. production of newsprint by 1928.[247] The third largest U.S. producer, the Crown-Zellerbach Corporation, also possessed substantial manufacturing investments in Canada. By 1928, Crown-Zellerbach produced 15 percent of total newsprint consumed in the United States and 3 percent of the Canadian supply.[248] The St. Regis Paper Company, the fourth largest U.S. firm, began manufacturing operations in Quebec during the decade.[249] In addition, the Kimberly-Clark Company owned the Canadian manufacturer, the Spruce Falls Power and Paper Company, which it expanded greatly in 1926 in order to become the *New York Times*' sole source of newsprint.[250]

A second feature of the U.S. firms' foreign operations was their sizable exports. These firms had highly integrated international operations; each plant was bound to the others through a web of intrafirm trading operations. The U.S. firms not only exported from Canada to the United States but also from Canada to major markets in the Far East and Europe. Overall, U.S. plants in Canada exported over 30 percent of their production.[251] The U.S. newsprint industry's multinationality was thus extensive and integrated, although concentrated in Canada among four large U.S. firms.

The U.S. and Canadian newsprint markets were also connected through the foreign sales operations and contracts of Canadian producers in the United States. Though Canadian manufacturers tended not to produce in the United States, they operated sales outlets there and entered into relationships with U.S. firms to sell their newsprint.

---

includes the rayon and wallboard sectors, this figure overestimates the value for just the newsprint industry; this overestimation is not, however, very significant.

[246] Senate, *FTC Report on the Newsprint Paper Industry*, 71st Cong., spec. sess., 1930, S. Doc. 214, pp. 79, 112-13.

[247] Louis Stevenson, *The Background and Economics of American Paper Making* (New York: Harper & Bros., 1940), pp. 174-75; Senate, *FTC Report on Newsprint*, Doc. 214, pp. 79, 112-13.

[248] Ibid.

[249] Moody's, *Manual: 1927*, pp. 2586-87.

[250] Ibid., p. 380; *NYT*, April 29, 1926, p. 25:8; *NYT*, September 27, 1927, p. 4:2.

[251] A. E. Safarian, *Foreign Ownership of Canadian Industry* (Toronto: McGraw-Hill, 1966), p. 125.

The Canadian firms did not have much capital invested in the United States, but by means of their oligopoly agreements at home and their U.S. contracts they controlled a substantial part of the U.S. newsprint market.[252] U.S. firms' control of the Canadian market was, nevertheless, greater than the Canadians' in the United States, because of the Americans' more extensive direct investments. The key point, however, is that the two markets were tightly linked through both sets of international ties. One observer claimed, "the American and Canadian newsprint paper industries [are] essentially one and the same entity, having the same primary markets and the same interest."[253]

Several other features of the industry are important. The American manufacturers were highly oligopolistic. In 1928, over 50 percent of total U.S. newsprint production was controlled by three U.S. firms.[254] This market control was accompanied by much monopolistic behavior; price fixing, market-sharing agreements, cooperative buying, and production quotas were constantly evident.[255] These practices were organized by the industry giants, especially by the International Paper Company, which operated as the "price leader" in the U.S. market.[256]

This oligopoly was reflected in the industry's tight political organization. The U.S. firms' interests were represented through the American Pulp and Paper Association, which had long operated as an effective political voice for the industry.[257] This association, however, appeared to be dominated by the largest firms in the industry, and so its political activities tended to favor the interests of the largest, multinational U.S. newsprint manufacturers.[258] The newsprint industry in the 1920s was thus economically powerful and politically well organized, largely as a consequence of its oligopolistic structure.

Another aspect of the industry in this period was its growing links to the newspaper publishing industry. These mounting ties resulted from both backward and forward integration of the publishers and

[252] Senate, *FTC Report on Newsprint*, Doc. 214, pp. 17-21, 85-89; *NYT*, November 24, 1928, p. 18:2; *NYT*, November 26, 1928, p. 45:1.

[253] Constant Southworth, "The Newsprint Paper Industry and the Tariff," *Journal of Political Economy* 30 (1922):694.

[254] Senate, *FTC Report on Newsprint*, Doc. 214, pp. 15-17.

[255] John Guthrie, *The Newsprint Paper Industry* (Cambridge: Harvard University Press, 1941), pp. 94-98.

[256] Senate, *FTC Report on Newsprint*, Doc. 214, p. 81; House, Judiciary Committee, *Study of Monopoly Power: Newsprint Paper Industry*, 81st Cong., 2nd sess., 1950, serial 14, pt. 6a, pp. 294-308, 922-25.

[257] Senate, *FTC Report on Newsprint*, Doc. 214, pp. 99-100.

[258] House, Judiciary, *Study of Monopoly Power*, 1950, serial 14, pt. 6a, pp. 294-310, 922-25; Senate, *FTC Report on Newsprint*, Doc. 214, pp. 99-100; *NYT*, February 6, 1921, p. 8:1.

manufacturers. In the 1920s newspaper publishers began acquiring substantial interests in U.S. and Canadian newsprint manufacturing operations.[259] Newsprint manufacturers also integrated forward. For example, by 1929 the International Paper Company had sizable holdings—about $10 million, or 10 percent of its total assets—in thirteen newspaper publishing companies.[260] In fact, all but two U.S. newsprint manufacturers had substantial ties to the publishing sector.[261] The development of these ties brought the two groups' interests into greater harmony by the end of the decade.

The Dependent Variable

The trade policy preferences of the U.S. newsprint manufacturers may be seen through the congressional tariff revisions, the U.S. Tariff Commission investigations, and intra-industry debates in the 1920s. Of these three, the congressional hearings of 1921 and 1929 provided the most information about the firms' preferences, but evidence from all three suggests that the firms preferred open home markets, especially in the latter part of the decade, when a very solid consensus emerged on this position.

The roots of this consensus began developing in the 1910s. In 1911 the United States and Canada negotiated a reciprocity treaty that was to place newsprint, wood pulp, and several other goods on the free list in both countries. The impetus for this agreement came from two sources. First, the U.S. newspaper publishers wanted the duties on newsprint eliminated so they could obtain it at lower prices. They also feared the enormous monopoly power of the U.S. newsprint producers, especially the International Paper Company; hence, publishers lobbied to reduce the tariff in order to increase competition among the manufacturers.[262]

The second source of pressure for tariff reductions was the U.S. manufacturers themselves. Although not as enthusiastic as the publishers, the newsprint manufacturers perceived an advantage in liber-

[259] Senate, *FTC Report on Newsprint*, Doc. 214, pp. 90-98; House, Judiciary, *Study of Monopoly Power*, 1951, Rept. 505, pt. 1, pp. 47-50. For example, the *New York Times* bought into the Spruce Falls Power and Paper Company of Canada, which was owned by the Kimberly-Clark Company. The *Chicago Tribune* integrated backward into newsprint manufacturing by purchasing the Ontario Paper Company of Canada in addition to several U.S. firms. Other publishers, such as the Hearst Papers, chose to integrate through contractual agreements rather than actual investments.

[260] *NYT*, May 1, 1929, pp. 1:8, 2:1-6.

[261] House, Judiciary, *Study of Monopoly Power*, 1951, Rept. 505, pt. 1, pp. 47-50.

[262] Lyman Weeks, *A History of Paper Making in the U.S.* (New York: Lockwood Trade Journal Co., 1916), pp. 316-17; Stevenson, *Background and Economics*, pp. 168-69.

alizing trade in wood pulp and newsprint between Canada and the United States. Many of these firms had acquired sizable forest holdings in Canada, and they wanted to make sure that the wood products derived from these holdings could be exported to the United States without interference.[263] The reciprocity treaty was designed to ensure this trade flow in return for opening the U.S. market to Canadian newsprint. Despite these pressures, the Canadians eventually vetoed the reciprocity treaty, believing it would only increase their economic dependence on the United States.[264]

U.S. pressure for liberalizing the market in newsprint did not die with this treaty. Rather, the momentum for a tariff reduction continued, and in the "liberal" atmosphere of the 1913 tariff revision, newsprint and wood pulp were placed on the free list.[265] Newspaper publishers were most actively involved in pushing for this change. U.S. manufacturers supported it but wanted an assurance, or a reciprocal action, from the Canadians promising they would not tax or forbid exports of the wood products used in newsprint manufacturing.[266] The U.S. producers became upset with the tariff reduction only when the Canadians refused to give such an assurance and later began implementing just such an export embargo.

In 1921, at the time of the Fordney-McCumber Tariff revision, U.S. newsprint manufacturers and newspaper publishers were the key participants in the debate over the newsprint tariff. Both wanted the duty-free status of newsprint to be retained; however, the manufacturers had other demands as well. In the congressional hearings, the American Pulp and Paper Association testified that newsprint should remain on the free list, but that a provision for raising the duty should be inserted to allow retaliation against foreign countries' unfair trade practices.[267] This provision, of course, addressed the manufacturers' complaints against the Canadian export taxes and their threatened export embargo on wood pulp. The U.S. firms wanted trade between the two countries liberalized even further; they wanted to use government policy to open the Canadian market to a greater extent. This free trade position was anomalous for the association, since on every

---

[263] Senate, Finance, *Tariff Act of 1929*, sch. 16, pp. 623-24.

[264] Wilkins, *Emergence of Multinational Enterprise*, pp. 144-45.

[265] Southworth, "Newsprint Paper Industry," pp. 681-90; John Glover and William Cornell, eds., *The Development of American Industries* (New York: Prentice-Hall, 1932), p. 100; Wilkins, *Emergence of Multinational Enterprise*, pp. 138-40; *NYT*, July 27, 1922, p. 7:1-3.

[266] Senate, Finance, *Tariff Act of 1929*, sch. 16, pp. 623-24; *NYT*, July 16, 1923, p. 20:1.

[267] House, Ways and Means, *General Tariff Revision of 1921*, sch. M, pp. 2902-2905.

other paper product it was demanding a tariff increase. The association's position on newsprint reflected the preferences of the major U.S. manufacturers.

In the 1921 hearings only two of the American newsprint firms testified independently. Their individual testimonies supported the basic position enunciated by the association but added one or two more specific demands. The St. Regis Paper Company lobbied to ensure that no duty was placed on newsprint and to divert attention from the retaliation provision suggested by the American Pulp and Paper Association.[268] St. Regis maintained that any such duty, or the threat to impose one, would simply provoke Canadian retaliation and thus hurt the industry. The company's large Canadian holdings and its sizable intrafirm trade between the two countries made it sensitive to the effects of any retaliation by Canada.

The International Paper Company, in contrast, was as deeply involved in Canada as was St. Regis but was willing to adopt a more aggressive strategy in its pursuit of freer trade between the two countries. International Paper had substantial landholdings in Canada in 1921 but few production facilities abroad. This firm favored inclusion of a retaliation provision; moreover, it wanted the United States to threaten actively to invoke this if the Canadians made any move to tax or halt wood pulp exports.[269]

The U.S. newspaper publishers also testified at the 1921 hearings. As in the past, these publishers remained ardent advocates of duty-free newsprint. They argued in favor of retaining newsprint's free status and against the retaliatory provision that International Paper wanted.[270] Like St. Regis, they maintained that the retaliation provision was likely to worsen U.S.-Canadian relations. Publishers feared that retaliation was a ploy developed by some major U.S. manufacturers to enable them to increase the tariff if their monopolistic position were ever threatened.[271]

The newspaper publishers' fears about the depth of the newsprint manufacturers' sentiment for freer trade proved unfounded. The U.S. manufacturers' extensive and growing investment relations with Canada made protectionism prohibitively costly. These manufacturers complained about the Canadians' attempts to tax and embargo wood

[268] Ibid., pp. 2967-68; Moody's, *Manual: 1927*, pp. 2586-87.

[269] Senate, Finance, *Tariff Act of 1921*, sch. 15, pp. 4866-68; *NYT*, July 8, 1923, pt. 2, p. 1:2.

[270] Senate, Finance, *Tariff Act of 1921*, sch. 15, pp. 4878-4910.

[271] House, Ways and Means, *General Tariff Revision of 1921*, sch. M, pp. 2944-66; Senate, Finance, *Tariff Act of 1921*, sch. 15, pp. 4878-4910.

pulp exports. In the mid-1920s, they pressured Congress and the executive branch to halt and/or retaliate against such Canadian efforts.[272] The U.S. manufacturers claimed that this export policy, because it would induce the movement of manufacturing operations to Canada and the export of finished newsprint from there to the United States, would mean the demise of the U.S. industry. In 1925 these manufacturers lost their fight: the Canadians imposed an export embargo on wood pulp at the provincial level; the United States did not retaliate; and U.S. firms rapidly moved their newsprint manufacturing to Canada.[273]

Before the 1929 tariff revision, the newsprint manufacturers pursued two other issues related to foreign competition. First, in 1921, manufacturers lodged antidumping complaints at the USTC against German and Scandinavian newsprint imports.[274] These manufacturers were joined by much of the U.S. paper industry in claiming that these countries were subsidizing and dumping all sorts of paper products in the U.S. market.[275] An investigation was begun. However, the newsprint manufacturers soon lost interest, and in the end no action was taken.[276]

The second issue involved attempts to alter the definition of "standard newsprint." The U.S. paper industry in general sought a precise and narrow definition of which paper goods would be admitted duty free. In the early 1920s, U.S. manufacturers of paper goods other than newsprint wanted this definition to be narrow to keep out competitive imports; some of the newsprint manufacturers also favored this at the time, because they viewed it as a possible way of keeping out German and Scandinavian imports.[277] Once again, the newsprint manufacturers lost interest in this issue. The rest of the U.S. paper industry, however, remained concerned, pressing the U.S. government for a narrowing, or "clarification," of the definition to no avail throughout the decade.[278]

[272] NYT, July 8, 1923, pt. 2, p. 1:2; NYT, February 2, 1925, p. 1:2.

[273] Wilkins, *Emergence of Multinational Enterprise*, pp. 138-39; Stevenson, *Background and Economics*, pp. 190-97; House, Judiciary, *Study of Monopoly Power*, 1951, Rept. 505, pt. 1, pp. 30-33.

[274] NYT, August 27, 1921, p. 3:5; NYT, August 28, 1921, p. 20:4.

[275] NYT, August 27, 1921, p. 3:5; NYT, October 21, 1922, p. 2:5; USTC, *5th Annual Report*, 1921, p. 41.

[276] House, Ways and Means, *Tariff Readjustment—1929*, sch. 15, pp. 9340-43. Imports from these countries fell somewhat, which may account in part for their decline in interest.

[277] Ibid., sch. 14, pp. 6821-24.

[278] Ibid.

On the dumping and newsprint definition issues, the U.S. newsprint manufacturers initially joined the rest of the paper industry in seeking to restrict trade. But the manufacturers' positions on these issues were half-hearted; they did not pursue them and were not upset over their demise. Their overall interest was in opening up international trade in newsprint, and this interest persisted, as the tariff revisions document. In fact, their preference for open markets was strengthened in the course of the 1920s, as their foreign operations intensified.

During the 1929 Smoot-Hawley Tariff revision, this consensus on free trade was evident. In the course of the most protectionist tariff revision in American history, not one U.S. newsprint manufacturer testified for increased duties, for a retaliatory provision, or for any other restrictive device. The manufacturers all favored keeping newsprint on the free list.[279] Once again, newsprint was the only item concerning paper in the tariff schedule on which the manufacturers did not want to elevate the tariff. The major reason for this free trade sentiment was the newsprint manufacturers' extensive ties to the international economy. Their substantial direct foreign investments in newsprint production by 1929 had solidified their position on the tariff. A representative of the paper manufacturers testified: "The whole economic situation [referring to the lower cost of foreign production operations of the U.S. manufacturers] is such that it would be foolish to attempt to put a duty on newsprint."[280]

During the Smoot-Hawley hearings the U.S. newspaper publishers also testified on the newsprint tariff issue. As before, they advocated the retention of its duty-free status and opposed any restriction of its trade.[281] The publishers also wanted to expand the open market in newsprint by enlarging the category of "standard newsprint." They wanted the Commerce Department's definition of newsprint to be broadened so that more types of paper could be imported duty-free.[282] This demand was linked to the publishers' own expanding international ties. As they had integrated backwards into newsprint and paper production in the United States and Canada during the 1920s, they had developed an interest in the duty-free import of all the newsprint and paper they now produced and used. At a minimum, these new international links induced them to oppose the American *paper* (not newsprint) manufacturers' attempts to restrict the definition of newsprint.

[279] House, Ways and Means, *Tariff Readjustment—1929*, sch. 13, pp. 6819-34; Senate, Finance, *Tariff Act of 1929*, sch. 14, pp. 1-9, and sch. 16, pp. 616-24.

[280] House, Ways and Means, *Tariff Readjustment—1929*, sch. 13, p. 6827.

[281] Ibid., sch. 15, pp. 9340-61; Senate, Finance, *Tariff Act of 1929*, sch. 16, pp. 616-24.

[282] Ibid.

Thus, by 1929 the U.S. publishers as well as the American manufacturers found their growing foreign operations shaping their trade preferences in the direction of freer trade.

Intra-industry debates regarding trade issues for the newsprint industry were limited in the 1920s. The central debate appeared to be not over the extent of protection but over the best strategy for opening markets. In 1921 this debate was reflected in the different positions adopted by St. Regis and International Paper. St. Regis felt the best way to ensure open markets was through unilateral policy moves; International Paper viewed aggressive, retaliatory policies as most effective. But even this muted debate over strategy was not evident in 1929. By that time, the extension of all the major U.S. firms' operations into Canada aligned their interests and strategies on the tariff issue. No internal debates over the industry's preference for free trade in newsprint were visible at this point.

Overall, the newsprint industry provides strong support for the argument advanced about Type IV industries. Having extensive and integrated foreign operations, the U.S. manufacturers found themselves tied tightly to the international economy, which in turn conditioned their trade preferences. They consistently supported the duty-free status of newsprint imports in the 1920s, despite the economic distress they were experiencing. In addition, their support for open markets increased as their foreign investment ties deepened in the late 1920s. As this case suggests, extensive, integrated multinational operations can pull firms away from preferences for protection generated by severe import competition and economic difficulty.

CHAPTER 4

The 1970s U.S. Case Studies

SIX AMERICAN INDUSTRIES in the 1970s are examined below to see whether they fit the hypothesis that industries with substantial links to the international economy are less protectionist than more domestically oriented industries, even if both are facing serious economic distress. As in chapter 3, each case study has two parts. First, the industry's economic difficulties and import problems are discussed in order to document its a priori interest in protecting its domestic market. The industry's ties to the international economy are detailed at both the industry and the firm levels, to allow classification of each case in terms of the argument and to generate expectations about its preferences on trade.

Second, the industry's preferences on trade issues, as expressed in three arenas, are examined. In the 1970s, trade law, rather than the tariff, was the major means of obtaining protection from imports in the United States. Thus a central focus here is the industry's activities in petitioning and lobbying the relevant executive agencies—i.e., the U.S. International Trade Commission (ITC), the Department of Commerce, the Department of the Treasury, and the office of the U.S. Special Trade Representative. Another consideration is each industry's involvement in Congress, especially its testimony concerning the GATT negotiations of the Tokyo Round and other attempts to introduce trade legislation. Finally, the industry's internal political divisions over trade issues are discussed. The focus is on divisions among the firms and the effects of these divisions on the industry's political activities. A survey of these three arenas provides a comprehensive picture of our dependent variable—the trade preferences of the selected 1970s industries and of the firms within them.

CASE 1: FOOTWEAR

The U.S. nonrubber footwear industry experienced tremendous economic distress and decline during the 1970s. Factory closings were numerous, with over 400 U.S. factories shut down between 1968 and

1983.[1] Total employment in the industry declined each year, and its profitability also suffered badly.[2]

The footwear industry was also besieged by imports. Its rate of increase in import penetration was one of the highest among U.S. manufacturers between 1971 and 1978.[3] Moreover, import penetration surged 111 percent between 1968 and 1976, and 54 percent between 1981 and 1983.[4] In absolute terms, nonrubber footwear imports accounted for 21.5 percent of U.S. consumption in 1968 and for 51 percent in 1979.[5] Because of this foreign competition and economic distress, the footwear industry was likely to seek protection.

In terms of its ties to the international economy, the manufacture of nonrubber footwear was a Type I industry, lacking significant exports and multinational operations. In all aspects, its trade dependence was limited. Its net trade balance became increasingly negative in the 1970s.[6] While imports as a percentage of domestic consumption surged during the decade, exports never moved beyond .05 percent of domestic consumption.[7] U.S. producers of nonrubber footwear were never successful exporters. At the same time, they experienced their keenest competition in their home market from foreign producers.

The U.S. footwear industry had little multinational production. Its direct foreign investment was small, about $53 million in 1977.[8] Its

[1] This case covers only nonrubber footwear (SIC 3143 and 3144). American Footwear Industry Association (hereafter AFIA), "Nonrubber Footwear Fact Sheet" (Washington, D.C.: AFIA, December 29, 1983); U.S. Dept. of Commerce, Bureau of the Census, *1974 and 1979 Annual Survey of Manufactures* (Washington, D.C.: GPO, 1976, 1983); John Mutti and Malcolm Bale, "Output and Employment in a 'Trade Sensitive' Sector: Adjustment in the U.S. Footwear Industry," *Weltwirtschaftliches Archivs* 117 (1981):353; U.S. International Trade Commission (hereafter U.S. ITC), *Footwear Investigation*, TA-201-18, pub. no. 799 (February 1977), p. A-10; U.S. ITC, *Footwear Investigation*, TA-201-7, pub. no. 758 (February 1976), p. C-44.

[2] U.S. Dept. of Commerce, *1974* and *1979 Annual Survey of Manufactures*; Michael Szenberg, John Lombardi, and Eric Lee, *The Welfare Effects of Trade Restrictions: A Case Study of the U.S. Footwear Industry* (New York: Academic Press, 1977), pp. 2-4; Mutti and Bale, "Output and Employment," pp. 353-54.

[3] U.S. Dept. of Commerce, *U.S. Commodity Exports and Imports as Related to Output, 1976/75* and *U.S. Commodity Exports and Imports as Related to Output, 1977/76* (Washington, D.C.: GPO, 1979, 1982).

[4] AFIA, "Nonrubber Footwear Fact Sheet."

[5] U.S. Dept. of Commerce, *U.S. Commodity Exports and Imports, 1976/75* and *1977/76*.

[6] Ibid.

[7] Ibid.

[8] U.S. Dept. of Commerce, Bureau of Economic Analysis, unpublished data printout. This data is for the two-digit SIC leather and leather products sector; it overstates the amount for the footwear industry.

ratio of foreign assets to total assets hovered around 4 percent, unchanged since the 1960s.[9] Whatever multinationality existed did not involve integrated global operations. Of footwear production done abroad by U.S. firms, little was exported back to the United States.[10] The largest firms, however, did develop into major importers into the U.S. market after the late 1970s.[11] Some of these firms began offshore production; others simply bought from foreign producers. By the early 1980s, the international ties of these large firms had become important and were often their primary source of profits. Overall, however, the multinational position of the U.S. footwear industry was relatively small, despite the dependence of the larger firms on foreign sources by the 1980s.

Two other aspects of the industry affected its trade policy preferences. First, the industry was relatively unconcentrated. It consisted of almost a thousand establishments in the early 1970s.[12] Most of these firms were small and privately owned.[13] The industry was homogeneous; most of its firms were similar in structure and possessed few, if any, international ties. This made political cooperation easier. Only the largest had any interest in the international market, and only after 1980 was this of any consequence. Second, footwear production was labor intensive and not technologically dynamic.[14] This made adjusting to foreign competition difficult. Little technology was available to reduce the industry's labor intensiveness, and most firms were too small to afford any large innovations. The U.S. footwear producers experienced great import competition over the decade, lacked international ties, and had little ability to adjust to this fierce new competition.

[9] U.S. Dept. of Commerce, *1972* and *1977 Enterprise Statistics*, (Washington, D.C.: GPO, 1977, 1981).

[10] Réal Lavergne, "unpublished data and appendices," used in Lavergne, *Political Economy of U.S. Tariffs*.

[11] Interviews with AFIA and EC. Examples are Melville, Endicott-Johnson, and R. G. Berry, all of whom left U.S. manufacturing for importing and moved to the VFRA from the AFIA.

[12] U.S. ITC, *Footwear Investigation*, no. 758, 1976, appendix C-83.

[13] OECD, *The Footwear Industry* (Paris: OECD, 1976); Szenberg, Lombardi, and Lee, *Welfare Effects of Trade Restrictions*, pp. 7-15; Mutti and Bale, "Output and Employment," p. 353; U.S. ITC, *Footwear Investigation*, no. 758, 1976, appendix C-83.

[14] For figures on labor intensity and R&D, see U.S. Dept. of Commerce, *Census of Manufactures, 1979* (Washington, D.C.: GPO, 1983); U.S. Dept. of Commerce, *Census of Manufactures, 1972* (Washington, D.C.: GPO, 1976). In general, see U.S. ITC, *Footwear Investigation*, no. 758, 1976, pp. A-71, A-75; OECD, *Footwear Industry*; David Yoffie, "Adjustment in the Footwear Industry," in *American Industry in International Competition*, ed. John Zysman and Laura Tyson (New York: Cornell University Press, 1983), pp. 325-27.

The Dependent Variable

The central political issue facing the U.S. footwear industry in the 1970s concerned imports, especially the rapid, disruptive adjustment problems they caused in the U.S. market. As the level of imports rose over the 1970s, the industry became increasingly adamant in its attempts to gain protection. Its activities in petitioning the ITC, in lobbying Congress, and in developing a unified industry position demonstrated the intensity of its desire for restraints on imports. By the early 1980s, however, this consensus for protection had begun to break down.

The industry was very active throughout the 1970s in pressing the ITC and various executive agencies for relief. Between 1973 and 1978, footwear manufacturers, workers, and unions petitioned the ITC approximately 355 times.[15] Although the majority of these petitions—333—were for trade adjustment assistance to individual workers or firms, the remaining 22 involved industry attempts to receive escape clause treatment or to have antidumping and/or countervailing duties imposed on imports.[16] Of these cases, the industry's three petitions for escape clause action, which demanded greatly increased tariff rates (or quotas) on all shoe imports, deserve special attention.

The first of these escape clause petitions was filed in 1970 at the urging of President Richard M. Nixon. This petition, one of the first concerted actions by the industry as a whole, was motivated in part by the surge of imports following the Kennedy Round tariff cuts on footwear duties implemented in 1968. U.S. footwear manufacturers, smarting from these rising foreign sales, began demanding a repeal of the tariff cuts and voicing strong opposition to any new bill granting the President authority to reduce tariffs in multilateral negotiations. To calm the industry, President Nixon instructed the ITC—then the USTC—to investigate whether the tariff cuts had indeed allowed imports to hurt the domestic industry. This escape clause investigation produced little. After months of inquiry, the ITC was evenly divided on whether the industry was being injured by imports. Under the laws then in effect, a split decision meant the President was not required to do anything, which was exactly the course he chose.[17]

The President's inaction surprised and upset the footwear industry,

---

[15] Judith Goldstein, unpublished data, used in her "Reexamination of U.S. Commercial Policy."

[16] Ibid.

[17] Yoffie, "Adjustment in the Footwear Industry," p. 353; David Yoffie, *Power and Protectionism* (New York: Columbia University Press, 1983), p. 172; Porter, *Presidential Decision-Making*, p. 159; AFIA interviews.

and unwittingly goaded it into an increased number of diversified activities to realize its demands. In addition to its efforts to shape trade legislation in Congress in the early 1970s, the industry filed a large number of countervailing duty complaints against various foreign manufacturers, including the Taiwanese, South Koreans, Brazilians, Spanish, and Argentineans. After months of investigation and no final determination, the footwear industry, through the American Footwear Industry Association (AFIA), decided to sue the U.S. government over the delay. Just prior to the lawsuit's resolution, however, the Treasury Department announced countervailing duties against Brazil, Spain, and Argentina.[18]

The imposition of these duties and the pressure exerted by the U.S. government to get Italy to "organize" its shoe exports to the United States met only a small part of the footwear industry's demands for import relief.[19] In 1975, the industry was once again pressing for escape clause action. In this petition the industry revealed its preference for global relief, calling for a stringent tariff-rate quota based on very low import levels. With new procedures for U.S. trade law by then in place, the ITC quickly investigated. Despite finding unanimously that imports had injured the industry, it remained divided in its recommendations for action. The case was sent to the President, who was authorized to make a final decision on the form of relief granted. The footwear industry expended substantial effort lobbying groups within the executive branch in order to affect the decision. President Gerald R. Ford, with the support of the office of the Special Trade Representative (STR), and the Treasury and State departments, refused to grant the industry the aid it desired; instead, he authorized only trade adjustment assistance to workers and the monitoring of footwear imports.[20]

This denial of relief prompted the industry to turn to Congress. Using their leverage as "important constituents," especially of various northeastern legislators, footwear manufacturers pressed the Senate Finance Committee to have the ITC begin a new escape clause investigation. This petition, initiated in 1976, was similar to the preceding one. The ITC investigation, in fact, produced almost the same conclu-

[18] Porter, *Presidential Decision-Making*, pp. 159, 163; U.S. ITC, *Footwear Investigation*, no. 758, 1977, p. A-3; AFIA interviews; Ralph Oman, "The Clandestine Negotiation of Voluntary Restraints on Shoes from Italy," *Cornell International Law Journal* 6, no. 7 (1974):6-11.

[19] Oman, "Clandestine Negotiation of Restraints," pp. 6-19; AFIA interviews.

[20] Porter, *Presidential Decision-Making*, ch. 5; AFIA interviews; Yoffie, "Adjustment in the Footwear Industry," pp. 336-38; U.S. ITC, *Footwear Investigation*, no. 758, 1976.

sions as before—a unanimous finding of injury from imports and a split decision on recommendations for relief. This time the case was sent to President Jimmy Carter. Though the industry's preference for a stringent, global tariff-rate quota persisted, negotiations between the industry and the administration, in particular, with Robert Strauss in the STR office, resulted in agreement on a less restrictive and yet global formula for relief. Carter decided to limit imports of shoes by negotiating orderly marketing agreements (OMAs) with two key importers, South Korea and Taiwan. In addition, the footwear industry claims, Strauss agreed to ensure that limits (or "caps") were negotiated on both exports to the United States from other countries and exports of close substitutes for the nonrubber footwear controlled in the OMAs. These promises, intended to prevent circumvention of the OMAs, were never acted upon by the administration. Thus, the limits imposed by the OMAs were avoided by the exporting firms. Although import rates slowed during the OMAs' four years, the footwear industry did not obtain the degree of protection it initially desired.[21]

More recent petitions to the ITC by the industry have also failed. In 1981 President Ronald Reagan rejected the industry's petition for extension of the OMAs; all import relief was terminated in June of that year. The industry's allegations of unfair trading practices against a number of developing countries were formalized in an ITC petition in 1982, which was subsequently dismissed. In January 1984, the industry filed its fourth major escape clause action, once again seeking heightened tariffs on all footwear imports.[22]

During the 1970s, the industry expended a great deal of effort not only to obtain import relief through the ITC, but also to shape congressional legislation on trade issues. Each time a trade bill was considered, the industry lobbied and testified. Its efforts were especially intense in the early part of the decade, when various trade bills enabling the President to negotiate reductions in tariff and nontariff barriers were under consideration, and in the late 1970s and early 1980s, when the industry organized a congressional caucus.

In the early 1970s, the industry lobbied to ensure that shoes would be treated specially in any multilateral negotiations to reduce tariffs

[21] Yoffie, "Adjustment in the Footwear Industry," pp. 338-46; Yoffie, *Power and Protectionism*, pp. 176-94; David Broder, "The Case of the Missing Shoe-Import Option," *Washington Post*, July 23, 1977; AFIA interviews; U.S. ITC, *Footwear Investigation*, no. 799, 1977.

[22] Christopher Madison, "The Troubled U.S. Footwear Industry Is Kicking for Relief from Imports," *National Journal*, February 5, 1983, pp. 283-85; AFIA interviews; AFIA, "Petition for Relief from Imports of Nonrubber Footwear under Section 201 of the Trade Act of 1974" (Washington, D.C.: AFIA, 1984).

and that the U.S. trade laws would be rewritten so that the costs of seeking import relief would be reduced. In 1970 and 1971, the shoe industry worked to obtain promises of quotas in the legislation on trade reform. In the Trade Bill of 1971, known as the Mills Bill, the House Ways and Means Committee drafted legislation granting import quotas to shoes as well as to textiles and apparel. Footwear would thus have obtained the special status that textiles and apparel had in their exemption from multilateral tariff-cutting negotiations,[23] but this never occurred. The initiation of the escape clause action by President Nixon in 1971 alleviated pressure on Congress to devise its own aid for the footwear industry. Moreover, the demise of the Mills Bill in the Senate meant that nothing was done for shoes.[24]

During consideration of a new trade reform bill in 1973 and 1974, the footwear industry continued to prefer exemption from the tariff-reduction negotiations and the development instead of a program of import controls similar to those on textiles and apparel in the Multifiber Agreement. The industry's efforts to realize this goal were largely fruitless.[25] But pressure from the footwear manufacturers, as well as from other industries, did help change U.S. trade laws. The alternatives to the existing laws favored by the industry included easing the conditions required for finding import injury in escape clause cases, forcing the President to act on cases where injury was found but relief recommendations were divided, providing congressional review of these presidential decisions, and placing time limits on investigations of trade petitions.[26] Many of these changes were adopted in the Trade Act of 1974. This act also contained three amendments designed specifically to help the industry by Senators from the shoe-sensitive New England area. These excluded certain footwear from GSP status, authorized presidential negotiations of special trade agreements on footwear, and forced the Treasury Department to impose countervailing duties on footwear if investigations showed such violations to be occurring.[27] These actions did not give footwear the special status it desired but did lean in that direction.

[23] Yoffie, "Adjustment in the Footwear Industry," p. 335; Oman, "Clandestine Negotiation of Restraints," pp. 6-10; I. M. Destler, *Making Foreign Economic Policy* (Washington, D.C.: Brookings Institution, 1980), p. 187; AFIA interviews.

[24] Ibid.

[25] Destler, *Making Foreign Economic Policy*, pp. 187-89; AFIA interviews.

[26] AFIA interviews.

[27] Destler, *Making Foreign Economic Policy*, pp. 187-89; AFIA interviews; House, Ways and Means Committee, *Trade Reform*, hearings, 93rd Cong., 1st sess., May 1973, pt. 1. GSP (Generalized System of Preferences) is a system by which developing countries can get preferential access to the markets of developed countries.

The next burst of congressional activity by the footwear industry occurred in the late 1970s. In 1979 the industry's pressure once again helped to generate changes in U.S. trade laws, which reduced the costs of gaining import relief. These revisions included shifting authority over antidumping and countervailing duty investigations from the Treasury Department to the Commerce Department, one more friendly to domestic industry.[28] The footwear industry also used its industry sector advisory committee in the Tokyo Round negotiations of the GATT to ensure that any tariff cuts on its products were minimal and reciprocal.[29] The industry also developed a formal congressional footwear caucus, comprised of Senate and House members sympathetic to the industry's demands. This caucus was used to ensure that proposals opposed by the industry were not included in the Trade Act of 1979. Today it provides a major source of pressure on the ITC and STR, and thus on the President, to take heed of the footwear industry's demands for import relief.[30]

We have seen that the U.S. footwear industry, beginning in 1970, worked through numerous channels in its mounting efforts to realize its objective of global relief from import competition. As a cohesive political force, the industry was increasingly determined in its efforts as imports surged and economic decline accelerated. Politically, the industry was organized into two opposing associations. U.S. manufacturers of shoes operated through the American Footwear Industry Association, which was the central force behind the industry's ITC petitions and its congressional lobbying. In fact, the AFIA did little in the 1970s besides pursuing the industry's desire for import relief. The problems posed by foreign competition were clearly its primary preoccupation over the decade.[31]

The AFIA's decision making on trade policy revealed a domestically oriented industry, fairly united in its desire for import protection. Participants in this decision making report that few, if any, divisions arose over the association's pursuit of import relief. Unanimous sentiment for such action among the association's members, which included all the major U.S. manufacturers, is claimed.[32] One association official

[28] Senate, Finance Committee, Subcommittee on International Trade, *Private Advisory Committee Reports on the Tokyo Round of the MTN*, hearings, 96th Cong., 1st sess., 1979, ISAC 9, pp. 164–80; AFIA interviews.

[29] Senate, *Private Advisory Committee Reports*, pp. 164–66.

[30] AFIA, *Petition for Relief*; Madison, "Troubled U.S. Footwear Industry"; AFIA interviews.

[31] Madison, "Troubled U.S. Footwear Industry"; AFIA interviews.

[32] AFIA interviews; Yoffie, "Adjustment in the Footwear Industry," pp. 327–35; Yoffie,

said, "It's easy to form policy in this industry because all the manufacturers make most of their profits and have most of their capital invested in the US market; so they know they have to protect that market first."[33]

The industry's unity and preference for import relief was thus related to its industrial structure. That few firms exported shoes, that most foreign markets were closed to U.S. footwear exports, and that few of the firms were multinational meant that the domestic market alone was of crucial importance. The weakness of these ties to the international economy fostered protectionist sentiment, which in turn inhibited the development of international ties.[34]

The primary opposition to the AFIA was led by shoe importers and retailers in the United States, organized in the Volume Footwear Retailers' Association (VFRA) Representing large importers like Matsushita and retailers such as Sears Roebuck, the VFRA consistently opposed the AFIA's attempts to obtain escape clause relief. The VFRA testified against the AFIA in ITC investigations and in congressional hearings.[35] The VFRA's opposition to restrictions on imports resulted from its members' ties to the international economy. As large-volume footwear importers, these firms did not want their supplies reduced and/or prices increased, which would be the likely effect of increased trade barriers. The VFRA was increasingly supported by a group of firms that were also members of the AFIA after the late 1970s. In the 1980s, large firms reduced manufacturing capacity in the United States and moved offshore, either manufacturing or simply importing. This movement abroad prompted changes in their political interests and activities. Many resigned from the AFIA and became active in the VFRA, thus be-

---

Power and Protectionism, p. 173, has suggested greater fragmentation of interests within the industry. He points out that a small core of large firms in the shoe business were extremely profitable in the 1970s and thus had little interest in the trade issue. These firms paid relatively small dues to the AFIA and lent little support to its political activities. The fact that the largest U.S. manufacturer, the Brown Shoe Company, testified on its own several times for escape-clause relief in the mid-1970s, however, challenges this claim.

[33] AFIA interview.

[34] AFIA interviews. One example of this latter phenomena occurred the late 1970s. At this time, several footwear manufacturers attempted to move production offshore, thus reducing costs by importing cheaper nonrubber shoe uppers for inclusion in their complete shoes. This move was vigorously opposed by the AFIA and by some of its members, who in return sought to have the imported uppers classified and taxed under the much greater tariff duty for complete shoes. Although hindered by this controversy, the offshore operations have continued.

[35] AFIA interviews; Madison, "Troubled U.S. Footwear Industry."

coming opponents of import barriers.[36] Indeed, the growing divergence of these large firms' interests from the AFIA's position was a critical factor enabling President Reagan to deny import relief to the industry in 1981.[37] Thus, it appears that firms chose between the two associations according in part to their degree of integration into the international economy. Those producing or buying abroad joined the VFRA and resisted efforts to close the U.S. market; those whose investment lay primarily in U.S. manufacturing facilities sided with the AFIA and perceived closure of the market as their only means of survival.

Although divisions within the footwear industry became increasingly evident after the late 1970s, the majority of U.S. footwear manufacturers sided with the AFIA. This group spent much time and money trying to secure relief from foreign competition in all political arenas. The AFIA sought global protection against imports. It resisted reductions in its tariff levels and pressed for strict tariff-rate quotas on all imports. Furthermore, its preference for a closed American shoe market grew stronger throughout the decade and prompted increased activity toward this end. As imports surged between 1968 and 1976, the industry devoted more and more resources to this political battle. Overall, the industry's strong preference for protection of its home market resulted from its manufacturers' dependence upon this home market and their lack of ties to the international economy.

CASE 2: MACHINE TOOLS

The U.S. machine tool industry experienced rising economic difficulties during the 1970s.[38] From a strong, if not preeminent, international position in the 1960s, the industry lost its comparative advantage. In its higher technology product lines, the industry was challenged by West German, and was later overtaken by Japanese, makers of machine tools.[39] In its older, more standardized products, various newly industrializing countries (NICs) captured world market shares from the U.S. firms.[40] The U.S. industry began losing both world and domestic market shares to these foreign competitors: imports as a percentage of domestic consumption doubled between 1970 and 1977, while the U.S. share of world exports fell from 23 percent in 1964 to

---

[36] Interviews at AFIA and EC; see examples cited in note 11 above.

[37] Interview at EC.

[38] The study involves only the metal-cutting sector of the machine tool industry (SIC 3541).

[39] *Business Week*, October 5, 1981, pp. 26-27; Fong, "Export Dependence," pp. 134-35, 180-85; *Business Week*, September 1, 1980, pp. 68-70.

[40] *Business Week*, February 5, 1979, pp. 25-26.

7 percent in 1977.[41] From its long-standing position as a net exporter, the U.S. industry was reduced to a net importer by 1977.[42] This loss of world leadership in technology and export performance was a central indicator of the industry's fundamental economic problems.

Signs of the industry's economic distress were widespread in the 1970s. Declining employment and profitability showed the deceleration of growth from the 1960s.[43] In addition, the number of firms in the industry dropped from the late 1960s to the mid-1970s.[44] Employment, profitability, and the number of firms all moved cyclically over the 1970s, but they generally closed the decade at a lower level than they started it.

The U.S. machine tool industry also encountered an import invasion during the 1970s. Imports surged from $126.1 million in 1970 to $1,027.6 million in 1979.[45] Import penetration rose from 7 percent to 14 percent between 1970 and 1977, increasing at an average of 3 percent annually over the period.[46] After 1977, import penetration continued rising at a rapid rate, reaching 27 percent by 1981 and 45 percent by 1985.[47] Within the industry, it was imports of lathes and machining centers that grew the most.[48]

The production of U.S. machine tools was a Type II industry throughout most of the 1970s. It had a strong export position and a small multinational position. After 1977, however, it was moving from Type II toward Type I—becoming a much more domestically oriented industry. By the early 1980s, its multinationality was receding, and its exports had fallen.[49]

---

[41] U.S. Dept. of Commerce, *U.S. Commodity Exports and Imports, 1976/75*, and *1977/76*; *The Competitive Status of the U.S. Machine Tool Industry* (Washington, D.C.: National Academy Press, 1983), pp. 8-9.

[42] Ibid.

[43] U.S. Dept. of Commerce, *Census, 1972* (Washington, D.C.: GPO, 1976); National Machine Tool Builders' Association (NMTBA), *Economic Handbook of the Machine Tool Industry* (Washington, D.C.: NMTBA, 1982), p. 63; Fong, "Export Dependence," p. 186; *Competitive Status*, pp. 21-23.

[44] U.S. Dept. of Commerce, *Census, 1972* and *1979*; NMTBA, *Economic Handbook*, pp. 62-63.

[45] NMTBA, *Economic Handbook*, p. 146.

[46] U.S. Dept. of Commerce, *U.S. Commodity Exports and Imports, 1976/75* and *1977/76*.

[47] *NYT*, February 3, 1986, p. D-2.

[48] NMTBA, *Economic Handbook*, pp. 146-54.

[49] The aggregate data from the U.S. Dept. of Commerce in *1972* and *1977 Enterprise Statistics* and in *U.S. Direct Investment Abroad—1977* (Washington, D.C.: GPO, 1981) all point to this conclusion, as did the NMTBA interviews. Firm-level data in Fong, "Export Dependence," and *Competitive Status* on firms or samples of the industry as well as evidence in *The American Machinist*, for the late 1970s and early 1980s, point to this conclusion.

The industry's international trade position was favorable during most of the 1970s, although this changed after 1977. The industry's net trade balance was positive, but decreasingly so, until 1977. It began the decade with a $142.1 million trade surplus, which turned into a deficit of $90.6 million in 1977.[50] The industry's export position remained strong throughout much of the 1970s. Exports as a percentage of domestic production of machine tools reached a relatively high 17 percent in 1970.[51] This percentage fell over the decade, slipping to 12 percent in 1977.[52] The machine tool sector's positive net trade balance and strong export position therefore mark it as a Type II industry in the 1970s, although moving toward Type I.

The industry had an average foreign investment position and a small but increasing amount of multinational-related trade. The direct foreign investment of the whole machinery sector was $519 million in 1977, $704 million in 1979, and $862 million in 1981.[53] As a proportion of total industry assets, the foreign investment of the industry was 12 percent in 1972, rising to 16 percent in 1977.[54] Earnings for the industry's foreign subsidiaries, as well as their return on capital, rose slightly.[55] The value of foreign trade conducted by the U.S. machine

[50] U.S. Dept. of Commerce, *U.S. Commodity Exports and Imports, 1976/75* and *1977/76*. These figures give an accurate picture of its trade balance since trade for TSUS items 806.30 and 807.00 was negligible, at least until 1978. See U.S. ITC, *Economic Factors Affecting the Use of Items 807.00 and 806.30 of the Tariff Schedules of the U.S.*, pub. no. 339, September 1970; U.S. ITC, *Import Trends in TSUS Items 806.30 and 807.00*, pub. no. 1029, January 1980; and U.S. ITC, *Tariff Items 806.30 and 807.00, US Imports for Consumption, Specified Years, 1966-79*, misc. pub., June 1980.

[51] U.S. Dept. of Commerce, *U.S. Commodity Exports and Imports, 1976/75* and *1977/76*.

[52] Ibid.

[53] See note 49; these aggregate-level data are for the entire nonelectrical machinery industry (three-digit SIC level) and thus should be used cautiously, since they differ substantially from just the metal-cutting machine tool sector. See also U.S. Dept. of Commerce, Bureau of Economic Analysis, unpublished data printout, 1984.

[54] U.S. Dept. of Commerce, *1972* and *1977 Enterprise Statistics*. Other data show a larger figure, about 36 percent of all corporate assets; see Internal Revenue Service (IRS), *Statistics of Income—1974-78, International Income and Taxes, U.S. Corporations and Their Controlled Foreign Corporations* (Washington, D.C.: GPO, 1981). Though these data suggest a sizable multinational position, other sources focusing more narrowly on only the metal-cutting machine tool sector yield much smaller estimates. For instance, data for five of the largest firms in the sector reveal in 1978 an average of 14.8 percent for their foreign assets compared to total assets, a figure about half that reported in some of the aggregate data. See Fong, "Export Dependence," p. 176.

[55] U.S. Dept. of Commerce, Bureau of Economic Analysis, unpublished data printout, 1984; U.S. Dept. of Commerce, Bureau of Economic Analysis, *U.S. Direct Investment Abroad, 1966* (Washington, D.C.: GPO, n.d.) and *U.S. Direct Investment Abroad, 1977*. Other sources differ on the direction of change in this sector's multinational position. At

tool multinationals was small but increasing.[56] Foreign operations of the U.S. machinery group were not geared to supplying the U.S. market; they were largely used to service the markets in which they operated. The sector's foreign investment position was thus not that sizable in the 1970s. Overall, its export dependence was more significant than its multinational operations, again making it a Type II industry before 1978.

Several other points should be noted. First, the industry was relatively unconcentrated. It was composed of over five hundred firms, although its leading eight firms accounted for 47 percent of its production.[57] The industry was homogeneous, with trade relations spread among many of its firms. Second, the U.S. machine tool builders were the earliest developers of the industry's leading technology, termed numerical control (NC). The U.S. firms introduced NC machines in the mid-1950s, but they did not sell widely until the 1970s.[58] By the mid-1970s, however, the U.S. industry had lost its technological advantage. Computer-controlled NC technology (CNC) had become the leader, and Japan was overtaking the United States in this area. By the early 1980s, the Japanese were recognized as the leaders in CNC technology.[59] This rapid loss of U.S. technological superiority helped explain the industry's quick transition from a dynamic exporter in the early 1970s to a more senescent, domestically oriented industry by the early 1980s.

The Dependent Variable

Throughout most of the 1970s, the U.S. machine tool industry displayed a strong preference for open world markets. Both the indus-

---

least three different sources maintain that the machine tool sector's multinationality began declining, not increasing, in the late 1970s. These sources, however, focus mainly on the late 1970s and early 1980s, and not as much on the period from 1970 to 1977, which is covered by the aggregate figures. See Fong, "Export Dependence," pp. 174-76; *The American Machinist*, various issues in 1978; U.S. ITC, *Competitive Assessment of the U.S. Metal-Working Machine Tool Industry*, investigation no. 332-149, pub. no. 1428, September 1983; OECD, *Technical Change and Economic Policy: The Machine Tool Industry* (Paris: OECD, 1980), pp. 63-64. See also note 49.

[56] U.S. Dept. of Commerce, *U.S. Direct Investment Abroad, 1966* and *1977*. The only data on re-export activity to the United States at the four-digit SIC level suggest a low but increasing amount of this trade; re-export relative to total imports was 6.1 percent in 1966 and 8.9 percent in 1977, according to Réal Lavergne, unpublished data, 1981, used in Lavergne, *Political Economy of U.S. Tariffs*.

[57] Fong, "Export Dependence," pp. 120-21; *Competitive Status*, pp. 16-18.

[58] Fong, "Export Dependence," pp. 122-26; *Competitive Status*, pp. 24-26.

[59] Fong, "Export Dependence," pp. 122-27, 180-85; U.S. ITC, *Competitive Assessment*, pub. no. 1428; *Competitive Status*, pp. 10, 30-34, 51-53; OECD, *Technical Change*, pp. 3-4.

try's public statements and trade policy activities reflected this. For instance, the industry, while pressing for greater export aid from the U.S. government and refraining from lodging formal complaints about imports, supported the Trade Act of 1974 and the resultant Tokyo Round negotiations' tariff reductions. Despite the industry's rising import penetration levels and other economic difficulties, it did not seek import relief in the 1970s. This would be expected from a Type II industry like machine tools. Because of their sizable dependence on foreign markets for exports, machine tool firms were cautious in demanding protection from imports. For them, closure of the U.S. market would hurt more than it would help, since it would probably lead to foreign retaliation and the loss of export sales.

Nonetheless, the industry's preference for free trade in the 1970s may seem a surprising contrast to its earlier preference for protection from import competition. During much of the 1960s, the machine tool builders had opposed trade liberalization of any sort and at times had sought heightened protection through new import surcharges.[60] In this period, however, when it voiced protectionist sentiment (though it took little action to realize this goal), the industry was under much less pressure from imports than in the 1970s, when foreign competition was more threatening.

In the 1970s, the machine tool builders were more politically active on trade issues than earlier. However, the industry's main political arena was Congress, not the executive branch; and its main trade concern was export promotion, not import competition.[61] Throughout the decade, the industry focused most of its political efforts pressing Congress to pass legislation that would aid its exports. The machine tool builders saw exports as critical for two reasons. First, foreign markets for exports were their largest potential and fastest growing markets.[62] Second, export sales provided a way to counterbalance the extreme cyclicality of the domestic market.[63] Since foreign demand tended to rise and fall countercyclically to U.S. demand, exports helped minimize the fluctuations in the industry's domestic performance.

The industry's testimony in Congress was devoted disproportionately to two export issues: East-West trade restrictions and export fi-

[60] Fong, "Export Dependence," pp. 163-66.

[61] NMTBA interview; Fong, "Export Dependence," pp. 212-16.

[62] NMTBA interview; *American Machinist*, 1977 and 1978; Fong, "Export Dependence," pp. 209-216.

[63] Fong, "Export Dependence," pp. 209-216, esp. p. 213; *Industry Week*, 1978 and 1977; *Competitive Status*, p. 40; NMTBA interview.

nancing.[64] East-West trade was important because the Communist, Eastern bloc countries were among the largest and most eager consumers of imported machine tools. Emerging from the Cold War period, the U.S. government had retained stringent restrictions on all high technology and national security–related exports to these Communist countries. In 1970 all machine tool exports to them were controlled.[65] The U.S. machine tool builders for the most part opposed this and claimed that, because all other Western bloc states had much less stringent restrictions, the Communist countries obtained the restricted items anyway.[66] The U.S. industry wanted to participate in this burgeoning export trade. Thus, it lobbied to have most favored nation (MFN) status conferred upon the Soviet Union, to have lists of restricted export products (both U.S. and COCOM lists) reduced, and to obtain export financing for sales to the Eastern bloc.[67]

This activity was successful in the early 1970s. The U.S. list of restricted machine tool products was cut in half, and trade with the Soviet Union surged.[68] In 1970, U.S. exports of machine tools to the Soviet Union were valued at $6 million; in 1975 they reached $90 million.[69] The Soviet Union had become one of the three primary export markets for the U.S. industry. With passage of the Jackson-Vanik Amendment in the Trade Act of 1974, however, the industry's export strategy toward the Communist countries ran into trouble. This amendment made MFN status for the Communist countries conditional on their emigration policies and effectively denied MFN status to the Soviet Union.[70] The amendment's effects on the industry were first felt in 1976, when U.S. exports to the Soviet Union dropped to $48 million.[71] The machine tool builders had worked hard to obtain greater access to these foreign markets. Their inability to increase exports to them after 1976 produced new concerns over import penetration in the United States.[72]

[64] NMTBA interview; Fong, "Export Dependence," pp. 212-16, 224-29.

[65] NMTBA interview; Fong, "Export Dependence," p. 210.

[66] NMTBA interview; House, Ways and Means Committee, Subcommittee on Trade, *Causes and Consequences of the U.S. Trade Deficit and Developing Problems in U.S. Exports*, hearings for November 3-4, 1973, 95th Cong., 1st sess., 1977; *Competitive Status*, pp. 41-42.

[67] Ibid.; Fong, "Export Dependence," pp. 209-211.

[68] Fong, "Export Dependence," p. 211.

[69] House, Ways and Means, *Causes of the Trade Deficit*, p. 411.

[70] Destler, *Making Foreign Economic Policy*, pp. 161-62; Fong, "Export Dependence," pp. 247-49; *Competitive Status*, p. 42.

[71] House, Ways and Means, *Causes of the Trade Deficit*, p. 411; Fong, "Export Dependence," pp. 247-49.

[72] NMTBA interview.

The other issue on which the industry pressed Congress involved export financing. The machine tool builders wanted Congress not only to continue programs that helped finance exports but also to expand these programs. The industry pushed for continuation and expansion of the foreign tax credit, the Domestic International Sales Corporation, Export-Import Bank financing, and other governmental programs to enhance U.S. export sales.[73] The industry's pressure for these export promotion devices was extensive and fairly successful. All of the programs were continued, and some were expanded. Although the machine tool builders did not obtain all the export aid they desired, their active interest in export promotion programs was apparent.

When the industry concerned itself with legislation relating to import problems in the 1970s, its position favored open world markets. In the early 1970s, it supported the Trade Act of 1974, which granted the President authority to cut tariffs in the multilateral trade negotiations.[74] It also opposed the earlier and more protectionist Mills Trade Bill of 1971 and the Burke-Hartke Trade Bill.[75] An industry spokesman said in 1973, "While the NMTBA is concerned over the inroads into the U.S. market by foreign competition, . . . it believes that in the long run *free trade*—assuming reciprocity, fair trading practices on all sides, and adequate governmental authority to deal with emergency situations—is both inevitable and desirable."[76] The machine tool builders maintained this preference throughout the 1970s. The industry approved of the Tokyo Round negotiations of 1979, and supported the tariff reductions and nontariff barrier codes.[77] Thus, in its most active political arena—the U.S. Congress—the machine tool industry supported trade liberalization, but focused its energy on export promotion.

During the 1970s, the industry rarely resorted to use of the U.S. trade laws to contain foreign competition. Only in 1977 did it consider filing a serious petition.[78] This marked the start of the industry's turn

[73] Ibid.; Fong, "Export Dependence," pp. 222-28; House, Ways and Means, *Trade Reform*, pt. 3, pp. 1505-1507.

[74] NMTBA interview; Fong, "Export Dependence," pp. 219-22.

[75] Fong, "Export Dependence," p. 217; NMTBA interview.

[76] House, Ways and Means, *Trade Reform*, p. 803. Emphasis added.

[77] Senate, Finance, *Private Advisory Committee Reports*, ISAC 17, August 1979, pp. 315-33; Fong, "Export Dependence," pp. 168-69.

[78] Judith Goldstein, unpublished data, used in "Reexamination of U.S. Commercial Policy"; NMTBA interview.

away from free trade, as it began complaining about Japanese firms' tactics.

In late 1977, during congressional hearings on the causes of the U.S. trade deficit, the U.S. machine tool builders began voicing complaints about Japanese imports. These objections concerned dumping and subsidization of exports to the United States by Japanese firms. The U.S. manufacturers charged that the Japanese were using unfair trading practices to seize U.S. market shares.[79]

At the urging of the chairman of the congressional Committee on Ways and Means, the industry decided to file a formal complaint with the ITC.[80] This unfair trade petition was never actually filed. The industry's political association, the National Machine Tool Builders' Association (NMTBA), publicly announced its intention to form a committee to develop antidumping charges against the Japanese in December 1977.[81] The Japanese responded immediately to this threat. They announced price increases on their machine tool exports to the United States and a government plan to "screen" machine tool export levels.[82] The U.S. industry then charged the Japanese with reactivating their machine tool cartel in order to undercut the U.S. builders' complaints.[83] Just as the NMTBA was preparing to file its charges with the ITC, however, the U.S. Justice Department began antitrust proceedings against the NMTBA, subpoenaing and impounding all of its documents. The Justice Department maintained that the NMTBA was acting collusively with the Japanese, seeking to control imports in order to raise machine tool prices.[84] This antitrust proceeding ended the industry's attempts to file its unfair trade petition. For the next two and a half years, it battled the Justice Department instead of its import problems.[85]

After termination of the Justice Department investigation in 1981, the machine tool builders returned to their concerns with Japanese imports. This time, however, the industry chose not to involve the NMTBA. Instead, a single firm, Houdaille Industries, decided to take action. With the support of the U.S. Special Trade Representative,

[79] House, Ways and Means, *Causes of the Trade Deficit*, pp. 382-438.

[80] Ibid., p. 393; Fong, "Export Dependence," p. 170; NMTBA interview.

[81] *American Machinist*, January 1978, p. 5; NMTBA interview.

[82] *American Machinist*, January 1978, p. 45, and May 1978, p. 45; Fong, "Export Dependence," p. 171.

[83] *American Machinist*, May 1978, pp. 5, 45; NMTBA interview; Fong, "Export Dependence," pp. 171-72.

[84] NMTBA interview; Fong, "Export Dependence," pp. 171-72.

[85] Ibid.

Houdaille filed its complaint against the Japanese in May 1982. Charging that the Japanese were employing all sorts of unfair trading practices to "target" the U.S. market, Houdaille requested that the President respond by denying all purchasers of Japanese machine tools a tax credit for this investment.[86] Although innovative, Houdaille's petition was rejected in April 1983.[87]

Finally, in March 1983, the NMTBA filed its own complaint with the ITC. This time the industry was demanding global import relief in the form of a quota limiting imports to 17.5 percent of domestic consumption, and no longer simply selective relief from the Japanese threat.[88] The NMTBA filed its charges under the national security provision of U.S. trade law (section 232), which allows the President to impose restrictions on products vital to the national security of the country. Angry because machine tool exports had been controlled in the 1970s due to their "national security implications," the industry was trying now to use the government's own arguments to obtain import relief.[89] This petition demonstrated the industry's departure from a free trade position, which was not unexpected, given its deteriorating international trade position.

The political divisions among U.S. machine tool manufacturers in the 1970s were minimal, or at least highly obscure. Despite the large number of firms and their diverse economic situations, few internal divisions over trade issues surfaced.[90] In part, the builders' similar ties to the international economy—i.e., their high levels of exports and low multinationality—accounted for this lack of division. But it also stemmed from the NMTBA, their well-established political association. Created in 1902, the NMTBA had long organized cooperation among the industry's firms in order to prevent, or mitigate, its cyclical behavior.[91] The NMTBA represented over four hundred firms, 90 percent of the industry. Its policy-making procedures appeared open and fair;

---

[86] NMTBA interview; Houdaille Industries, "Petition to the President of the U.S. through the U.S. STR for the Exercise of Presidential Discretion Authorized by Section 103 of the Revenue Act of 1971," May 1982.

[87] NMTBA interview; U.S. ITC, *Competitive Assessment*, pub. no. 1428, p. 35.

[88] NMTBA, "Summary of the NMTBA's Section 232 Petition," October 1983; *NYT*, July 5, 1983, p. D-2; NMTBA interview; U.S. ITC, *Competitive Assessment*, pub. no. 1428, p. 35.

[89] NMTBA interview. Protection was eventually given to the industry through the negotiation of voluntary export restraint accords in 1986; see *Wall Street Journal*, November 20, 1986, November 21, 1986, November 24, 1986, and December 17, 1986; *NYT*, December 17, 1986.

[90] NMTBA interview.

[91] Harless Wagoner, *The U.S. Machine Tool Industry from 1900 to 1950* (Cambridge: MIT Press, 1968), p. 74; NMTBA interview; Fong, "Export Dependence," pp. 159-62.

and consensus building seemed essential.[92] Its policy-making bodies tended to include spokesmen for all segments of the industry, thus suggesting its positions were representative of the entire industry's preferences.[93] In general, the NMTBA was able to present a unified industry position on trade issues in the 1970s.

The NMTBA's expressed preference for free trade and its activities in support of exports and trade liberalization in the 1970s seem to have represented a consensus position. In any case, no machine tool firm spoke out against the NMTBA's position. The only individual effort by a machine tool builder was the 1982 trade petition by Houdaille Industries. Although this firm was less multinational than other large firms in the industry and thus perhaps more likely to take action against imports, its petition was evidently supported by much of the industry.[94] Because it was worried about renewed Justice Department antitrust action if it tried to collect the data necessary for the suit and because the suit was focused on a few narrow product lines, the NMTBA refrained from involving itself in the Houdaille case, even though it tacitly supported the action.[95] Furthermore, the association had its own petition to file, which demanded global relief and was supposedly supported by "every single firm in the industry."[96]

The trade policy preferences of the U.S. machine tool industry were focused on freer trade and export promotion during the 1970s. Much as one would expect of a Type II industry, the machine tool builders were most concerned with access to foreign markets and were willing to open their home market up in return for greater access abroad. The industry acted upon these preferences and resisted the pressures for protectionism emanating from its economic difficulties and rising imports during much of the 1970s. By 1978, however, changes in the machine tool builders' economic situation were registered in their trade policy preferences. As their ties to the international economy weakened and their competitive advantage—in the form of a superior technology—eroded, the industry embarked on a more protectionist course, turning away from its support of trade liberalization and its concerns with exports. The machine tool industry's attempts to obtain import relief in the early 1980s were a manifestation of its weakened international economic ties.

[92] NMTBA interview; Fong, "Export Dependence," pp. 160-62.
[93] NMTBA interview.
[94] Ibid.
[95] Ibid.
[96] Ibid.

CASE 3: SEMICONDUCTORS

The U.S. semiconductor industry had grown throughout the 1950s and 1960s, but the 1970s, in contrast, was a turbulent economic period. Foreign competition, especially from Japan, eroded the U.S. industry's hold over both its own and world markets; import penetration in the United States surged, and the U.S. share of world semiconductor exports fell by over 12 percent.[97] Direct foreign investment in the United States also skyrocketed from a mere $4.7 million in 1975 to $515.3 million in 1979.[98] Most of this investment was by large West European electronics companies, who acquired smaller U.S. semiconductor firms. Thus the U.S. industry faced a double challenge from foreign producers: rising import penetration by the Japanese and growing foreign investment by the West Europeans.

Far-reaching technological changes also swept the semiconductor industry. By the early 1970s, the industry had begun selling its third wave of new products: large-scale integrated circuits (LSI).[99] This group of products was introduced even more rapidly than previous generations.[100] The accelerated development was largely due to the increased foreign competition. Japanese companies produced new versions of LSI circuits in quick succession, forcing the U.S. firms to behave similarly and thereby thrusting them into development of their fourth generation of products, the very large-scale integrated circuits (VLSI).[101] This rendered the industry increasingly volatile.

The economic distress in the U.S. semiconductor industry caused by these challenges was highly cyclical. Problems were worst in the periods from 1969 to 1972, from 1974 to 1976, and from 1978 to 1983. Reversing its steadily increasing trend, employment in semiconductor

[97] This case covers semiconductors as defined in SIC code 3674. U.S. Dept. of Commerce, International Trade Administration (ITA), *An Assessment of the Competitiveness in U.S. High Technology Industries* (Washington, D.C.: GPO, February 1983), p. 45.

[98] U.S. ITC, *Competitive Factors Influencing World Trade in Integrated Circuits*, investigation no. 332-149, pub. no. 1013, November 1979, pp. 37-39.

[99] Y. S. Chang, *The Transfer of Technology: The Economics of Offshore Assembly*, UNITAR report no. 11 (New York: United Nations, 1971), pp. 5-7; U.S. Dept. of Commerce, *A Report on the U.S. Semiconductor Industry* (Washington, D.C.: Commerce Dept., 1979); Michael Borrus, James Millstein, and John Zysman, "Trade and Development in the U.S. Semiconductor Industry," in *American Industry in International Competition*, ed. Zysman and Tyson, pp. 153-66.

[100] John Tilton, *The International Diffusion of Technology: The Case of Semiconductors* (Washington, D.C.: Brookings Institution, 1971), pp. 19-48; Chang, *Transfer of Technology*, pp. 5-7.

[101] Borrus, Millstein, and Zysman, "Trade in the Semiconductor Industry," pp. 178-248.

production rose and fell throughout the 1970s.[102] Profitability was also volatile, falling between 1969 and 1972, between 1974 and 1975, and between 1978 and 1979.[103] Thus, while not a period of absolute secular decline for the industry, the 1970s were a time of increasing instability and severe cyclical distress.

Import penetration of the U.S. market rose on average between 3 and 4 percent per year from 1971 to 1977. From 9 percent of domestic supply in 1970, imports rose to 22 percent in 1977. In absolute terms, the value of imports surged from $167.7 million in 1970 to $1,349.8 million in 1977.[104] In addition to its economic difficulties, then, competition from imports grew constantly, making the industry a likely candidate to seek protection.

U.S. semiconductor production was a Type III industry in the 1970s. It had extensive multinational and intrafirm trading operations and substantial export activities. The industry's international trade position was mixed. Without adjusting for its own offshore assembly trade, the industry had a net trade deficit through much of the decade and a rising proportion of exports relative to domestic production.[105] Since offshore assembly trade was significant in this industry, however, these figures must be adjusted to eliminate double counting.[106] Making these adjustments reveals that over the decade the net trade balance in semiconductors was positive, although decreasingly so.[107] The industry's export position, after adjusting for offshore trade, also shows a steady decline. Exports as a percentage of domestic production fell from a high of 21.7 in 1970 to 19.5 in 1977 and to 17.2 in 1979.[108] Thus, the industry's international trade position over the 1970s, when adjusted for its offshore assembly operations, reveals a declining trade surplus and a strong but declining export position.

The industry had a substantial and growing foreign investment position in addition to a well-developed system of multinational trade, mostly in the form of offshore assembly. This direct foreign invest-

---

[102] U.S. Dept. of Commerce, *Census, 1972*; U.S. Dept. of Commerce, *1979 Annual Survey of Manufactures*; U.S. ITC, *Competitive Factors*.

[103] U.S. ITC, *Competitive Factors*, p. 33.

[104] U.S. Dept. of Commerce, *U.S. Commodity Exports and Imports 1976/75 and 1977/76*.

[105] Ibid.

[106] U.S. ITC, *Competitive Factors*, p. 16.

[107] Grunwald and Flamm, *Global Factory*, pp. 73-74, 108.

[108] U.S. Dept. of Commerce, *U.S. Commodity Exports and Imports 1976/75 and 1977/76*; Grunwald and Flamm, *Global Factory*, pp. 84, 108, for adjusted figures. *Without* the adjustments, exports of semiconductors as a percent of domestic production grew irregularly over the 1970s; the percentage increased from 26 in 1970 to 35 in 1974 and then dropped to 33 in 1977.

ment position grew during the 1970s, as did the magnitude of this foreign investment relative to the industry's total investment. For the electronic components sector, the proportion of foreign assets to total assets rose from 6 percent in 1972 to 24 percent in 1977, a very substantial figure.[109] In addition, the earnings of these foreign operations were healthy and important for the industry.[110] Trade related to the semiconductor industry's multinational operations also was sizable. Foreign subsidiaries produced substantial amounts for export. In 1977, these exports back to the United States accounted for 32.4 percent of foreign subsidiaries' total sales.[111] All told, the semiconductor industry had a substantial and growing multinational position and intrafirm trade network during the 1970s.

These extensive international ties, unevenly distributed in the industry, were concentrated among the largest eight or nine producers. Moreover, of the top eight firms in 1978, two of the largest were the most multinational: IBM and Texas Instruments. These two possessed widespread foreign production and intrafirm trading operations. Only they had plants operating in Japan.[112] The other leading producers—Motorola, Fairchild Camera, National Semiconductor, Intel, Mostek, and Advanced Micro Devices—were less involved in this internationalization of production, although they did possess some foreign operations.[113]

Two additional features of the industry should be noted. First, the nature of the industry's international ties was different from those of many other industries because semiconductor producers engaged heavily in offshore assembly operations, in which components fabri-

[109] U.S. Dept. of Commerce, *1972* and *1977 Enterprise Statistics*. IRS, *Statistics of Income—1974-78*, shows the total assets of U.S.-controlled foreign corporations as a percentage of their total U.S. parents' assets was even higher, 31.8 percent in 1974. This figure is for the two-digit SIC level, one larger than just the semiconductor industry.

[110] U.S. Dept. of Commerce, *U.S. Direct Investment Abroad—1966* and *U.S. Direct Investment Abroad—1977*. These data are suggestive, since the data for each period are at different levels of aggregation.

[111] Ibid. Similarly, their MOFA (majority-owned foreign affiliates') exports to the United States as a percentage of their MOFAS' total sales were 31.7 percent in 1977. Data at the four-digit SIC level indicate a very sizable increase in the value of U.S. foreign subsidiaries' exports to the United States as a percentage of total semiconductor imports over the 1970s. Rising from 38 percent in 1966, MOFA exports to the United States relative to total imports reached 86.8 percent in 1977. See Réal Lavergne, unpublished data, used in his *Political Economy of U.S. Tariffs*.

[112] *Electronic News* (hereafter *EN*), March 13, 1978, p. 66; *EN*, December 12, 1977, p. 6; Borrus, Millstein, and Zysman, "Trade in the Semiconductor Industry," p. 175; Semiconductor Industry Association (SIA) interviews.

[113] Ibid.

cated in the United States were exported to foreign subsidiaries for further processing and then returned to the United States for final assembly and/or sale. This worldwide integration of production differed from mere exporting or the establishment of foreign production facilities to service local or third-country markets. This trade tied firms tightly to the international economy and made them sensitive to trade barriers, since the heightening of these barriers could destroy their global network of production and sales.

Second, the U.S. semiconductor industry was relatively concentrated. Though populated by many firms, the largest four accounted for 41 percent of all domestic shipments in 1977, and the largest eight for 60 percent.[114] These firms were divided into two separate groups, which increased concentration within the industry. Among these top eight, the two largest—IBM and Western Electric—were "captive" semiconductor producers, producing only for their own consumption and not for sale in the marketplace.[115] Captive production was common in the industry, accounting for over 50 percent of all domestic shipments.[116]

The noncaptive, or "merchant," U.S. producers of semiconductors were numerous but dominated by three or four firms, who controlled 60 percent of the shipments of merchant semiconductor devices.[117] The leading firms were Texas Instruments, Motorola, Fairchild Camera, and National Semiconductor. After these four were Intel, Mostek, and Advanced Micro Devices.[118] These top seven merchant producers were the domestic industry's economic and political leaders.

The Dependent Variable

During the 1970s, the trade policy preferences of the U.S. semiconductor industry were gradually shaped into explicit demands for greater openness of markets worldwide. Early in the decade, the in-

[114] U.S. Dept. of Commerce, *Concentration Ratios in Manufacturing* (Washington, D.C.: GPO, 1977); Chang, *Transfer of Technology*, pp. 11-12; Douglas Webbink, *The Semiconductor Industry: A Survey of Structure, Conduct, and Performance* (Washington, D.C.: FTC, 1977), pp. 18-28; Borrus, Millstein, and Zysman, "Trade in the Semiconductor Industry," pp. 157-63. The top eight U.S. producers in 1978 were IBM, Western Electric, Texas Instruments, Motorola, Fairchild Camera, National Semiconductor, Intel, and Mostek.

[115] Borrus, Millstein, and Zysman, "Trade in the Semiconductor Industry," pp. 150-67; U.S. ITC, *Competitive Factors*.

[116] U.S. ITC, *Competitive Factors*, p. 25.

[117] Chang, *Transfer of Technology*, p. 11.

[118] Borrus, Millstein, and Zysman, "Trade in the Semiconductor Industry," pp. 159-63; *Business Week*, September 10, 1979, p. 86-87; *Business Week*, October 22, 1979, pp. 127-28.

dustry did not possess a trade policy of its own. Instead, working through the political organization for the electronics industry, the Electronic Industry Association (EIA), it quietly supported efforts to reduce tariff and nontariff barriers (NTBs) at home and abroad.[119] In addition, the semiconductor producers followed the association's opposition to repeal of TSUS items 806.30 and 807.00 and to the protectionist Burke-Hartke Trade Bill.[120] As foreign, especially Japanese, competition rose over the 1970s, the semiconductor industry initiated its own activities to deal with these trade issues. Even in this later phase, when the semiconductor industry leaders were threatening to use U.S. trade laws against the Japanese, the U.S. semiconductor producers remained primarily concerned with securing greater access to the Japanese market. Their strategy was to employ the threat of demanding trade restrictions in order to induce greater Japanese willingness to negotiate tariff and NTB reductions.[121] As would be expected of this type of industry, the semiconductor producers were interested primarily in maintaining and/or increasing the openness of their home and foreign markets.

In the 1970s, despite rising import levels, the semiconductor industry did not seek protection through the primary avenue available, U.S. trade law. Some producers did, however, tacitly use these as well as put pressure on the President to achieve their liberal aims. Only two trade petitions to the ITC were filed by the semiconductor industry in this period. One, submitted in 1976 by a small firm, Sprague Electronics, charged the Japanese with dumping capacitors. This petition, eventually rejected by the ITC, had little if any industry support and concerned a first generation product.[122] The other petition, which concerned unfair trading practices and is discussed in greater detail below, was never actually filed.

Though the industry did not formally charge the Japanese with trade law violations, it did use the threat of filing such charges to realize its preferences for greater access to the Japanese market. Toward the end of 1976, a group of merchant producers started complaining about Japanese trading practices, as the Japanese began to corner ma-

[119] EIA interview; SIA interviews; House, Ways and Means, *Trade Reform*, 1973, pp. 3216-78.

[120] Ibid. TSUS—Tariff Schedule of the United States.

[121] SIA interviews; SIA, *The International Microelectronics Challenge* (Cupertino, Calif.: SIA, 1981); SIA, *The Effect of Government Targeting on the World Semiconductor Industry* (Cupertino, Calif.: SIA, 1983).

[122] *EN*, November 1, 1976, p. 28; SIA interviews; Judith Goldstein, unpublished data, used in her "Reexamination of U.S. Commercial Policy."

jor portions of the world and U.S. market in large-scale memory integrated circuits, especially 16K and 64K RAM devices. The U.S. producers charged the Japanese with export subsidization, dumping, targeting, and nonreciprocal trade behavior.[123] In part, these complaints arose from the surge of Japanese imports into the United States; however, they were also generated by the U.S. firms' inability to penetrate the Japanese market. At the time, U.S. tariffs on semiconductors averaged only 6 percent, while the Japanese tariffs were 12 percent.[124] Moreover, U.S. foreign investment by the *merchant* producers in the Japanese semiconductor industry was limited to one major investment by Texas Instruments.[125] The U.S. firms felt that this situation was biased against them.

After circulating these complaints and establishing their own industry organization, the Semiconductor Industry Association (SIA), several leading merchant producers—Intel, Motorola, Advanced Micro Devices, Mostek, National Semiconductor, and Fairchild Camera—decided that the SIA should develop an unfair trading practices (section 301) petition against the Japanese in 1978 and 1979. These SIA members hoped to use the case to scare the Japanese into adopting fairer trade practices.[126] The association, however, ran into opposition over the petition from both the U.S. government (the office of the Special Trade Representative, in particular) and, most important, other semiconductor and computer firms. The U.S. government, or at least the executive branch as represented by the STR, opposed the filing of the petition because it was worried about another political confrontation with the Japanese government.[127] Certain U.S. semiconductor firms opposed it for two reasons. First, captive semiconductor producers, like IBM and Western Electric, and computer manufacturers, like IBM, DEC, CDC, and Hewlett-Packard, bought a substantial portion of their semiconductor devices from Japanese producers; they feared such a trade case would disrupt their supply of Japanese imports.[128]

[123] *EN*, April 18, 1977, pp. 1, 4; U.S. ITC, *Competitive Factors*, p. 60; Borrus, Millstein, and Zysman, "Trade in the Semiconductor Industry"; SIA, *International Microelectronics Challenge*; House, Ways and Means Committee, *Competitive Factors Influencing World Trade in Semiconductors*, hearings, 96th Cong., 1st sess., November 30, 1979, pp. 74-76.

[124] *EN*, April 18, 1977, pp. 1, 4; SIA interviews; U.S. ITC, *Competitive Factors*; SIA, *International Microelectronics Challenge*; SIA, *Effect of Government Targeting*.

[125] *EN*, March 13, 1978, p. 66; *EN*, December 12, 1977, p. 6; Borrus, Millstein, and Zysman, "Trade in the Semiconductor Industry," p. 175.

[126] SIA interviews; SIA, *International Microelectronics Challenge*; SIA, *Effect of Government Targeting*.

[127] SIA interviews.

[128] Ibid.; U.S. ITC, *Competitive Factors*.

Second, some firms, like Texas Instruments and IBM, had major semiconductor production facilities in Japan; they were concerned that the Japanese government might retaliate against their investments if the United States pursued the case.[129] Facing opposition from parts of the U.S. government and from the leading multinational semiconductor producers, the SIA decided not to file the unfair trade case.

The SIA did decide to use the threat of such a case to realize its firms' preferences for greater reciprocity in U.S.-Japanese trade.[130] Agreeing to this strategy, other major semiconductor producers, mainly IBM, joined with the association in 1979 in pressuring the U.S. government (again mainly the STR and the President) to open negotiations with the Japanese to accelerate the tariff cuts and ensure implementation of the NTB codes developed in the Tokyo Round.[131] The United States and Japan began these semiconductor negotiations in 1980, largely because of the SIA's prompting. In 1981, the Japanese agreed to accelerate their tariff reductions. The negotiated agreement called for harmonization of U.S. and Japanese semiconductor tariff rates at 4.2 percent, beginning in 1982.[132] Further pressure from the U.S. industry led to the resumption of these negotiations in 1983 to eliminate all tariffs on semiconductors in the two countries.[133]

In addition to these negotiations, the SIA pressed the U.S. government to ensure greater Japanese compliance with the Tokyo Round's NTB codes and, most important, to obtain Japan's agreement on opening up the country's telecommunications industry, controlled by Nippon Telephone and Telegraph, to the procurement of foreign supplies.[134] The negotiations were initiated and eventually resulted in an agreement acceptable to the U.S. industry. In fact, in 1981, Motorola won the first foreign contract ever from Nippon Telephone.[135] The SIA maintained that none of these initiatives to reduce trade barriers would have occurred or been successful without its threatening to

---

[129] SIA interviews; *EN*, March 13, 1978, p. 66. For suggestions about the likelihood of Japanese retaliation, see *EN*, May 9, 1977, p. 1.

[130] SIA interviews; SIA, *International Microelectronics Challenge*; U.S. ITC, "Testimony of the SIA on Investigation no. 332-102," May 30-31, 1979; *EN*, March 28, 1977, p. 1; *EN*, April 18, 1977, pp. 1, 4; *EN*, July 31, 1978, p. 1.

[131] SIA interviews; SIA, *International Microelectronics Challenge*; Alex Lidow, "Testimony before the House Ways and Means Committee," December 15, 1981.

[132] SIA interviews.

[133] Ibid.

[134] Ibid.; SIA, *International Microelectronics Challenge*; T. Skornia, "Testimony before the House Ways and Means Committee," September 18, 1980; George Scalise, "Testimony before the House Ways and Means Committee," July 9, 1981.

[135] *Washington Post*, February 26, 1981, p. B-1.

launch an unfair trading case against the Japanese. Furthermore, it claimed that the trade case was just a means to realize the industry's actual preferences for greater openness in markets throughout the world.[136]

If a first consequence of the SIA's pressure was these U.S.-Japanese efforts to reduce trade barriers, a second consequence was the initiation of an investigation of the integrated circuit industry and its trade by the ITC in 1979. The SIA's numerous complaints and testimony to Congress about the Japanese threat in 1977 and 1978 prompted the lawmakers, in particular the House Ways and Means Committee, to request an investigation by the ITC.[137] This action was intended to appease the SIA and to increase pressure on the Japanese to adopt reciprocal and fair trading practices. The SIA's attempt at using the U.S. trade laws against the Japanese prompted a flurry of activity in the executive and legislative branches that eventually resulted in the reduction of tariffs and NTB's between the two countries.

After 1982, increasing economic distress and import competition generated renewed activity by the merchant semiconductor producers on trade issues. In the mid-1980s the SIA and several firms filed trade complaints against the Japanese that charged them with dumping, subsidization, and patent infringement.[138] The firms did not seek import restraints as a solution, however. Rather, the firms once again resorted to the strategy of using these petitions to force the Japanese to open their market and to halt their unfair trade activities.[139] These complaints did not mean the semiconductor manufacturers had turned protectionist. They revealed the industry's keen and continuing interest in seeing Japanese markets further opened. Not all of the firms supported these trade petitions. Once again, the most international producers—IBM, Texas Instruments, and Motorola—opposed some of these activities.[140] The SIA's complaints, nevertheless, got a great deal of political attention, and the U.S. government initiated its own investigation of the industry.[141] All of this pressure resulted in 1986 in the negotiation of an agreement between the United States

[136] SIA interviews.

[137] U.S. ITC, *Competitive Factors*; House, Ways and Means, *Competitive Factors*.

[138] *Business Week*, July 1, 1985, p. 23; *NYT*, June 5, 1985; *NYT*, June 14, 1985; *NYT*, June 16, 1985; *NYT*, September 28, 1985; *The Economist*, August 24, 1985, p. 69; *Wall Street Journal*, September 30, 1985.

[139] *Business Week*, July 1, 1985; *NYT*, June 14, 1985.

[140] Ronald Gutfleich, "Why Protection? U.S. Corporate and State Responses to a Changing World Economy" (Ph.D. dissertation, University of California, Berkeley, 1987), ch. 8, pp. 33-34.

[141] *NYT*, December 7, 1985; *Wall Street Journal*, December 9, 1985.

and the Japanese to monitor Japanese semiconductor export prices and to allow U.S. firms a larger piece of the Japanese market.[142]

In Congress, the industry's activity during the 1970s went through three phases, in all of which their interest in trade liberalization was maintained. These activities paralleled their efforts with the executive branch. In the early part of the decade, as already mentioned, the semiconductor industry was not very active in Congress. When it was, it operated through organizations representing a wide spectrum of electronics industries, such as the EIA and the WEMA (Western Electronics Manufacturers' Association). The semiconductor industry's general disinterest in political issues at the time was evident from its lack of political organization. When the industry did concern itself with political matters, it supported the larger association's positions, which generally advocated freer trade. On the key trade issues of the early 1970s, the semiconductor industry gave its support to legislation to begin a new round of multilateral trade negotiations (the Trade Act of 1974) and opposed the protectionist Burke-Hartke Bill and repeal of TSUS items 806.30 and 807.00.[143] The industry's political activity in Congress prior to 1976, although minimal, was congruent with its interest in open world markets.

The industry's second phase of congressional activity, beginning in 1976 or so, coincided with the founding of the SIA, which will be discussed in more detail when the industry's internal debates are examined. Created primarily to deal with trade issues, the SIA pressed its case in Congress, voicing its complaints about the Japanese to generate pressure on both the U.S. executive and the Japanese government. The SIA thus testified extensively on Capitol Hill between 1976 and 1979 and began transforming its grievances into legislative proposals.[144]

The third phase of the industry's congressional activity saw a return to explicit support for freer trade and a broadening of the agenda for aiding the industry. This phase, beginning around 1979 or 1980, coincided with the SIA's expansion to include large U.S. and foreign multinationals engaged in the semiconductor and computer businesses. As already discussed, the new multinational members did not support the unfair trade case against Japan. They wanted instead to develop policy

[142] *Wall Street Journal*, August 1, 1986; *Wall Street Journal*, August 4, 1986; *NYT*, July 26, 1986; *NYT*, August 1, 1986; *NYT*, August 2, 1986; *Business Week*, August 18, 1986.

[143] House, Ways and Means, *Trade Reform*, pp. 3216-78; SIA interviews.

[144] SIA interviews; SIA, *International Microelectronics Challenge*; House, Ways and Means, *Competitive Factors*; Skornia, "Testimony" (1980); U.S. ITC, "Testimony of the SIA on Investigation no. 332-102," May 30-31, 1979.

proposals helpful to the multinationals (and the entire industry). The SIA was forced to abandon its filing of the unfair trading practices petition and to turn its complaints into wider proposals for action. The association broadened its agenda, moving away from trade issues to larger questions of industrial policy, and focused on issues like tax policy, antitrust policy, and provisions to reduce capital costs to the industry.[145] On questions directly related to trade, the U.S. semiconductor industry supported trade liberalization, as in its backing of the Trade Act of 1979, endorsing the Tokyo Round results.[146]

The industry's relations with the U.S. government on trade issues were affected by its own internal politics. Lack of organization and divisions among the firms initially constrained their political activity. As we have seen, prior to 1976, the semiconductor producers were represented by associations for the electronics industry. The EIA and WEMA were dominated by the large U.S. multinationals and evinced little concern for the interests of the merchant semiconductor firms.[147]

With the mounting Japanese import threat beginning in 1976, merchant producers, such as Intel, Motorola, Advanced Micro Devices, National Semiconductor, and Mostek, increasingly sought a political solution to their trade problems. When the EIA and WEMA were not forthcoming, these producers established their own association, the SIA.[148] Remaining aloof from the SIA were not only firms in the other electronics industries, which were the major users of semiconductor devices and were represented by the EIA and WEMA, but also two of the largest and most multinational semiconductor producers, IBM and Texas Instruments. These firms did not share the SIA's belief that "something had to be done" to halt the Japanese invasion of the U.S. semiconductor market.

The SIA members soon realized that without an industry-wide consensus, and in particular without the support of the leading producers—IBM and Texas Instruments—their trade complaints were not likely to be politically successful. Around 1979 the association began seeking to develop such a consensus by expanding its membership. In this process, it brought in IBM and some of the computer manufac-

---

[145] SIA interviews; Robert Noyce,"Testimony to the Subcommittee on International Finance of the Senate Banking Committee," January 15, 1980; SIA, *International Microelectronics Challenge*; SIA, "An American Response to Foreign Industrial Challenge to High Technology Industries," congressional staff briefing, July 23, 1980; Scalise, "Testimony"; Lidow, "Testimony."

[146] Senate, Finance, *Private Advisory Committee Reports*.

[147] *EN*, March 28, 1977, p. 1; *EN*, April 18, 1977, p. 1; SIA interviews; EIA interviews.

[148] Ibid.

turers and major semiconductor users like DEC, CDC, Honeywell, and Hewlett-Packard.[149] Texas Instruments, however, still declined to join, both out of fear of the Japanese reaction and out of a desire to be represented only by its own employees.[150] As noted, this expansion of the SIA changed its political focus, shifting its primary concentration from trade policy to broader industrial policy questions, on which a general consensus could be formed. The enlarged membership of the SIA in turn seems to have increased its political influence, since only after this expansion were its preferences for greater access to the Japanese market acted upon by the U.S. government.

Overall, the semiconductor producers fit our argument about Type III industries. The industry advocated free trade at home and abroad throughout the 1970s. Its international trade and multinational ties meant that protection was not a viable solution to its problems. It maintained this preference throughout the 1980s, despite fearsome import competition and mounting economic problems. The SIA's complaints and petitions in the 1980s were intended less to close the U.S. market than to open the Japanese market. Many U.S. manufacturers felt the Japanese were playing unfairly, and after much frustrating negotiation they decided to use the threat of trade action to compel the Japanese to change their ways. The U.S. manufacturers had become more aggressive in their strategy of dealing with their overseas competitors. Their trade policy preferences had not changed, but their method of pursuing them had.

CASE 4: RADIOS AND TELEVISIONS

U.S. manufacturers of radio and television sets suffered severe economic difficulties in the 1970s. The decade brought declining U.S. capacity, profitability, and employment for the industry. Plant closings were a common experience; the plants that survived operated at low levels of capacity.[151] Profitability declined every year between 1970 and 1977; and employment in the industry fell almost 50 percent from its peak in 1971 by 1975.[152]

This economic hardship accompanied rapidly rising import competition. Import penetration rates increased about 6 to 8 percent an-

---

[149] SIA interviews; SIA, *International Microelectronics Challenge*.

[150] SIA interviews.

[151] The industry studied here is those firms producing radios and televisions as defined in SIC 3651. U.S. ITC, *Television Receivers, Color and Monochrome*, pub. no. 808, March 1977.

[152] Ibid.; Office of Technology Assessment (hereafter OTA), *International Competitiveness in Electronics* (Washington, D.C.: GPO, November 1983), pp. 114-15.

nually between 1971 and 1977, with imports capturing 43 percent of the domestic market by 1977.[153] For certain segments of the industry, imports were even more dominant: in 1977, imports accounted for 65 percent of domestic consumption of radios, nearly 50 percent of the market in audio equipment, and close to 63 percent of the sale of black and white television sets in the United States.[154] In fact, by the late 1970s most domestic production of these commodities had ceased, and what remained were U.S. assembly operations on components produced elsewhere.[155] Only color television sets, the best-selling product in the industry, were still produced in some number in the United States in 1977; imports of these claimed over 27 percent of the domestic market in that year.[156] All of these problems made the radio and television manufacturers prime candidates to demand protection.

U.S. radio and television manufacturing was a Type IV industry. It had significant multinational production, but few exports and limited intrafirm trading operations. The international trade position of the industry was not strong. Its net trade balance grew more and more negative over the 1970s, falling some 200 percent between 1970 and 1977.[157] Exports as a percentage of domestic consumption, however, increased in the period, from 5 percent in 1970 to 10 percent in 1977.[158] Much of this increase resulted from heightened use of off-shore assembly. Despite this rising export activity, the U.S. industry's global trade position was weakening throughout the period.

The industry's multinational position also points to its categorization as Type IV. The industry began developing multinational production facilities in the 1960s, early in its history. This phase of expansion was accompanied by U.S. domination of the entire industry. After this, U.S. direct foreign investment stabilized, and in the 1970s the Japanese assumed domination of the world market. Only in the latter part of the decade did U.S. firms renew their movement abroad, but now

[153] U.S. Dept. of Commerce, *U.S. Commodity Exports and Imports, 1976/75* and *1977/76.*
[154] Ibid.; U.S. ITC, *Television Receivers*, pub. no. 808.
[155] OTA, *Competitiveness in Electronics*, pp. 112-14.
[156] U.S. Dept. of Commerce, *U.S. Commodity Exports and Imports, 1976/75* and *1977/76.*
[157] Ibid.; OTA, *Competitiveness in Electronics*, pp. 116-18. Since trade in TSUS items 806.30 and 807.00 accounts for a substantial proportion of imports, approximately 32 percent in 1976, this figure alone is inadequate. When the trade figures are adjusted for these imports, the net balance for the industry remains negative but less so.
[158] U.S. Dept. of Commerce, *U.S. Commodity Exports and Imports, 1976/75* and *1977/76.* Subtracting out the value of the U.S. content of trade in TSUS item 807.00, the export to domestic consumption ratio is much less robust. See OTA, *Competitiveness in Electronics*, pp. 118-19; U.S. ITC, *Economic Factors Affecting the Use of the Items 807.00 and 806.30*, pub. no. 339; U.S. ITC, *Import Trends in TSUS Items 806.30 and 807.00*, pub. no. 1029.

this occurred as a response to economic difficulty and rising competition in the domestic market. Direct foreign investment by the U.S. firms was stable between 1972 and 1977. Foreign assets as a percentage of total assets were about 10 percent in both 1972 and 1977.[159] Multinational trade in the industry was small but increasing. For instance, the proportion of all multinational affiliates' exports to the United States relative to their affiliates' total sales totaled 31 percent in 1977 for the industry, an increase from the early 1970s.[160] U.S. multinationals producing radio and television sets had thus established some trading operations among their subsidiaries and parent corporations, which they were intensifying during the decade.

Multinational production and trade ties were unevenly distributed in the industry. Among the leading U.S. firms in the early 1970s, RCA and General Electric were the most international; GTE-Sylvania, Magnavox, and Zenith were the least; and Motorola was in between these two groups.[161] For example, RCA received almost as much revenue from its television technology licenses to Japanese firms ($50 million per year) during the 1970s as it did from its own sales of televisions.[162] On the other hand, Zenith received 80 percent of its revenues from its television manufacturing operations, which until 1978 were almost entirely concentrated in the United States.[163] By 1980, these rankings had changed to some extent; U.S. firms remaining in the industry had increasingly shifted production offshore, thus rendering RCA, General Electric, and Zenith more similarly dependent on multinational operations.[164]

Three other features of the industry are pertinent. First, the technological advantages held by U.S. manufacturers in this industry had

[159] U.S. Dept. of Commerce, *1972* and *1977 Enterprise Statistics*.

[160] U.S. Dept. of Commerce, *U.S. Direct Investment Abroad—1966* and *1977*. The value of MOFA exports to the United States (for the radio, television, and communication equipment industry, one somewhat larger than SIC 3651) in 1977 was $569 million. Estimates for MOFA exports to the United States as a percentage of total imports for the smaller four-digit SIC sector point to a substantial increase in this ratio from a relatively low 6.5 percent in 1966 to 13.5 percent in 1977. See Lavergne, unpublished data, used in his *Political Economy of U.S. Tariffs*; and U.S. Dept. of Commerce, *U.S. Direct Investment Abroad—1977*.

[161] *EN*, February 14, 1977, p. 2; James Millstein, "Decline in an Expanding Industry: Japanese Competition in Color TVs," in *American Industry in International Competition*, ed. Zysman and Tyson, p. 125; Moody's, *Moody's Manual of Industrial Securities* (New York: Moody's, 1975); Katherine Hughes, *Corporate Responses to Declining Rates of Growth* (Lexington, Mass.: Lexington Books, 1982), ch. 4.

[162] OTA, *Competitiveness in Electronics*, p. 108.

[163] Ibid., p. 111.

[164] Ibid., p. 113; *EN*, October 3, 1977, p. 1; *EN*, December 12, 1977, p. 2.

eroded by the late 1960s. At this time, Japanese firms moved to the forefront, mainly through the early introduction of solid-state technology. Ninety percent of Japanese production of radios and televisions in 1971 involved solid-state components instead of the older vacuum tubes; U.S. firms did not produce this new technology in any volume until 1973 or later, which indicates the loss of the U.S. technological lead.[165] Once this new technology was standardized, competitive advantage shifted further away from U.S. producers to other low-wage producers in East Asia.

A second feature involves the degree of foreign investment in the United States in this industry. With the loss of technological superiority, U.S. firms faced two related problems: increased U.S. imports and rising foreign investment in the U.S. market. In 1974, Japanese and West European electronics producers began U.S. production and/ or assembly operations. By 1982, of the fifteen manufacturers of televisions in the United States, eleven were foreign owned.[166] A central implication of this was the enormous threat foreign producers posed to U.S. producers in their own home market.

Third, the industry was relatively concentrated. The largest eight firms produced over 60 percent of total shipments; and the two largest U.S. firms—RCA and Zenith—accounted for 40 percent of total sales of all color televisions.[167] Only a handful of U.S. firms were important players in the industry: RCA, Zenith, General Electric, Curtis-Mathes, GTE-Sylvania, Magnavox, and Motorola.

All this points to U.S. radio and television manufacturing as a Type IV industry, with substantial multinational operations and limited international trading capacity. These international ties, however, were concentrated among the largest firms. Among these firms, a key division existed between on the one hand, General Electric and RCA, the dominant multinationals, and on the other hand, Zenith, GTE-Sylvania, and Magnavox, who were domestically oriented companies.

The Dependent Variable

During the 1970s, the trade policy preferences and activities of the radio and television manufacturers reflected the divisions in the industry associated with the firms' different degrees of multinationality. In general, the producers with production located mainly in the

---

[165] Millstein, "Decline in an Expanding Industry," p. 107.

[166] OTA, *Competitiveness in Electronics*, p. 107.

[167] The industry concentration figure is from U.S. Dept. of Commerce, *Concentration Ratios*; the firms' market share figure is from OTA, *Competitiveness in Electronics*, pp. 114, 115.

United States—Zenith, GTE-Sylvania, and Magnavox—waged a continuous battle against selected importers, using all types of trade policy measures. Domestic labor unions eventually joined with these firms in their protests against imports, as did various U.S. manufacturers of components (e.g., glass tubes) for the television industry. In opposition were the industry's highly multinational U.S. firms, such as RCA and the foreign multinationals, who gradually bought out many of the opponents of imports. Though not as vocal, this multinational group weakened the force of the domestic firms' arguments against imports simply by refusing to join them.

In the late 1960s and throughout the 1970s, the domestically oriented firms employed a variety of trade laws to force the executive branch to take action against imports. These manufacturers leveled charges of dumping, export subsidization, antitrust violation, and unfair trading practices against selected importers, finally resorting to demands for escape clause relief to staunch the flood of imports. Between 1973 and 1978, the industry filed twenty-four petitions for trade relief with the ITC.[168]

Two features of these charges are noteworthy. First, they were selective in whom they were directed against: the firms' concerns were related to Japanese imports only, not to all imports. Second, only particular products were involved in the charges. Color televisions, usually those already assembled, and citizen-band radios (CBS) were the prime targets. Other products, such as radios and monochrome televisions, were less an object of concern, since by 1973 they were not produced in any number in the United States.

The U.S. television manufacturers' battle against imports began in 1968 when Zenith, supported by allies in the Electronics Industries Association (EIA), brought antidumping charges against Japanese television imports. Zenith claimed that the Japanese were selling sets in the United States at prices lower than in Japan in order to gain U.S. market share. The charges were referred to the Treasury Department, which was responsible for determining whether such price discrimination was occurring. Two years later (December 1970) the Treasury Department ruled that dumping was indeed being practiced, thus sending the case to the ITC, which had to decide if the dumping had caused injury to the domestic industry. Almost a year later, the ITC found for Zenith and referred the case back to Treasury

[168] Judith Goldstein, unpublished data, used in her "Reexamination of U.S. Commercial Policy."

to establish the size of the antidumping fines.[169] The department, however, experienced difficulties. The Japanese refused to cooperate by providing the requisite information, and Zenith demanded steep fines. When the fines were finally set in 1972, both groups objected to them, and because of the controversy, they were only partially collected for several years. By 1980, only $13 million of the original assessment of $130 million in fines had been collected.[170] This was only the first unsatisfactory battle in Zenith's ten-year war against the Japanese.

In the midst of this antidumping case, Zenith and other manufacturers brought countervailing duty (CVD) charges against the Japanese. In April 1970, Zenith charged that the Japanese government was providing export subsidies to its television exporters through its rebates of their value-added commodity taxes.[171] In 1972 Magnavox and GTE-Sylvania initiated similar CVD cases against the Japanese.[172] These cases also engendered controversy. After a long delay, the Treasury Department ruled in 1975 against the domestic firms, maintaining that the VAT rebates were not a "bounty or grant" to which CVDs were applicable.[173] Angered by this decision, Zenith took the case to U.S. Customs Court, which in 1976 ruled in Zenith's favor.[174] Pressure from the Japanese government in part prompted the Treasury Department in 1977 to appeal the Customs Court's decision, and later that year the U.S. Appeals Court ruled against Zenith. Zenith then took the case to the U.S. Supreme Court, which in 1978 upheld the Appeals Court decision.[175] Zenith and its allies, Magnavox and GTE-Sylvania, had lost another battle in the war against Japanese imports.

Several other actions were taken by these U.S. manufacturers against Japanese importers. Zenith brought antitrust charges in 1974 against a number of Japanese firms for conspiracy to restrain trade. In particular, Zenith was concerned with the attempt of a Japanese

[169] David Yoffie, "Zenith Radio Corporation vs. the U.S.," case no. 0-383-070, Harvard Business School, 1982; Millstein, "Decline in an Expanding Industry," pp. 125, 133.

[170] Millstein, "Decline in an Expanding Industry," p. 125; OTA, *Competitiveness in Electronics*, pp. 439-41; *EN*, April 10, 1978, pp. 1, 72.

[171] Yoffie, "Zenith Radio Corporation," pp. 9-11.

[172] Yoffie, "Zenith Radio Corporation"; Millstein, "Decline in an Expanding Industry," pp. 125-27.

[173] Yoffie, "Zenith Radio Corporation," p. 9; Dean De Rosa, J. Michael Finger, Stephen Golub, and William Nye, "What the 'Zenith Case' Might Have Meant," *Journal of World Trade Law* 13 (January-February 1979):47-54.

[174] Yoffie, "Zenith Radio Corporation"; *EN*, April 18, 1977, p. 1.

[175] *EN*, August 1, 1977, pp. 1, 13; Yoffie, "Zenith Radio Corporation," pp. 9-11; *EN*, June 26, 1979, p. 1; OTA, *Competitiveness in Electronics*, p. 444.

firm, Matsushita, to buy Motorola's television operations. The Justice Department refused to do anything about the charges, and the case ended quietly four years later in 1978.[176] In another effort, GTE-Sylvania, alleging dumping, filed an unfair trading practices suit (section 337) in 1976 against Japanese importers. Strongly opposed, the U.S. Special Trade Representative and Treasury Department pressured GTE-Sylvania to drop the charges.[177]

Prior to 1976, the efforts of these U.S. television manufacturers to obstruct Japanese imports were made individually. In 1976 a coalition of labor unions, two U.S. television manufacturers, GTE-Sylvania and Wells-Gardner, and three U.S. suppliers to the domestic television industry, Corning Glass, Owens-Illinois, and Sprague Electric, calling themselves the Committee to Preserve American Color Televisions—COMPACT—petitioned the ITC to provide escape clause relief. Unlike earlier actions, COMPACT's demands were for *global* relief via quotas.[178] Zenith, the only large domestically oriented producer left, did not join COMPACT but did eventually support the petition for quotas on assembled televisions.[179] This move was strongly oppose by RCA. In the industry association's debate on this petition, RCA vocally disapproved of it.[180]

The ITC not only accepted this escape clause petition but also began its own investigation of all types of television imports. This latter investigation was opposed vigorously by other executive branch departments and was eventually terminated.[181] The escape clause petition filed by COMPACT was investigated by the ITC, which in 1977 found that injury to the domestic industry existed. The ITC's recommendation to increase the tariffs on color televisions for five years, which was applauded by COMPACT, was sent to President Carter for a final deci-

[176] *EN*, October 25, 1976, p. 6; *EN*, April 4, 1977, p. 21; *EN*, January 2, 1978, p. 38; Yoffie, "Zenith Radio Corporation," pp. 11-13.

[177] U.S. ITC, *Investigation of Televisions*, 337-TA-23 (January 1976); OTA, *Competitiveness in Electronics*, pp. 445-46; Yoffie, "Zenith Radio Corporation," pp. 7-8; *EN*, March 28, 1977, p. 22.

[178] Millstein, "Decline in an Expanding Industry," pp. 128-33; Yoffie, "Zenith Radio Corporation"; Yoffie, *Power and Protectionism*, pp. 215-21; *EN*, September 27, 1976, p. 1; COMPACT, *Petition to the U.S. ITC for Import Relief* (Washington, D.C.: COMPACT, September 1976); *EN*, October 25, 1976, p. 6; *EN*, January 17, 1977, p. 1.

[179] *EN*, September 27, 1976, p. 1; *EN*, October 25, 1976, p. 6; *EN*, January 17, 1977, p. 1; Millstein, "Decline in an Expanding Industry," pp. 128-29.

[180] Electronic Industries Association (EIA) interview; Millstein, "Decline in an Expanding Industry," p. 131; *EN*, March 21, 1977, pp. 1, 14.

[181] *EN*, April 12, 1976, p. 49; *EN*, April 19, 1976, p. 18; *EN*, October 4, 1976, p. 28; *EN*, October 11, 1976, p. 32; *EN*, November 15, 1976, p. 56; *EN*, December 20, 1976, p. 11.

sion.[182] For a variety of reasons, he rejected the ITC recommendation and instead negotiated an orderly marketing agreement with the Japanese. The choice of the OMA was partially dictated by fears that if nothing were done for the industry, COMPACT would appeal to Congress, which might overrule the President's decision and impose higher tariffs.[183] In May 1977, a three-year OMA with Japan on complete and incomplete color televisions was signed.[184] In 1978 two new OMAs with Taiwan and South Korea were arranged to prevent their imports from filling the gap left by the Japanese limits.[185]

These selective restraints—selective because they affected only certain importers and did not pertain to subassemblies or components—were in general accepted by the U.S. television manufacturers. Zenith was satisfied because it obtained some limits on imports from its major competitors, and RCA did not actively fight the restraints since they did not affect its multinational trade operations.[186] The domestic industry's response to the OMAs was either to accelerate their movement offshore or to sell their operations to a foreign company. For instance, in 1978 Zenith began reducing its U.S. television production operations and moving them to Mexico and Taiwan, and in 1981 GTE sold its Sylvania television operations to the Dutch firm, N. A. Philips.[187] This exodus of U.S. television producers relieved much of the pressure for limits on imports.

This diverse activity during the 1970s to use U.S. trade laws against Japanese importers of televisions suggests the continuous and increasing preference that domestically oriented television manufacturers had for restraint of Japanese competition, as the Japanese seized a technological lead in the industry. Their harassment of the Japanese abated only when the U.S. firms increased their international identity by moving offshore or by being acquired by a foreign multinational.

The U.S. manufacturers' battle against imports did not, however,

---

[182] U.S. ITC, *Television Receivers*, pub. no. 808; Yoffie, "Zenith Radio Corporation," pp. 13-14; Millstein, "Decline in an Expanding Industry," pp. 130-31.

[183] Millstein, "Decline in an Expanding Industry," pp. 132-35; Yoffie, "Zenith Radio Corporation," pp. 13-15; Yoffie, *Power and Protectionism*, pp. 215-21; *EN*, March 21, 1977, pp. 1, 14; EIA interview.

[184] Yoffie, *Power and Protectionism*, pp. 215-21; *EN*, May 23, 1977, p. 1; OTA, *Competitiveness in Electronics*, pp. 446-48; Millstein, "Decline in an Expanding Industry," p. 135.

[185] OTA, *Competitiveness in Electronics*, p. 448; Yoffie, *Power and Protectionism*, pp. 215-21; Millstein, "Decline in an Expanding Industry," p. 138.

[186] *EN*, May 23, 1977, pp. 1, 22; Millstein, "Decline in an Expanding Industry," p. 128; EIA interviews; *NYT*, May 21, 1977, p. 25.

[187] OTA, *Competitiveness in Electronics*, p. 116; *EN*, October 3, 1977, p. 1; *EN*, December 12, 1977, p. 2; *EN*, September 26, 1978, p. 1.

extend to pressuring Congress for legislation against the Japanese. They never called for separate legislation to deal with the radio and television industry's import problems, as the footwear industry did. Nor did they develop an explicit caucus in Congress devoted to solving their trade problems, as the textile, steel, automobile, and footwear industries all did. As a group, they were represented by the EIA, which testified frequently but kept its statements broad and oriented toward "free but fair" trade.[188] Without a coherent, industry-wide policy position or political organization and with a preference for selective import relief, these domestically oriented television manufacturers found it difficult to press for congressional action.[189]

The U.S. television manufacturers did seek to change the laws relating to trade. As in the footwear case, the costly, protracted, and unsatisfactory resolution of the television manufacturers' petitions against imports prompted these firms to seek to alter the trade laws during their congressional reviews in 1973-74 and 1979-80. The experience of television manufacturers, especially Zenith, with long delays in the investigation of antidumping and countervailing duty cases led them to desire time limits on these investigations, which the EIA proposed in hearings on the Trade Reform Act of 1974.[190] These limits were adopted in the final bill.

Later in the 1979 trade bill hearings to ratify the Tokyo Round agreements, some television manufacturers, along with other groups, expressed their dissatisfaction with the Treasury Department's handling of their trade petitions. Citing Treasury's reluctance to help domestic manufacturers, they proposed that the more friendly Commerce Department be given responsibility for these investigations.[191] The final bill once again reflected these desires, as jurisdiction for the

---

[188] See EIA, *Electronics and International Competition* (Washington, D.C.: EIA, 1978), for views of EIA.

[189] These domestic television producers did pressure Congress in order to pressure the executive branch into granting import relief under the trade laws. Several times these producers were able to obtain congressional help in their petitions. After experiencing much delay, Zenith got Senator Edward Kennedy, head of the Senate Judiciary Committee, to request that the Justice Department speedily investigate Zenith's antitrust charges against the Japanese. This request had little effect, for the Justice Department rejected the case. In another instance COMPACT pressured President Carter into the OMA action by prompting the Senate Finance Committee to urge the President to do something for the industry. This pressure was apparently more effective; Carter responded by negotiating OMAS for the industry. See *EN*, September 4, 1978, p. 74; *EN*, March 21, 1977, pp. 1, 74.

[190] EIA interviews; OTA, *Competitiveness in Electronics*, pp. 438-42, 450; *EN*, October 25, 1976, p. 6; House, Ways and Means, *Trade Reform*, pp. 3216-78.

[191] EIA interviews; OTA, *Competitiveness in Electronics*, pp. 440-42; Senate, Finance, *Private Advisory Committee Report*, pp. 365-410.

investigations was shifted to Commerce. Thus, in addition to pressuring the executive branch, the television manufacturers desiring import relief sought the help of Congress to alter the trade laws to make this more attainable.

The industry remained internally divided throughout the 1970s on trade issues. The basis of this political division related to the firms' differing multinational positions. Those with extensive multinational ties—like RCA and General Electric—maintained their preference for open markets, fighting to ensure that any import restrictions would be selective and not affect their operations.[192] Those firms whose production was concentrated in the United States—like Zenith, GTE-Sylvania, and Magnavox (until it became part of the Dutch N. A. Philips in 1974)—sought action against the Japanese importers. Having only their home market to lose, these firms felt impelled to resist the Japanese invasion.

These internal divisions had two important ramifications. First, the divisions were reflected in the lack of political organization in this sector. Though the electronics industry as a whole was represented by the EIA, the television manufacturers had no organization to represent them. Within the EIA, the industry was represented on trade issues in two different forums, which were controlled by the two different factions in the industry. In the International Business Council of the EIA, where general trade policy positions were discussed and adopted, the large U.S. and foreign multinationals held sway, and the councils' positions were pro–free trade. In the EIA's consumer electronics products' division, the domestically oriented television manufacturers outnumbered the large international firms, and the policy stances issuing from this group were supportive of trade actions against Japanese imports.[193] The EIA was thus riven by the same political divisions as the industry.

This lack of consensus forced the EIA to avoid taking positions on trade issues or to adopt only the most general ones. The inadequacy of representation provided by the EIA induced the firms wanting trade restrictions to form another organization to promote their interests. In 1976, as mentiond above, several domestic manufacturers helped create, along with a number of labor unions and domestic suppliers of television components, the Committee to Preserve American Color Televisions, which thereafter became the major force for trade restrictions on television imports. This organization, involving a labor-man-

---

[192] E.g., *EN*, February 14, 1977, p. 2.
[193] EIA interviews.

agement coalition, proved more successful than the earlier individual and EIA-backed efforts.

Despite COMPACT's apparent success, the industry ultimately possessed only a weak position because of its serious internal divisions. The inability to develop a consensual position on trade issues and its lack of political organization contributed to it's political weakness. When they did not find support among or, worse, were contradicted in their charges by the largest U.S. television manufacturers—RCA and General Electric—those firms fighting against Japanese imports found their cases weakened in the eyes of U.S. government officials. Similarly, without an organization to speak for their cause, the domestically oriented television manufacturers were less able to appeal directly to Congress. These internal divisions, generated by divergences in the multinational ties of the firms, reduced the pressures for actions against imports that might otherwise have arisen, given the economic distress felt by the industry in the 1970s.

CASE 5: WATCHES AND CLOCKS

The U.S. watch and clock industry experienced great economic upheaval during the 1970s. The technological change from conventional jeweled watches to nonconventional solid-state (digital and analog) watches forced the industry to reorganize. In effect, the industry was bifurcated into two distinct segments—conventional and nonconventional watch producers. The former group was composed of the long-standing American watch makers, led by Timex and Bulova. The latter group was composed mainly of U.S. semiconductor producers—such as Texas Instruments, National Semiconductor, and Fairchild Camera—and Japanese imports. Over the decade, conventional watches were displaced by nonconventional ones, and the traditional manufacturers either left the industry or moved into the nonconventional segment.[194]

The industry, especially the conventional sector, also faced much economic distress. In the decade, employment in conventional watch production was first steady and then declined, while in the nonconventional sector employment rose from 1974 to 1978 and then fell.[195] In

[194] This industry includes the products under SIC code 3873. Frost and Sullivan, *The U.S. Watch Market* (New York: Frost and Sullivan, 1978), pp. 1-35; U.S. ITC, *Report on Watches and Parts*, investigation no. 332-80, in House, Ways and Means Committee, *Report on Watches and Parts*, hearings on H.R. 14600, May 30, 1977.

[195] U.S. ITC, *Report on Watches*, investigation no. 332-80, p. 107; U.S. Dept. of Commerce, *Census: 1972*.

addition, the industry experienced a decline in the number of firms producing watches, despite the entrance of many semiconductor firms into the nonconventional segment.[196] The industry's economic performance in terms of its capacity utilization and profitability also suffered. Makers of conventional watches experienced periods of substantial excess production capacity in the early and mid-1970s before they were able to switch to nonconventional watch production. The industry encountered profit problems over the period; significant ups and downs in these firms' profitability between 1972 and 1976 were evident.[197]

The industry was also beleaguered by import competition. The watch and clock industry had always faced import competition, but the 1970s brought rapidly increasing rates of import penetration as well as new heights in import penetration levels. Between 1971 and 1977, import penetration of the U.S. market grew an average of 8 percent annually.[198] Imports accounted for 18 percent of domestic supply in 1970, and 35 percent in 1977.[199] The sector experiencing the greatest surge in imports was the nonconventional one. While conventional watch imports maintained a steady proportion of the U.S. market between 1972 and 1976 (between 35 and 28 percent), the nonconventional imports gained market share rapidly, jumping from 12 percent of domestic consumption in 1972 to 33 percent in 1976.[200] This foreign competition, combined with their economic difficulties, made the watch producers likely candidates to seek protection.

U.S. watch and clock manufacture was a Type IV industry, with substantial multinational operations but limited exports and intrafirm trade. However, the nonconventional watch segment was most like Type III, with substantial foreign production and trade activities, as in the semiconductor industry. The net international trade position of the industry over the 1970s was one of increasing deficits.[201] Its export

---

[196] Ibid.; Frost and Sullivan, *U.S. Watch Market*, pp. 1-35.

[197] U.S. ITC, *Report on Watches*, investigation no. 332-80, pp. 102-103, 120-21; Frost and Sullivan, *U.S. Watch Market*.

[198] U.S. Dept. of Commerce, *U.S. Commodity Exports and Imports 1976/75* and *1977/76*.

[199] Ibid.

[200] U.S. ITC, *Report on Watches*, investigation no. 332-80, p. 59.

[201] From a deficit of $160 million in 1970, the red ink rose to $536 million in 1977. See U.S. Dept. of Commerce, *U.S. Commodity Exports and Imports, 1976/75* and *1977/76*. These figures need to be corrected for the offshore assembly trade of U.S. firms. Significant use of TSUS items 806.30 and 807.00 in the watch industry began after 1974 and was largely concentrated in the nonconventional watch segment. In 1972, these offshore-assembly imports totaled about $1 million, or 0.7 percent of total imports. By 1976, these imports had soared to $189 million, or 43 percent of total imports. Recalculating the industry's

dependence was limited but advancing. Exports as a percentage of domestic supply grew from 2 percent in 1970, to 6 percent in 1974, to 13 percent in 1977.[202] Much of this increase was due to rising exports of watch parts and components for offshore assembly into nonconventional watches or modules.[203] Exports of conventional watches and parts from the United States rarely amounted to much, averaging 1 to 2 percent of total shipments in the late 1960s and early 1970s.[204] The export surge of the 1970s was not their doing.

The extent of multinational investment and trade for watches and clocks also indicates the conventional segment to be a Type IV industry. Its foreign investment was sizable. For example, foreign assets approximated 19 percent of total assets in 1972 and 1977, a large percentage.[205] The industry, however, had small intrafirm trade operations. Only 4 percent of all U.S. instrument producers' foreign affiliates' sales were imports to the United States in 1977.[206] Overall, the industry was characterized by a strong foreign investment position and limited export and multinational-related trade flows.

Two other features of this industry should be noted. First, the domestic industry had two segments, the conventional watchmakers and the nonconventional ones. The conventional segment was a Type IV industry, but the nonconventional segment was composed of U.S. semiconductor firms, which were Type III multinationals. This split within the industry had important economic and political conse-

---

net trade data to exclude the double counting of this offshore-assembly trade reveals that, though remaining in deficit throughout the period, the industry's trade position deteriorated much less than the original data suggests. By 1976, the deficit for watches and parts without the double counting was $265.4 million, while originally it was nearly double this figure. See U.S. ITC, *Report on Watches*, investigation no. 332-80, pp. 134-39; U.S. Dept. of Commerce, *U.S. Commodity Exports and Imports, 1976/75* and *1977/76*.

[202] U.S. Dept. of Commerce, *U.S. Commodity Exports and Imports, 1976/75* and *1977/76*.

[203] Nonconventional watch and parts exports rose from 21 percent of total exports in 1972 to 93 percent in 1976. See U.S. ITC, *Report on Watches*, investigation no. 332-80, p. 126. Additionally, exports related to TSUS items 806.30 and 807.00 (the nondutiable component) increased from 2 percent of total watch and parts exports in 1972 to almost 38 percent in 1976. As these figures demonstrate, the portion of U.S. exports of watches that was actually growing in the 1970s was the nonconventional sector of its offshore-assembly trade. U.S. ITC, *Report on Watches*, investigation no. 332-80, pp. 136-39; U.S. Dept. of Commerce, *U.S. Commodity Exports and Imports, 1976/75* and *1977/76*.

[204] U.S. ITC, *Report on Watches*, investigation no. 332-80, pp. 136-39; U.S. Dept. of Commerce, *U.S. Commodity Exports and Imports, 1976/75* and *1977/76*.

[205] U.S. Dept. of Commerce, *1972* and *1977 Enterprise Statistics*. These figures seem very high and are probably overstated.

[206] U.S. Dept. of Commerce, *U.S. Direct Investment Abroad—1966* and *1977*. These figures are the larger sector of all instruments and thus are too highly aggregated. The ratio for MOFA exports to the United States was similar: 3 percent.

quences. Second, the industry had another sizable segment, composed of importers and assemblers, who imported incomplete watches or watch components requiring little further assembly and had U.S. subsidiaries that sold the watches under well-known brand names. This group, though not considered to be domestic producers, controlled a substantial share of the U.S. watch market.[207] All three of these segments were linked to the international economy, but the traditional domestic manufacturers depended most on the domestic U.S. market, because that was where most of their investments and profits related to watches were located.

The Dependent Variable

The trade policy preferences and activities of the U.S. watch and clock industry in the 1970s were affected much by these splits within it. The traditional manufacturers, led by Timex, were advocates of selective protection of the U.S. market. They opposed any new tariff reductions in 1974 and later sought to have duties on certain imports elevated by congressional legislation.[208] This move to raise some watch tariffs was related to the intra-industry competition between the traditional and solid-state manufacturers. It was part of the traditional firms' strategy to slow down the solid-state watch firms' rapid takeover of the entire U.S. watch market. Having failed to anticipate consumer demand for solid-state watches, these traditional manufacturers hoped that by raising solid-state prices, tariff increases in nonconventional watches would dampen demand and give them time to initiate large-scale production of these new watches.

These manufacturers had a history of dependence on selective trade barriers. After World War II, they worked to obtain protection from Swiss imports. In 1954 they succeeded in getting escape clause relief, which raised the tariff on (high quality) watch imports for thirteen years.[209] Even after the escape clause relief was terminated in 1967, tariff rates for the industry remained above the national manufacturing average.[210] In general, though these traditional manufacturers became more linked to the international economy through their growing worldwide sourcing and production of watches and compo-

---

[207] U.S. ITC, *Report on Watches*, investigation no. 332-80.

[208] Timex testimony in House, Ways and Means, *Trade Reform*, pp. 3185-92; U.S. ITC, *Report on Watches*, investigation no. 332-80.

[209] House, Ways and Means, *Trade Reform*, p. 3181.

[210] The nominal, post-Kennedy Round, trade-weighted average for the industry was almost 24 percent; the effective rate was 45 percent. U.S. ITC, *Protection in Major Trading Countries*, pub. no. 737, August 1975.

nents in the postwar period, they continued to prefer selective protection of the home market against their major sources of foreign competition: high-quality Swiss imports before 1970 and low-cost solid-state imports after 1973.

Opposition to the protectionist desires of the domestic manufacturers was weak before the 1970s. Led by importer/assembler firms, this group of opponents had little political influence, because it involved foreign firms and few American jobs. It was strengthened by the growing participation of the U.S. solid-state watch manufacturers. These were large, American semiconductor firms, which possessed substantial political as well as economic clout. In the battle over tariff rates, the interests of the nonconventional watchmakers and of the importer/assemblers coincided, since both preferred an open U.S. market.[211] An increase in U.S. watch tariffs would hurt these two groups both by increasing their watch prices and thus decreasing their sales in the U.S. market and by inviting retaliation by other countries. The battle over trade policy in the 1970s became part of the watchmakers' intra-industry competition, with the traditional manufacturers pressing for selective protection and the solid-state producers and importer/assemblers opposing such a policy.

The watch industry in the 1970s expended most of its efforts on Congress and in internal political activities. It spent little time petitioning the executive branch through the use of U.S. trade laws. Unlike the U.S. radio and television manufacturers, who sought import relief almost exclusively by petitioning the ITC over trade law violations of various importers, the domestic watch manufacturers infrequently employed this method. Between 1973 and 1978, they filed six ITC petitions, five of which were begun as a result of the industry's pressure on Congress and one of which was an unfair trade petition, which was later withdrawn.[212] When domestic watchmakers' pressure on Congress did result in ITC investigations of the industry's trade problems, the ITC usually found unanimously against these domestic manufacturers' claims.[213] This negative reception strengthened the conven-

---

[211] U.S. ITC, *Report on Watches*, investigation no. 332-80; Robert Plishkin (American Watch Association [AWA]), "Testimony to the U.S. ITC on HR 14600 for investigation no. 332-80," March 1977; AWA interview; *EN*, March 8, 1976, p. 33; *EN*, March 15, 1976, p. 66.

[212] Thirteen petitions total were filed. Of these, seven (and the only successful ones) were for workers' trade adjustment assistance. See Judith Goldstein, unpublished data, used in her "Reexamination of U.S. Commercial Policy"; U.S. ITC, *Report on Watches*, investigation no. 332-80.

[213] Ibid.

tional manufacturers' penchant for going to Congress with their complaints.

Throughout the 1970s, the traditional domestic manufacturers—Timex, Bulova, Benrus, and Armin—sought to realize their preference for a more protected U.S. market by lobbying Congress. Their goal in 1973 and 1974 was to have legislation enacted that would exempt the industry from further tariff reductions in the Tokyo Round negotiations and from inclusion in the lists of products in the Generalized System of Preferences (GSP). Pressure to obtain these exemptions was evident in their testimony to and lobbying of Congress during consideration of the Trade Reform Act of 1974 (and its predecessors). These domestic manufacturers opposed delegation of tariff-setting authority to the President for the new multilateral trade negotiations. This opposition resulted partially from a desire to stifle any new multilateral trade talks and partially from a desire to exchange their opposition to the whole bill for promise of the industry's exclusion from the tariff cutting. Timex and Benrus testified against the trade act and worked to obtain President Nixon's promise that the watch industry would be exempted from duty-free GSP status.[214] These efforts were not very successful. The act was passed, and watches were not given a special status, except in their exemption from GSP.

Failure to receive exemption from the multilateral tariff-cutting negotiations, combined with rising competition from solid-state watches, prompted a new search for protection by the domestic watch manufacturers. In 1976 these manufacturers—in particular, Timex, Bulova, and Benrus—induced the House Ways and Means Committee to introduce a bill (H.R. 10176, later H.R. 14600) to alter the tariff classification of solid-state watches and to increase duties upon them dramatically from 75 cents per unit to $5.37.[215] Wilbur Mills, chairman of the committee, introduced the bill. The fact that Timex had several plants and its headquarters in his district was frequently noted.[216] The bill was an instrument of selective protection, since it only affected solid-state watches, and this evoked great opposition. The importer/assemblers, organized in the American Watch Association (AWA), and the U.S. semiconductor firms involved in solid-state watch production all worked against the bill.[217]

[214] House, Ways and Means, *Trade Reform*, pp. 3186-95.

[215] *EN*, February 16, 1976, p. 1; U.S. ITC, *Report on Watches*, investigation no. 332-80, esp. pp. 23-29.

[216] AWA interview; *EN*, February 16, 1977, p. 1; *EN*, March 14, 1977, p. 8.

[217] AWA interview; U.S. ITC, *Report on Watches*, investigation no. 332-80; Plishkin, "Testimony"; *EN*, March 8, 1976, p. 33; *EN*, March 15, 1976, p. 66.

Despite the fact that provisions of the bill would have been "inconsistent with certain tariff concessions granted by the U.S. under the GATT and could [thus] result in claims for compensation by the [countries]," the bill initially seemed likely to pass, largely because of Mills' support.[218] When Mills was forced to leave the committee, however, the new chairman, Al Ullman (D.-Oreg.), halted activity on the bill and requested that the ITC investigate the industry. The ITC determined unanimously that the industry did not need protection and that the bill was merely an attempt by several domestic producers—mainly Timex—to reduce competition from nonconventional watches.[219] The Ways and Means Committee accepted the ITC's conclusions. Not bowing to Timex's threats to abandon all U.S. production if the bill was not passed, it tabled the bill in 1977.[220]

In part the bill's failure was attributable to Mills' departure from the Ways and Means Committee and to vigorous opposition from the major nonconventional watch producers—Texas Instruments, National Semiconductor, Fairchild Camera, and Hughes Aircraft. But the bill also lost the support of many of its original proponents. Over the two-year period of the bill's consideration, many of the traditional manufacturers began their own production, usually offshore, of solid-state watches, and others simply closed shop or sold out to foreign firms. By March 1977, Benrus, Bulova, and Armin had ended their support for the bill, as they now produced and imported digital watches from offshore.[221] Only Timex continued to support the bill, and even its support was waning, as the firm initiated sizable offshore assembly of watch components and began purchasing quartz components from Hughes Aircraft, which opposed Timex's stance on the bill.[222] The traditional producers' economic responses to the solid-state watch manufacturers' competition thus deepened their ties to the international economy and thereby diminished their preference for protection.[223]

---

[218] U.S. ITC, *Report on Watches*, investigation no. 332-80, letter to ITC findings, p. vii.

[219] U.S. ITC, *Report on Watches*, investigation no. 332-80.

[220] *EN*, March 21, 1977, p. 72; AWA interview.

[221] *EN*, March 21, 1977, p. 72.

[222] *EN*, March 14, 1977, p. 8; *EN*, March 21, 1977, p. 72.

[223] The only other trade policy action by the watch industry in the 1970s involved pressure on Congress to deal with a rather minor issue: revoking the duty-free status of Soviet imports to the United States from the Virgin Islands. The issue here pitted the foreign and American importers and assemblers represented by the AWA, who wanted to end the duty-free entry of Soviet parts, against several Virgin Islands watch assemblers and importers who used Soviet-made parts. The debate did not involve the major U.S. watchmakers. In the end, this minor issue—the Soviets only imported some $3.7 million

The U.S. watch and clock industry's battle over trade policy, though fought primarily in Congress, reflected divisions in the industry that resulted from the introduction of solid-state technology. The three central segments of the industry were defined largely by the differences in their linkages to the international economy.[224] The traditional domestic manufacturers, a Type IV industry, much like U.S. radio and television manufacturing, carefully targeted their political attacks on imports, not wanting to disrupt trade globally for fear that this would injure their own multinational operations. As in the radio and television industry, this response to import competition had two components: a political one, involving efforts to get import relief, and an economic one, involving further movement of production out of the United States and/or increasing ties to foreign firms. The latter response weakened these manufacturers' preferences for any kind of import relief, since they became major importers themselves.

Finally, in a third similarity to the domestic radio and television manufacturers, the traditional watch producers lacked a political organization. Timex, much like Zenith, seemed to prefer to operate on its own politically. Unlike Zenith, though, it chose congressional legislation over U.S. trade law remedies as its primary weapon against imports. The domestic component of the traditional watch industry behaved like a Type IV industry. Being multinational but dependent largely on the home market, it could afford only to press for selective protection from its main import threat—nonconventional watches.

The other two segments of the watch industry possessed different international ties and different trade policy preferences. The importer/assemblers were mainly foreign firms that had U.S. sales subsidiaries. Their dependence on imports into the United States for all their sales made their preference for an open U.S. market understandable. Surprisingly, these firms were also well organized politically. Represented by the AWA, they were visible and respected proponents of freer trade for the watch industry.[225] Because they could not claim to speak for any sizable domestic political constituency, how-

---

in watch components from the insular possessions in 1977—was resolved by Congress through a compromise: the Soviet imports were monitored but not taxed. See Senate, Finance Committee, Subcommittee on International Trade, *The Use of 'Low Labor' Components in the Insular Possessions' Watch Industry*, 95th Cong., 2nd sess., August 21, 1978, pp. 1-65.

[224] U.S. ITC, *Report on Watches*, investigation no. 332-80; Frost and Sullivan, *U.S. Watch Market*, pp. 1-35; Plishkin, "Testimony"; AWA interview.

[225] AWA interview; *EN*, March 8, 1976, p. 33.

ever, they lacked political influence relative to the traditional manufacturers.

The third segment of the watch industry possessed greater political influence. This group, composed of large U.S. semiconductor firms, was interested in open U.S. markets for watches and their components. Producing and assembling most of their solid-state watches abroad and then shipping them back to the United States, these firms had no desire to see tariffs on these goods increased. Their preference for open markets was conveyed both individually and jointly through their industry associations, originally through the WEMA and later through the SIA. In testimony to Congress, these associations expressed their staunch opposition to any attempts to erect trade barriers in the watch industry.[226] Their efforts, combined with those of the AWA, eventually proved successful.

After 1978, vicious competition within the industry drove many of the U.S. semiconductor firms involved in watchmaking out of the business. National Semiconductor bowed out in 1978 and Fairchild was acquired by the French-based firm Schlumberger in 1979, which thereby eliminated two of the biggest U.S. nonconventional watchmakers.[227] By 1979, three major forces were left in the U.S. watch market: Timex, Texas Instruments, and Japanese imports.[228] In the early 1980s Texas Instruments also stopped producing electronic watches.[229] In the space of a decade, then, the restraints against protectionist forces—i.e., the nonconventional domestic watch producers—had evaporated. The Japanese at this point began quietly "monitoring" their watch exports to the United States, due to fear that the United States might otherwise impose trade restraints on them.[230]

CASE 6: TIRES

Throughout the 1950s and 1960s, the U.S. rubber tire and inner tube industry registered high growth and profitability. It was the world's technological and sales leader, its fortunes having risen in tandem with those of the U.S. auto industry. Beginning in the late 1960s, however,

    [226] EIA interviews; *EN*, March 8, 1976, p. 33; U.S. ITC, *Report on Watches*, investigation no. 332-80; *EN*, March 15, 1976, p. 66.

    [227] *EN*, June 13, 1977, pp. 1, 6; Borrus, Millstein, and Zysman, "Trade and Development in the Semiconductor Industry," pp. 171-72; *EN*, January 9, 1978, p. 60; *EN*, January 30, 1978, p. 1.

    [228] *EN*, January 9, 1978, p. 60.

    [229] *Wall Street Journal*, September 17, 1981, p. 29:1; *Wall Street Journal*, June 1, 1981, p. 4:1; *NYT*, May 30, 1981, p. 29:3; *EN*, June 1, 1981, p. 27:1.

    [230] *EN*, May 15, 1978, p. 60.

U.S. producers began losing their preeminent position, and they experienced substantial economic upheaval in the 1970s.

First, the U.S. industry lost its technological advantage by failing to adopt the new radial tire technology.[231] Foreign tire companies, especially the French-based Michelin, moved aggressively into radial production in the late 1960s. After the quadrupling of oil prices in 1974, the fuel-saving radials developed a massive popular following and moved from about 5 percent of the U.S. passenger tire market in 1972 to 100 percent in 1982.[232] The U.S. industry was not prepared when this dramatic shift began in 1975, and the foreign radial imports seized market share rapidly.

Second, foreign autos, trucks, and motorcycles with their own, foreign-made tires were increasingly imported to the United States in the 1970s. As these imports gained U.S. market share, U.S. tire manufacturers lost sales. Not surprisingly, the tire industry gaining the most in this process was that of Japan, led by Bridgestone Tire Company.[233] By 1980 the radial tire threat begun by Michelin had been superceded by the tire import threat led by Bridgestone.

The U.S. industry experienced increasing economic difficulties over the 1970s. From its expanding position throughout the 1950s and 1960s it slowed down in the early 1970s and then declined in the later part of the decade. Between 1970 and 1982, twenty-six U.S. tire plants were closed and capacity in the industry was reduced significantly.[234] U.S. tire firms also shifted the bases of their operations geographically, moving operations from Akron, Ohio, to newer, nonunionized plants in the southern United States in search of lower-cost production.[235] Employment grew slowly until 1976 but declined sharply after 1977.[236] The profitability of the tire makers also suffered.[237]

---

[231] The industry covers the manufacturers of rubber tires and inner tubes (SIC 3011). *Rubber and Plastics News* (hereafter *RPN*), April 12, 1982, p. 4; Rubber Manufacturers Association (RMA) interviews. Although a U.S. firm, Goodrich, originally developed the radial tire in the late 1950s, U.S. firms decided not to produce and market it at that point. The fact that radials last substantially longer than normal tires and hence need to be replaced less often may have influenced this decision.

[232] *RPN*, April 12, 1982, p. 4.

[233] *RPN*, October 12, 1981, pp. 59-60.

[234] U.S. Dept. of Commerce, *Census, 1972*; *Business Week*, October 29, 1979, pp. 150-54; *RPN*, April 12, 1982, p. 4.

[235] *Industry Week* (hereafter *IW*), vol. 195, November 21, 1977, pp. 70-76.

[236] U.S. Dept. of Commerce, *Census, 1972*; U.S. Dept. of Commerce, *1979 Annual Survey of Manufactures*.

[237] *IW*, vol. 184, March 24, 1975, pp. 57-59; *IW*, vol. 192, March 28, 1977, pp. 58-59; *IW*, vol. 197, March 20, 1978, pp. 57-59.

This economic distress was accompanied by rising foreign competition from all sides. As noted, for different reasons, both West European and Japanese imports steadily took over U.S. market share. In terms of import penetration, the industry saw a surge from about 3 percent in 1972 to 12 percent in 1976, or an average annual increase of 4 percent between 1971 and 1976.[238] Imports reached $991.6 million in 1977 from a value of $202.2 million in 1970.[239] The tire industry thus was a likely candidate to demand protection.

U.S. tire manufacturing was a Type IV industry. It had a sizable but declining multinational position and lacked substantial trading operations. Its international trade position was weak. It experienced a net trade deficit throughout the 1970s that grew substantially each year, except for 1974 and 1975 immediately after countervailing duties (CVDs) had been placed on certain Canadian imports.[240] Its export position over the decade was also small and unchanging. Exports averaged about 3.5 percent of domestic consumption.[241]

The tire industry had a significant multinational component that declined slightly in this period. Its ratio of foreign assets to total assets was 23 percent in 1972 and 19 percent in 1977.[242] The industry's declining multinational position was also reflected in its foreign earnings, which fell between 1966 and 1977 from 18 percent to 3 percent.[243] Though substantial, its foreign operations were performing poorly.

Direct foreign investment by the industry was unevenly distributed. The leading four firms were large multinationals in the early 1970s.[244] These firms accounted for almost all of the industry's foreign production; the rest was domestically oriented. Among these leading firms, moreover, multinationality was increasingly unevenly distributed. The leader, Goodyear, who alone controlled one-third of the U.S. market, was by far the most multinational. It received almost 40 percent of its

[238] U.S. Dept. of Commerce, *U.S. Commodity Exports and Imports, 1976/75* and *1977/76*.

[239] Ibid.

[240] Ibid.

[241] Ibid.

[242] U.S. Dept. of Commerce, *1972* and *1977 Enterprise Statistics*. Other data on the percentage of total foreign assets to total parent assets show the figure to be slightly higher, around 43 percent in 1974. See IRS, *Statistics of Income—1974-78*. Data on the affiliates' sales as a percentage of their parents' total sales point to a figure of 35 percent for 1977. See U.S. Dept. of Commerce, *U.S. MNC's: U.S. Merchandise Trade, Worldwide Sales, and Technology-Related Activities in 1977* (Washington, D.C.: GPO, 1983).

[243] U.S. Dept. of Commerce, *U.S. Direct Investment Abroad—1966* and *1977*. This figure represents foreign earnings as a percent of total foreign investment position.

[244] *RPN*, June 7, 1982, p. 1.

net income from foreign earnings in 1974.[245] Its dominant position increased over the decade, as other firms pulled out of foreign markets when they got into trouble.

The U.S. tire industry had a weak international trading network in the 1970s. Not only were its U.S. exports very small, but its foreign operations were geared less to trade than to serving the local market. Exports to the United States were only 8 percent of the total sales of all foreign affiliates in 1977.[246] All in all, this was a Type IV industry, facing the loss of its international competitive advantage both at home and abroad.

Two other features of the industry deserve mention. The U.S. tire industry has long been very concentrated. In 1977 its largest four firms accounted for 71 percent of all shipments, while the top eight firms controlled 90 percent.[247] The five firms dominating the U.S. market in the 1960s and 1970s were Goodyear—the largest, with over 33 percent of the market, Firestone—a distant second with 17 percent, B. F. Goodrich, General Tire, and Uniroyal.[248] Goodyear far surpassed the others in size and multinationality.

Within the industry, differences in firms' participation in its sectors were also apparent. The largest sector, passenger car and truck tires, was highly concentrated and dominated in the 1970s by the five largest firms.[249] Other sectors, such as off-the-road and agricultural equipment tires, bicycle tires, and inner tubes, were controlled by different, smaller U.S. firms.[250] The second- and third-tier firms dominating these particular sectors—like Armstrong, Cooper, and Carlisle—were small domestic producers. Unlike "the big five," who in some cases had

[245] Moody's, *Manual: 1975.*

[246] U.S. Dept. of Commerce, *U.S. Direct Investment Abroad—1966* and *1977.* MOFA exports to the United States accounted for 5 percent of total MOFA sales in 1977. More disaggregated data demonstrate that the tire industry's MOFA exports to the United States as a proportion of all tire imports accounted for 39 percent in 1966 but only 19 percent in 1977. See Réal Lavergne, unpublished data, used in his *Political Economy of U.S. Tariffs.*

[247] U.S. Dept. of Commerce, *Concentration Ratios.*

[248] *RPN*, June 7, 1982, pp. 1, 11.

[249] *RPN*, January 18, 1982, p. 8.

[250] For instance, bicycle tires were produced in the United States in 1975 by only two firms, Carlisle Tire and Goodyear; after 1977, only Carlisle remained in the market. See U.S. ITC, *Bicycle Tires and Tubes,* investigation no. TA-201-33, pub. no. 910, September 1978; *RPN*, June 7, 1982, p. 1. The production of inner tubes in the United States was also controlled by a different set of small firms. Armstrong Rubber Company, Cupples, Cooper Tire, Carlisle, and to a much lesser degree Firestone, Goodrich, and Goodyear were the key inner tube producers in the United States in the 1970s. *RPN*, March 15, 1982, p. 1.

up to one-third of their operations outside the United States, these small firms were completely dependent upon the U.S. market.[251]

A second notable feature was the rising direct foreign investment in the U.S. industry during the 1970s, which accompanied foreign penetration of the U.S. market by imports. Beginning in the mid-1970s, every major foreign tire maker initiated plans to build or acquire production facilities in the United States. By 1983, four of the leading foreign tire manufacturers were operating American plants.[252] This was one more sign of the mounting competition faced by the American firms.

The Dependent Variable

The trade policy preferences of the U.S. tire and inner tube industry in the 1970s were geared largely to the maintenance of open markets for tires throughout the world. The industry's preferences revolved around retention of the status quo. Formal trade barriers in the industry were low in the early 1970s,[253] and informal barriers to trade in tire products were also insignificant. Operating on a global basis and dominant in it, the "big five" U.S. firms had long preferred a world of free trade.

The industry's political activities reflected this preference. The industry remained satisfied with the existing situation in the 1970s and did little beyond supporting efforts like renewed Tokyo Round negotiations that would keep markets open. Rising import penetration and economic difficulties, however, prompted some activity to obtain relief. The industry initiated a few trade-related actions in particular product lines that were greatly suffering from foreign competition. In these cases, which involved three products—radial tires, bicycle tires, and inner tubes—firms in the industry, after a good deal of internal

[251] U.S. ITC, *Bicycle Tires*, pub. no. 910; RMA interviews.

[252] Dunlop, the British tire maker, who had production operations in the United States already, increased its investment and production in the United States during the 1970s. See *NYT*, April 3, 1974, p. 65; *RPN*, August 16, 1982, p. 4; *RPN*, September 26, 1983, p. 1. Michelin opened its first plant in the United States in 1975, and by 1981 its American production accounted for a substantial 8 percent of U.S. tire sales. See *RPN*, January 18, 1982, p. 8; *RPN*, July 5, 1982, p. 4. Buying a Firestone plant in Tennessee, the Japanese firm Bridgestone moved to the United States in 1982. See *RPN*, March 1, 1982, p. 4; *RPN*, December 19, 1983, p. 1; *RPN*, January 3, 1983, p. 1. Continental, the German tire manufacturer, acquired production facilities in the United States in 1982. See *RPN*, August 16, 1982, p. 4.

[253] The U.S. post–Kennedy Round, trade-weighted average duty was 3.9 percent; the average in 1973 for the thirteen major industrial countries was 7.1 percent. U.S. ITC, *Protection in Major Trading Countries*, pub. no. 737.

debate, took actions that were intended to make it more difficult for imports to be sold in the United States.[254] These actions were few and were targeted against specific products and importers.

These initiatives to curb imports relied upon use of the U.S. trade laws. When the industry did infrequently approach executive agencies, it attempted to do so with a united front, which was developed only after much intra-industry discussion. No single firm or small group of firms persistently sought import relief of any type in the 1970s. Nor did the tire industry ever try to have legislation introduced in Congress to provide it special import relief.

Between 1968 and 1978, the industry was involved in only eight petitions to the ITC. Of these, only one involved the largest market segment—auto tires—where the five large multinationals controlled the market.[255] The other cases focused on smaller sectors where the second- and third-tier domestic firms dominated. In addition, of the eight petitions, only one sought import relief through increased tariffs or quotas. The remaining petitions dealt with charges of export subsidization and dumping by specific importers. Despite its economic difficulties, the industry's attack on imports was mild and limited.

The first petition, the only one in the 1970s involving car tires, was initiated by the Rubber Manufacturers Association (RMA) in 1972. In this petition the RMA charged that Canadian exports to the United States of radial auto tires produced by Michelin were being subsidized and argued that a CVD should therefore be imposed on them. The Canadian government and Michelin acknowledged that the tire operations were subsidized, but they maintained that the subsidies were intended to promote regional domestic development in Canada and not exports. Thus the issue was not whether subsidization was occurring, but whether it was directed toward export or domestic economic promotion. In a surprising decision, the U.S. Treasury Department ruled that export subsidization was occurring, and it imposed CVDs (a 6.6 percent duty) against Canadian radial tire imports by Michelin in 1973.[256]

In a sense, this petition represented a valid use of U.S. (and GATT)

[254] U.S. ITC, *Selected Publications of the U.S. ITC, through September 1979*, pub. no. 1031, January 1980, pp. 15-30; U.S. ITC, *Bicycle Tires*; RMA interviews.

[255] Of a total of twenty, twelve concerned trade adjustment assistance for workers; the remaining eight petitions were initiated by the industry. Judith Goldstein, unpublished data, used in her "Reexamination of U.S. Commercial Policy."

[256] RMA interviews; Robert Guido and Michael Morrone, "The Michelin Decision," *Law and Policy in International Business* 6 (Winter 1974):237-66; *NYT*, January 5, 1973; House, Ways and Means, *Trade Reform*, pp. 3364-68.

trade laws to prevent unfair trading practices by other countries. But the subsidization was of a type that the GATT system often recognized as legitimate, since it was for domestic economic purposes. This argument was the one Michelin and the Canadian government used in their long battle to have the CVDS repealed. In fact, Michelin claimed that U.S. firms were using the CVD complaint as a means of dealing with Michelin's technological advantage in radial tires.[257] As one analyst of the case phrased it, "Michelin argued the complaint lodged by the U.S. RMA was actually a disguised attempt to protect [the U.S. firms'] monopoly position by preventing the better, safer, although higher priced Michelin product from competing in the US market."[258] As in other cases, this petition for trade action was related to intra-industry competition, and in this case involved an effort to offset a competitor's technological advantage through other means.

The industry's decision to file against Michelin required substantial internal discussion and consensus building. Goodyear, having received similar subsidies for other products from the Canadians and fearing retaliation, was not favorably disposed to the action.[259] As the world and U.S. industry leader, Goodyear was opposed to protectionist activity. Goodyear, an official stated, "refused to be identified with any formal protectionist activity because it feared foreign retaliation."[260] Since the chairman of Goodyear in much of the 1970s, Charles Pilliod, was also head of the RMA, protectionist sentiment arising within the tire industry met with opposition from the RMA.[261] In fact, by the end of the 1970s, Goodyear would no longer support the continuing imposition of CVDS against Michelin. In 1981, it convinced the RMA to end its case against Michelin and thereby helped to terminate the CVDS.[262]

The other industry petitions for trade action were related to product lines where the smaller, domestically oriented firms were most affected. The bicycle tire manufacturers—mainly, Carlisle Tire—filed several petitions for help, demanding escape clause relief and anti-dumping action. Carlisle's petitions were not joined by the RMA, but the association did not prevent the petitions from being filed.[263] In the

---

[257] RMA interviews; Guido and Morrone, "Michelin Decision."

[258] Guido and Morrone, "Michelin Decision," p. 253.

[259] RMA interviews. Goodyear might have been against the CVD because it received similar subsidies from the Canadians; see Guido and Morrone, "Michelin Decision," p. 252, note 106.

[260] RMA interviews.

[261] Ibid.; *RPN*, May 24, 1982, p. 1.

[262] *RPN*, June 21, 1982, p. 1; RMA interviews.

[263] *RPN*, June 7, 1982, p. 1; RMA interviews; U.S. ITC, *Bicycle Tires*, pub. no. 910.

case of the U.S. inner tube manufacturers who filed antidumping and CVD petitions, the actions were initiated by the small domestic firms like Armstrong Rubber and Cooper Tire, although the large multi-nationals ended up signing the petitions.[264] The RMA, however, did not participate; instead, these small firms began their own ad hoc committee to develop an industry-wide consensus on the issue.[265] Action concerning the inner tube imports was also targeted against specific importers, such as Taiwan and South Korea. Thus, the petitions filed by the U.S. tire industry against imports were few, selective, and prompted by the small domestic firms in the industry.

The industry's activity in Congress concerning international trade issues was minor in the 1970s. Other issues, such as product liability and safety, labor relations, and tax policy consumed much more of the RMA's attention.[266] And even in the trade area, the industry's concerns involved exports and the treatment of multinationals as much as they did the issue of import trade barriers. The industry expressed some interest in export promotion legislation and in matters concerning the tax treatment of multinationals—i.e., the foreign tax credit issue.[267] The RMA's main activity concerning trade barriers involved supporting the idea of a new round of multilateral trade negotiations in 1973-74 through its endorsement of the Trade Act of 1974.[268] The industry by 1979 was less interested in further reductions in U.S. tariffs on tires, but it did support the Trade Act of 1979, endorsing the Tokyo Round negotiations' results.[269] The industry never tried to organize a congressional caucus to promote its trade policy preferences. Throughout the 1970s, it was content with the trade policies in place.

The industry's internal politics reflected the differences in economic position among its firms. Though all segments of the industry faced rising import competition and serious economic difficulties, the ones most frequently resorting to trade relief petitions were those dominated by the smaller, domestically oriented firms. The bicycle tire and inner tube makers petitioned for help, while the major auto tire manufacturers refrained from such political activity and preferred to re-

[264] U.S. ITC, *Bicycle Tires*, pub. no. 910; RMA interviews; *RPN*, March 15, 1982, p. 1; *RPN*, August 30, 1982, p. 1.

[265] *RPN*, August 30, 1982, p. 1; RMA interviews.

[266] RMA interviews.

[267] RMA interviews; Senate, Finance Committee, Subcommittee on International Trade, *Multinational Corporations*, 93rd Cong., 1st sess., February 1973, pp. 176-206; House, *Trade Reform*, pp. 3364-68.

[268] RMA interviews; House, Ways and Means, *Trade Reform*, pp. 3364-68.

[269] RMA interviews; Senate, Finance Committee, *Private Advisory Committee Reports*, pp. 143-61; *RPN*, November 23, 1981, p. 5; *RPN*, January 18, 1982, p. 11.

spond economically to their problems. In the face of serious economic decline, the large firms opted to diversify and/or to increase their international operations rather than to call for protection.[270]

These differences within the industry were not reflected as much in its political organization. All the firms in the tire industry, except McCreary Tire, belonged to the RMA. Although dominated by the large multinational tire makers, the RMA's tire division also represented the small U.S. manufacturers. It lent support to their petitions for trade relief in the late 1970s and the early 1980s but did not participate in decision making on these cases for two reasons. First, not all the major firms liked the idea of pursuing the petitions, and the RMA refused to take action whenever unanimous consent was lacking.[271] Second, the RMA was legally forbidden by the Federal Trade Commission from collecting and circulating data on industry prices necessary for the filing of CVD and antidumping suits.[272] Apparently, fear of antitrust violations kept the RMA out of the petition process.

Because of these two factors, the RMA refused to handle the smaller firms' trade complaints. These firms then decided to form their own ad hoc committee, as already mentioned, to develop consensus within the industry on the trade complaints. Consensus building was very important in this industry, largely because the petitioners' problem was obtaining the support of the industry leader, Goodyear, who preferred freer trade. Without Goodyear's tacit support, any petition lacked credibility; hence, Goodyear had to be convinced, along with the other major firms, not to oppose the petitions. The industry's economic structure thus rendered political consensus building a necessity, while the major firms' well-developed links to the international economy made trade policy actions to hinder imports undesirable and difficult to undertake, even in the face of tremendous economic distress. Rather than seek protection, the major firms adjusted on their own, shedding unprofitable operations, diversifying, and/or developing new products.

[270] *RPN*, January 18, 1982, p. 1; *RPN*, March 29, 1982, p. 1; *RPN*, April 26, 1982, pp. 1, 75; *RPN*, September 27, 1982, p. 59; RMA interviews.

[271] RMA interviews.

[272] Ibid. One interviewee claimed the RMA feared the antitrust implications of collecting the antidumping and countervailing-duty data; the other interviewee claimed this was not a concern, since they collected this data for the excise tax calculations.

CHAPTER 5

The French Case Studies, 1970s

WE NOW TURN to six French industries of the 1970s, and examine them in terms of our primary hypothesis: that industries with greater links to the international economy should be less protectionist than more domestically oriented industries, even when both face serious economic distress. As in chapters 3 and 4, each case is divided into two parts. First, the industry's economic distress and import problems, which indicate its a priori interest in protecting its domestic market, are discussed. The industry's ties to the international economy are also detailed, generating predictions about its preferences on trade policy issues. Other relevant features of the industry are then examined as well.

The second section of each case explores the preferences of the industry vis-à-vis trade policy. For French firms in the 1970s, four different arenas for communicating their trade policy views existed. The industry expressed its *national* trade policy interests, usually involving its complaints about foreign trade and its desire for import surveillance or limitation, to French government officials. Second, the industry made known its demands for *industrial* policy measures through pressure on the appropriate French officials for increased aid, subsidies, reduced tax burdens, and new norms and standards affecting foreign competition. Third, the industry's desire for trade policy actions at the *European Community* (EC) level may be seen in its preferences expressed regarding the tariff negotiations of GATT, its complaints about foreign dumping, subsidization, or injury by imports, and its demands for import surveillance or limitation by the EC. The fourth arena was internal, involving the industry's own discussions and determination of strategies to deal with its problems.

CASE 1: FOOTWEAR

Prior to the mid-1970s, the French footwear industry was a success. The industry was the second largest in Europe, just behind Italy, and the world's third largest footwear exporter. This success was reversed after 1975; from this point on, the industry declined steadily and experienced severe economic distress due to increasing imports, declining demand within France, and closure of the traditional export markets.[1] Decreasing numbers of firms, rising unemployment, falling investment, and low profitability marked the industry. Between 1971 and 1978, 20 percent of all French footwear firms disappeared.[2] French footwear production, after reaching its highest volume in 1971, declined some 15 percent between 1975 and 1981.[3] These firm closures and production declines led to rising unemployment in the industry.[4] By the late 1970s, investment levels and profit margins were very low.[5]

Its troubled domestic situation after 1974 was accompanied by a deteriorating international trade position, as manifested in rising import levels, mounting import penetration, and declining exports. The footwear industry in France initially benefited from the opening of the European Common Market. Between 1969 and 1974, its exports grew phenomenally, around 25 percent per year, while its imports remained moderate.[6] After 1974, however, footwear imports surged, doubling in value almost every two years between 1974 and 1980.[7] As a percentage of the domestic market, imports also rose: in 1970, import penetration was around 12 percent; by 1977 it was over 25 percent and by 1981 it accounted for almost 50 percent of the French market.[8] The worst periods for the industry were the years from 1975 to 1977 and from 1979 to 1983. The first period was marked by a sudden surge in Italian imports, as well as by a sharp decline in ex-

[1] *Les Echos*, March 17, 1972; *Le Point*, September 8, 1975; Fédération Nationale de l'Industrie Chaussure Française (hereafter FNICF), *Chaussures de France* (Paris: FNICF, September 1984), pp. 12-17; DAFSA, *L'Industrie de la Chaussure en Europe* (Paris: DAFSA, 1979), pp. 24-26; Christian Stoffaës, *La Grande Menace Industrielle* (Paris: Calmann-Lévy, 1978), p. 225.

[2] DAFSA, *L'Industrie de la Chaussure en Europe*, 1979, p. 51.

[3] *Libre Service Actualité* (hereafter *LSA*), no. 864, November 5, 1982, p. 257; DAFSA, *L'Industrie de la Chaussure en Europe*, 1979, pp. 7-20.

[4] *La Vie Française*, February 7-13, 1983, p. 35; *La Croix*, September 5, 1975; FNICF, *Chaussures de France*, September 1984, p. 11; European Confederation of Footwear Industries (hereafter ECFI), *Sectoral Study of the European Footwear Industry* (Brussels: ECFI, November 13, 1978), pp. 45-46; INSEE, *Les Comptes de l'Industrie: Situation en 1979* (Paris: Documentation Française, 1980), pp. 129-32.

[5] INSEE, *Annuaire Statistique de la France* (Paris: Documentation Française, 1983), p. 511; DAFSA, *L'Industrie de la Chaussure en Europe*, 1979, intro.

[6] *Le Point*, September 8, 1975; *Les Echos*, December 3, 1969; *Les Echos*, March 17, 1972; *Les Echos*, August 28, 1975.

[7] Figures from French Customs Service (Douanes fiche for NAP 600-4601).

[8] Unpublished INSEE data on import penetration; Bernard Bobe, "Les Importations des Biens de Consommation en Provenance de Tiers Monde," *Revue d'Economie Industrielle*, no. 14 (4th trim., 1980):52; FNICF, *Chaussures de France*, pp. 16-17; *Les Echos*, March 14, 1985.

ports due to the closure of traditional markets abroad.[9] In the second period, imports surged once again, but their primary source was now the countries of East Asia, mainly Taiwan, South Korea, Hong Kong, and China.[10] Between 1975 and 1981 French footwear imports rose by 67 percent, while its exports fell by 7 percent.[11] Overall, the industry's economic difficulties and rising foreign competition made it a likely candidate to seek protection.

The industry's links to the international economy in the 1970s were moderate but declining. In general, French footwear was a Type I industry, with limited trade ties and few multinational operations. The ties that did exist were concentrated in the hands of a few large firms. The industry's international trade position in the 1970s deteriorated. From an increasingly positive trade balance in the early part of the decade, the industry's position turned negative in 1975 for the first time.[12] Its trade deficit ballooned from 400 million francs in 1976 to 2.4 billion francs by 1982.[13] The industry's export dependence—that is, its export sales relative to its domestic production—was stagnant if not falling after 1975. In 1970, the industry exported about 21 percent of its production. This held constant through the 1970s, reflecting the fact that both exports and national production declined; but by the early 1980s, footwear's export dependence was beginning its decline, dropping to about 18 percent.[14] By the early 1980s its primary

[9] *Le Monde*, October 17-18, 1976; *Forum International*, June 11, 1979; FNICF, *Chaussures de France*, pp. 16-17; *Chaussure Industrie*, no. 105 (July 1981); *Le Figaro*, September 9, 1977; ECFI, *Sectoral Study*, pp. 20-26.

[10] Although Italy remained the largest importing country, these Asian imports were the most rapidly expanding, especially in terms of lower-priced footwear. See FNICF, *Chaussures de France*, pp. 14-17; Parlement Européen, *Rapport du Parlement Européen*, by E. Romagnoli (Strasbourg: Parlement Européen, November 1981), pp. 11-12 esp.; *Chaussure Industrie*, no. 105 (July 1981); *La Vie Française*, February 13, 1983, p. 35; ECFI, *Sectoral Study*, pp. 24-29. This new source of import competition was combined with (and in part a consequence of) the further closure of other footwear markets. American restraints on Asian footwear begun in 1978, in particular, caused problems for the Europeans, because their market then remained the last one open to footwear exports and thus served as the area to which the Asian exports were diverted. See *Chaussure Industrie*, no. 95 (February-March 1980):7-10; Parlement Européen, *Rapport du Parlement Européen*, pp. 11-12 esp.; DAFSA, *L'Industrie de la Chaussure en Europe*, 1979, p. 28.

[11] *LSA*, no. 864, November 5, 1982, p. 257.

[12] DAFSA, *L'Industrie de la Chaussure en Europe*, 1979, pp. 29-30; ECFI, *The Situation of the European Footwear Industry* (Brussels: ECFI, 1983).

[13] French Customs Service data (Douanes fiche).

[14] Bobe, "Les Importations des Biens de Consommation en Provenance de Tiers Monde," p. 52. French Customs Service data (Douanes fiche) for exports; INSEE, *Annuaire Statistique*, 1983, p. 514; *Chaussure Industrie*, no. 105 (July 1981).

trade ties to the international economy were through imports and not exports.

The significance of its export dependence was also reduced, since only the few, largest firms in the industry exported. Of a total of nearly five hundred firms, the sixty largest accounted for over 75 percent of all exports, and 90 percent of all exports were done by the ninety largest firms in the late 1970s.[15] French export dependence in footwear was declining in the 1970s, highly concentrated among a few large firms, and limited to high-priced leather footwear and to a few developed countries' markets.

The industry had few multinational ties. Its foreign production was limited, no more than 2 percent of total production.[16] Among the producers, however, different levels of multinationality were apparent. Foreign penetration of the industry was substantial; in fact, of the ten largest firms in France in 1978, three were completely foreign owned. These three—Adidas, Charles Jourdan, and Bata—were large multinationals and some of the most important exporters in France.[17] In addition, for the top three French-owned firms—André, Eram, and Myrys—the international market also played an important role.[18] These firms had foreign production, sizable export sales, and extensive import operations. After 1975, they adapted to rising foreign competition by shifting production abroad to lower-wage areas and by moving increasingly into footwear distribution (commercial operations), rather than production, in France.[19] These three large French

---

[15] FNICF, *Chaussures de France*, pp. 9-11; *Chaussure Industrie*, no. 87 (July 1978):37.

[16] Michel Delapierre and Charles-Albert Michalet, in Centre d'Etudes et de Recherches sur les Entreprise Multinationale (hereafter CEREM), *Crise, Concurrence Internationale, et Stratégies des Multinationales Françaises* (Paris: CEREM, 1981); Charles-Albert Michalet, ed., *L'Intégration de l'Economie Française dans l'Economie Mondiale* (Paris: Economica, 1984), pp. 77-102; Julien Savary, *Les Multinationales Françaises* (Paris: Presses Universitaires Françaises, 1981), p. 28.

[17] In 1976, direct foreign investment was estimated to equal 15 percent of total value-added for the industry. STISI, *Les Entreprises Moyennes dans l'Industrie* (Paris: Documentation Française, 1976), pp. 174-75. However, for these firms foreign operations were very significant. Adidas (West Germany) and Charles Jourdan (U.S.) exported over 50 percent of their total French sales, and Bata (Swiss) was regarded as the "IBM" of footwear with ninety factories worldwide. *La Vie Française*, February 7-13, 1983, pp. 32-36; DAFSA, *L'Industrie de la Chaussure en France* (Paris: DAFSA, 1976), pp. 16-17; *La Vie Française*, June 18, 1979.

[18] DAFSA, *L'Industrie de la Chaussure en Europe*, 1979, p. 53.

[19] *La Vie Française*, February 7-13, 1983; DAFSA, *L'Industrie de la Chaussure en Europe*, 1979. For example, André, France's largest footwear firm, exported about 20 percent of its production in the mid-1970s but had no foreign production before 1970; however, by the early 1980s, André had several factories in Germany and Spain and was importing

firms, who accounted for most of the multinationality in the footwear industry, were thus import centered and *not* export oriented.

In sum, the French footwear industry's international ties in the 1970s were limited and concentrated in the hands of the few largest firms. Its trade linkages grew on the side of imports, while exports stagnated. Foreign production operations were never significant for the industry, although they did increase in importance for the largest firms over the decade. Finally, the different levels of international linkages among the firms prompted divergences of interests on trade issues.

Three other features of the French footwear industry deserve comment, since they illuminate facets of its political organization, strength, and activity. First, the industry was composed of many small firms, and its largest lacked substantial control over the market.[20] The large number of firms and the limited importance of the largest firms meant that industry-wide organization was critical for political success. On the other hand, the differences between the largest firms and the mass of smaller ones were considerable. The problems and interests of the large firms were unlike those of the rest of the industry. In fact, a majority of the industry felt that their problems were caused by the large firms' activities in foreign production, distribution, and importing.[21] The industry was increasingly divided over this issue during the 1970s.

Second, the industry was regional. The masses of small footwear producers were concentrated in three rural areas—the Cholet in the Loire, Romans in the Rhone-Alps, and Alsace.[22] Though each of these centers had some export activity, the Alsatian region led in this respect, exporting 47 percent of its total regional footwear production.[23]

into France over two-thirds of the footwear it sold there. See *La Vie Française*, February 7-13, 1983, pp. 32-36; *Le Figaro*, February 9-10, 1985, p. 13; *Le Monde*, February 5, 1985; *Usine Nouvelle*, December 3, 1981, p. 75; 1985 André *Bulletin*. Similarly, Eram increasingly moved production abroad and established a larger presence in distribution in the late 1970s. By 1983, it produced in France only 40 percent of the footwear it sold there and imported much of the rest from its factories in Spain, Portugal, and Brazil. See *Le Matin*, June 6, 1977; *La Vie Française*, February 7-13, 1983, pp. 32-36; DAFSA, *L'Industrie de la Chaussure en France*, 1976, pp. 16-17.

[20] FNICF, *Chaussures de France*, pp. 9-11; ECFI, *Sectoral Study*, pp. 47-48; DAFSA, *L'Industrie de la Chaussure en Europe*, 1979, p. 49. For example, the largest firm, André, held only 9 percent of the total market in 1982. *Le Figaro*, February 9-10, 1985.

[21] *Le Monde*, April 2, 1977; interviews.

[22] FNICF, *Chaussures en France*, pp. 9-10; *La Vie Française*, February 7-13, 1983, p. 34; *Economie-Géographie*, no. 171 (January 1980):6-7.

[23] *La Vie Française*, February 7-13, 1983, p. 34; *Forum International*, March 25, 1980; *Le Figaro*, March 25, 1980; *Le Matin*, March 28, 1980.

This difference in the regions' extent of international activity was reflected in their preferences on trade matters. In addition, the producers' concentration of activity in each region enhanced their influence with the regional government.

Third, the industry-wide association of footwear producers (FNICF) represented over 90 percent of all French footwear producers and was well organized and powerful. The association served not only as the industry's main conduit to the French government and the EC but also as an industry leader, organizing and conducting R&D, defining product standards, and aiding ailing firms. Although influential within all segments of the industry, the association encountered increasing problems reconciling the two main groups' interests in the late 1970s, which eventually prompted some of the larger firms to seek representation, especially on trade issues, elsewhere.

The Dependent Variable

Parts of the footwear industry in France showed a strong preference for protection of the domestic market after 1975. In the latter part of the decade, the industry's internal coherence decreased, as the large and small firms' adjustment strategies diverged. The development of international ties by the largest firms provoked increasing intra-industry divisions on trade issues. The lack of export or multinational ties to the international economy among most footwear firms meant that protection was a low-cost strategy with potentially high benefits for them, while it was more costly for the larger producers.

Throughout the 1970s, the industry's concern about trade issues rose and fell with the degree of economic distress it faced. As its difficulties grew, concern with trade mounted. Three periods of intense activity by footwear manufacturers at the national level on trade and industrial policy can be identified. In each, activity on trade issues was couched in the terms of an industry-wide industrial policy, or *plan*. The solutions promoted by the industry followed similar lines; they called for reduction of the "social costs" paid by firms, increased government aid to "restructure," and measures to deal with trade problems. Not surprisingly, in the latter two episodes, which coincided with periods of severe economic distress, the trade measures proposed were protectionist.

The first period of the footwear industry's attention to trade issues, between 1968 and 1970, was prompted by the opening of the Common Market in 1968. The French industry saw this as a great opportunity and wanted to capture more of the European market. In particular, the FNICF, led by an active president, José Bidegain, and the large

French footwear exporters realized the opportunities of the European market and designed a plan to enhance the French industry's position within it. The plan they developed called for substantial government aid (worth about 400 million francs, much through low-interest loans) to promote exports and to aid firms in restructuring.[24] This set of measures contained none that served to protect the domestic market, although the export aid measures did aim at strengthening France's trade abroad. In 1970, after a year of negotiations over the exact amount of aid to be given, the footwear industry's plan was accepted by the French government.[25]

The second period, which began in 1975, was shaped by the industry's growing economic difficulties. Parts of the footwear industry began complaining about imports, especially from Italy, which accounted for 60 percent of all French footwear imports.[26] In the face of workers' strikes, plant occupations, and plant closures, the industry association, still led by Bidegain, devised a new footwear plan. It was similar to the earlier one, except that it also contained measures intended to protect the French market.[27] This plan embodied a compromise between the two groups of firms with different preferences. Although all firms in the industry supported price liberalization and reductions in social costs and taxes, only the largest pressed for increased government aid, especially concerning exports.[28] As the principal exporters, the large firms gained the most from this kind of assistance.

On the other hand, the small firms concentrated in the regions near Fougères and Cholet, who faced the brunt of the import invasion, wanted protection. Supported by unions and the regional government, they demanded that something be done to halt the precipitous decline of the region's footwear industry; they viewed protection as a means to fight the problem.[29] The large firms opposed protection,

[24] *Le Figaro*, October 25, 1968; *Les Echos*, August 28, 1975; interviews; *L'Humanité*, February 26, 1976.

[25] Ibid.

[26] DAFSA, *L'Industrie de la Chaussure en Europe*, 1979, pp. 29-30.

[27] The 1975-76 plan called for price-control liberalization, a new injection of export and restructuring aid from the government, reductions in social costs and taxes paid by firms, and the imposition of border controls on imports. *Rapport de la Commission Industrie*, 7th Plan (Paris: Documentation Française, 1976), pp. 187-88; *Les Echos*, February 26, 1976; *Le Figaro*, September 9, 1977; *L'Aurore*, September 10, 1975; interview.

[28] *Libération*, March 10, 1978; *Le Nouvel Economiste*, no. 71, March 7, 1977, pp. 38-39; interviews.

[29] *Le Monde*, February 19, 1976; *Le Monde*, March 9, 1976, p. 46; *Les Echos*, April 1, 1976.

however, for two reasons. They feared its effects on their exports and, most important, being large importers themselves, they realized import limits might upset their intrafirm trade.[30]

These divisions within the industry did not prevent the association led by Bidegain from pushing its new plan containing protectionist measures. Bidegain and the regional authorities from Fougères and Cholet lobbied the French government, especially the Ministry of Industry, during 1975 and 1976. Finally, the government adopted a plan in 1976 to force Italian footwear importers to use "technical visas," a procedure designed to slow imports and raise their costs.[31] Bidegain also negotiated an agreement on footwear imports with the Italian industry. But this arrangement, under pressure from French footwear distributors and the EC, collapsed quickly.[32] In this case, intra-industry divisions prevented the implementation of a protectionist scheme.

The association launched a new plan to protect the industry in 1976. Demands for the industrial policies involved in the 1975 plan were combined with a new demand for "safeguarding" the industry from injury caused by imports.[33] After much industry lobbying, the French government initiated a new series of measures, similar to the industry's plan, including a system of import surveillance and quotas to keep the market "orderly."[34]

When these policy measures were instituted in 1977, they provoked a breakdown of consensus within the industry. The large firms, mainly André, Eram, and Labelle, objected to any new protection; in fact, they used the distributors' association to lobby the government against these measures.[35] When the government initiated them over these protests, the large firms provoked a crisis within the footwear industry association and succeeded in ousting Bidegain. These firms claimed that he was trying to ruin the industry and that the protection he advocated only hurt French producers.[36] The large firms seized control

---

[30] *Le Nouvel Economiste*, no. 71, March 7, 1977, pp. 38-39; interviews.

[31] *Les Echos*, February 26, 1976; *Le Monde*, October 17-18, 1976; *Le Nouvel Economiste*, no. 71, March 7, 1977, pp. 38-39; interviews; *Les Echos*, June 6, 1977.

[32] *Le Monde*, October 17-18, 1976.

[33] *Le Nouvel Economiste*, no. 71, March 7, 1977, pp. 38-39; *Le Monde*, February 27, 1976; *Rapport de la Commission Industrie*, pp. 187-88.

[34] *L'Unité*, March 19, 1976; *Le Figaro*, March 10, 1976; *Le Monde*, March 10, 1976; *L'Humanité*, March 10, 1976; *Les Echos*, September 13, 1977, p. 16; interview; Ministère de l'Industrie, *Note d'Information*, no. 66 (Paris: Ministère de l'Industrie, September 13, 1977), pp. 2-3.

[35] *Le Monde*, April 2, 1977; interviews.

[36] Ibid.

of the FNICF and pressed their interest in having the protectionist system dismantled. Once again, divisions of interests within the industry limited the protectionist policies adopted. In the end the government maintained surveillance (a posteriori) on imports but never instituted the quota system.[37]

The third episode of industry activity occurred between 1979 and 1982. Coinciding with the worsening of economic problems, this period was marked by increasing concern over imports from East Asian and other less developed countries. Before 1979, however, the industry association, now controlled in large part by the big, international firms, had steered clear of any protectionist activity. The association waged an increasingly public war between 1977 and 1980 against the import limits of other countries and attempted to increase its exports.[38]

When these measures had done little to help the industry by 1979, complaints against East Asian imports were renewed. In response, the footwear association proposed a new set of measures in 1981. The industry once again demanded increased government aid to restructure the industry, reduced taxes and social costs for footwear producers, formalization of the quality certificate system, a "buy French" campaign waged against footwear distributors, and the negotiation of import "autolimitation" agreements with South Korea and Taiwan.[39] Coinciding with the Socialists' entry into government and their campaign to "reconquer the domestic market," these ideas were favorably received. In 1981, the new footwear plan was announced, and later that year the industry negotiated its own import limits with the South Korean and Taiwanese industries.[40]

This time, the large French firms did not appear to object. These firms seemed to feel that this might calm the rest of the industry's growing demands for strict, global quotas. Moreover, these import limitation agreements were "loose."[41] Most important, they did not interfere with the large firms' import trade, because these firms neither

[37] Interview.

[38] ECFI, *Sectoral Study*, pp. 16-20, 63-65. With French government help, it created an industry export center and obtained a collective export insurance guarantee from the government (from COFACE). *Forum International*, June 26, 1979.

[39] *Le Monde*, September 5, 1980; *Les Echos*, September 4, 1980; *La Vie Française*, February 7-13, 1983, p. 35; *Le Monde*, December 7-8, 1982; *Le Figaro*, June 5, 1981.

[40] *La Vie Française*, February 7-13, 1983, p. 35; *Le Figaro*, June 5, 1981; *Le Monde*, December 7-8, 1982; *Les Echos*, March 22, 1983; *Le Monde*, April 23, 1981; interviews.

[41] They were administered by the industry association itself, and they placed such large ceilings on imports that they were not very restrictive. Interviews.

imported from Asia nor imported the types of shoes the Asians did.[42] For these reasons, the large, more international firms accepted the protectionist measures, though they never liked them.

In the mid-1970s and again in the early 1980s, the industry attempted to obtain increased protection at the European level. Here again, the industry's internal differences limited its protectionist demands. During the Tokyo Round negotiations of the GATT, the French footwear industry, claiming that further opening of its market would mean its demise, sought to have its tariffs exempted from all proposed reductions.[43] Later, it pressed to be included in some global import limitation program, like the textile sector's Multifiber Agreement (MFA).[44] In 1978, before GATT negotiations were concluded, it proposed that its tariffs be increased.[45]

Although footwear tariffs were reduced by less than the average cut agreed to on other products, the French firms' demands were not met for two reasons. First, the large French producer-distributors did not support these proposals and probably did their best to see them defeated.[46] Second, the Italian footwear manufacturers, being the number one exporters in the world, opposed any such protectionist measures. Because the EC operated on a unanimity system, the opposition of the Italians meant that these measures could not be instituted or even proposed in the GATT negotiations.[47] Thus once more, intra-industry divisions, based on differences in firms' international ties at both the national and European levels, mitigated pressures for protection.

The second period of European pressure by the French industry occurred at the end of the decade. In 1978, mounting concern over East Asian imports and over growing trade barriers in all other countries prompted many European producers, led by the French, to agree on the need for a more "organized" trading system. Pressure from the European industry confederation prompted the EC to initiate a statistical import surveillance system on Asian footwear.[48] The closure of the U.S. footwear market in 1978 to Asian imports created fears that the Asians would then make a massive attack on the European market. This united the European producers. In the early 1980s when the

[42] Interviews.
[43] *Les Echos*, October 23, 1975; *Le Monde des Affaires* (July-August 1977):59-60.
[44] *Les Echos*, September 28, 1978; interview.
[45] *Les Echos*, January 24, 1978.
[46] Interviews.
[47] Ibid.
[48] *Le Nouvel Economiste*, no. 129, April 24, 1978; *Les Echos*, April 20, 1978; interviews.

Asian import "invasion" reached new heights, the European industry demanded that the EC develop a permanent system of import surveillance.[49] By the early 1980s, the rise of the Asian footwear importers, which constituted a threat to all the European firms, had led to a coordinated, mildly protectionist action against them. As on the national level, the European footwear industries grew increasingly protectionist over the 1970s, as imports surged and their international ties weakened.

In the 1970s the French footwear industry's internal divisions also deepened. The main cleavage existed between the large firms, who imported and exported significantly, and the small firms, whose orientation was domestic. Over the 1970s this division grew, as the large firms increased their size and foreign operations in response to rising import competition. They moved production abroad and imported more into France, and this activity brought their interests into conflict with those of the smaller firms. Policy outcomes were affected by these disputes, as protectionist pressures before 1979 were reduced by the opposition of the large firms.

After 1979, when the problem became Asian imports, the resistance of the large firms nationally and at the European level to protectionist forces declined. The large firms had few trade relations and no production activity in the Asian countries; their ties to this part of the international economy were weak. Imports from this area could be selectively limited without infringing upon the intrafirm trade of the large firms. The leaders of the French industry were thus less active in their opposition to protection, although the organization of distributors (SNCICF), which they had used earlier to lobby against protection, did attempt to dissuade the French government from adopting any protectionist measures.[50]

Overall, the French footwear industry in the 1970s had limited ties through exports or multinational production to the international economy. As expected, the lack of these ties meant that when problems arose, the industry was likely to demand protection. However, the international economic ties that did exist within the industry were concentrated among the largest firms, and they turned out to be antiprotectionist in the 1970s. Their efforts centered on promoting exports and reducing trade barriers elsewhere. Their opposition to the smaller firms' preferences for market closure seemed, in the end, to have diluted the protectionist measures adopted.

[49] Parlement Européen, *Rapport du Parlement Européen*, pp. 5-7; interviews.
[50] Interviews.

CASE 2: WATCHES AND CLOCKS

The French watch and clock industry underwent dramatic changes in the 1970s. The industry shifted first toward the production of watches in response to declining consumer interest in clocks and second, in a more significant change, toward the development of electronic watches. This technological revolution caught French producers unaware. The industry was both unwilling and unable to make the change to electronic watches and clocks. By 1981, a decade into the technological shift, France had only two producers of electronic watches, accounting for a mere 15 percent of total consumption.[51] Not surprisingly, this cost the industry dearly. Within France, the firms suffered a great deal; their market was invaded by imports and many of them disappeared. From an industry with hundreds of firms in the early 1970s, it was grouped entirely around one firm by the early 1980s.[52] Internationally, the French also declined. In 1977, they were the fifth largest producers in the world; in four years they had fallen to seventh.[53]

Falling demand and shifting consumer preferences in view of the electronics revolution forced rapid adjustment on an already weak industry. Problems began in the early 1970s with mounting firm losses and closures, rising unemployment, falling profitability, and declining investment.[54] These problems continued throughout the 1970s and returned with renewed impact in the early 1980s.[55] In 1982-83, the industry's two largest firms were forced to lay off large numbers of workers and close various operations.[56] The industry thus faced serious, mounting economic distress between 1970 and 1983.

The technological change also brought new foreign competition, as imports from East Asia surged. Before 1968, the watch and clock pro-

---

[51] *La Vie Française*, November 9, 1981.

[52] Centre pour le Développement Horloger (hereafter CPDH), *Rapport sur l'Horlogerie Française* (Paris: CPDH, 1986), p. 2; *Economie-Géographie*, no. 202 (February 1983):2; *Les Echos*, June 22, 1979.

[53] *Economie-Géographie*, no. 202 (February 1983):1.

[54] CPDH, *Rapport*, pp. 8-9; *LSA*, no. 860, October 8, 1982, pp. 66-70; *Usine Nouvelle*, no. 9, March 1, 1984, p. 44; *Economie-Géographie*, no. 202 (February 1983):10-11; CPDH, *Bilan des Activités du CPDH depuis 1982 et Propositions pour un Nouveau Programme à Moyen Terme* (Paris: CPDH, 1985), annex, pp. 4-5; DAFSA, *L'Industrie Horlogère* (Paris: DAFSA, 1978), pp. 47-50, 59-60.

[55] CPDH, *Bilan des Activités*, p. 4; *Economie-Géographie*, no. 202 (February 1983):6; *Usine Nouvelle*, no. 9, March 1, 1984, pp. 41-42; *Les Echos*, April 26, 1979; *La Vie Française*, December 6-12, 1982, p. 94; *Economie et Statistique*, no. 144 (May 1982):22.

[56] CPDH, *Bilan des Activités*, p. 4; *Le Nouvel Economiste*, May 3, 1985, pp. 64-65; *La Vie Française*, December 6-12, 1982, p. 94; interview.

ducers faced little import pressure. In the late 1960s, imports accounted for no more than 10 percent of French production.[57] Foreign competition greatly increased after this due to important reductions in trade barriers in the late 1960s.[58] The industry's tardiness in developing electronic watches also induced a spate of imports. This import invasion began in the mid-1970s and entailed a shift in suppliers from Swiss, German, and American producers to those from Hong Kong, South Korea, Taiwan, and Japan.[59] This change in suppliers had an important effect. The French industry had few ties to these new importers and viewed this competition ominously.

Imports increased about five fold in the 1970s as a consequence of the surge in electronic watches from East Asia.[60] Imports as a share of the domestic market also rose dramatically from 31 percent in 1970 to close to 60 percent in 1979.[61] Import penetration nearly doubled in the decade, eventually claiming more than half of all sales. The need to adjust to the new technology, combined with the intensified foreign competition, produced serious challenges for the French producers, and made them likely candidates to want protection.

In the 1970s the watch- and clockmakers had strong trade dependence and low multinationality, although the industry was penetrated by foreign investment. The industry's international ties were mixed and changing over the decade. As the industry failed to meet the technological challenge, its trade ties, especially its export capacity, weakened. By the mid-1980s the industry was moving from being a Type II to becoming more like a Type I, especially in the electronic watch sector.

In the 1970s the industry's trade dependence was extensive, although beginning to weaken. It had a small positive net trade position until 1979, when it turned negative.[62] Exports by the industry increased over the decade, although they too slowed by the early 1980s.[63] Exports as a percentage of national production rose from 44

[57] Banque de France, *L'Industrie de l'Horlogerie* (Paris: Banque de France, 1974), pp. 23-25.

[58] The opening of the Common Market, the GATT Kennedy Round tariff reductions, the removal of quotas on Japanese products, and a new Swiss-French trade treaty augmented the openness of the French market. Banque de France, *Horlogerie*, pp. 23-25; *Economie et Politique* (March 1976):45-46; DAFSA, *Horlogère*, p. 15.

[59] DAFSA, *Horlogère*, pp. 12-14; *LSA*, no. 860, October 8, 1981, p. 70; *Economie-Géographie*, no. 202 (February 1983):14.

[60] French Customs Service data.

[61] Unpublished INSEE data.

[62] French Customs Service data.

[63] Ibid.

percent in 1971 to 68 percent in 1977, falling back, however, to 63 percent in 1982.[64] The French export trade in watches and clocks was distinct, as it involved mainly (90 percent) *parts* of watches and clocks. The French firms did not export the parts directly but rather sold them to a large retailer/distributor who did the exporting.[65] This weakened the firms' connection to the international market and reduced their interests in exports. Exports of watch and clock parts were not concentrated within the industry. Many small, specialized firms exported the parts they fabricated, usually through a large distributor, while the largest French producers were important exporters as well.[66] As in the industry overall, the exports of all large French firms, except one, declined after 1978. They could not compete with the new electronic watches made in Asia.[67]

The French watch and clock producers' multinationality was limited in the 1970s. The producers were small and specialized and thus less likely to develop foreign operations. Instead of multinational production, they employed a web of trade flows and international licensing agreements to obtain access to foreign markets. Foreign production relative to total production for them equaled 1.7 percent in 1974, the lowest percentage for any industrial sector in France.[68]

Foreign investment in the industry was more significant than French operations abroad. Of the largest French producers, excluding the foreign controlled firms, only one appeared to have any production operations outside France.[69] The other large producers before 1979 were either controlled by foreign firms or were subsidiaries of large foreign producers.[70] In fact, over half of the top seventeen firms

[64] DAFSA, *Horlogère*, p. 6; *Usine Nouvelle*, no. 9, March 1, 1984, p. 44.

[65] DAFSA, *Horlogère*, intro and pp. 6, 8, 11; *Economie et Statistique*, no. 144 (May 1982):13-15; CPDH, *Bilan des Activités*, p. 18.

[66] *Quotidien de Paris*, April 30, 1985; *Forum International*, November 29, 1980; *Les Echos*, April 16, 1971; *Le Figaro*, March 8, 1978; *Le Figaro*, May 2, 1979.

[67] *La Vie Française*, November 9, 1981; *Les Echos*, February 15, 1975; *Le Figaro*, May 2, 1979.

[68] This is for the larger sector containing watches and clocks ("construction mécanique" or "mécanique de précision"); Savary, *Multinationales Françaises*, p. 28. The sector also had one of the lowest percentages of subsidiaries abroad among all French industries in 1978. Michel Delapierre, in *L'Intégration de l'Economie Française*, ed. Michalet, pp. 88-89, 99.

[69] In the mid-1970s, Jaz had about five plants operating outside France and had financial ties to the large Franco-Belgian group Empain-Schneider. *Usine Nouvelle*, no. 39, September 28, 1978, pp. 36-38; DAFSA, *Horlogère*, pp. 27-31; *L'Expansion* (March 1978):96-99.

[70] *Usine Nouvelle*, no. 39, September 28, 1978, pp. 36-38; *Economie et Politique*, no. 260 (March 1976):44.

were foreign controlled in 1976.[71] The largest firm, the American Timex, held some 25 percent of the total French market.[72] Indeed, U.S., German, and Swiss control over the French industry through foreign investment rivaled the penetration that imports claimed on the market.

Unlike trade dependence, which declined after 1979, the industry's multinational ties increased. After 1979 the industry was restructured around one large firm, Matra, which was an electronics and military equipment producer and exporter. Matra, although not highly multinational, sought to build a series of international alliances to strengthen its watch division.[73] Principally, it allied with the Japanese firm Seiko to obtain new technology and export bases. By 1983, this left two groups, Matra allied with the Japanese, on the one hand, and about 150 small French producers allied in the industry association, on the other.

Although constituting a small industrial sector, the French watch and clock producers commanded much national political attention for three reasons. First, the producers were concentrated geographically. Ninety percent of the firms were located in the Haut Doubs Department, near the city of Besançon.[74] The industry had a tremendous regional impact and commanded the interest of its local political leaders.[75] Second, the industry became infamous for its labor unrest. The "Lip Affair" in the early 1970s symbolized a new wave of labor problems, involving plant takeovers, and focused national attention on the industry.[76] Third, the industry was extremely well organized. Despite the large number of firms, it had a strong, centralized industry association with a number of different organizations devoted to helping the firms financially and technologically. The producers were able to speak publicly with a single voice, and their association had good ac-

[71] DAFSA, *Horlogère*, pp. 27-31, 33.

[72] Ibid.

[73] Groupe ESCP, "Le Développement International des Groupes Français," *Cahier d'Etudes et de Recherche*, no. 82-30 (October 1982):12, shows Matra's multinationality to be very low: 5 percent. Evidence of its strategy is in *La Vie Française*, November 24, 1980, p. 32; *Les Echos*, December 23, 1983; *Les Echos*, November 26, 1982; *La Vie Française*, December 6-12, 1982, p. 95; *Le Monde*, October 23, 1980; *Le Nouveau Journal*, July 10, 1979; *La Vie Française*, November 9, 1981; interviews.

[74] *Economie-Géographie*, no. 202 (February 1983):4.

[75] Two of whom—Edgar Faure and Jean-Pierre Chevènement—were national political figures. Interview.

[76] *Le Monde*, April 19, 1973; *L'Express*, August 13, 1973; *Le Figaro*, February 19, 1976; *Le Figaro*, January 31, 1976; *Les Echos*, April 6, 1976; *Le Monde*, August 17, 1977; *Le Nouvel Observateur*, August 15, 1977; *Les Echos*, June 22, 1984.

cess to the French government.[77] In the late 1970s this unity was, however, disrupted by Matra's move into the industry. Matra had different interests than the small watchmakers and its own connections to the government; both of these factors brought it into conflict with the industry association.[78] From a highly unified industry, it had evolved by the early 1980s into a more bifurcated one.

The Dependent Variable

The French firms' strong trade dependence, weak multinationality, strong organization, and high foreign penetration shaped their responses to their economic problems. These responses changed significantly over the period from 1970 to 1983 as their international ties weakened and foreign competition grew. In the late 1960s and early 1970s, the industry was increasingly integrated into a web of international trade flows and was interested in promoting this trade by reducing the barriers hindering it. In the mid-1970s, as its problems and especially foreign competition grew, the industry backed off from its interest in greater market openness. It made few trade policy demands and concentrated instead on conversion to the new electronics technology. In this period, industrial policy demands were central. After 1980, as the French industry weakened and its exports fell, the producers took new interest in trade issues, but this time in protectionist policies. Unable to adjust, the French producers demanded that foreign competition be reduced.

The French watch and clock industry's national trade policy preferences revealed the industry's shifting interests during the 1970s. Before 1973, the producers were oriented toward free trade. The French producers willingly accepted the end of French quotas on Japanese watch and clock imports in the late 1960s. They agreed to the full level of tariff reductions on their products in the Kennedy Round of the GATT negotiations. They also helped negotiate a trade treaty with the Swiss, in which they accepted the progressive elimination of all tariffs on their trade in return for greater access to the Swiss market.[79]

In the mid-1970s, as trade grew and as the French failed to shift to the new electronic products, their interest in open markets declined. No attempts to close their market were made, however. Given the

[77] CPDH, *Rapport*, pp. 2-5, 10-12; *Economie et Statistique*, no. 144 (May 1982):17; *Economie-Géographie*, no. 202 (February 1983):2-3; *La Croix*, April 15, 1976.

[78] Interviews.

[79] Banque de France, *Horlogerie*, pp. 23-25; *Economie et Politique* (March 1976):45-46; DAFSA, *Horlogère*, p. 15; interview.

rapid rise in foreign competition, this was surprising. At this time the industry was still a major exporter with substantial trade flows. Despite rising bankruptcies, labor unrest, and mounting import penetration, the producers resisted any temptation to demand protection.

By 1980 the situation had changed. Export growth was falling and the trade balance had turned negative. The French producers had been unable to adjust to the new technology, and electronic watch imports surged. The industry made its first demand for protection when its association called for a quota on electronic watch imports. In 1981 the industry was granted this quota; however, it was restricted to imports from Hong Kong.[80] Apparently Matra, the largest French producer, with substantial trade ties to Japan, did not want quotas on all Asian countries. Unlike much of the rest of the industry, Matra was unexcited about quotas in general and opposed to quotas on countries with which it had sizable trade ties.[81] Matra's resistance thus helped reduce the scope of the French quotas imposed.

This trade action was taken nationally and outside of both GATT and EC rules, and it prompted swift retaliation. The government of Hong Kong imposed a boycott on one of France's largest export items, cognac.[82] In addition, a French firm partially controlled by the largest Hong Kong watch producer, Remex, lodged a complaint with the GATT over the quota. The French firm was a major exporter and importer of watches and their parts, and the quota restricted this intra-firm trade.[83] These two actions shifted further demands for protection to more approved channels—i.e., the EC.

The other national arena in which the French watch and clock producers voiced their preferences concerning foreign competition involved industrial policy debates. In the 1970s, the watch and clock producers began making industrial policy demands through their strong industry organization. As the producers' problems mounted after 1973, the association designed restructuring plans and negotiated with the government for aid. Four different plans were demanded and implemented by the industry between 1970 and 1983. The plans reveal the industry's gradual turn to protection and increasing internal disarray.

The first plan was developed around 1971, when trade was growing

[80] *La Vie Française*, December 6-12, 1982, pp. 94-95; *Journal Officiel de la Communauté Européen* (hereafter *JOCE*), no. L, 106/34, April 19, 1984; *LSA*, no. 860, October 8, 1982, pp. 66-70; interview; *Les Echos*, July 15, 1980.

[81] Interviews.

[82] *La Vie Française*, no. 1956, December 6-12, 1982, pp. 94-95.

[83] Ibid.

and the electronics revolution just beginning. The industry association sought to promote adjustment within the industry. It wanted aid to help firms develop the new technology and to foster concentration in order to increase firms' competitiveness.[84] This resulted in a government plan to give aid to the largest and most innovative firm, Lip.[85] It also prompted the creation of a new firm, Montrelec, allied with Thomson-Brandt and Lip and geared to the development of electronic watches.[86]

With the failure of these measures, the industry was even in deeper trouble by 1976, when it began designing a new plan. This plan focused on the same two elements as the earlier one had—financial aid and restructuring. This time the industry sought to have the government give aid not to any single firm but rather to the association, for distribution to deserving projects. In addition, the industry was to restructure around one large firm, Jaz.[87] In the end this second plan increased concentration in the industry a bit and gave the firms new financial aid. Like the first plan, it had little protectionist intent or effect and instead focused on improving competitiveness.

With the limited success of this plan, the industry was again reeling from the effects of foreign competition by 1979. It was hardly producing any electronic watches, and imports were now exceeding exports. A new strategy was devised. The industry felt that it must have a leader, that is, a large firm with the electronics technology and foreign markets to produce and sell the new products.[88] The government also wanted such an industry "federator," and it finally forced Matra to take on this role. In 1979 Matra unhappily bought controlling in-

[84] *La Croix*, March 8, 1970; *Le Figaro*, February 9, 1971; *La Croix*, April 15, 1976; *Financial Times*, February 4, 1970; *Les Echos*, May 24, 1971.

[85] *Les Echos*, May 24, 1971; *Le Figaro*, February 17, 1972; *Le Monde*, March 12, 1974; *Les Echos*, February 1, 1974; *L'Express*, February 4, 1974; *Le Monde*, June 17, 1976; *L'Express*, April 12, 1976, pp. 58-59; *Le Figaro*, February 9, 1976.

[86] *La Croix*, April 15, 1976.

[87] Later on, this restructuring plan was altered as another large firm, Jaeger, refused alliance with Jaz and sought to create its own "pole" of alliances. *Le Figaro*, October 7-8, 1978; *Les Echos*, September 6, 1978; *L'Expansion*, no. 89 (October 1975):141-43; *Le Nouvel Economiste*, no. 28, April 26, 1976, pp. 32-35; DAFSA, *Horlogère*, p. 30; *Usine Nouvelle*, no. 9, March 1, 1984, pp. 41-42; *Le Monde*, December 8, 1977; *Le Monde*, December 10, 1977; *L'Expansion* (March 1978):97-99; *La Vie Française*, August 20, 1979, p. 17; *La Vie Française*, February 12, 1979, p. 30; *Economie-Géographie*, no. 202 (February 1983):3-4; *Le Nouvel Economiste*, no. 149, September 18, 1978; *Le Monde*, September 10-11, 1978; *Le Monde*, January 19, 1979; *Les Echos*, January 18, 1979; interview.

[88] *Le Matin*, June 29, 1979; *Forum International*, July 2, 1979; *La Vie Française*, August 20, 1979, p. 17; interview.

terests in the largest firms, Jaz and Jaeger, thereby becoming a major force in the industry.[89] Protection was still not demanded.

The fourth plan for the industry was announced in 1982. This plan was more ad hoc and protectionist. Designed in part by the industry association and in part by the local prefect of Franche-Comté, a region where the industry produced, the plan called for increased aid, to expand R&D and save employment, and for the imposition of quotas on electronic watches from Asia.[90] As part of the Socialist government's attempt to help industry "reconquer the domestic market," the plan sought to halt decline rather than promote adjustment. The industrial policy preferences of the industry thus evolved in an increasingly defensive, protectionist direction, as its trade ties weakened and imports took over the domestic market.

A similar evolution in preferences was apparent at the EC level. The French producers began the 1970s with an interest in freer trade. Their agreement to end traditional French quotas on Japan, to reduce by the full amount their tariffs in the Kennedy Round of GATT, and to negotiate a trade liberalization treaty with Switzerland all testify to this preference for greater market openness before the mid-1970s. By the Tokyo Round GATT negotiations, however, the industry's preferences were beginning to shift. The French were not interested in seeing European watch and clock tariffs reduced by the full amount; indeed, they hoped that certain products would be exempted from any tariff cuts.[91] Though not explicitly protectionist, the industry's preferences were no longer as oriented toward free trade as previously.

By 1979, the industry's demands had become more protectionist. In the late 1970s a large number of dumping complaints were lodged by the industry. These complaints involved many different products—from mechanical alarm clocks to quartz crystal pieces—and were directed against a wide spectrum of countries—from Japan and the United States to China and the Soviet Union.[92] In 1983, the French

[89] Les Echos, June 27, 1979; Les Echos, June 29, 1979; Les Echos, August 27, 1979; La Vie Française, August 20, 1979, p. 17; interview.

[90] CPDH, Rapport, pp. 3, 12, 20-26; La Vie Française, December 6-12, 1982, p. 95; La Vie Française, February 7-13, 1983, p. 66; Les Echos, July 15, 1980; Economie-Géographie, no. 202 (February 1983):4; interview.

[91] In the end, EC tariffs on watch and clock products were substantially reduced in exchange for similar reductions by other developed countries, but some products were completely exempt from any further liberalization. EC, Rapport de la Commission de la CE sur les Négociations Multilatérales, Bilan par Secteur (Brussels: EC, 1979), p. 23; Economie et Politique (March 1976):45-46; interview.

[92] EC, "Official List of Anti-Dumping and Anti-Subsidy Complaints" (Brussels: EC, 1981), pp. 6, 30, 32.

industry, supported by its government, lodged an escape clause petition, seeking to organize all trade in this sector.[93] The EC watch and clock industry had been reduced over the 1970s to the French producers alone.[94] Opposition to the French firms' demands for protection was thus limited, unlike in the footwear case. In the end, the French industry's requests were granted; quotas were imposed in 1985 on electronic watch imports from China, Taiwan, Hong Kong, Japan, India, Pakistan, the Philippines, and Singapore.[95] The beginning of an "organized trading system" for French watches and clocks was thus created, as much of the industry desired.

Matra's role in the erection of these trade barriers was unclear. Although it opposed the French quotas in 1982, its preferences in the 1983-84 escape clause action appeared mixed. Matra had fared poorly in the watch business since its start in 1979. By 1982 it was losing huge sums and had forged alliances with the Japanese in order to remain in the business. On the one hand, the threat of protection allowed Matra to negotiate these accords; without it, the Japanese would have kept importing.[96] On the other hand, the quotas imposed affected Matra's trade with Seiko adversely and fortified the firm's desire to sell its watch operations.[97] However, because Matra was not a substantial extra-European exporter of watches and clocks and because it wanted the alliance with Seiko, the largest Japanese producer, Matra's position toward the escape clause action tended to be favorable. Its opposition in any case seemed weak, while the protectionist demands of the other producers and the industry association were loud, united, and insistent.[98] By the mid-1980s, the industry was more protectionist than before, even if somewhat divided as a result of Matra's mixed interests.

The French watch and clock industry thus responded to its economic difficulties as predicted for a Type II industry moving toward being a Type I. Throughout the early 1970s, when its exports and trade dependence were expanding, the industry pushed for freer trade at both the national and EC level. By the mid-1970s, as economic pressures and imports mounted, the industry sought to foster adjust-

[93] *JOCE*, no. L, 106/34, April 19, 1984; *Financial Times*, April 19, 1984; interview.
[94] By the 1980s, the French industry produced 70 percent of all EC watches; only one or two British and German firms remained. *JOCE*, no. L, 106/34, April 19, 1984.
[95] Chambre Française de l'Horlogerie (CFH), circular no. 1099, Paris, June 7, 1985, p. 4.
[96] *Les Echos*, December 23, 1983, p. 7; interview.
[97] Ibid.
[98] *Les Echos*, December 23, 1983, p. 7; *La Vie Française*, December 6-12, 1982, p. 95; interview.

ment through a national industrial policy, though it never demanded protection. This resistance to protection before 1980 was surprising, given the industry's serious difficulties. By 1982, the French producers had seen their trade dependence and export growth reduced as they failed to move into the new electronic products. They began demanding protection with increasing insistence. First at the national level and then at the EC level, they pressed for import quotas. Their pursuit of protection on both fronts was successful. Unified in a strong industry association and lacking EC industry opposition, the mass of small French watch and clock producers were able to impress their trade preferences upon the entire European industry in the 1980s.

CASE 3: FLAT GLASS

The French flat glass industry was one of the world's largest and most powerful; in the early 1970s, it was the sixth largest producer in the world.[99] In addition, the industry was dominated by two of the world's largest producers, St. Gobain and BSN, who controlled well over 70 percent of the French market and maintained a virtual duopoly on glass manufacturing within continental Europe during the 1970s.[100] In the course of this decade, however, the industry underwent a technological revolution, which created problems for it and in time altered its structure by breaking this duopoly and inducing the entry of new foreign competitors.[101]

[99] It comprised the largest component of the glass manufacturing sector, with over 35 percent of the sector's total sales; Patrick Sergent, "L'Industrie Verrière Française de 1962 à 1971" (Thesis, Paris, Fondation Nationale des Sciences Politiques, 1973), p. 7. Data on international position from *Economie-Géographie* (November 1977):8-10.

[100] Institut de Recherche et d'Information Socio-économique (hereafter IRIS), *Restructuration de l'Appareil Productif Français* (Paris: Documentation Française, 1976), pp. 110-11; *Economie-Géographie* (November 1977):2-10; Sergent, "L'Industrie Verrière," pp. 22-24; Christian Mille, "Evolution de la Branche Verre Plat en France et en Europe" (Ph.D. dissertation, Paris, Université de Paris I, 1981), pp. 365-67.

[101] In the mid-1960s a new glass-making technique, called "float" glass processing, was introduced. Though the flat glass industry had long been characterized by very large-scale economies of production, necessitating extremely large plants, huge capital investments, and sizable labor forces, this new technique created even larger-scale economies and made obsolete the old plants. The building of these huge new plants created significant overcapacity problems and initially reinforced concentration within the European industry in the mid-1970s. See Mille, "Evolution de Verre Plat," pp. 307-308; Sergent, "L'Industrie Verrière," p. 3; DAFSA, *L'Industrie du Verre dans le Monde* (Paris: DAFSA, 1976), intro. The fact that this change occurred at the same time that the industry's main consumers, the automobile and construction industries, were falling into a deep recession only aggravated their problems. See DAFSA, *L'Industrie du Verre,* 1976, intro. and p. 41; FCSIV, *Rapport d'Activité pour 1983* (Paris: FCSIV, 1983), p. 8; *J'Informe,* December 12, 1977.

Between 1970 and 1982, the French flat glass industry experienced several periods of severe economic difficulty. In the years between 1974 and 1977 and after 1979, the glass manufacturers faced serious recessions. The technological shift to "float" glass beginning in the late 1960s, the oil shock of 1973-74, and the consequent decline in the glass industry's main consumers—the automobile and construction industries—sent the French industry into a tailspin between 1974 and 1977.[102] The number of glass plants in France fell, and given the large size of these plants, this entailed a substantial decline in employment.[103] This declining demand, coupled with the erection of new float plants, led to sizable overcapacity and falling prices.[104]

Problems at the firm level, especially for the two industry giants—St. Gobain and BSN—were also manifest. In particular, St. Gobain experienced tremendous difficulties in France between 1974 and 1977 because it had built ten huge new float glass plants between 1968 and 1975. When demand fell in 1974, the firm was left with substantial unused and unprofitable capacity.[105] In fact, without its profitable foreign operations, St. Gobain would have gone out of business in France in the late 1970s, according to its president.[106] Like St. Gobain, BSN experienced great problems with its flat glass operations in the 1970s. In 1972, BSN was the largest producer in Europe; by 1980, it had sold all of its flat glass plants. Unlike St. Gobain, BSN failed to modernize early and developed only one "float" plant before 1973. Thus, it was forced to build these new plants in the mid-1970s, amid industry-wide overcapacity and falling prices.[107] This late modernization made BSN's flat glass operations even less profitable than St. Gobain's.[108]

The glass industry recovered for several years after 1977, but the same problems hit it again after the second oil shock. Once more, construction activity and auto manufacturing declined, which reduced de-

[102] *La Vie Française*, February 27, 1975.

[103] DAFSA, *L'Industrie du Verre dans le Monde* (Paris: DAFSA, 1981), p. 68.

[104] IRIS, *Restructuration*, pp. 112-13; *J'Informe*, December 12, 1977; DAFSA, *L'Industrie du Verre*, 1981, intro., p. 28; *La Vie Française*, February 27, 1975; FCSIV, *Rapport*, p. 5; INSEE, *Annuaire Statistique*, 1983, p. 99.

[105] *La Vie Française*, December 8, 1975. This left its glass divisions with negative net after-tax balances between 1975 and 1979, and it reduced the whole company's profit margins to about 1 to 2 percent of its revenues, a very low figure. DAFSA, *L'Industrie du Verre*, 1981, pp. 154-56; *L'Expansion*, December 21, 1979–January 10, 1980, p. 96.

[106] *La Vie Française*, February 20, 1978.

[107] Mille, "Evolution de Verre Plat," pp. 334-37; *La Vie Française*, December 8, 1975; *La Vie Française*, March 10, 1980.

[108] In fact, between 1973 and 1979, these operations lost a total of 620 million francs. Mille, "Evolution de Verre Plat," p. 337, note 1.

mand for flat glass. The result, as before, was overcapacity, price-cutting wars, declining production, and falling profit margins for several years after 1980.[109] Moreover, a new form of foreign competition entered the French and European markets: direct foreign investment in the flat glass sector. After 1980, four new foreign firms bought or built plants in Europe. These four, from the United States, Japan, and Britain, represented another powerful foreign threat to the industry in Europe.[110] They were disliked by the existing firms, especially St. Gobain, because they broke its virtual monopoly.

These intermittent economic crises were compounded by the steady growth of imports in the French (and European) market over the decade. Imports rose every year, quadrupling between 1973 and 1982.[111] Their share of the total French market doubled between 1970 and 1980. Rising from a relatively low level of 18 percent in 1970, imports captured approximately 35 percent by 1980 and close to 40 percent by 1982.[112] In addition, this import threat came from new sources, such as Italy, Eastern Europe, and East Asia, which had recently developed new capacity and were shifting from importing to exporting. Their appearance on the world glass market was doubly disturbing for the French industry: it signaled the decline of French glass exports to them and meant increased competition at home and in Europe.[113] Overall, the French flat glass industry faced constantly mounting foreign competition at home (and abroad) in the decade, which should have induced serious concerns about imports and perhaps demands for protection.

The manufacture of French flat glass was a Type III industry, with substantial export dependence and sizable, integrated multinational production capacity in the 1970s.[114] During the 1970s, the flat glass industry in France had extensive international trade relations. Although the industry's trade balance was negative every year except

---

[109] FCSIV, *Rapport*, p. 5; *JOCE*, "Communications," no. C232, September 3, 1984, p. 19; *Financial Times*, July 24, 1985; Mille, "Evolution de Verre Plat," pp. 365-67.

[110] *La Vie Française*, March 10, 1980; *Financial Times*, July 24, 1985; Mille, "Evolution de Verre Plat," pp. 364-67.

[111] French Customs Service data.

[112] Unpublished INSEE figures (for 1970); *Les Echos*, January 7, 1983 (for 1980 and 1982). These figures understate the actual penetration of flat glass imports by a substantial amount, since they do *not* account for any of the glass brought into France on imported motor vehicles, whose penetration of the French market was itself rising over the decade.

[113] IRIS, *Restructuration*, pp. 112-13; *J'Informe*, December 12, 1977; interviews; Mille, "Evolution de Verre Plat," p. 267.

[114] Sergent, "L'Industrie Verrière," pp. 22-24; see note 100 above.

1979, 1981, and 1982, it was a substantial exporter.[115] The value of its exports grew fivefold between 1973 and 1982, climbing slightly faster than its imports. Its percentage of exports to domestic production also rose over the decade, from about 25 to 30 percent in 1970 to nearly 42 percent in 1979.[116] At the firm level, exports also played a crucial role. Exports of glass from France for St. Gobain and BSN grew over the 1970s and were their most important exports globally.[117] The French glass industry and its two leading producers were thus large and growing exporters, dependent on these sales for a substantial part of their revenues.

In addition to being export dependent, the French flat glass industry was very multinational. The internationalization of this industry began early and was well advanced by the 1970s. This international activity also involved a great deal of intrafirm trade; its foreign and domestic production were well integrated due to the large-scale economies of production that induced the building of specialized plants used to service a number of markets.[118] Its percentage of foreign production relative to total production was 28.3 percent, the highest for all French industrial sectors in the 1970s.[119]

The firms St. Gobain and BSN also had extensive and rising multinationality over the decade. By the end of the 1960s, St. Gobain dominated production throughout continental Europe and also had plants in the United States, Brazil, and Lebanon.[120] In 1971, the firm realized only 57 percent of its revenues from glass in France, and this multi-

[115] French Customs Service data.
[116] INSEE, *Les Comptes de l'Industrie, 1979*; Bobe, "Les Importations des Biens de Consommation en Provenance de Tiers Monde," p. 52.
[117] For St. Gobain, approximately 13 percent of its total global sales in 1979 and over 15 percent in 1984 were accounted for by its French exports. See DAFSA, *L'Industrie du Verre*, 1981, p. 98; St. Gobain, *Annual Report, 1984* (Paris: St. Gobain, 1984), p. 4. Moreover, of its total export sales, 70 percent were those from France. See St. Gobain, *Annual Report, 1984*, pp. 3-4. St. Gobain was also the thirteenth largest exporter among French firms in 1981. See *Economie-Géographie*, no. 207 (September 1983):10. For BSN, the figures were lower but still very significant. Around 10 percent of its total global sales involved its French exports during the 1970s. (This figure is estimated from data in Sergent, "L'Industrie Verrière," pp. 27-31; DAFSA, *L'Industrie du Verre*, 1981, p. 98; interviews.) Other data reveal that exports for both firms grew at a rate of 10 percent over the period from 1974 to 1979. Groupe ESCP, "Le Développement International," pp. 11-12.
[118] Mille, "Evolution de Verre Plat," pp. 261-63; INSEE, *Annuaire Statistique*, 1983, p. 417.
[119] Savary, *Multinationales Françaises*, table 6, p. 28. This figure is for the larger glass and minerals manufacturing sector.
[120] Mille, "Evolution de Verre Plat," pp. 304-305, 337-41; DAFSA, *L'Industrie du Verre*, 1976, p. 86.

nationality grew more throughout the 1970s, as the firm began new production operations in Latin America, Egypt, Nigeria, and Portugal.[121] By 1979, the company was generating 53 percent of its sales through its foreign operations[122] and was among the one hundred largest multinationals in the world.[123]

St. Gobain's operations were integrated worldwide. Its intrafirm trade, especially within Europe, was important in the 1970s. Most of the flat glass exported from West Germany and Belgium to France was part of the firm's internal trade.[124] Moreover, after 1974, the only profit-making glass operations of St. Gobain were those outside France.[125] St. Gobain's multinational production operations were large and growing, highly integrated, and profitable in this decade.

Like St. Gobain, BSN was an early international producer. Although less multinational than St. Gobain, BSN had 47 percent of its total employees outside France and earned 42 percent of its revenues abroad by 1979.[126] It was also ranked the tenth largest multinational in France in the 1970s.[127] Like St. Gobain, it had significant intrafirm trade in Europe and was responsible as well for much of France's flat glass imports from West Germany and Belgium.[128] Thus BSN too was a large multinational, rivaling its domestic competitor, St. Gobain. Overall, the French flat glass industry was highly export dependent and multinational in this period.

While the industry was concentrated in France, it was also concentrated regionally and globally. In Europe, three producers—St. Go-

---

[121] Sergent, "L'Industrie Verrière," p. 1; interview.

[122] DAFSA, L'Industrie du Verre, 1981, p. 98; Economie et Politique, no. 82/355 (February 1984), p. 69; St. Gobain, Annual Report, 1984, pp. 3-4.

[123] St. Gobain, Annual Report, 1984, pp. 3-4. Furthermore, St. Gobain was the second largest multinational in France among industrial companies in terms of both its amount of foreign production and its number of employees abroad relative to the firm's total (50 percent and 58 percent, respectively, in 1979). Groupe ESCP, "Le Développement International," p. 13; Julien Savary, "Les Multinationales Françaises," Economie et Humanisme, no. 257 (January-February 1981):76.

[124] No figures on this intrafirm trade are available. Information from interviews; INSEE, Annuaire Statistique, 1983, p. 417. Since these two countries were France's largest sources of flat glass imports (with 28 percent and 22 percent, respectively, of all these imports), St. Gobain's intrafirm trade among these two countries was very significant. FSCIV, Rapport, pp. 11-12.

[125] La Vie Française, February 20, 1978; DAFSA, L'Industrie du Verre, 1981, pp. 154-56; interviews.

[126] DAFSA, L'Industrie du Verre, 1981, p. 98; Groupe ESCP, "Le Développement International," p. 12.

[127] Savary, "Multinationales Françaises," p. 76.

[128] INSEE, Annuaire Statistique, 1983, p. 417; interviews.

bain, BSN, and Pilkington in the United Kingdom—controlled the entire market. In North America, Pittsburgh Plate Glass (PPG) played the dominant role, while in East Asia the Japanese firm, Asahi, a subsidiary of Mitsubishi, controlled much of the flat glass market.[129] These top five producers controlled about 80 percent of the world market in 1976.[130]

This concentration was significant for two reasons. First, it meant that the large French firms were primarily European in their operations and not French. St. Gobain and BSN may be termed "European" firms in the 1970s.[131] This European identity and the market domination of these two French firms led to collusion between them. Infrequently clashing, the two often ran an effective and "cozy" cartel, dividing the European market and controlling prices within it, until their lucrative practice attracted foreign attention.[132]

A second point about this European organization of flat glass production in the 1970s was that it broke down after 1979. BSN's sale of its glass operations between 1979 and 1982 ended the European duopoly. Since St. Gobain was not interested in these operations, they were acquired by foreign firms. The entry of these new firms destabilized the old cartel and brought new foreign competition.[133] More worrisome, the construction of new glass operations in Luxembourg by the U.S. firm, Guardian, provoked further deterioration in the cartel and generated rising concern about overcapacity.[134] The entry of

[129] Interviews; IRIS, *Restructuration*, pp. 110-11.

[130] *Bulletin du Crédit National* (1er trim., 1983):13-16; IRIS, *Restructuration*, pp. 110-11.

[131] For example, not only did St. Gobain do its accounting in ECU rather than in francs, but it also organized its decision making for the sector at the European, and not the French, level. See *Le Monde*, July 28-29, 1985, p. 14; interview; Mille, "Evolution de Verre Plat," pp. 345-46; St. Gobain, *Annual Report, 1984*, pp. 4-7. This European identity was highly ironic given St. Gobain's history; it was created in 1665 by Colbert to be the national monopolist in glass and to halt the glass import invasion from Italy. Mille, "Evolution de Verre Plat," pp. 283-84.

[132] *Financial Times*, July 24, 1985; Mille, "Evolution de Verre Plat," pp. 369-85; DAFSA, *L'Industrie du Verre*, 1976, p. 89; Sergent, "L'Industrie Verrière," pp. 22-24, 33-34.

[133] Pilkington, the British giant, bought the German operations; Asahi, the Japanese firm, moved into Belgium; and PPG, the United States's and world's largest firm, acquired its French operations. See *Financial Times*, July 24, 1985; Mille, "Evolution de Verre Plat," pp. 323-26, 359-67; *La Vie Française*, March 10, 1980; interviews. Direct foreign investment in the French industry prior to 1976 accounted for at most 10 percent of total investment in the industry; however, by 1983, this figure had risen to 50 percent. IRIS, *Restructuration*, pp. 109-110; *Economie et Politique*, no. 82-355 (February 1984):69.

[134] Mille, "Evolution de Verre Plat," pp. 354-58, 365-67; *La Vie Française*, March 10, 1980; *Financial Times*, July 24, 1985; interviews; *JOCE*, "Communications," c232, September 3, 1984.

these new firms and particularly the competitive pressures it un-
leashed were likely to have inspired attempts by the French firms to
close the French or European markets to foreign investment as well as
to imports.

The Dependent Variable

Understanding the French flat glass industry's reaction to the foreign
competition it faced in the 1970s requires asking whether the French
(or European) flat glass industry wanted to protect its market from
either foreign imports or direct foreign investment; that is, was the
industry protectionist toward any aspect of foreign competition? In
general, the industry's lack of protectionist demands and activity at
both the national and the European level and the importance attributed to its own internal adjustment strategies are evident.

In the 1970s, the French flat glass industry was minimally involved
with the national government on issues of trade or industrial policy.
The industry showed little interest in trade issues and made no demands for surveillance or limitation of imports.[135] In fact, during the
industry's worst crises, the presidents of St. Gobain expressed their
preferences for free trade and the maintenance of an open European
market.[136] This preference was linked to the firm's international character—that is, its need to ensure continuous flows of exports and imports of glass among its far-flung plants.

This disinterest in trade restrictions in the face of severe economic
difficulties was combined with a similar disinterest in controlling foreign investment. During the decade, the two leading firms made no
efforts to limit foreign investment in French glass production. In 1979
when BSN announced its intention to sell its glass plants, neither BSN
nor St. Gobain tried to block their purchase by the giant American
firm, PPG.[137] The flat glass industry's preferences for foreign trade
and investment policies at the national level thus tended toward market openness, despite the rising pressures from foreign competition.

In the industrial policy arena, the makers of flat glass again showed
little interest in governmental aid. Apparently, the manufacturers
wanted little to do with the government. Relations between the industry and government in the 1970s were described as "not very smooth"

---

[135] Interviews; no other sources reveal any interest by the industry in such measures.

[136] *Le Nouvel Economiste*, no. 151, February 10, 1978, pp. 52-53; Stoffaës, *Grande Menace Industrielle*, p. 486; *La Vie Française*, February 20, 1978; *Bulletin du Crédit National* (1er trim., 1983):5-7.

[137] Interviews; no other sources make any mention of attempts to forestall such direct foreign investment in France.

and rather "strained."[138] The industry dealt mainly with three ministries, two of which it tended to fight with constantly. Battles over price controls with the Ministry of the Economy and Finance and over environmental rules with the Ministry of Health and the Environment were a continuous focus of attention. In addition to these contacts, there were good relations with the Ministry of Industry.[139] But throughout the 1970s no "plan" ever existed for the glass industry, and it received little government aid.[140] Moreover, the lack of a plan or aid did not concern the industry.[141] Both BSN and St. Gobain prided themselves on their independence from the government, and both remained largely self-financed through their crises.[142] The French glass industry was slightly more active at the European level. This greater interest reflected the European scale of its operations. For BSN and St. Gobain, the European market, rather than the French, was more important, due to their concentration of trade and production operations throughout Europe. Preferences for closure of the European market were never voiced by the industry; indeed, in traditional trade policy areas, it sought greater openness of markets worldwide.

The trade policy demands of the industry concerning European issues were evident in its activities during the GATT Tokyo Round negotiations in the mid-1970s. By and large, the French producers of flat glass preferred the application of the full tariff reduction to their products. Even when the United States refused to reduce its glass rates, the Europeans went ahead with a 23 percent reduction in their schedule.[143] The industry's interest was in having other countries open their markets further, but even when this was not possible it did not oppose greater opening of its market. The European industry also worked to harmonize glass tariff classifications among different countries, another effort intended to facilitate trade.[144]

On other European trade issues, the glassmakers also showed no interest in protection. In the 1970s the industry never lodged a formal

[138] Interviews.

[139] Ibid.

[140] Ibid. Unpublished data from INSEE on aid show very minimal amounts to the glass sector; St. Gobain did get some aid for its electronics operations in the late 1970s.

[141] Interviews; *Le Figaro*, February 21, 1978; *Bulletin du Crédit National* (1er trim., 1983):5-7; *Les Echos*, January 7, 1983.

[142] Interviews; Mille, "Evolution de Verre Plat," pp. 292-94, 344; St. Gobain, *Annual Report, 1984*, pp. 7-14; *Les Echos*, January 7, 1983.

[143] EC, *Rapport de la Commission de la CE sur les Négociations Multilatérales*, p. 27; interviews.

[144] Interview; FSCIV, *Rapport*.

trade complaint against any of its foreign competitors. No evidence of antidumping, antisubsidy, or escape clause petitions by the industry before 1982 exists.[145] Given that East European imports surged, that the United States was protecting its market against the European glassmakers while beginning to export to Europe, and that East Asian imports were growing during this decade, the lack of any such complaints by the Europeans was remarkable.[146]

Concerning the problem of foreign investment within Europe, the flat glass manufacturers also showed little interest during the decade. The industry's constant fears of overcapacity should have produced concerns about potential new foreign entry, but little attention was directed toward this problem. The French industry did nothing to block the sale of BSN's operations in Europe to foreign producers. The entry of Pilkington (U.K.), PPG (U.S.), and Asahi (Japan) into the European market did not elicit any attempt by St. Gobain to preserve its monopolistic status.[147]

Only in the early 1980s, when the U.S. firm, Guardian, attempted to build new glass plants in Luxembourg did the existing producers complain. St. Gobain, along with the rest of the industry—i.e., the other foreign firms, lodged a complaint against the Luxembourg government for encouraging this new capacity by giving Guardian huge subsidies to build in the country. Concerned about both overcapacity problems and the price effects of these subsidies, the existing glass manufacturers hoped the new float plants would never be built. After negotiations, the subsidies were reduced and a first plant built.[148] In this case, the industry used the EC to help negotiate reductions in the subsidies with the Luxembourg government. The issue, then, was one of concern over the deleterious effects of national subsidies to industry. In general, the French glass producers in the 1970s and early 1980s were as disinterested in EC intervention to help them as they were in French government aid. One EC official maintained that the sector had adopted a position aimed at persuading the EC to allow the

[145] Interviews; EC Commission, *lst Annual Report of the Commission of the EC on the EC's Anti-Dumping and Anti-Subsidy Activities* (Brussels: EC, 1983) and *2nd Annual Report of the Commission of the EC on the EC's Anti-Dumping and Anti-Subsidy Activities* (Brussels: EC, 1984).

[146] Mille, "Evolution de Verre Plat," pp. 264-67; interviews. In interviews, the rising concern over East Asian production and exports was voiced. Since 1982 this concern has increased, but as of 1986 no complaints had been filed or other actions taken.

[147] Interviews.

[148] Interviews; Mille, "Evolution de Verre Plat," pp. 354-58; *JOCE*, "Communications," c232, September 3, 1984, esp. p. 19; *Financial Times*, July 24, 1985.

evolution of the industry to proceed with as little public intervention as possible.[149]

Disinterest in French or EC intervention did not mean that the flat glass industry was inactive in trying to deal with its economic problems in the 1970s and early 1980s. The industry did not choose to seek public resolution of its foreign competition problems through protectionism, but it did pursue solutions on its own. Three basic strands of its strategy can be discerned.

The first part of this strategy involved efforts by the French firms to increase their international operations in the 1970s. Further multi-nationalization was viewed as a means to enhance competitiveness by augmenting the firm's size and its presence in many markets.[150] Both BSN and St. Gobain expanded their operations globally in the 1970s. Moreover, after BSN's exit and the entry of new giant competitors like PPG and Asahi, St. Gobain felt more compelled to move abroad in order to remain competitive with its new global rivals.[151]

The second element in the industry's adjustment strategy involved diversification. Though St. Gobain and BSN both had sizable operations outside of flat glass production before the 1970s, the two opted to diversify more extensively after 1968. Hence, in 1971 BSN had 43 percent of its sales in flat glass; in 1981, it had no flat glass operations left. The success of its diversified activities led to BSN's sale of its money-losing flat glass operations in 1980.[152] For BSN, the rising competitive pressures in flat glass initially induced diversification and then exit from the industry; it never tried to protect its market to stave off these pressures. St. Gobain also chose to accelerate its diversification. It initially integrated downstream, acquiring a large consumer for its glass products, and later moved further afield into the high technology area.[153] Through this diversification, St. Gobain sought to reduce its dependence on the difficult glass industry. Like BSN, it worked to resolve its problems in glass by means of its corporate strategy, not protection.

---

[149] *JOCE*, "Communications," c232, September 3, 1984, p. 19.

[150] Mille, "Evolution de Verre Plat," pp. 295-97, 302-305, 337-43; DAFSA, *L'Industrie du Verre*, 1976, p. 86; interviews.

[151] *Les Echos*, January 7, 1983; interview.

[152] Sergent, "L'Industrie Verrière," pp. 27-31; *Financial Times*, July 24, 1985; Mille, "Evolution de Verre Plat," pp. 346-49.

[153] Sergent, "L'Industrie Verrière," pp. 33-34. In 1979, it began a joint venture with National Semiconductor to produce semiconductors in Europe. Additionally, St. Gobain sought to position itself for the future by moving into the computer field. In 1980, it acquired a 20 percent interest in Machines Bull, the French computer maker. *Journal des Finances*, December 7, 1978; *L'Expansion*, December 21, 1979–January 10, 1980, pp. 94-96; *Les Echos*, November 8, 1979.

The final element in the industry's strategy involved collusion and cartelization of the European market. BSN's and St. Gobain's control of most of the flat glass industry in Europe allowed the two to exercise a duopoly.[154] Ultimately, however, this did less to protect the European market than to encourage further attempts at entry. While precluding much market share movement by producers within Europe and holding back new investment, this collusion created stable, high prices for glass that made foreign producers eager to enter the market. This collusion attracted both imports and attempts to invest in the market. Indeed, when BSN was selling its operations, the major foreign producers fought to buy them. As one manager in the French glass industry said, the foreign firms saw BSN's sale as a "big opportunity" to finally get into the European market.[155] In the end, this element of the industry's strategy induced foreign competition instead of forestalling it.

Overall, the French flat glass industry's response to its economic problems in the 1970s principally involved its own internal economic strategies, especially internationalization, diversification, and collusion. The glassmakers rarely used more public, political strategies. In large part, this preference stemmed from the industry's international character. Having a global web of trade and production activities, the industry did not see protectionism or other forms of public intervention as desirable, because they would have upset the firms' trade and production flows. This is the view expected of a highly export-dependent, multinational industry.[156]

CASE 4: PHARMACEUTICALS

The specialties sector of the pharmaceutical industry in France was divided into two distinct groups.[157] A large number of its firms were

[154] Sergent, "L'Industrie Verrière," pp. 22-24; Mille, "Evolution de Verre Plat," pp. 369-85; DAFSA, *L'Industrie du Verre*, 1976, p. 89; *Financial Times*, July 24, 1985. The French government apparently even encouraged it, believing that it would lead to more rational investment decisions and calmer market conditions. See Mille, "Evolution de Verre Plat," pp. 376-379. On the other hand, the EC investigated and condemned these two firms' collusive activities numerous times. DAFSA, *L'Industrie du Verre*, 1976, p. 89; Mille, "Evolution de Verre Plat," pp. 379-84.

[155] Mille, "Evolution de Verre Plat," pp. 354-58; *Financial Times*, July 24, 1985; interviews.

[156] This point was made repeatedly in interviews; see also *Financial Times*, July 24, 1985; *Les Echos*, January 7, 1983.

[157] The pharmaceutical sector had two main sectors: basic pharmaceuticals (NAP 1901) and specialty ones (NAP 1902). Although somewhat arbitrary, because the producers of each were essentially the same firms, this division was important because the two areas

small, independent laboratories producing a limited selection of pharmaceutical products. The second group, which dominated the industry, consisted of a few large, diversified firms, often with only a minority interest in pharmaceuticals. Though the industry was not very concentrated, the large firms controlled it by virtue of their overwhelming size.[158] Over the 1970s the gap between these two groups widened, and the balance of power shifted increasingly in favor of the large firms.[159]

During the 1970s the pharmaceutical industry in France experienced severe economic difficulties coupled with mounting foreign competition. A serious downturn between 1974 and 1978 resulted in declining firm numbers, stagnant employment, and falling rates of profit, investment, and production. The effects of the first oil shock in 1973, which raised production costs and reduced demand, hurt the pharmaceutical industry. Between 1970 and 1984, its number of firms decreased by 25 percent.[160] This consolidation and closure of firms also reduced employment.[161] The severity of the industry's problems was revealed further by its declining profitability and investment. The industry was caught in a profit squeeze. This in turn reduced investment in it after 1975 and, given the importance of R&D investment, hurt its competitiveness.[162] These problems affected all parts of the pharmaceutical sector; in 1975 and 1976, 50 percent of its firms reported financial losses.[163] The biggest firms also suffered. Rhône-Poulenc Santé, Sanofi, and Roussel-Uclaf, the three largest, experienced declines in profits, employment, and exports in the late 1970s.[164]

The effects of this recession were aggravated by growing import competition. After the late 1960s, pharmaceutical trade globally and

had different international trade positions. Due to its trade problems, the specialties sector is the one focused on here. The specialty pharmaceutical industry consists of firms manufacturing active substances, the basic input for pharmaceutical products, and specialty medicines for human use.

[158] Jacqueline Sigvard, *L'Industrie du Médicament* (Paris: Calmann-Lévy, 1975), pp. 36-42.

[159] Sigvard, *Médicament*, pp. 36-51; *Economie et Politique* (September 1980):62; *Le Matin*, April 23, 1977; *Entreprise*, no. 1008, January 3, 1975, pp. 46-50.

[160] Sigvard, *Médicament*, p. 25; Syndicat National de l'Industrie Pharmaceutique (hereafter SNIP), *Dossier Economique* (Paris: SNIP, 1985); *Le Nouvel Economiste*, no. 496, June 28, 1985.

[161] INSEE, *Les Comptes de l'Industrie, 1979*, pp. 120-22.

[162] Sigvard, *Médicament*, pp. 59, 61, 96-97; SNIP, *L'Industrie Pharmaceutique et Ses Realités* (Paris: SNIP, 1982), p. 17; *Economie-Géographie*, no. 151 (February 1978):10; *Le Nouvel Economiste*, no. 496, June 28, 1985.

[163] *La Vie Française*, November 3, 1975; *Le Monde*, July 16, 1976.

[164] *La Vie Française*, April 4, 1977, p. 19; *Le Nouvel Economiste*, no. 489, May 10, 1985, p. 78; *Le Nouvel Economiste*, no. 502, August 9, 1985, p. 27.

in Europe particularly exploded due to the creation of the Common Market and the reduction of numerous trade barriers.[165] The growing threat posed by imports of specialty pharmaceuticals was apparent in France during the 1970s. Between 1973 and 1981, imports multiplied over ten times in value.[166] The share of imports in total domestic consumption rose between 1970 and 1977 from 16.5 percent to over 25 percent.[167] Moreover, this increase was doubly significant because foreign penetration in the 1960s was virtually unknown.[168] Among all French industries, the pharmaceuticals sector experienced the fourth largest rate of increase in import penetration between 1974 and 1980.[169] Combined with its economic difficulties, this import invasion should have prompted concern among the firms over trade issues, and perhaps even demands for protection.

Pharmaceuticals was a Type III industry. Trade and multinational ties were significant for the industry and rising over the 1970s, although multinationality remained its primary form of international activity. But exports and foreign production operations were concentrated in the hands of the largest firms; the majority of small labs focused only on the domestic market.[170]

The trade relations of the French pharmaceutical manufacturers grew over the 1970s. The liberalization of markets in the period between 1965 and 1972 prompted an expansion of imports and exports. France increased the value of its pharmaceutical exports by more than five times between 1973 and 1980.[171] Exports as a percentage of national production rose impressively from 13.4 percent in 1970 to 20 percent in 1980.[172]

Three features of this export trade should be noted. First, the industry derived a great deal of foreign income from licenses and patents with foreign firms, although it ran an increasingly negative balance in this area.[173] This sizable trade in licenses and patents

[165] Sigvard, *Médicament*, pp. 147-51.

[166] French Customs Service data (Douanes fiche for NAP 1902).

[167] Unpublished INSEE data (NAP 1092).

[168] Sigvard, *Médicament*, pp. 147-51; *Economie-Géographie*, no. 151 (February 1978):10.

[169] Ministère de l'Industrie, *Les Chiffres Clés de l'Industrie, 1984* (Paris: Documentation Française, 1985), p. 48, for sector including "parachimie et pharmacie."

[170] *Les Echos*, October 30, 1975.

[171] SNIP, *Dossier Economique*, p. 41; Sigvard, *Médicament*, pp. 147-51. Although this increase was from a low initial level, it was not as rapid as that experienced by imports, and in consequence, imports overtook exports in 1976, which produced an increasingly large trade deficit. See French Customs Service data.

[172] Bobe, "Les Importations des Biens de Consommation en Provenance de Tiers Monde," p. 52; *Info Chimie*, no. 238 (June 1983):102.

[173] Taking into account the net trade through licensing agreements, which were almost

constituted an essential part of the industry's linkage to the international economy. Second, it imported mostly lower value-added active substances, which were then used in the production of higher value-added medicines, which in turn formed the core of the industry's exports.[174] The manufacturers were thus dependent on imports for their production and exports. Third, export dependence was not equally shared by all firms. Of a total of over 300 firms, only 180 exported at all, and the largest ten exporters sold over 40 percent of the industry's exports.[175] This concentration of export activity meant that the largest firms were more dependent on exports than the industry as a whole.[176]

The pharmaceutical producers in France were extensively involved in foreign production operations. Many of these were begun early in the postwar period as a means to obtain access to foreign markets, which were then largely closed to imports.[177] Multinationality thus had come first and was more significant for the pharmaceutical industry than were its exports. Although its production abroad relative to its total production was about 8 percent in the early 1970s, its percentage of the total number of French foreign operations was the highest for all French industry. It possessed 25 percent of all French production facilities abroad in 1978.[178]

This multinationality grew over the 1970s. The French producers felt they had to expand abroad or lose competitiveness.[179] Movement

---

five times the size of direct exports, the trade balance becomes more negative. French pharmaceutical producers were involved in many such agreements, but on balance they earned less from their patents than they paid for the use of foreign companies' licenses. *Economie-Géographie* no. 151 (February 1978):10; *Les Echos*, October 30, 1975; DAFSA, *L'Industrie Mondiale de la Pharmacie: Structure et Stratégies* (Paris: DAFSA, 1981), pp. 70-71.

[174] Sigvard, *Médicament*, pp. 147-51; DAFSA, *L'Industrie Mondiale*, pp. 55, 65; SNIP, *L'Industrie Pharmaceutique*, 1982, pp. 25-29.

[175] *Les Echos*, October 30, 1975.

[176] Rhône-Poulenc, the largest firm in the industry, was the eighth largest exporter in France in 1981. For the firm's pharmaceutical division, exports accounted for 30 percent of all sales. The figure for Sanofi, the fourth largest French producer, was 20 percent for 1980. Pharmuka, the seventh largest firm, also had an above-average export dependence; the figure for its parent corporation, Pechiney-Ugine-Kuhlmann, was 25 percent in 1976. *Economie-Géographie*, no. 207 (September 1983):10; *Info Chimie*, no. 238 (June 1983):111; "Les Multinationales," *Cahiers Français*, no. 190 (Paris: Documentation Française, March-April 1979), p. 23.

[177] *Les Echos*, August 21, 1980; INSEE, *Annuaire Statistique*, 1983, p. 418; EC, *The Community's Pharmaceutical Industry* (Brussels: EC, 1985), pp. 19-22. This figure is for pharmaceuticals as a whole and other chemicals.

[178] Savary, *Multinationales Françaises*, p. 28; Michel Delapierre in *L'Integration de l'Economie Française*, ed. Michalet, p. 99.

[179] DAFSA, *L'Industrie Mondiale*, pp. 1, 70-79; *Le Figaro*, January 28, 1980; *Info Chimie*, no. 238 (June 1983):127.

abroad enabled firms to spread their high production (especially R&D) costs over larger markets, which increased profits.[180] These operations were woven together through webs of intrafirm trade. Producers manufactured active substances in certain markets and then shipped these to other areas where they were used in the production of medicines, many of which were then exported. This intrafirm trade was increasingly significant for the French industry during the decade.[181] These foreign operations were more profitable for the firms than were their domestic ones. In some cases, without their foreign profits, the pharmaceutical firms would have generated such losses in France their survival would have been questionable.[182] Multinationality was clearly important for the industry.

This multinationality was concentrated in the hands of the largest firms. Rhône-Poulenc Santé, the leader of the French industry, had subsidiaries worldwide in the 1970s, with an especially strong presence in Europe, Africa, and the Middle East. Its multinational operations accounted for 30 percent of its sales in the late 1970s. Moreover, this percentage grew rapidly over the 1970s and early 1980s.[183] The second largest firm in France, Roussel-Uclaf, which in 1974 was bought by the German firm, Hoechst, also increased its foreign operations over the 1970s. Its foreign operations accounted for 40 percent of its total sales in 1975.[184] Sanofi, another large French producer, made some 40 percent of its sales outside of France and was actively expanding into Japan, the United States, and West Germany in the 1970s and early 1980s.[185] All of France's large pharmaceutical producers were thus heavily multinational.[186]

[180] *Info Chimie*, no. 238 (June 1983):111.

[181] DAFSA, *L'Industrie Mondiale*, pp. 53, 78; *Le Nouveau Journal*, March 29, 1980.

[182] *Info Chimie*, no. 238 (June 1983):107-110, 118-19; *Le Figaro*, September 22, 1978; *Les Echos*, May 20, 1980; *La Vie Française*, April 4, 1977, p. 19; *La Vie Française*, September 25, 1978, p. 25; *La Vie Française*, April 14, 1980; *Le Monde*, April 11, 1980.

[183] *Info Chimie*, no. 238 (June 1983):107-112; *Le Nouvel Economiste*, no. 489, May 10, 1985; EC, *The Community's Pharmaceutical Industry*, p. 20; Groupe ESCP, "Le Développement International," p. 12.

[184] Groupe ESCP, "Le Développement International," p. 12; *La Vie Française*, February 16, 1981, p. 50; *Les Echos*, December 22, 1976; *La Vie Française*, April 4, 1977, p. 19; *Le Monde*, December 7, 1977; DAFSA, *L'Industrie Mondiale*, pp. 69-70; EC, *The Community's Pharmaceutical Industry*, p. 20.

[185] DAFSA, *L'Industrie Pharmaceutique*, pp. 69-70; *Info Chimie*, no. 238 (June 1983):118-19, 124; *Les Echos*, March 24, 1981; EC, *The Community's Pharmaceutical Industry*, p. 20; *Le Figaro*, June 19-20, 1980.

[186] The French firms were not as multinational as the large U.S., Swiss, and German firms that dominated the industry globally. See DAFSA, *L'Industrie Mondiale*, intro. and p. 1; *Le Nouvel Economiste*, no. 496, June 28, 1985. Rhône-Poulenc and Sanofi were twentieth and thirty-first, respectively, in size among the world's largest pharmaceutical pro-

The firms in the business were highly trade dependent and multi-national. In fact, these two forms of international activity accounted for the majority of the industry's sales. The revenues generated by exports, technical licenses, and foreign operations accounted for 61 percent of domestic revenues in 1968, 75 percent by 1973, and 90 percent in 1980.[187] These high levels and growth rates of international operations for the industry attest to its strong ties to the world economy.

In addition to its international ties, the movement of foreign firms into the French industry increased its international character and competitive pressures. Not only did import competition rise, but foreign competition through direct investment accelerated. In the 1960s, only some 20 percent of capital in French pharmaceuticals was controlled by foreigners; by the end of the 1970s the figure had risen to 50 percent.[188] The early penetration by Swiss firms was followed later by the Germans and Americans. As already mentioned, the second-largest French firm, Roussel-Uclaf, was acquired by the giant German corporation, Hoechst, in 1974.[189] Indeed, of the top five firms in France, two were foreign owned.[190] Direct foreign investment, therefore, constituted another crucial aspect of foreign competition for the industry.

Dependent Variable

Did the French pharmaceutical industry respond to its economic difficulties by seeking to close its market to foreign competition, either imports or investment? The role played by the industry's growing international ties in the formulation of its demands was critical. In general, these links fostered its attempts to open its market further.

At the national level, the French pharmaceutical manufacturers

---

ducers. See EC, *The Community's Pharmaceutical Industry*, table on p. 20. Moreover, the large French producers had small market shares in the biggest world markets—that is, in the United States, West Germany, and Japan. By the early 1980s, the French had improved their international standing somewhat. Their consolidations at home and expansion abroad increased both their size and presence, bringing them into closer competition with the world leaders. Sigvard, *Médicament*, pp. 43-47; *Le Monde*, January 22, 1980, p. 43; *Le Monde*, April 11, 1980; *Les Echos*, supplement, February 28, 1979, pp. 13-20.

[187] SNIP, *L'Industrie Pharmaceutique*, 1982, p. 28; Sigvard, *Médicament*, pp. 141-47; *Les Echos*, October 30, 1975.

[188] *Le Matin*, April 23, 1977; DAFSA, *L'Industrie Mondiale*, pp. 74, 206; Stoffaës, *Grande Menace Industrielle*, pp. 267-68; Sigvard, *Médicament*, pp. 47-51.

[189] *Les Echos*, February 13, 1974; *La Vie Française*, January 2, 1974; *Le Nouvel Economiste*, no. 489, May 10, 1985.

[190] Sigvard, *Médicament*, pp. 74-75.

pursued no efforts whatsoever in the 1970s to protect their domestic market from rising foreign competition. Prior to 1972, neither imports nor direct foreign investment was appreciable. The French market in pharmaceuticals was virtually closed to all foreign pressures due to the very strict system of industry price controls and national drug regulations. Between 1968 and 1972, however, a number of initiatives were taken that reduced the constraining effects of this system.[191] Imports increased greatly as a result. Despite this import surge, the producers never sought to have the French government protect the industry, even when they ran into economic difficulties after 1975.[192] Furthermore, the pharmaceutical manufacturers never pressed for restrictions on the entry of foreign producers.[193] Overall, the industry had little interest in trying to restore restrictions on access to its home market.

In the postwar period, the French pharmaceutical industry was involved in the government's health policy; it was seen as an integral element in the social security system. As such, it was subjected to a great deal of government regulation, ranging from price controls to new product rules. Although related to national health policy, these regulations had strong effects on trade. Their severity made importing practically impossible before the late 1960s. In the late 1960s and early 1970s efforts were made to reduce the protectionist effects of these measures, often at the behest of the industry itself. Moreover, during the period after 1972, the industry and its association, SNIP, became involved in attempts to open the French market and to create a European market in pharmaceuticals.

The industry's activities to alter its industrial policies focused on three key goals. First, the pharmaceutical producers wanted an end to the strict price control scheme regulating their products. The French government used this to set prices for pharmaceuticals purchased as part of its health insurance and social security policies. These prices were kept at low levels to control the social security system's chronic deficit,[194] but they pervaded the whole French market. They basically determined the range of all drug prices in France and the price of

[191] DAFSA, *L'Industrie Mondiale*, pp. 31-33, 53, 75-79; Sigvard, *Médicament*, pp. 79-83, 136-39; Chambre de Commerce, *La Concurrence Etrangère et les Importations Sauvages* (Paris: Chambre de Commerce, 1977), p. 33; INSEE, *Annuaire Statistique*, 1983, p. 418.

[192] Interviews.

[193] Ibid.; EC, *The Community's Pharmaceutical Industry*, pp. 36-45; *Economie et Politique* (September 1980):62; *Les Echos*, January 27, 1981.

[194] Sigvard, *Médicament*, pp. 79-83, 18; EC, *The Community's Pharmaceutical Industry*, pp. 36-45; *Les Echos*, supplement, February 28, 1979, pp. 46-58, 67; *Les Echos*, July 15, 1976.

exports, since foreign purchasers negotiated on the basis of the publicly known domestic prices.[195] Price controls were a major source of concern for the industry, because they reduced its profitability, thus limiting R&D and hurting its competitiveness.

The pharmaceutical producers fought for greater pricing flexibility throughout the 1970s. They launched three major efforts to force the government to alter its policy and were successful in two of them. The battle over pharmaceutical prices was waged between the industry and the Ministry of Industry, on the one hand, and the ministries of Health and of Finance, on the other. The first group desired to end, or at least reduce, price controls in order to restore the industry's profitability and competitiveness; the second group advocated retention of controls in order to keep the social security deficit from increasing and to retain influence over the industry.[196] In 1972 the industry launched its first campaign for price liberalization and relaxation of various regulations. Some of the industry's demands were realized, mostly in regard to the latter issue. The net effect was to encourage importing by making it easier and by making pharmaceuticals more profitable.[197]

The decade's major effort to reduce price controls occurred in 1975-76. The French producers were experiencing severe economic difficulties, which prompted them to seek changes in the policies affecting them. Taking the initiative, the industry designed a long-term industrial policy for itself, a central element of which was price liberalization. In alliance with the Ministry of Industry, the pharmaceutical producers presented their plan to the President of the Republic.[198] The industry received no satisfaction of its demands at this point, but it continued and intensified its campaign.[199]

The final episode in the battle over price controls took place in the late 1970s. The industry, as its problems worsened, found a new ally in the Ministry of Health. By the late 1970s, the producers, with the

[195] Sigvard, *Médicament*, pp. 136-39; DAFSA, *L'Industrie Mondiale*, p. 15; *Les Echos*, April 14, 1976; interview.
[196] Sigvard, *Médicament*, pp. 97-103; *La Vie Française*, November 3, 1975; *La Vie Française*, March 26, 1979, p. 26; *Le Monde*, July 16, 1976; *Info Chimie*, no. 238 (June 1983):115; *Le Figaro*, November 14, 1979; interview.
[197] *Les Echos*, supplement, February 28, 1979, p. 67; interview; DAFSA, *L'Industrie Mondiale*, pp. 31-32, 53.
[198] *Le Point*, no. 179, February 23, 1976, pp. 85-86; *Le Point*, no. 209, September 20, 1976, p. 112; *Le Monde*, July 16, 1976; *Les Echos*, January 10, 1977; *Le Matin*, June 22, 1978; interview.
[199] *Le Figaro*, February 13, 1976; *Le Nouvel Observateur*, June 28, 1976, p. 43; *Le Point*, no. 179, February 23, 1976, pp. 85-86; *Economie-Géographie*, no. 151 (February 1978):2-3.

backing of the ministries of Industry and Health, impressed their concerns on the government and were allowed some price liberalization, which encouraged imports.[200] The industry's demand for reductions in price controls was directed at its own domestic situation, but the industry understood and approved of the trade effects—i.e., both higher-priced exports and more imports—attached to such liberalization.

The industry's second goal was to restore its competitiveness by reorganizing. In 1975, as part of its price liberalization scheme, the industry proposed to regroup itself around several of the largest firms, but only in exchange for greater pricing flexibility. When the Ministry of Finance and the President rejected the changes in the pricing scheme, the pharmaceutical producers refused to regroup, something that the government strongly desired.[201] When the government agreed to price liberalization in 1979-80, the industry then reorganized itself around the four largest firms.[202] What is interesting about the industry's demands for new industrial policies is that they did not involve protectionism. Despite the industry's mounting problems and import penetration, it never sought to close its market. Indeed, it actively sought to reduce trade barriers and promote foreign investment.

The industry's demands also were not focused on receiving more government aid. Although considered a sector of the future, the pharmaceutical industry was not a major requester or recipient of state aid. Largely self-financed, it did not depend on the government.[203] The aid it did receive went mainly toward its R&D efforts; it was a way of making up for profits lost due to the price controls.[204]

The third goal sought by the pharmaceutical producers was the relaxation of rules governing the introduction of new drugs. In the early 1970s, the industry sought to loosen testing requirements and to re-

[200] *La Vie Française*, March 30, 1981, p. 33; *Les Echos*, January 27, 1981; *Le Matin*, January 7, 1980; *Le Figaro*, March 7, 1980; *Le Point*, no. 390, March 10, 1980, p. 100; *Les Echos*, March 7, 1980.

[201] *Le Point*, no. 209, September 20, 1976, p. 112; *Le Monde*, August 6, 1976; *Le Monde*, August 9, 1976; *France Nouvelle*, May 23, 1977; *La Vie Française*, January 17, 1977; *Le Matin*, June 22, 1978; *Les Echos*, July 15, 1976.

[202] *Le Monde*, March 7, 1980; *Le Point*, no. 390, March 10, 1980, p. 100; *Journal des Finances*, March 13, 1980; *Journal des Finances*, February 12, 1981.

[203] *Les Echos*, supplement, February 28, 1979, p. 27; Sigvard, *Médicament*, pp. 59, 61, 64; *La Vie Française*, November 26, 1979; *Le Nouveau Journal*, September 13, 1979; *Les Echos*, June 13, 1978.

[204] *Les Echos*, supplement, February 28, 1978, pp. 71-78; *Les Echos*, June 13, 1978; *Le Nouveau Journal*, September 13, 1977.

duce waiting periods for new products. In 1972 measures were adopted by the French government to ease such restrictions, which thereby further opened the market to imports.[205] After this, however, the industry's efforts concerning drug regulations shifted to the European level.

There, pharmaceutical industry's efforts were more focused on reducing trade barriers than its efforts in France had been. In terms of traditional trade policy instruments like tariffs and quotas, the industry was already unencumbered by them in the 1970s. In the GATT negotiations of the Tokyo Round, the European industry did not resist further cuts in its tariffs, but these were not a central concern.[206] The industry also favored increased international harmonization of product classifications to facilitate trade.[207] In addition, the industry's involvement in the negotiations with the United States to end its policy of "American Selling Price" (ASP) on chemical imports was part of its preferences for trade liberalization globally.[208] The pharmaceutical manufacturers' central concern with trade involved the European Common Market. As the firms increased their operations throughout Europe, their interest turned more toward the creation of a single European market.[209] Toward this goal, a major attempt to harmonize pharmaceutical regulations in Europe was made in the early 1970s. Beginning in 1972, the EC initiated negotiations to eliminate various national regulations and to establish European-wide standards, rules, and testing procedures. This process was backed by the European pharmaceutical producers, who saw the myriad of diverse national policies as an impediment to their European trade and production flows. In 1975, the negotiations produced a set of European codes for the pharmaceutical industry, which aided trade within the Community.[210]

The French industry's disinterest in protection was further dis-

[205] *Economie-Géographie*, no. 151 (February 1978):2-3; Sigvard, *Médicament*, pp. 79-83, 136-39; *Les Echos*, supplement, February 28, 1979; EC, *The Community's Pharmaceutical Industry*, pp. 36-45; interview.

[206] DAFSA, *L'Industrie Pharmaceutique*, pp. 75-76; interview. Duties on pharmaceutical specialties in France were reduced in the Tokyo Round from 5.5 percent in 1974 to 2.5 percent in 1981, according to figures from the French Customs Service.

[207] Interview.

[208] *Les Echos*, February 21, 1979, p. 7.

[209] *Le Matin*, June 22, 1978; *Les Echos*, October 31, 1974; Sigvard, *Médicament*, pp. 19, 278-81; interview.

[210] Sigvard, *Médicament*, pp. 19, 79-83, 278-81; EC, *The Community's Pharmaceutical Industry*, pp. 36-45; *Economie et Politique* (September 1980):62; *Les Echos*, supplement, pp. 58-61, 67; interview.

played by its lack of complaints to the EC over foreign dumping, subsidization, or other unfair trade practices. The chemical sector as a whole was one of the most frequent complainers, but the pharmaceutical producers were not involved in this activity.[211] Despite growing foreign competition from both within and outside of the EC, the industry showed little desire to have this limited. Not even the relatively restrained step of complaining to the EC was taken. The industry at home and in Europe appeared far more interested in meeting foreign competition than in halting it.

The industry's own, internal efforts to adjust were most important. Its strategy to restore its competitiveness had two central elements, neither of which entailed efforts to reduce imports or foreign investment. The first element in the French producers' strategy was to increase their multinationality. The large producers realized that to remain competitive they had to have large markets over which to spread their costs. Only by exporting and operating in large, profitable markets could they make the revenues necessary to finance the R&D efforts crucial to their future. This realization prompted the largest firms to extend their foreign operations and to seek ways to reduce barriers impeding their sizable intrafirm trade flows.[212] As part of this, the French producers also increased their technical agreements with foreign producers in an effort to acquire new technology and/or foreign outlets.[213] The success of this internationalization increased the industry's insertion into the global economy and provided a key means for dealing with its economic problems.

The second element in the pharmaceutical industry's strategy was to increase firm size by consolidating the industry. The large firms believed that only further growth would enable them to be competitive with the giant Swiss, German, and U.S. firms that dominated the industry globally. This view led to acquisitions of smaller labs by the big producers as well as acquisitions by large firms outside the industry.[214] These efforts were initially not favored by the French government, but by the late 1970s the government had become a full partner in

[211] EC, *First* and *Second Annual Report on Anti-Dumping and Anti-Subsidy Activities*; interviews.

[212] *Info Chimie*, no. 238 (June 1983):127; DAFSA, *L'Industrie Mondiale*, intro. and pp. 1, 53, 68; Sigvard, *Médicament*, pp. 282-83; *Les Echos*, May 2, 1983, p. 7; *Le Matin*, June 22, 1978; *Le Figaro*, October 21, 1977; *Economie-Géographie*, no. 151 (February 1978):3-4.

[213] DAFSA, *L'Industrie Mondiale*, pp. 70-74; *Economie-Géographie*, no. 151 (February 1978):10.

[214] Sigvard, *Médicament*, pp. 43-47; *Le Monde*, May 24, 1973; *Le Monde*, January 22, 1980, p. 43; *Le Monde*, April 11, 1980; *Les Echos*, supplement, February 28, 1979; *Les Echos*, May 20, 1980.

these efforts. In the plan agreed to in 1980, the industry reorganized itself around the largest four firms and increased its concentration and competitiveness.[215] The French pharmaceutical industry's response to its economic difficulties in the 1970s did not involve protectionism. Its efforts were focused on lowering the barriers to trade both in France and within the EC. Its attempts to reduce price controls, relax national regulations and standards, and harmonize procedures in Europe contributed to freer trade, and its own strategies of internationalization and consolidation aimed at restoring its competitiveness. The industry's growing interests in trade liberalization were related directly to its growing international operations. The fact that close to 70 percent of its revenues came from foreign sales made foreign markets crucially important to the industry.

CASE 5: TIRES

The French have one of the largest, most powerful tire industries in the world. In 1974 they were the world's third largest tire producer, after the United States and Japan.[216] France's strong position was due to one firm, Michelin. It controlled the French market and accounted for about 50 percent of all sales in 1974. It also dominated the European market, where it held 31 percent of the market there in 1973.[217] Moreover, Michelin rose from being the third largest world producer in 1973 with 14 percent of the global market to being a close runner-up to the number one firm, Goodyear, in 1982 with 18 percent of the market.[218] The story of the French tire industry, and indeed the European one as well, in the 1970s, was largely the story of Michelin, since the only other French producer, Kléber-Colombes, was partially controlled by Michelin.

Michelin played a central role in the industry globally. Worldwide, the industry was concentrated; the five largest producers held over 65 percent of the global market by the late 1970s, and this concentration was increasing.[219] Until the mid-1970s, world competition involved

---

[215] *Les Echos*, supplement, February 28, 1979, pp. 71-78; *Journal des Finances*, February 12, 1981. Concentration within the industry rose over the decade; in 1970, the biggest firms held about 35 percent of the market; by the end they accounted for 75 percent. *La Vie Française*, June 16, 1980.

[216] EC, *Etude sur l'Evolution de la Concentration dans l'Industrie des Pneus en France* (Brussels: EC, August 1977), p. 11.

[217] EC, *Etude sur l'Industrie des Pneus*, pp. 17, 22; *La Vie Française*, February 8, 1973.

[218] *La Vie Française*, February 8, 1973; *L'Expansion*, June 22-July 5, 1984, pp. 76-77.

[219] DAFSA, *L'Industrie Mondiale des Pneumatiques* (Paris: DAFSA, 1980), intro. and p. 1.

two American firms, Goodyear and Firestone, and Michelin.[220] After this, the market underwent a dramatic restructuring, mainly because of Michelin's aggressive strategy.

In the early 1970s, Michelin began fiercely marketing the new radial tires and internationalizing in an attempt to gain market share. This strategy was successful, but it upset the industry's structure. Michelin moved into new markets, acquired larger market shares, and became the world's largest radial producer.[221] It also helped bring about the radial revolution, which caught other firms unprepared. The rapid consumer shift to radials, combined with the recessions caused in part by the oil shocks, led to the demise of numerous large and small tire makers. By the early 1980s, all of the American firms, except Goodyear, and all of the European firms, except Michelin, were in retreat. The market now centered around the intense, global competition of Goodyear, Michelin, and the Japanese firm, Bridgestone.[222] The tire industry in France and elsewhere was thus restructured during the 1970s, becoming increasingly international and concentrated.

The French tire industry experienced severe economic distress in the 1970s as well as rising foreign competition due to the oil crises and the change to radials. Radial production required huge capital investments in new facilities, and the oil shortage flattened consumer demand for autos and thus for tires. These problems squeezed industry profits and induced overcapacity, plant closures, and falling employment. The difficulties were particularly evident between 1974 and 1977 and between 1980 and 1985.[223] Tire production grew until 1975, then leveled off, and began falling by the decade's end.[224] Employment in the industry fell in the last half of the 1970s, although for Kléber it dropped severely between 1970 and 1975.[225]

Problems were even worse after 1979. Michelin, though hurt in France during the first recession, was spared worse damage because of its lead in radial technology and its strong sales abroad. After 1979, this changed, and Michelin, like Kléber, closed plants, laid off increasing numbers of workers, and encountered mounting financial losses,

---

[220] *Economie-Géographie*, no. 125 (June 1975):4.

[221] *L'Expansion*, June 22-July 5, 1984, pp. 75-76; *Les Echos*, December 28, 1977; DAFSA, *L'Industrie des Pneus*, pp. 80-84, 93.

[222] *L'Expansion*, June 22-July 5, 1984, pp. 75-77; *La Vie Francaise*, May 4, 1981.

[223] DAFSA, *L'Industrie des Pneus*, intro., pp. 3-4, 20, 28; EC, *Etude sur l'Industrie des Pneus*, pp. 11-18; *Les Echos*, December 28, 1977; *Le Figaro*, August 1, 1985, p. 11.

[224] INSEE, *Annuaire Statistique*, 1983, p. 536; EC, *Etude sur l'Industrie des Pneus*, pp. 11-18; *La Vie Française*, May 8, 1978, p. 23; *Economie-Géographie*, no. 125 (June 1975):9.

[225] INSEE, *Annuaire Statistique*, 1983, p. 533; EC, *Etude sur l'Industrie des Pneus*, pp. 30-34.

especially after 1981.[226] Indeed, every tire producer suffered: sales in France fell 18 percent, exports dropped 13 percent, and 10,000 jobs were lost in the industry between 1980 and 1983.[227] Excess capacity and losses also forced several firms out of business in France—e.g., Dunlop and Uniroyal.[228]

Foreign competition also intensified over this period. Tire imports into France increased fourfold in value between 1973 and 1981.[229] Imports claimed a growing share of the domestic market. In 1970, they held 10 percent of domestic consumption; by 1979 they claimed 21 percent.[230] In addition, the nature of this competition changed, becoming more threatening. Early in the decade, imports had come almost entirely from other European countries; these imports were usually high quality, specialized tires. By the late 1970s, the competition involved large volumes of low-priced tires imported from East Asia or Eastern Europe.[231] Foreign tire competition in France thus accelerated and shifted ominously over the decade, which created serious problems for the French producers and made them likely to seek protection.

Tire manufacturing was a Type III industry. Both its trade dependence and multinationality were substantial and growing over the decade. Moreover, the French producers took part in its rising internationalization.

Export trade in the French tire industry was extensive, and increasingly so, over the 1970s. France exported more tires as a percentage of its total tire production than any other country.[232] Not surprisingly, the industry's trade balance was positive in the decade. While imports experienced significant growth, exports began at a substantial level and rose rapidly until the early 1980s.[233] As a proportion of domestic production, exports of tires climbed from 40 percent in the early 1970s to nearly 50 percent by 1979, revealing the industry's sizable

---

[226] *Le Figaro*, August 1, 1985, p. 11; *Le Monde*, April 21, 1984; *Le Matin*, July 6, 1984; *L'Expansion*, June 22-July 5, 1985, pp. 75, 77-78; *Les Echos*, May 5, 1980; *La Vie Française*, July 21, 1980; *La Vie Française*, February 4-10, 1985, p. 41; *Wall Street Journal*, December 12, 1984, p. 34.

[227] *Le Monde*, April 11, 1984; *Le Monde*, April 19, 1984; *La Vie Française*, March 14-20, 1983, p. 34; *Quotidien de Paris*, February 16, 1985.

[228] *L'Expansion*, June 22-July 5, 1984, pp. 75-76; *Les Echos*, August 23, 1979.

[229] French Customs Service data.

[230] Unpublished INSEE data.

[231] French Customs Service data; EC, *Etude sur l'Industrie des Pneus*, p. 18; DAFSA, *L'Industrie des Pneus*, p. 52; *Le Nouvel Economiste*, no. 503, August 23, 1985, p. 40.

[232] DAFSA, *L'Industrie des Pneus*, pp. 49-51.

[233] French Customs Service data.

overall dependence on exports.²³⁴ For Michelin, over 36 percent of its total sales in 1970 were due to its exports,²³⁵ and this percentage increased as the firm internationalized. Indeed, Michelin probably accounted for a large part of both French imports and French exports of tires. Through its integrated global production strategy, the firm shipped tires to and from about ninety countries.²³⁶

In terms of multinationality, the tire makers also revealed their integration into the world market. Foreign production by the French firms was large, accounting for almost 15 percent of total production in 1974,²³⁷ a proportion that was the second largest among all sectors of the nation's industry.²³⁸ This foreign production was highly integrated and profitable,²³⁹ and production abroad rose during the 1970s. For Michelin, multinational operations were crucial. Michelin began its internationalization early; by 1970 it had seventeen plants outside of France.²⁴⁰ Between 1970 and 1974, this number rose to twenty-two, as the firm advanced into Canada and the United States.²⁴¹ By 1974, Michelin was the third largest multinational in France. It had close to 60 percent of its total employees located outside France and realized about 50 percent of its total sales abroad.²⁴² During the decade this multinationality increased further, so that by 1980, the firm had thirty-five plants worldwide and almost 70 percent of its revenues from operations outside France.²⁴³

²³⁴ DAFSA, *L'Industrie des Pneus*, pp. 49-51, 94; *Economie-Géographie*, no. 125 (June 1975):7; EC, *Etude sur l'Industrie des Pneus*, p. 18. These figures understate the actual importance of exports since they do not include indirect tire exports—i.e., those already on French cars or trucks sold outside of the country. *Economie-Géographie*, no. 125 (June 1975).

²³⁵ *La Vie Française*, October 8, 1971.

²³⁶ *Entreprise*, no. 941, September 21, 1973, p. 81; *L'Humanité*, December 1, 1981; Michelin, unpublished corporate documents, 1985; interviews. The other firms in the French market also moved different types of tires around Europe to balance production and demand. Kléber and the other producers—most of whom were foreign multinationals—thus contributed to the sizable trade flows of tires in and out of France. Interviews; DAFSA, *L'Industrie des Pneus*.

²³⁷ Savary, *Multinationales Françaises*, p. 28.

²³⁸ Ibid.

²³⁹ See note 236; see also Savary, *Multinationales Françaises*, pp. 90-91, 171.

²⁴⁰ *Entreprise*, no. 941, September 21, 1973, pp. 71, 73; *La Vie Française*, September 18, 1970.

²⁴¹ *Le Monde Diplomatique*, June 1974.

²⁴² Savary, "Multinationales Françaises," p. 76; "Les Multinationales," p. 23; *Le Monde Diplomatique*, June 1974; Alain Jemain, *Michelin: Un Siècle des Sécrets* (Paris: Calmann-Lévy, 1982), pp. 210-23.

²⁴³ *L'Humanité*, June 10, 1980; Jemain, *Michelin*, pp. 230-36. Michelin's movement abroad in the 1970s was partly offensive and partly defensive. The firm's technological

Michelin also had very integrated production operations. It operated a complex web of international facilities that greatly depended on intrafirm trade flows.[244] This web was especially important in Europe. Michelin was largely responsible for the tire trade among France, Spain, Italy, and West Germany. Indeed, its plants in these countries exported close to 50 percent of their production, most going to Europe or the United States.[245] Michelin was thus a central force in tire trade and production globally.

Because they were its main source of profits in the 1970s, these foreign operations were of crucial importance for the firm. François Michelin, the firm's largest owner and its director, stated that without its foreign plants and sales, the company would have gone bankrupt in France.[246] The greater profitability of these foreign operations not only made them essential to the firm but also encouraged their growth at the expense of French operations. By the end of the decade, Michelin was the largest multinational in tire production.[247]

The other French tire maker, Kléber-Colombes, was also a multinational, although smaller than Michelin. In 1975, Kléber earned 37 percent of its revenues outside France.[248] This percentage rose as the

---

advantages prompted it to adopt an aggressive marketing strategy, which targeted the North American market since this was the least "radialized." Michelin built plants in Canada to service the entire continent in the early 1970s, but the firm eventually moved into the United States as part of a more defensive strategy. Michelin's Canadian exports to the United States exploded, and several American tire producers launched a trade complaint. When in 1973 duties on its imports to the United States were raised as a result of this complaint, Michelin began U.S. production. By 1977, it held 8 percent of the American tire market, which made it the third or fourth largest producer there. *L'Express*, July 27, 1970; *Entreprise*, no. 941, September 21, 1973, pp. 73, 75; *L'Expansion*, September 7-20, 1979, p. 108; *Financial Times*, July 14, 1971; *NYT*, October 8, 1972; *Le Monde*, October 6, 1972; *London Times*, May 6, 1973; Jemain, *Michelin*, pp. 210-23; *L'Expansion*, June 22-July 5, 1984, pp. 76-77.

[244] *La Vie Française*, July 21, 1980; EC, *Etude sur l'Industrie des Pneus*, pp. 30-33; *Le Nouveau Journal*, September 16, 1970.

[245] DAFSA, *L'Industrie des Pneus*, pp. 53-55; EC, *Etude sur l'Industrie des Pneus*, pp. 11-18.

[246] *La Vie Française*, May 8, 1978, p. 23.

[247] Even in comparison to the large American firms, it was unique, having over 50 percent of production abroad compared to Goodyear's 44 percent and Goodrich's 22 percent, which indicated the full range of the American firms' multinationality. DAFSA, *L'Industrie des Pneus*, pp. 53-56, 33; *Economie et Politique*, no. 240 (July 1974):32-45.

[248] EC, *Etude sur l'Industrie des Pneus*, p. 34. In essence, Kléber operated as an independent firm, but throughout the 1970s Michelin had a growing interest in it. Only in the early 1980s, when Kléber ran into severe economic difficulties, did Michelin assume management control over it. Prior to this, however, Kléber acted in fact as an autonomous French tire manufacturer. *Entreprise*, no. 941, September 21, 1973, p. 71; *International Herald Tribune*, September 17, 1980; Jemain, *Michelin*, pp. 137-55.

firm branched out in Europe, and by 1980, the proportion had reached 54 percent.[249] Kléber limited its operations to Europe and had substantial trade flows as well among its subsidiaries.[250]

The French industry, in addition to being multinational, was penetrated by foreign capital. This foreign presence accounted for about 48 percent of the industry's total investment in 1974.[251] Before 1979, of the top seven French producers, five were foreign and were subsidiaries of some of the world's largest tire firms—e.g., Goodyear, Firestone, Dunlop, and Uniroyal.[252] The industry's poor economic fortunes during the decade altered the character, but not the extent, of this foreign presence, leaving only three foreign producers in France: Goodyear, Continental, and Sumitomo.[253] It also left the industry in France and Europe more concentrated, with four firms controlling the market and with Michelin the clear leader in Europe.[254]

The Dependent Variable

What was most striking about the French tire industry's response to its economic difficulties between 1974 and 1982 was that despite the severity of its economic situation, it resorted little to demanding public help from either the French government or the EC. The industry chose to adjust through its own mechanisms.

The tire industry's economic crisis did not lead to greater "concertation" between the manufacturers and the French government. The relationship between these two groups has never been extensive or amicable in the postwar period, largely as a consequence of the problems between Michelin and the government.[255] Unlike most large French firms, Michelin has not had a special relationship with the government; indeed, Michelin has avoided having anything to do with it. This attitude comes from the company's family owners and directors. The long line of Michelins who control the firm has always distrusted the government—whether on the right or left—and preferred to op-

---

[249] *Les Echos*, May 5, 1980.

[250] *Entreprise*, no. 941, September 21, 1973, p. 82.

[251] Savary, "Multinationales Françaises," p. 258.

[252] DAFSA, *L'Industrie des Pneus*, pp. 96-100, 103, 109, 112-13.

[253] After 1979, Uniroyal and Firestone pulled out of Europe altogether, the first selling its operations to a German firm, Continental, and the second simply ending production. Later, Dunlop ended its operations in France, selling them to the Japanese firm, Sumitomo. *L'Expansion*, June 22-July 5, 1984, pp. 75-76; *Financial Times*, June 4, 1985; *Les Echos*, August 23, 1979; *L'Usine Nouvelle*, no. 21, May 24, 1979; *Le Monde*, April 11, 1984; *La Vie Française*, May 4, 1981.

[254] DAFSA, *L'Industrie des Pneus*, pp. 109-113.

[255] Jemain, *Michelin*, chs. 10, 11.

erate independently of any political organization. Largely self-financed and privately owned, Michelin has long operated in a cloud of secrecy.[256] In part, this independent posture has allowed the firm to continue its conservative style of management without interference from unions or the state.

Michelin's attitude toward the government was backed by its actions. Despite mounting imports and rising difficulties in the 1970s, the firm did not go to the government and demand any aid. It did not ask for protection against either imports or new foreign investments; Michelin did not desire any type of protectionism. In fact, Michelin officials maintained protection was "not the right way to go" because it would lead to more government interference and because it would upset the firm's international operations and reduce its competitiveness.[257] Michelin's concern with the international market and its desire to remain independent led it to resist any urge to protect its home market.

In terms of industrial policy measures, the firm also avoided contact with the French government. Michelin's development of the radial tire and its large investment program abroad were financed independently of the French Treasury. The firm used its own cash flows and organized a large international loan to finance these massive investments.[258] In addition, Michelin never demanded any form of subsidy or aid from the government in the 1970s. No "plan" for the industry existed, and none was desired.[259]

The other firms in the industry also had little to do with the French government. All the others, save Kléber, were foreign owned and tended to have less contact with the government. The French government did give aid to Dunlop-France in 1982. It is unclear, however, whether Dunlop requested this. The firm desired to sell its operations,

---

[256] *L'Expansion*, September 7-20, 1979, pp. 101-108; *L'Expansion*, June 22-July 5, 1984, p. 82; *L'Express*, July 27, 1970, pp. 51-52; *Le Monde Diplomatique*, June 1974; Jemain, *Michelin*, pp. 154-59, 161-67, 170-73. The firm even refused to allow President de Gaulle to visit its factories, and it pulled out of the main industry organization, the CNPF, in 1968 after condemning it for accepting the union demands involved in the Grenelle Accords. Moreover, many have speculated that Michelin internationalized with such a vengeance to escape the confines of the French government and was keen to operate in the United States where its philosophy was better accepted. Jemain, *Michelin*, pp. 154-59, 161, 216-23; interviews; *Entreprise*, no. 941, September 21, 1973, p. 84; *Le Monde Diplomatique*, June 1974; *L'Expansion*, September 7-20, 1979, pp. 101-108.

[257] Interview.

[258] *L'Express*, July 27, 1970, pp. 51-52; *Le Monde Diplomatique*, June 1974; *L'Expansion*, June 22-July 5, 1984, p. 82.

[259] Jemain, *Michelin*, pp. 154-59, 161-67; *Les Echos*, August 23, 1979; *L'Expansion*, September 7-20, 1979, pp. 101-108; interviews.

but the only interested buyers were foreign. The French government did not want a foreign purchaser but wanted to preserve employment in the area. After Michelin refused to purchase Dunlop's operation, the government found another answer. The compromise was to give Dunlop money to enable it to continue. This proved an ephemeral solution: Dunlop sold out to Sumitomo, the Japanese firm, in 1984.[260]

The other area of government intervention involved Kléber, which fell into deep trouble in the late 1970s and recorded growing losses each year. As rumors of bankruptcy spread, Kléber began seeking a buyer. Once again, the French government desired a "French solution"; it did not want a foreign buyer. When the German firm, Continental, agreed to buy a controlling interest in 1979, the government nevertheless acceded, accepting a "European solution." This deal fell through in 1980, however, as Continental grew fearful of Kléber's huge and mounting losses. Michelin at this point decided to try to sell its large interest in Kléber to a Japanese firm. The French government rejected this sale and instead forced Michelin to increase its holding in Kléber. In the battle, the government proposed to inject new funds into Kléber if Michelin would take it over. Though unhappy about them, Michelin finally accepted these terms.[261]

Except for the interventions in Dunlop and Kléber, which were not the firms' first preferences, the tire industry received and demanded little government aid. Despite growing import penetration, the firms never sought protection, which they viewed as more of a problem than a solution. In terms of industrial policy, the government appeared more eager to offer help than the firms were to receive it. No industrial plan was ever sought or designed; all the interventions were ad hoc and frequently government-initiated. Moreover, the interventions

---

[260] Le Monde, April 11, 1984; Le Matin, October 11, 1983.

[261] Jemain, Michelin, pp. 243-55; International Herald Tribune, September 17, 1980; Les Echos, November 14, 1980; L'Humanité, December 1, 1981; Le Monde, April 19, 1984; Le Figaro, March 7, 1985. In 1984, Michelin's forced marriage to Kléber and its own difficulties prompted it to seek government help. When Michelin announced 5,000 layoffs that year, all located in the region around Clermont-Ferrand, the regional government offered to help Michelin and encouraged it to contact the national government to get further aid. Some months later, Michelin entered into negotiations with the national government for the first time ever; it attempted to secure loans at preferential rates. Thus Michelin succumbed finally to seeking aid from the French government, but only after being forced to take over the unprofitable Kléber by the government. See Le Point, no. 530, November 15, 1982, pp. 125-26; Wall Street Journal, December 12, 1984, p. 34; L'Expansion, June 22-July 5, 1984, pp. 77-78; Le Monde, April 21, 1984; Le Matin, July 6, 1984; Le Monde, August 19-20, 1984; L'Express, April 26, 1985, p. 34.

were not in the least intended to restrict foreign trade; they aimed most at preserving employment in France.

At the European level, the industry's dearth of activity was also evident. In spite of mounting import penetration by East European and East Asian products, the industry made little attempt to halt this trade. Some of its activities were even aimed at further opening the market. During the GATT Tokyo Round negotiations, the European tire manufacturers offered to cut their tariffs by more than the accepted percentage if other countries would likewise reduce their barriers to trade. The industry also sought greater harmonization of industrial classifications with other countries in order to facilitate trade. And it did not seek to have the GSP status of products from its leading importers ended; this special status, allowing East European and East Asian tires to enter with almost no duty at all, was a major factor contributing to these imports' growth.[262] All of this suggests the industry's resistance to protectionism and its interest in open markets. As EC officials stated, if Michelin did not like the policies adopted, it would only have to make that known for them to be changed.[263] Apparently, Michelin had no such objections to these trade-liberalizing measures.

In terms of unfair trade complaints, the tire manufacturers also were inactive at the European level. Before 1979, no complaints of any sort were ever lodged by the industry.[264] In general, the tire industry was little involved with the EC. Michelin maintained its policy of avoiding public attention and governmental, whether French or EC, involvement, and tended to solve problems on its own. Being oligopolistic and well organized, the producers had little need for EC help. Indeed, as one EC official stated, the EC needed the manufacturers more than they needed it, since all reliable data on the industry available to the EC came from the producers themselves.[265] The EC's ma-

---

[262] *Le Monde*, April 19, 1984; DAFSA, *L'Industrie des Pneus*, p. 52; interviews.

[263] Interviews.

[264] Ibid. In 1979, however, a dumping complaint against four East European countries was lodged. The source of this complaint was apparently the British Rubber Manufacturers Association (BRMA), which was run primarily by Pirelli-UK, Goodyear-UK, Dunlop, and Avon Tires. The EC pursued this complaint, eventually finding for it. Duties were never raised since the countries agreed to raise their prices to some acceptable level. This complaint was not of major importance and did little to reduce imports from these countries. Imports have continued to flood the Community, yet no new complaints have been made to date. EC, *First Annual Report on Anti-Dumping and Anti-Subsidy Procedures*; EC, *JOCE*, no. 113, May 1, 1980, pp. 70-73; interviews; DAFSA, *L'Industrie des Pneus*, p. 52; *Le Monde*, April 19, 1984; *Le Nouvel Economiste*, no. 503, August 23, 1985, p. 40.

[265] Interviews.

jor contacts with the industry were adversarial and involved investigations of its anticompetitive behavior.[266]

The most important means by which the French tire manufacturers responded to their economic distress in the 1970s were internal. Both Kléber and Michelin sought to deal with the new conditions in the industry on their own, and their strategies emphasized renewed competitiveness and not protection against competition. For Kléber, the strategy was initially to internationalize further; in the early 1970s, hoping to expand its scale economies and capture new sales, it moved into new foreign markets.[267] The failure of this strategy led in the late 1970s to attempts to find a suitable buyer, a large firm to take over its operations. Kléber, despite its near bankruptcy, never sought protection against foreign competition, and chose instead to exit the industry.[268]

Michelin's strategy in the 1970s had two main elements. First, like Kléber, it sought to increase its presence abroad in order to become one of the world's leading producers. Michelin aggressively promoted its radial tires throughout the world. Exports and foreign production were used to capture market share worldwide. The firm's movement into the United States was viewed as absolutely necessary if Michelin was to remain a world-class competitor. Michelin's strategy was to compete as hard as it could wherever it could, moving abroad to meet the challenge.[269]

The second element in Michelin's strategy involved the acquisition and maintenance of a monopolistic position within the European market. By the early 1970s, the firm already controlled 60 percent of the sales in France and over 30 percent in Europe, and also held a dominant market position in nearly every European country.[270] Michelin maintained this dominance through a variety of means, none of which included protectionism.

A central method involved the creation of strong ties with tire dealers. The firm even bought an interest in these dealer networks, so that

[266] Ibid.

[267] *Les Echos*, May 5, 1980; Jemain, *Michelin*, pp. 246-52.

[268] *International Herald Tribune*, September 17, 1980; Jemain, *Michelin*, pp. 251-55.

[269] Jemain, *Michelin*, pp. 177-85, 212-27; interviews. This strategy was successful until 1982. Michelin moved heavily abroad in the 1970s and increased its global market share significantly. The problems it began facing after 1982, moreover, seemed to have led *not* to the abandonment of this strategy but to a temporary hiatus in order to regroup. Jemain, *Michelin*, pp. 225-36, 258-61; interviews.

[270] *La Vie Française*, June 19, 1970, and February 8, 1973.

by 1973 it controlled directly some 30 percent of all European sales.[271] A second way of holding market share involved the industry's primary customer, the automobile industry. Being the largest tire buyers, auto manufacturers were a primary target for Michelin's attentions and held the dominant position in this relationship. Michelin did, however, own a large portion of Citroën, the number three French car maker, during the 1970s. Not surprisingly, it sold Citroën 100 percent of the tires it needed.[272] But this was unusual for the industry. In both France and the United States, the relationship between tire and auto manufacturers tended to be distant and adversarial, because the auto firms liked to get the best price possible by playing suppliers off against one another. Hence, even Michelin's relationship with the main French car producer, Renault, was not marked by any cooperation. In this case, a possible means of protection through government procurement policies—i.e., to require Renault to buy only Michelin tires—was not employed.[273]

In conclusion, the French tire industry, with its extensive foreign trade and production activities, chose to adjust to foreign competition and not to protect itself in the 1970s. The industry's strong international ties prevented it from seeking protection either in France or in Europe. Led by Michelin, the industry avoided public intervention as much as possible and managed its problems through its own internal strategies.

CASE 6: RADIOS AND TELEVISIONS

In the early 1970s the production of radios and televisions in France was controlled by three firms, only one of which, Thomson-Brandt, was French.[274] The other two were Radiotechnique, owned by Philips,

[271] This arrangement and other exclusive sales deals were disliked by the EC, which received numerous complaints about Michelin's behavior. The firm evidently promised to sell its high quality tires to dealers only if they refused to sell certain other tires. Michelin saw this as a way to retain its high quality image, but this policy had a way of limiting other firms' sales. Indeed, one East European tire maker went bankrupt because its European dealer went out of business when Michelin refused to sell to it. Interviews; *Entreprise*, no. 941, September 21, 1973, p. 81.

[272] *Entreprise*, no. 941, September 21, 1973, p. 73; *L'Expansion*, September 7-20, 1979, p. 104; Jemain, *Michelin*, pp. 187-203; DAFSA, *L'Industrie des Pneus*, pp. 46-47.

[273] DAFSA, *L'Industrie des Pneus*, pp. 46-47; *Entreprise*, no. 941, September 21, 1973, p. 82; Jemain, *Michelin*, pp. 190-207, 213-27, 234-36; interviews.

[274] DAFSA, *L'Industrie des Téléviseurs en Europe* (Paris: DAFSA, 1975), p. 64; *Stratégies*, no. 227, May 26-June 1, 1980, p. 61; EC, *Etude sur L'Industrie de l'Electronique Grand Public en Europe* (Brussels: EC, 1978), pp. 146-51.

and Oceanic, controlled by ITT. Thomson-Brandt held about 40 percent of the French market in 1973, but this share dropped in the late 1970s, as Radiotechnique and imports grabbed increasing market share.[275] The French radio and television manufacturers had developed late and, despite being protected, they had never become strong international competitors.

Throughout the late 1960s and into the early 1970s, producers of radios and televisions in France operated profitably as a result of strong import barriers. When these barriers were reduced and new products, such as color televisions, were introduced that were not controlled by these barriers, the situation began to deteriorate for the French producers. The industry suffered simultaneously from reduced demand, sharp technological changes, and vigorous foreign competition. These difficulties, manifested in declining firm numbers, falling employment, and low profitability,[276] were apparent even among its largest producers. Radiotechnique was forced to restructure its operations, close several plants, and lay off large numbers of workers twice in the 1970s.[277] Thomson-Brandt fared poorly after 1976 as its profits fell.[278]

Foreign competition also plagued the industry. Over the 1970s the French radio and television producers lost control of their market to imports. The value of imports quadrupled between 1973 and 1980, and imports' share of the domestic market rose from 17 percent in 1970 to 39 percent in 1979 and to 50 percent by 1983.[279] These figures suggest the magnitude of the import invasion that the industry faced in the decade and the likelihood of its seeking protection.

[275] EC, *Etude sur L'Electronique Grand Public*, pp. 272-73; Arthur D. Little (ADL), *Analyse des Marchés et des Grandes Tendances Technologiques dans le Domaine de l'Electronique Grand Public* (Paris: Ministère de l'Industrie, 1979), p. 84, table 19.

[276] EC, *Etude sur L'Electronique Grand Public*, pp. 70-72, 83, 86, 91-92, 97-100, 271-73; SIMAVELEC, *L'Electronique Grand Public Français en 1983-84* (Paris: SIMAVELEC, 1985), p. 6; DAFSA, *Electronique Grand Public* (Paris: DAFSA, 1983), p. 145, 161. DAFSA, *L'Industrie Mondiale des Appareil de Radio, Télévision, et Electroacoustique* (Paris: DAFSA, 1978), pp. 63, 66.

[277] *Les Echos*, March 27, 1973; *Le Figaro*, November 26, 1974; *Les Echos*, January 14, 1981; *Les Echos*, January 21, 1981.

[278] *Le Figaro*, November 26, 1974; *Les Echos*, March 11, 1977; *Le Monde*, September 24, 1977; *L'Expansion*, January 25-February 7, 1980, p. 70.

[279] French Customs Service data; unpublished INSEE data (1970, 1979); *Libération*, March 11, 1982. For radios, imports grew from 39 percent of the market in 1970 to close to 90 percent in 1977. Imports of black and white televisions surged from 9 percent of the French market in 1970 to 34 percent in 1979. Color television imports augmented their share of the market from 6 percent in 1970 to 18 percent in 1979. DAFSA, *L'Industrie Mondiale des Appareil*, pp. 24-25; *Politique Hebdo*, October 17, 1977; DAFSA, *L'Industrie des Téléviseurs*, pp. 16-20; *Stratégies*, no. 227, May 26-June 1, 1980, p. 60.

The industry's links to the international economy were weak, especially before the late 1970s. French radio and television manufacture was a Type I industry before the mid-1970s but a Type IV after that. The French industry had been sheltered from foreign competition from its inception. These protectionist policies, in particular the adoption of a different standard for television reception and broadcasting (the SECAM system), limited French exports since French televisions were unusable elsewhere. The policies also limited French foreign operations; the French could not produce under other systems in foreign countries because they did not possess the know-how or the licenses to these technologies.[280] The industry was thus created behind artificial barriers, which in turn restricted its international development.

French radio and television manufacturers did not have strong trade ties to the international economy. The industry's trade balance grew increasingly negative over the decade. Even though exports grew, increases in imports overwhelmed this growth.[281] Exports did not amount to a significant part of total industry production; in 1972, their share of the French market was a mere 3.7 percent.[282] Moreover, the French share of the European and global market in radios and televisions was low and falling in the 1970s.[283]

At the firm level, exports were also unimportant. The consumer products section of Thomson-Brandt exported at most 17 percent of its production in 1976, and much of this was television parts and other nonrelated goods.[284] In addition, Thomson's exports were directed to-

[280] Rhonda Crane, *The Politics of International Standards* (Norwood, N.J.: ABLEX, 1979), chs. 3-6; *Usine Nouvelle*, no. 26, June 30, 1977, pp. 30-31.

[281] French Customs Service data; DAFSA, *L'Industrie Mondiale des Appareils*, pp. 33-35; *Les Echos*, June 5, 1979; Stoffaës, *Grande Menace Industrielle*, p. 226. From a low level, exports tripled between 1973 and 1980.

[282] DAFSA, *L'Industrie des Téléviseurs*, pp. 37, 48. The French exported very few radios, and between 4 and 5 percent of their consumption of televisions in the 1970s. *Stratégies*, no. 227, May 26-June 1, 1980, p. 60; EC, *Etude sur l'Electronique Grand Public*, pp. 122, 123, 125.

[283] DAFSA, *L'Industrie des Téléviseurs*, p. 37, 48. In 1978, French products accounted for a mere 4 percent of all European television and radio exports; by 1983, for 2 percent. DAFSA, *L'Industrie Mondiale des Appareils*, p. 5; DAFSA, *Electronique Grand Public*, p. 61.

[284] Figures for the firms are problematic. For Thomson-Brandt as a whole (that is, for CSF and Brandt) exports accounted for about 30 percent of production in the 1970s. But this figure overstates greatly the amounts involved in the radio and television sector, since it includes the data for CSF which was a strong, high technology, export-oriented division of Thomson. Brandt produced more mundane consumer goods; it had nowhere near the exports that CSF did. Jean-Marie Fourier, "Développement d'une Entreprise à

ward small countries that were former French colonies; it was not a player in large, competitive foreign markets.[285] Radiotechnique, controlled by the large Dutch multinational Philips, exported nearly 40 percent of its total sales in the early 1970s. Much of this trade, however, was with its parent firm.[286] Radiotechnique was thus a more important exporter; but, like the French firm, many of its exports were not destined for sale in competitive world markets.

The French industry's multinationality was restricted. The French producers had neither the technological edge nor the presence in foreign markets that might have induced foreign production. The industry's overall direct foreign investment position was limited. The percentage of foreign production to total production for the sector in 1974 was 4.1, one of the lowest for all French industrial sectors.[287] Indeed, before 1974 Thomson-Brandt's radio and television division had no production capacity outside of France.[288]

In the early 1970s, Thomson-Brandt changed its strategy, deciding that the only way to remain in business was to increase its size and produce abroad. In particular, the firm saw the European market as its target and set out in the mid-1970s to "Europeanize" its operations.[289] The firm accelerated its expansion abroad toward the end of the decade, so that by 1983 it controlled over 20 percent of the European television market.[290] This expansion made Thomson the second largest radio and television producer in Europe, behind Philips, and among the top ten producers globally.[291]

Vocation Internationale," *Humanité et Entreprise*, no. 106 (December 1977): 41-43, 48-49; Groupe ESCP, "Le Développement International," p. 13.

[285] Fourier, "Développement d'une Entreprise," pp. 48-49; *Stratégies*, no. 227, May 26-June 1, 1980, p. 62; EC, *Etude sur L'Electronique Grand Public*, p. 108.

[286] Over one-third of its French exports were sent to other subsidiaries of Philips in Europe. Furthermore, much of its exports were radios or parts for televisions to be processed outside of France. *Les Echos*, March 27, 1973.

[287] Savary, *Multinationales Françaises*, pp. 28-29. Other reports note the feebleness and tardiness of foreign investment by French firms in this sector. Michel Delapierre in *L'Intégration de l'Economie Française*, ed. Michalet, p. 92; interviews; Stoffaës, *Grande Menace Industrielle*, pp. 189-90.

[288] DAFSA, *L'Industrie Mondiale des Appareils*, pp. 49-52, 56; interviews.

[289] DAFSA, *Electronique Grand Public*, pp. 80-82; interview; *L'Expansion*, January 25-February 7, 1980, pp. 68-69; EC, *Etude sur L'Electronique Grand Public*, pp. 100-101; *L'Express*, June 2-8, 1979, pp. 94-95; *Usine Nouvelle*, no. 40, October 6, 1977, pp. 52-53.

[290] *Le Monde*, September 24, 1977; *La Vie Française*, March 14-20, 1983, p. 33; *Financial Times*, March 25, 1980; *Usine Nouvelle*, no. 40, October 6, 1977, pp. 52-53; *Libération*, March 11, 1983; *Usine Nouvelle*, no. 11, March 17, 1983, pp. 64-65.

[291] Christian Moretti, "Les Restructurations Industrielles en Europe: Le Cas de l' Elec-

Thomson-Brandt's acquisitions in the 1970s made it an important European producer. It had sizable production outside France and a substantial amount of intrafirm trade by 1983, as it exported throughout Europe from its plants in Spain and Germany.[292] But for many reasons Thomson remained a primarily French firm, never finding its foreign operations that important. First, the firm lost money on these foreign acquisitions, and so they were never viewed as integral.[293] Second, Thomson-Brandt never became a leading world producer because it did not innovate. Thomson's strategy was instead to buy the technology from other foreign producers or to import the products.[294] For these reasons, Thomson-Brandt, while possessing substantial European operations by the 1980s, still depended heavily on its home market. At most, Thomson-Brandt was an important European producer by the 1980s; however, its role outside of Europe was minimal. The French industry's multinational ties were therefore limited and less extensive than foreign operations in the French market.

A large number of foreign firms were producing radios and televisions in France. Of the three leading firms, two were foreign owned, and by the early 1970s over 50 percent of total investment in the industry was controlled by foreign firms.[295] The foreign firms involved were huge multinationals, such as Philips and ITT. Although controlling a large portion of the French market, they viewed their operations in France as only one small part of their global strategies. Philips, the second largest world producer, controlled 40 percent of the French television market through Radiotechnique, but its operations in France were tiny in comparison to its global capacity.[296] It was a global firm with integrated production operations and an international focus, unlike Thomson-Brandt.[297] This difference between

tronique Grand Public," *Cahiers d'Etudes et de Recherche*, no. 81-16 (1981):24-25; *Le Matin*, September 14, 1981; *Usine Nouvelle*, no. 11, March 17, 1983, pp. 64-65.

[292] EC, *Etude sur L'Electronique Grand Public*, pp. 78-79, 104-109, 113.

[293] *L'Expansion*, January 25-February 7, 1980, p. 69; *La Vie Française*, September 21, 1981, p. 31.

[294] It employed this strategy for color televisions, small televisions, television tubes, and video cassette recorders. *Le Nouvel Economiste*, no. 322, February 1, 1982, p. 52; *La Vie Française*, March 14-20, 1983, p. 33; *Le Figaro*, April 26, 1983; *Le Monde*, January 25-26, 1981; *Les Echos*, May 8, 1981; *L'Expansion*, January 25-February 7, 1980; *La Vie Française*, February 7, 1977, p. 13.

[295] DAFSA, *L'Industrie des Téléviseurs*, p. 68; EC, *Etude sur L'Electronique Grand Public*, pp. 109-112.

[296] EC, *Etude sur L'Electronique Grand Public*, p. 276; DAFSA, *L'Industrie des Téléviseurs*, p. 68.

[297] Moretti, "Les Restructurations Industrielles," pp. 24-25; DAFSA, *L'Industrie des Téléviseurs*, p. 68; *Le Figaro*, January 21, 1981; *La Vie Française*, March 31, 1980.

Thomson and Philips was central to the distinct approaches the two adopted to their similar economic problems.

The Dependent Variable

The industry's responses to the economic challenges of the 1970s were conditioned by its late, sheltered development and its lack of international ties. The industry basically chose to seek greater protection. It sought protection on the national level through trade and industrial policy measures. Gradually, as this national protection became less effective, the industry sought help at the European level. As it developed greater ties to the European economy, the French industry realized its need for protection on an EC-wide basis. Internally, the industry also made efforts to help itself by reorganizing, establishing operations in Europe, and attempting various anti-Japanese alliances.

At the national level, the French radio and television producers demanded and received protection against their main foreign competitors, the Japanese, before the 1970s. In the 1960s, the industry was protected in two ways. Weak and also afraid of Japanese competition, the producers lobbied in the mid-1960s to be included in the set of selective safeguards imposed on Japan as it became a regular GATT member.[298] The industry, and especially Thomson-Brandt, pushed for quotas on Japanese television imports on the grounds that they were necessary for the late-starting French industry to catch up.[299] The producers portrayed themselves as an essential element in the electronics industry and claimed that without profitable, large-scale consumer electronics operations they could not finance or support the substantial R&D costs necessary to a healthy, high technology electronics sector. This demand for protection fit in with the government's desire to create a strong, independent electronics industry.[300] In 1969 the French radio and television producers negotiated their first in a series of quotas with the Japanese. Although backed by the French government, the accords, limiting Japanese television exports to 4 percent of the French market, were negotiated by the industries themselves.[301]

In addition to these quotas, the French also protected the industry

[298] Robert Hine, *The Political Economy of European Trade* (Brighton: Wheatsheaf, 1985), pp. 239-41; *La Vie Française*, November 15-21, 1982, p. 28.

[299] Interviews; Fourier, "Développement d'une Entreprise," p. 52.

[300] *London Times*, November 6, 1982.

[301] European Research Associates (ERA), *EEC Protectionism* (Brussels: ERA, 1982), pp. 197-98, 211; *La Vie Française*, November 15-21, 1982, pp. 28; *La Vie Française*, December 15-21, 1982, pp. 28-30; *L'Expansion*, January 25-February 7, 1980, pp. 68-69.

by technical barriers. The 1960s saw the development of color televisions, and different systems for their operation proliferated. The United States early in the decade adopted one system (NTSC), which was soon taken up by other countries. The Europeans, however, later developed two different systems; the French invented the SECAM system and the Germans, the PAL system. These three were incompatible, and the Europeans fought a long battle over which one would be selected as the Community standard. In the end, no common choice was made; the French used SECAM and most of the rest of Europe adopted PAL.[302] This segmented the world market into three zones, the smallest of which was SECAM's. In this way the French protected their market, for any of the major importers would have to build special SECAM television production facilities in order to export televisions to France. But the French also limited their own capacity to export and reduced incentives to produce in non-SECAM countries, since they did not have licenses to build NTSC or PAL systems.[303]

The French industry's preferences concerning this technical barrier changed over time. It initially favored the decision because of its protective effects and the profits the SECAM licenses generated. But the industry, and Thomson in particular, feared that later when the industry had grown strong in France and needed larger, foreign markets, these would be denied because of the difficulties created by the different standards.[304] The industry's initial ambivalence later changed to outright opposition. In the 1970s, as Thomson grew dominant in France and sought to expand its operations, it pushed for the adoption of a bistandard system, one capable of using either PAL or SECAM.[305] The only way that Thomson could become a European player was through adoption of PAL standards. Apparently, Thomson's demands were heard; in the late 1970s the French government introduced a new television norm, allowing only bistandard televisions to be sold.[306]

Thus beginning in the late 1960s, the French radio and television market was doubly protected, once by quotas and once by the techni-

---

[302] Crane, *Politics of International Standards*, esp. chs. 3-6.

[303] DAFSA, *L'Industrie des Téléviseurs*, p. 3; *Le Figaro*, January 16, 1974; Crane, *Politics of International Standards*, chs. 3-6; Moretti, "Les Restructurations Industrielles," p. 21; *Le Figaro*, June 19, 1975; *Les Echos*, February 12, 1975.

[304] Crane, *Politics of International Standards*, esp. p. 71, also chs. 3-6; *Stratégies*, no. 227, May 26-June 1, 1980, p. 62; *Les Echos*, February 12, 1975; interview.

[305] *Les Echos*, February 12, 1975; interview; Crane, *Politics of International Standards*, chs. 3-6; DAFSA, *Electronique Grand Public*, p. 11.

[306] *Les Echos*, September 20, 1976; *LSA*, March 19, 1982, pp. 88-90. DAFSA, *Electronique Grand Public*, p. 11.

cal standard. This protection, which continued well into the 1970s, did not halt increases in imports. Despite the barriers, imports from Japan and East Asia surged after the mid-1970s.[307] The French firms, dependent on the domestic market, responded to this by demanding help from the French government. The industry sought a new quota with the Japanese in the early 1970s, as the initial one expired. They negotiated an agreement, only to have it challenged as unfair by the EC.[308] With this quota abrogated, the industry lodged safeguard complaints, and the French government used article 115 of the EC's Treaty of Rome to impose formal quotas on Japanese televisions and to begin surveillance of all television imports.[309]

Later, as the Japanese shifted production and export capacity to other East Asian countries, the French industry responded by demanding quotas on imports from South Korea, Taiwan, and Hong Kong. Under the provisions of article 115, new restraints were negotiated.[310] In terms of their preferences for trade policy nationally, the French television producers sought selective protection against East Asian producers, while simultaneously hoping to reduce technical trade barriers within Europe. Selective protection outside the EC and creation of a more unified European market were the goals Thomson pursued to accompany its strategy of "Europeanizing" its operations.

The producers were also involved in industrial policy deliberations. As part of the electronics sector, they took part in the government's attempts to promote it. Indeed, Thomson was selected as the "national champion" in French consumer and professional electronic goods, and Radiotechnique was also active in planning. With the government, these firms devised three plans for the industry in the period between 1970 and 1982. Each one had similar elements, usually entailing aid for R&D and exports and the use of government procurement policy, especially military contracts.[311] In general, the industry's preferences

[307] Les Echos, January 7, 1976; Moretti, "Restructurations Industrielles," pp. 14-16; Libération, March 11, 1982; DAFSA, Electronique Grand Public, p. 74.

[308] ERA, EEC Protectionism, pp. 197-98, 211; La Vie Française, December 15-21, 1982, pp. 28-30; Usine Nouvelle, no. 38, September 21, 1978, pp. 40-41; L'Expansion, January 25-February 7, 1980, pp. 68-69.

[309] Les Echos, September 20, 1976; Edgar Pisani, Enjeux et Conditions des Equilibres Extérieurs de la France, French Senate, Report 31, pt. 2, 1978, pp. 42, 184-85; La Vie Française, November 15-21, 1982, p. 28; interviews.

[310] DAFSA, Electronique Grand Public, p. 12; ERA, EEC Protectionism, p. 199.

[311] Yvonne Giordano, "Analyse de la Politique Française du Commerce Extérieur depuis le 6em Plan" (Ph.D. dissertation, University of Nice, 1982), p. 206; Le Nouvel Economiste, no. 322, February 1, 1982, p. 50; Revue d'Economie Industrielle, no. 23 (1st trim., 1983):298-99, 302.

were similar to its other demands: it sought to preserve its position in the French market.

The first plan for the industry was finalized in 1972, after much government-industry negotiation. In essence Thomson received government aid for R&D and exporting, and the government worked to persuade other countries to adopt the SECAM system and import French televisions.[312] In the early 1970s, the industry was provided with two thirds of its financing by the government.[313] The second plan was established in 1977-78. The first oil crisis and renewed Japanese competition had prompted the industry to seek help again. The government, concerned about the sector's deteriorating trade balance, unemployment problems, and loss of an independent high technology industry, was ready to lend assistance and ultimately gave some 600 million francs to the electronic components industry.[314] The third plan was initiated in 1982, after further economic difficulty beset the industry. Drawn up in negotiations between the industry and the government, this plan was written by the head of one of Thomson's subsidiaries and gave all aid in the consumer electronics area to Thomson.[315] Thomson took part in the negotiation of all three plans and was seemingly satisfied with their outcome, since it never complained.

While the French radio and television producers sought selective protection and subsidies nationally in the 1970s, they also were active at the European level, where they worked to protect the European market from Asian competition. In terms of traditional trade policy measures, the industry wanted to limit their reduction. During the Tokyo Round GATT negotiations, the industry was opposed to tariff reductions.[316] Initially, the EC planned to offer full reductions in this sector, but by the late 1970s it decided to reduce the amount of tariff

[312] Crane, *Politics of International Standards*, p. 42, chs. 3-6; *Les Echos*, September 15, 1972. As part of the "Plan Calcul," the industry was given about 70 million francs a year beginning in 1971, a part of which went to Thomson's radio and television production. OECD, *Selected Industrial Policy Instruments* (Paris: OECD, 1978), pp. 84-86.

[313] *London Times*, November 6, 1972.

[314] *Les Echos*, March 11, 1977; *La Vie Française*, April 10, 1978, p. 24; *Financial Times*, June 2, 1978; *Les Echos*, March 11, 1977; *Libération*, April 6, 1982. Radio and television operations were not directly subsidized, but as a later review of the plan noted, the firms used this money to help all their operations and thus "patch up" their overall balance sheets. *Libération*, April 6, 1982.

[315] *Les Echos*, May 13, 1982. Radiotechnique apparently received no aid. *Le Nouveau Journal*, July 30, 1982; *La Vie Française*, October 11-17, 1982, pp. 77-79; *Revue d'Economie Industrielle*, no. 24 (2nd trim., 1983):54-60.

[316] EC, *Rapport Sur Les Négociations Multilaterales*, p. 22; interviews.

cutting and applied only a 13 percent cut instead of the standard 25-30 percent.[317]

The European television makers also filed complaints with the EC concerning Asian imports. In 1973 the French industry tried to have its informal, national quotas instituted formally at the EC through a safeguard clause. This attempt failed because the German and British governments, as well as Philips, the Dutch multinational, opposed any such action.[318] This internal battle continued throughout the 1970s, with Thomson and the French government on the one hand, pushing for concerted European action against the Asian imports, and Philips and the British and German governments on the other, strongly resisting protectionist moves.[319]

Philips opposed protection because it was a large, integrated multinational producer with substantial operations in Asia.[320] The British opposed the French demands because they were home to numerous Japanese radio and television manufacturers[321] and were concerned about the repercussions that protection might have on the Japanese investments they subsidized. The Germans opposed the French out of a desire to see the German industry return to international competitiveness, which they felt protection would hinder.[322] Throughout the 1970s, these battles forestalled the erection of uniform barriers to Asian radio and television imports in the EC.

By the 1980s, much of this opposition to protection had dissolved. In 1981, a dumping case against Korean television imports was filed at the EC, a first step toward having the French demands met.[323] Although nothing came of this case, by 1982 negotiations were under way with the Japanese on a range of products, including stereos, televisions, television tubes, and VCRs.[324] Producers throughout the Com-

[317] EC, *Rapport sur les Négociations*, pp. 22, 56; *Le Figaro*, January 29-30, 1983.

[318] *Les Echos*, April 17, 1973; ADL, *Analyse des Marchés*, pp. 44-47; *La Vie Française*, March 31, 1980.

[319] ERA, *EEC Protectionism*, ch. 6; EC, *The Consumer Electronics Industry* (Brussels: EC, 1985), pp. 87-96, 124-31; interviews; *Le Figaro*, April 26-27, 1980.

[320] EC, *Consumer Electronics Industry*, pp. 6, 87-96, 98-100; EC, *Etude sur L'Electronique Grand Public*, pp. 104-109; *La Vie Française*, January 17-23, 1983, p. 30; interview; *Le Figaro*, April 26-27, 1980.

[321] By the 1980s, the Japanese had almost 10 plants in the U.K. and covered some 10 percent of European production from this direct foreign investment. ADL, *Analyse des Marchés*, p. 71; ERA, *EEC Protectionism*, pp. 215-17; Moretti, "Restructurations Industrielles," pp. 29-31; *Usine Nouvelle*, no. 38, September 21, 1978.

[322] ADL, *Analyse des Marchés*, pp. 44-47.

[323] *JOCE*, "Communications," c25, February 5, 1981, p.3.

[324] Hine, *Political Economy of European Trade*, pp. 240-42; DAFSA, *Electronique Grand Public*, p. 12.

munity were now unified in their fears of a Japanese takeover of the electronics industry and were demanding that something be done.[325]

By 1982, Thomson was European in scale and thus was interested in European-wide protection, not in national barriers. It became active at the EC in seeking protection against Japanese imports. Resistance by Philips to Thomson's demands was weakened. It had ended some operations in Asia and was losing crucial markets in new product areas—VCRs and compact discs—to the Japanese.[326] The Germans no longer had much of a television industry left, since by 1983 Thomson and Philips controlled nearly all production in the country.[327] And British opposition had waned due to growing trade problems in other sectors, which were included in the agreement, and to a feeling that the Japanese were not playing the trade game fairly.[328] In 1983, an EC-Japanese agreement was concluded, providing for import surveillance of "voluntary" export limits on ten sensitive products, including radios and televisions. By the early 1980s, then, selective protection for Europe on audio equipment and televisions had been instituted.[329] These actions were in line with Thomson's growing interest in a European solution to its problems.

Selective protection at the national level and increasingly at the European level was the French radio and television producers' preference during the period from 1970 to 1985. The industry relied upon this protectionist strategy, combined with French industrial policy aid, to meet the economic challenges of the 1970s. While attempting to expand internationally, Thomson-Brandt's internationalization never became central to its survival or its prosperity. This was due in part to its late and sheltered development and its inability to become an innovative force in the industry. Thomson was dependent on the French market and government, and movement abroad was not a

[325] Les Echos, January 5, 1983, p. 6; Les Echos, January 21, 1981; Le Point, no. 530, November 15, 1982.

[326] Le Point, no. 530, November 15, 1982; Les Echos, January 21, 1981; LSA, March 19, 1982, pp. 88-90; La Vie Française, March 31, 1980; EC, Consumer Electronics Industry, pp. 124-25, 185-86; ERA, EEC Protectionism, pp. 204-11.

[327] ERA, EEC Protectionism, pp. 215-17; LSA, March 19, 1982, pp. 88-90; La Vie Française, March 31, 1980. By 1982 only three major producers were left in Europe: Philips, Thomson, and the Japanese.

[328] Hine, Political Economy of European Trade, pp. 240-42.

[329] Le Monde, June 15, 1985, p. 20; Le Monde, July 27, 1985, p. 13; Hine, Politcal Economy of European Trade, pp. 240-42. Pressures for further action arose in 1984, as Thomson and Philips filed new complaints demanding tariff increases on VCRs. In 1985, tariffs on this good were elevated, and compensation was accorded through the lowering of duties on other electronic goods.

strategy favored by French governments in the 1970s.[330] Thomson's operations in Singapore and Spain as well as its joint ventures and import agreements with various Japanese firms were disliked by the French government, which sought to bring Thomson's production back home.[331]

The government did not, however, discourage Thomson's European strategy. Thomson and the government agreed that increasing the firm's size and moving to a strong position within the European market were crucial. But Thomson "Europeanized" its operations only after 1977. This strategy of increasing its presence in the European market coincided with its desire for reduced intra-EC barriers and its demand for selective protection against Asian producers.

In this case, the industry's weak international ties in the early 1970s led to a response to foreign competition and other serious difficulties that centered on closing the home market. As Thomson-Brandt expanded into Europe, developing a European network of trade and production relations, its interests shifted from protection of the French market to a European solution which entailed reduced intra-EC trade barriers and heightened selective extra-EC protection. Global protection was not desired, because this would hurt the firm's operations in Europe. The industry's changing international ties over the decade thus helped alter its trade preferences. It increasingly behaved like a Type IV industry in its quest for selective protection.

[330] Giordano, "Analyse de la Politique Française," p. 214, shows Thomson as one of six largest aid receivers; *Les Echos*, March 11, 1977; *London Times*, November 6, 1972.

[331] *La Vie Française*, February 7, 1977, p. 13; *Usine Nouvelle*, no. 26, June 30, 1977, pp. 30-31; *Les Echos*, May 8, 1981; *Libération*, July 31, 1981; *Libération*, September 12-13, 1981; *Le Nouvel Economiste*, no. 322, February 1, 1982, p. 50; *Le Figaro*, April 26, 1983; interview.

CHAPTER 6

Firms' Trade Policy Preferences

ARE FIRMS' TRADE POLICY preferences shaped by the extent of their integration into the international economy? To what degree do the three sets of cases confirm our four hypotheses? This chapter considers the answers to these questions and, in doing so, examines similarities and differences among the cases. Three related points are also developed. First, several other explanations of firms' demand for trade policy are discussed to see how the cases here shed light on these theories. Second, the logic behind the central argument is evaluated. Do the case studies reveal that rational behavior is the basis for firms' decisions? Again, other interpretations of firms' behavior, focusing on past behavior, ideology, and context, are analyzed. Finally, an explanation of how the micro arguments about firms' preferences provide the basis for a macro argument about the aggregate differences between the 1920s and the 1970s—the initial puzzle—is presented.

INTERDEPENDENCE

Greater interdependence should reduce some firms' interests in protection. Firms with greater export dependence, multinational production, and global intrafirm trade should be less protectionist than more domestically oriented firms, even under similar conditions of economic distress. The four hypotheses detailing this argument are reviewed in table 6.1. These hypotheses link firms' different levels and types of international operations to different trade policy preferences. We may now ask whether the cases in chapters 3, 4, and 5 support the idea that firms with more extensive ties to the international economy in the 1920s and 1970s, as well as in the United States and France, have less protectionist preferences than do more domestically oriented firms. Because the firms in each case were in economic difficulty and were experiencing the greatest increases in imports among their contemporaries, all of them should have been likely to desire protection. That some did not is surprising. As listed in table 6.2, the more international firms are generally less protectionist, despite their problems.

The first hypothesis (Type I) refers to industries lacking linkages to the international economy. Firms in Type I industries are oriented

TABLE 6.1 The Four Hypotheses

	Low	High
High	TYPE IV Mixed interests; less protectionist than Type I; selective protectionist	TYPE III Least protectionist; most free trade
Low	TYPE I Most protectionist; for global protection; intensity of demand varies with economic difficulty	TYPE II Less protectionist than Type I; most favored is open markets abroad

MULTINATIONALITY (left axis: High / Low)

Low   High

EXPORT DEPENDENCE

primarily to the domestic market, since they possess limited export dependence and little multinationality. When experiencing economic difficulty and rising imports, these firms are likely to seek protection. Indeed, such firms are expected to devote increasing amounts of effort to obtain import barriers as their situation worsens, and they are expected to seek global, not selective, protection of their market. They should prefer to reduce all imports, not just those from certain countries or of certain products. This preference is rational, given the extensive dependence of these firms on the domestic market. For them, protectionism is not a costly policy. It benefits them by reducing imports but cannot hurt them by affecting their export or multinational operations, because these are minimal or nonexistent. Industries composed of firms without these international ties should be the most actively and intensely protectionist of all.

Among the American and French cases, four industries can be classified as Type I: the 1920s U.S. woolen goods manufacturers, the 1920s U.S. watch and clock manufacturers, the 1970s U.S. nonrubber footwear manufacturers, and the 1970s French footwear producers. As the case studies document, these four industries exhibited low export dependence and limited multinationality. They were also the most protectionist.

When World War I ended and imports and other difficulties mounted, firms in the U.S. woolen goods industry began lobbying for

TABLE 6.2 The Industries and Their Preferences

Industries, by International Ties	Type	Trade Preferences
U.S. Woolens (1920s)	I	Protection
U.S. Footwear (1970s)	I	Protection
U.S. Watches and Clocks (1920s)	I	Protection
French Radios and TVs (1970s)	I/IV	Selective protection
U.S. Textile Machinery* (1920s)	II	Divided; some free trade, some moderate protection
U.S. Radios and TVs (1970s)	IV	Divided; RCA free trade, others selective protection
French Footwear* (1970s)	II/I	Divided; selective protection
U.S. Machine Tools* (1970s)	II	Free trade; selective protection in mid-1980s
French Watches and Clocks* (1970s)	II	Divided; free trade until 1980s, when selective protection favored
U.S. Fertilizer (1920s)	III	Free trade
U.S. Newsprint (1920s)	IV	Free trade
U.S. Tires (1970s)	IV	Free trade; some divisions
French Pharmaceuticals (1970s)	III	Free trade
U.S. Photo Equipment (1920s)	III	Moderate protection; increasingly free trade
U.S. Watches and Clocks (1970s)	IV	Divided; some moderate, selective protection
U.S. Semiconductors (1970s)	III	Free trade; increasing strategic protection demands in mid-1980s.
French Tires (1970s)	III	Free trade
French Glass (1970s)	III	Free trade

NOTE: Industries are ranked in terms of increasing international ties. The order is a rough approximation only. It was constructed by adding together each industry's value of export dependence and percentage of foreign investment from tables 2.7 and 2.8. Not all of these measures are strictly comparable; thus the ranking is suggestive at best. The asterisked industries were moved out of their numerical order because the numbers used were clearly inaccurate. They were placed in order using data the cases suggested was more appropriate.

closure of the domestic market. They demanded increased tariffs during the 1921 Emergency Tariff debate, and later they called for a duty increase of 130 percent in the Fordney-McCumber tariff hearings. When new difficulties arose in the late 1920s, they demanded even higher tariff levels before and during the Smoot-Hawley hearings. In addition the industry favored the protectionist American valuation plan and opposed the flexible tariff provision, which allowed the President to adjust rates up or down unilaterally. Protectionist pressure was also directed against the U.S. Tariff Commission. This pressure came mainly from small, specialty firms, but it underscored the industry's eagerness for extensive protection. The wool manufacturers' preferences for protection rose in intensity with the level of economic difficulties, were voiced in all possible political arenas, and were focused on obtaining global protection.

The U.S. watch and clock manufacturers in the 1920s were also limited in their international economic ties. These producers had strong preferences for protection during the decade, especially in the first half. In 1921 they lobbied Congress for sizable increases in their tariffs and demanded a return to the highest rates ever adopted. They sought to alter their tariff classification to evade the freer trade influences of other metals manufacturers. In the mid-1920s the watch and clock manufacturers followed up their protectionist lobbying of Congress with pressure on the USTC. In 1929, after suffering a renewed onslaught of import penetration, they demanded further protection. The growth of foreign sales and import-assembly operations over the decade, however, moderated the duty increases desired and prompted some interest in tariff reductions.

Given their lack of strong foreign ties, these domestic producers saw protection as a congenial solution to their problems. But the intensity of their preferences for market closure varied with their economic situation. Desire for protection increased after the two periods (1919-21 and 1925-27) of most rapid import growth. Like the woolens industry, they lobbied all available political arenas for help: Congress, the Tariff Commission, and the public. The industry began the decade united in its preferences for tariff increases on all products. However, as some firms developed exports and import-assembly operations, the consensus for global protection dissolved. Firms involved in these trading operations sought to have their products exempted from the protectionist upswing. Growing interdependence within the industry reduced pressures for market closure, an outcome different from the case of the woolens industry, where such international ties never developed.

American nonrubber footwear producers also had a domestic orientation in the 1970s. Throughout the decade, these producers had limited international ties. After imports surged in the late 1960s, the industry began its campaign for protection. In the early 1970s it filed both an escape clause petition and numerous countervailing duty cases. As new difficulties arose, the industry renewed its protectionist activities, filing more escape clause actions in 1975 and 1976. The industry also lobbied Congress for aid. It sought exemption from the Tokyo Round tariff cuts and inclusion in bills designed to protect the domestic market for textiles. Overall, the industry was unified and intensely protectionist in the 1970s. Like the two 1920s cases, its activities to obtain protection increased dramatically as its imports and economic difficulties mounted. Moreover, its lobbying was widespread; all possible political arenas were used to voice its preferences: the ITC, the executive branch, Congress, and the public. The industry's most preferred outcome was for global protection on all products. Like the 1920s watch and clock manufacturers, however, its unity was reduced in the 1980s as its largest firms developed import-assembly operations and multinational production.

The final Type I industry was French footwear. Among the four cases, this industry was the most divided. The majority of French footwear producers were small and national, lacking international ties. The four largest firms were, however, significant importers and foreign producers. Not surprisingly, the industry was divided in its trade policy preferences. The bulk of producers, organized in the FNICF, became protectionist after 1975 when imports surged and exports fell. This group sought protection in the European Community and in France. In the 1970s these producers were opposed by the four large firms, and protection was limited in its scope as a result. Later, when further protection was desired by the majority of producers, this too was limited so as not to interfere with the large firms' international operations.

The French footwear case confirms the propositions about domestically oriented, Type I industries. Closure of the domestic market was preferred by the majority of firms. The intensity of their demands for protection, varying with the level of import penetration, rose after 1975 when imports overtook exports. The industry, lobbying both European and French officials as well as taking action on its own, sought protection from all potential sources. Divisions within the industry limited the scope of protection it sought. Global protection was the preference of the bulk of domestic producers, but the trading relations of the largest firms gave them an interest in shielding their trade from any new barriers. The industry compromised and sought selective restraints. Global protection is most desirable only in industries where all of the firms lack significant international ties, as in the 1920s U.S. woolen goods industry.

A Type II industry is one with extensive exports but limited multi-nationality. Such industries should be less protectionist than those in Type I, even when the Type IIs face similar levels of import competition and economic distress. In fact, these export-oriented firms are likely to press for greater market openness, especially abroad. Despite import pressure, these firms are expected to maintain an interest in open markets largely because the costs of protection, due to retaliation or loss of export markets, are greater than its benefits. According to our hypothesis, the three Type II industries among our cases should have similar trade preferences despite their different contexts. In particular, they should be most concerned with increasing the openness of their export markets and secondarily interested in maintaining their home market's openness. Interest in the latter will increase when linked explicitly to progress in the former. In any case, demands for protection from such industries are expected to be unusual even in times of great economic distress, as long as exports remain significant.

The U.S. manufacturers of textile machinery in the 1920s made up one such export-oriented industry. Though appearing export dependent in the aggregate, these builders were divided in two: the woolen machinery sector had few exports, while the cotton machinery sector had significant exports. This division reduced its capacity to develop a single trade policy preference. In the early 1920s when exports were most significant, the industry was unable to lobby Congress during its tariff hearings. Severe economic distress and rising imports did not drive these producers to embrace protectionism. Rather, the export interests of some firms divided the industry and muted preferences for protection. Over the decade these export interests declined, and so did the interests of these firms in avoiding protectionist demands. In 1929 a group of firms, mainly in woolen machinery, pressed for moderate tariff increases on their machines. Despite being beseiged by imports, these producers refrained from demanding protection for much of the decade and remained moderate in their later demands.

The U.S. machine tool industry in the 1970s was also export oriented. Export dependence in it was significant but declining over the decade. These manufacturers lost market share to imports and experienced other economic difficulties; however, they did not resort to demands for protection but instead pressed for help in promoting their exports. In the early 1970s the industry lobbied Congress and the executive branch for aid to its exports. In particular, the industry wanted major foreign markets (such as those of the Soviet Union and the Eastern bloc) to be opened to its exports. The failure of these initiatives, the decline of the industry's trade, and the increase of imports into the United States eventually pushed the industry to seek aid against imports. After 1978, interest in protection rose. However, it was targeted mainly against one country, Japan, and was fueled by the decline in U.S. exports. Throughout much of the 1970s the industry's export orientation led it to support trade liberalization both at home and abroad, despite mounting imports. This orientation shifted, however, when the significance of its exports declined, especially relative to that of its import competition.

The French producers of watches and clocks had significant export sales for most of the 1970s. With the advent of electronic watches, however, for which the industry was not prepared, its export dependence began falling and import penetration surged. During the 1970s the industry never demanded protection despite its problems. In fact, in the early part of the decade the industry supported trade liberalization, as is evident in its interest in the GATT tariff reductions and a Swiss-EC trade treaty. Later the industry did seek aid in adjusting through various industrial policy plans, but these efforts had little protectionist intent. Although beginning in 1980 the industry sought protection, this was primarily against Asian imports of electronic watches, a product the French barely produced, let alone exported. More surprising than this interest in protection was the industry's lack of such interest in the decade. In the early 1970s, when its trade dependence was rising, the industry pushed for freer trade both at the national and EC level. Even in the late 1970s, when its difficulties and imports mounted, the watch and clock producers resisted the temptation to demand protection and sought rather to foster adjustment to the new competitive situation. Only when the importance of exports declined, especially relative to that of imports, did their interest in protectionism grow.

These three cases demonstrate the importance of export dependence as a barrier against protection. In each, when export dependence was rising and/or strongest for the industry, interest in protection was insignificant despite surging imports. Indeed, trade liberalization was preferred at this time. These export-oriented industries were distinct in their trade preferences from the more domestically oriented, Type I industries. The similar competitive difficulties of the two sets of industries prompted divergent preferences as a result of their different ties to the international economy.

In each case, however, these industries eventually sought some protection. Declining export dependence coupled with rapidly rising import penetration unhinged these firms' resistance to protection. In all three cases, when import penetration rose above export dependence—i.e., when imports overtook exports as a percent of domestic production—protection became more desirable. This shift in preferences occurred as the the export constraint declined. This finding suggests two caveats for the argument. First, export dependence may not lead to *stable*, long-run preferences for freer trade. Exports in themselves may be unstable, and when they decline shifts in firms' preferences are expected. Even if exports are stable, moreover, rapidly surging imports may turn firms' attention from their export interests to their import problems. Export dependence may thus operate only at a high "threshold." When export dependence is high and increasing, especially relative to import penetration, then firms will be most likely to resist the temptation to demand protection in times of economic distress.

A third type of industry involves those with significant export dependence and sizable, integrated multinational operations. Because they are the most integrated into the international economy, these Type III industries are expected to be the least protectionist, since the costs of protection are very high for them. These firms should show a durable interest in continued openness, or further opening, of the home market, as well as a secondary interest in the maintenance of openness in foreign markets even in the face of rising imports and other difficulties. Once again, the preferences of these firms should appear more similar to one another, despite their different contexts, than to other types of firms.

Among the six cases of Type III industries, two are from the 1920s: the fertilizer producers and the photographic equipment manufacturers. The U.S. fertilizer producers were highly export dependent and multinational by the early 1920s. They proved to be very free trade oriented despite their economic problems. In the 1921 tariff hearings they requested the retention of the duty-free status of their products. In the 1929 hearings, this preference still prevailed, although strategic considerations were introduced. Certain producers demanded protection on some goods unless they could receive tariff reductions on others. This strategy was aimed at, and resulted in, greater openness of the home market, since no new tariffs were enacted and several were reduced. Throughout the decade the major producers, those with the largest international operations, opposed the attempts of some small domestic producers to have tariffs on various products increased. In general, the fertilizer manufacturers were more interested in preserving their home markets' openness than in erecting new barriers, despite mounting import competition.

The U.S. photographic equipment industry in the 1920s was also an important exporter with growing international production. This industry, dominated by the Eastman Kodak Company, was initially divided on the tariff issue. The few small domestic producers desired greatly increased tariffs on cameras and film, while Kodak in 1921 sought only moderate increases. Kodak's interest in even minor increases appears somewhat unexpected, but two factors help explain it. First, at this time Kodak had no foreign operations and a declining export position. Its foreign ties were not strong enough to outweigh the temptations of protection. Second, these temptations were all the greater since Kodak was a monopolist at home. Closing the domestic market would effectively eliminate all of Kodak's competition, which consisted chiefly of imports. By 1929 Kodak's position had changed. Its foreign operations were now more developed. Not surprisingly, Kodak began advocating tariff reductions on the products it traded most actively—i.e., films. Although still seeking protection for certain products in order to retain its monopoly position, the firm altered its policy preferences on those goods for which its foreign trade and production operations were most developed.

In the 1970s, the U.S. semiconductor industry had substantial export dependence and integrated multinational operations. Firms in this industry favored trade liberalization throughout much of the decade. In the late 1970s a split developed: the largest and most international firms retained the industry's original preferences, but some smaller firms organized to demand action against Japan's unfair trade practices. In time the largest firms were able to convince the smaller ones that further trade liberalization both at home and abroad was the best strategy. Using the threat of a future trade petition, the industry then pressed both the U.S. government and the Japanese government and firms to agree to negotiations to reduce tariff and nontariff barriers in the semiconductor market. The U.S. firms were thus most interested in enhancing market openness, despite mounting import problems. The threat of petitioning for relief against Japanese imports was a strategic maneuver designed to improve U.S. access to Japan's market, but this approach was disliked by the largest, most multinational firms. The industry's later petitions against the Japanese were also strategic, designed more to open the Japanese market than to close the U.S. one.

Three of the French cases fall into this category of highly international industries: the pharmaceutical, glass, and tire makers. The French pharmaceutical industry was by the 1970s much engaged in exporting, multinational production, and intrafirm trading operations, especially within Europe. Despite rising import penetration and severe economic difficulty, this industry never sought protection. In fact, the producers made efforts throughout the decade to reduce trade barriers. They worked to dismantle and/or reduce nontariff barriers (price controls and regulations regarding drug introduction and testing) in France. The industry also actively encouraged European efforts to harmonize drug procedures and standards within the Community, thus facilitating trade. And, rather than rely upon government aid or policy, the pharmaceutical manufacturers pursued their own strategies to maintain and enhance their competitiveness. These French producers responded to their problems not by seeking to close their home market but by acting to promote trade liberalization and their competitiveness.

The French glass industry in the 1970s also was export dependent and multinational. Like other industries of this type, it did not show any interest in protectionism despite rising foreign competition. The industry did not appeal to either the French government or the EC for help. Indeed, it supported the Tokyo Round tariff reductions and fought to keep American glass producers from closing their market. Like the pharmaceutical industry, it was little interested in government aid and chose to adjust to the new international competitive situation on its own. Internal adjustment and continued support of an open trading system were the hallmarks of the glass producers' responses to their economic difficulties.

Another highly international industry in France was the tire manufacturers, which involved primarily one firm, Michelin. By the 1970s Michelin was a large exporter with production and trading operations throughout the world. This firm's response to the difficulties of the decade did not involve seeking protection or government aid. Nor did it seek protection at the European level, where the industry in general and Michelin in particular supported the trade liberalizing measures of the GATT negotiations. Much like the pharmaceutical and glass manufacturers, Michelin sought to adjust through its own internal strategies and continued to support the liberal international trading system. Rising foreign competition, then, did not prompt a protectionist response from the internationally oriented French tire producers.

The six cases that are classified as Type III, highly export dependent and multinational, fit the argument quite well. In each case, except perhaps for Kodak, the firms did not respond to rising import com-

petition by demanding protection. Quite often, their response was to
seek further openness of their markets. Two other features common
to these cases should be noted. First, in a number of cases, strategic
behavior by firms, involving threats to close the home market if markets abroad were not further opened, was evident. The fertilizer and
semiconductor cases are two examples. These multinational firms
were not merely rational actors reacting to their environment; they
were strategic game players, seeking to shape that environment. Second, these firms had a number of options for responding to economic
difficulty. Political action in the form of demands for aid or protection
did not need to be the first response. Many firms never entered the
political arena. Instead they adjusted through their own internal strategies, as in the three French industries. This option was probably
more significant for large, international firms than for small, domestic
ones, since the former could more easily expand and reshape their
international operations to take advantage of the industry's new global
situation. In any case, the firms with extensive exports and multinational production were purposeful, strategic actors intent on remaining a part of the international system, rather than reactive agents who
preferred the security of a tightly sealed domestic market.

The fourth type of case involves firms with little export activity but
substantial foreign production. Unlike Type III firms, Type IVs use
foreign production almost entirely to service the host market and tend
to lack integrated international operations. Because of the disinte-
grated character of their production, these firms have less interest in
the global trading system than do Types II and III. But these firms are
likely to be less protectionist than Type Is. In particular, these multinationals will, if they show any interest in protection, desire selective
protection, directed specifically against particular countries and/or
products. It will be limited protection, designed to avoid disrupting
the industry's international operations but to deal with the most
threatening foreign competition.

Among the five industries in this category, one was the 1920s U.S.
newsprint manufacturers. Firms in this industry were multinational
but only minor exporters. Their foreign operations were concentrated
in Canada, where they exported a great deal to the United States. This
industry thus did possess a substantial amount of international intrafirm trade, and hence it was more like a Type III industry. Throughout the 1920s the newsprint producers supported freer trade in their
product. In neither 1921 nor 1929 did they try to have the duty-free
status of newsprint altered. The U.S. newsprint producers, despite rising imports, never sought protection in the 1920s. Much like Type III

firms, they were active players in the international system and perceived its openness to be in their interest. For these firms, even selective protection was not desired, since they did possess substantial world-trading operations and integrated global production. In such conditions protection was not desirable.

In the 1970s, three American cases fit into this fourth category. The U.S. tire producers were large multinationals with few U.S. exports. Only the largest firm, Goodyear, was a highly integrated global producer. This difference produced a split within the industry: Goodyear versus the rest of the firms. The industry for the most part remained in favor of a free trade system throughout the decade. Several divergences from this general orientation occurred, however. In the early 1970s, when imports first surged, the industry began a countervailing duty case against its most threatening rival, Michelin. Goodyear did not support this case, but it was filed and decided in the U.S. industry's favor. Goodyear and Michelin later took action to have it halted and were successful. In the late 1970s, as Asian imports rose, some tire manufacturers again filed petitions on particular products against specific countries. Considering the industry's serious problems, these were restrained actions. These attempts at selective protection were combined with internal activity to adjust to the new international environment. The smaller, less international U.S. tire makers chose internal adjustment and selective protection, while the global giant, Goodyear, preferred a response without recourse to any protection.

The U.S. watch and clock industry was also composed of several large multinationals, who had limited trading operations. This industry underwent major changes in the 1970s as new electronic watches were introduced and rapidly took over the market. The traditional manufacturers' response to this was to seek protection against the new products, and they lobbied both the executive branch and Congress for help. This selective protection was opposed, however, by the sizable group of U.S. importer/assemblers. It was opposed also by the semiconductor firms who had developed electronic watch production. The failure of the conventional producers' efforts to obtain selective protection led them to adjust on their own by increasing their imports and foreign operations. After this, explicit pressure for protection was reduced. Like other industries in this category, the watch producers chose a strategy of selective protection combined with internal adjustment. Global protection was not desired, because this would have upset the firms' other trading and production operations.

The U.S. radio and television industry was fairly multinational, with limited exports. Like the tire industry, it was also divided: its largest firm, RCA, had a well-developed network of international production and trade, while the others were much more domestically oriented. This latter group responded to rising import pressures by waging a continuous battle against certain imports. Led by Zenith, these firms filed a large number of trade petitions against Japanese television imports, beginning in 1968. These actions were opposed by RCA, who feared their impact on its own foreign operations. When protection was granted, it was selective, directed against several countries and specific products in order to avoid hurting RCA's and other U.S. producers' growing offshore-assembly and import operations. In time the industry also pursued its own internal adjustment strategies, which by the 1980s left little radio or television production in the United States and hence little interest in protection.

The French radio and television industry became multinational in the 1970s, but it never developed substantial export operations. The French industry, composed of Thomson-Brandt and several foreign multinationals, had long been a sheltered domestic one—a Type I industry. Preferences for protection against Japanese imports developed early and were retained throughout the 1970s. This selective protection against the Japanese was combined, however, with attempts to open the French market. As Thomson developed production operations in Europe, it increasingly sought a more integrated European market. This was best accomplished by reducing barriers to the French market while erecting barriers to Japanese production at the European level. Thomson increasingly pursued this strategy as the European character of its operations grew. Again the firm sought selective protection in addition to making its own internal adjustments to the heightened competition it faced.

Industries with substantial foreign production but limited exports revealed preferences for selective protection. In fact, their behavior was a cross between that of purely domestic firms (Type I) and highly international ones (Type III). These firms pursued their own adjustment strategies but usually less actively than Type IIIs. To compensate and preserve their international operations, they sought selective protection against their most threatening competition. A combination of resisting adjustment through protection and attempting to adjust internally characterized their behavior. The more like Type III firms they were, the more emphasis they placed on adjustment in contrast to protection. For instance, the 1920s newsprint firms, Goodyear, and RCA were firms with substantial global trade and production activities. These firms did not favor even selective protection, which distinguishes them from the other Type IV cases, who had smaller international operations.

The trade policy preferences of foreign multinationals operating abroad are also part of our argument. The preferences of these foreign subsidiaries depend on whether the subsidiary is part of a Type III or Type IV firm. If the subsidiary services only the domestic host market and was built originally to circumvent trade barriers to that market, the subsidiary will have little interest in reducing those barriers. As part of a Type IV firm, the foreign enterprise will desire at least the maintenance of barriers and perhaps even their elevation in times of rising import penetration.[1] On the other hand, if the operation is part of a parent's global production and trade network, then the subsidiary is unlikely to seek further protection and may want existing barriers reduced. In this case, as part of a Type III firm, the foreign subsidiary should prefer freer trade, much like its parent.

The trade preferences of a variety of the foreign subsidiaries evident in the cases support this argument. In the 1920s, for instance, the British textile machinery firms located in the United States were the spearheads of the British manufacturers' export drive into America. As part of this export strategy, these subsidiaries were tightly integrated into a global trading network run by their parent firms, whose interests were served by an open American market. These subsidiaries not only were ardent opponents of protection but also sought tariff reductions in the United States. Similar to this case were the Japanese and European subsidiaries in the U.S. tire, semiconductor, and radio and television industries. Most of these subsidiaries acted as part of their parent firms' global trade and production networks. Although they serviced mainly the U.S. market, the subsidiaries provided both substitutes and complements for their parents' exporting activities. As part of their parents' global strategy, these firms generally opposed new protection in the United States, especially any targeted against them. Their interest in the reduction of barriers was less apparent. Once in the United States, they may not have become active free traders; nonetheless, they did become active opponents of further protectionism.

Among the French cases, the preferences of foreign subsidiaries were more complicated. The subsidiaries that were developed before the 1970s—those in watches and clocks and radios and televisions—

[1] Richard Caves, *Multinational Enterprise and Economic Analysis* (Cambridge: Cambridge University Press, 1982), pp. 40-43; and Bergsten, Horst, and Moran, *American Multinationals and American Interests*, pp. 297-300.

were intended to service the closed French market. Firms such as Timex-France and Radiotechnique were less a part of their parent's global trading operations; they produced primarily for the protected French market and greeted rising import competition in the 1970s with cries for help. The aid they sought, however, was in the form of industrial policy and not tariff protection. They wanted subsidies from the government but were not vocal proponents of further protection, although they probably did not actively oppose it. On the other hand, subsidiaries developed in the 1970s were different from those begun earlier. In part these subsidiaries were developed less to service the French market than to augment their parents' international operations. In industries like tires, glass, and pharmaceuticals, these new foreign entrants behaved more like Type III firms. They tended to be vocal opponents of any new protection and were silent partners in steps toward trade liberalization, especially within Europe.

Overall, the preferences of these foreign firms varied, depending on their role in their parent firms' strategies. The less integrated into a global trading network and thus the more like a purely domestic firm they were, the more protectionist the foreign subsidiary appeared.[2] When part of a globally integrated multinational, these subsidiaries will be more free-trade oriented. The behavior of these foreign subsidiaries confirms our arguments about Type III and IV firms.

OTHER EXPLANATIONS

How do the case studies shed light on other explanations of firms' trade policy preferences? Although the preferences of industries have been less studied than other factors affecting trade policy outcomes, several different explanations do exist. These have focused on predicting firms' demands for protection; much less has been written about firms' preferences for further trade liberalization.[3] Despite these limitations, the cases here provide new evidence for these other theories.

  [2] Although little is known about the amount of influence foreign subsidiaries have on trade policy outcomes in developed countries, it is likely that the more they resemble a domestic firm, the greater their influence will be. This appearance will enhance their legitimacy within the policy process. However, it will make their preferences more like those of domestic firms: more protectionist than their multinational character might predict.
  [3] For a summary of this literature, see chapter 2, note 1. Only export dependence is explicitly used to explain antiprotectionist pressures and outcomes.

In part, firms' preferences for protection have been accounted for by their competitive position. That is, indicators of competitive disadvantage have been used to predict protectionist demands. One factor indicating disadvantage that is linked to demands for protection is an industry's labor intensity.[4] The claim is that the more labor (especially unskilled labor) intensive an industry in a developed country is, the more disadvantaged it is and the more likely it is to seek protection. The cases here support this argument to an extent. The most labor-intensive industries among the cases were usually domestically oriented, Type I industries, and hence ones preferring protection. The cases also suggest that the movement of labor-intensive segments of firms' production abroad can enhance firms' willingness to resist protection. As this movement further internationalizes their operations, it thereby increases the costs of protection. Examples of this abounded: the U.S. semiconductor producers, U.S. and French watch and clock manufacturers, U.S. and French radio and television producers, and U.S. newsprint firms. This migration of labor-intensive production abroad has been an important force in the internationalization of production occurring in the past several decades. It has also been a major reason for the growing divergence between the trade preferences of labor unions and multinationals in developed countries.

Other explanations of industry's preferences on trade focus on the characteristics that enhance the rents obtained from trade barriers.[5] This line of inquiry has pointed to the degree of industry concentration—as a proxy for its monopoly power—as a determinant of protectionist demand. One economist explains:

Ceteris paribus, monopolistic industries can be expected to have a relatively larger stake in tariffs than competitive industries since the latter can enjoy only ephemeral excess quasi-rents before increased investment by the industry and the consequent expansion of supply sends excess capital returns back to zero. . . . Certainly industries which also enjoy monopoly rents are in a better position to exploit the advantages of tariff protection and could be expected, therefore, to lobby relatively intensely.[6]

[4] E.g., Caves, "Economic Models of Political Choice"; Baldwin and Anderson, "Political Market for Protection in Industrial Countries"; Ray, "Determinants of Tariff and Non-tariff Trade Restrictions in the U.S."; R. Baldwin, *Political Economy of U.S. Import Policy*, pp. 150-72; Lavergne, *Political Economy of U.S. Tariffs*, pp. 75-87.

[5] Anne Krueger, "Political Economy of the Rent-Seeking Society," *American Economic Review* 64 (1974):291-303; Brock and Magee, "Economics of Special Interest Politics"; Lavergne, *Political Economy of U.S. Tariffs*, pp. 88-90, 92-93.

[6] Lavergne, *Political Economy of U.S. Tariffs*, p. 92.

Tests of this hypothesis have generally not supported it, and the cases here also cast some doubt on it.[7] Many concentrated industries, like U.S. semiconductors or glass and tires in France, were much less protectionist than more competitive industries, like footwear in the 1970s in the United States or France and U.S. woolens and watches and clocks in the 1920s. On the other hand, one case strongly supports this argument. Of all the cases studied, the photographic industry was the most dominated by one firm. Kodak in the 1920s photographic equipment sector was a monopolist using trade barriers to increase its profits. Indeed, Kodak's interest in protection was largely attributable to its monopoly position. This case suggests that only very high levels of concentration may induce firms to seek protection, and that more oligopolistic structures may have mixed effects on firms' preferences.

The amount of protection previously supplied has also been seen as influencing firms' later trade preferences. In general, past protection is expected to have a consistent, positive effect on future demands.[8] Past protection is seen as leading to future demands for protection. The logic behind this argument is that "highly protected industries [will] resist tariff reductions more intensely than low duty industries since, ceteris paribus, the former sectors stand to lose more from the cuts."[9] The cases provide mixed support for this argument. In some, high levels of protection did not seem to influence industries' later preferences. For example, watches and clocks, semiconductors, and machine tools in the United States all had relatively high levels of duty protection prior to the 1970s.[10] During much of that decade, however, these industries favored tariff reductions. For other industries, past protection did engender further similar demands. For instance, the U.S. woolens industry in the 1920s, the U.S. footwear industry, and the French radio and television producers in the 1970s were all highly protected before the period examined and remained protectionist throughout it. In these cases, past protection appeared unsuccessful; that is, the industry's problems continued and/or intensified. This unsuccessful past protection, then, led to demands for new protection.

A more nuanced argument relates the success or failure of past protection to later industry preferences for it. "If protectionism fails to raise profits for a domestic industry, then, ceteris paribus, firms will

---

[7] Ibid., pp. 152-56; R. Baldwin, *Political Economy of U.S. Import Policy*, pp. 150-72.

[8] On outcomes, see Lavergne, *Political Economy of U.S. Tariffs*, pp. 164-66.

[9] Robert Baldwin, "Political Economy of U.S. Import Policy," 1981, typescript, p. 194.

[10] USTC, *Trade Barriers: An Overview*, 1:56-58; Robert Hawkins and Ingo Walter, eds., *The U.S. and International Markets: Commercial Policy Options in an Age of Controls* (Lexington, Mass.: Heath, 1972), pp. 50-52, 57-62.

increase their demand for future trade barriers. . . . [while] on the other hand if trade barriers improve an industry's economic health, the firms in that industry will reduce the intensity of their lobbying efforts."[11] The claim is that the success of past barriers weakens demands for them later. Some cases here support the first half of this argument, as the U.S. footwear and woolens, and French radio and television industries reveal.

The second part of this argument is more complicated. Demands for protection may be extinguished not only because the earlier barriers were successful but also because the industry adjusted to the foreign competition. In this argument, low barriers to exit in an industry also reduce protectionist demand, because firms can then easily shift to new, more profitable enterprises.[12] Again, the cases underline the importance of adjustment as an alternative to protection. They suggest that two adjustment strategies are particularly salient. Exit from an industry and internationalization of production by firms seem to weigh most strongly in their decisions not to seek protection. In the U.S. radio and television, tire, footwear, and the French tire, glass, and footwear industries, the firms' decisions to leave the industry or to develop significant, new international operations discouraged them from seeking protection. Internationalization of production can serve as an alternative to protection. Not only may strong international ties prevent firms from demanding trade barriers, but having the capacity to internationalize may also alter firms' preferences in a more free trade direction.

This brings us to a final set of factors that have been seen as influencing firms' trade preferences—their international ties. First, export dependence, it is claimed, affects firms' trade preferences.[13] Various studies show that demands for protective measures are much less common among firms that export a substantial part of their production. This study confirms this observation. Export-dependent firms (Type II) were likely to resist protectionist urges even in times of increasing imports. But the cases here suggest a less robust relationship. Export dependence among highly import-penetrated firms was an unstable

[11] Aggarwal, Keohane, and Yoffie, "Dynamics of Negotiated Protectionism," p. 350.

[12] Ibid., p. 356; and Pugel and Walter, "U.S. Corporate Interests," use levels of diversification as an indicator of capacity for adjustment.

[13] Fong, "Export Dependence," ch. 2; R. Baldwin, *Political Economy of U.S. Import Policy*, pp. 150-72; Lavergne, *Political Economy of U.S. Tariffs*, pp. 160-64; Becker, *Dynamics of Business-Government Relations*; Wilson, *American Business and Foreign Policy*; I. M. Destler and John Odell, *Anti-Protection: Changing Forces in United States Trade Politics* (Washington, D.C.: Institute for International Economics, 1987).

bulwark against demands for market closure.[14] In the three cases
when exports declined and imports overtook them as a percentage of
domestic production, the firms became alarmed and gradually developed an interest in protection. These firms were in transition, moving
from a strong export position to an increasingly weak one, which was
undoubtedly associated with the industry's growing competitive disadvantage. Export dependence thus may be a less stable deterrent
against protectionist demands than extensive, integrated multinationality.

Recent work has attempted to deal with the rise of multinational
corporations and their influence on trade policy. It has been argued
that multinationals have an interest in reduced trade barriers as a result of concerns about their foreign operations and global intrafirm
trade.[15] But in these studies the industry's degree of multinationality
has often not been a significant determinant of its preferences,[16] and
this finding is supported here. Industry-wide levels of multinationality
are not good predictors of firms' trade preferences. One must look
both at the individual firms' multinational relations and at the character of that multinationality. First, industry-level data obscures the
distribution of international ties among firms. In a highly multinational industry, some firms may have few, if any, international ties and
may thus be protectionist. Because of this uneven distribution, data on
individual firms may give a more accurate picture of their trade preferences. Indeed, firm-level data collected elsewhere strongly confirm
the importance of multinational ties as a brake on protectionist demands, as this study also does.[17] Second, multinational firms organized
in different ways may have distinct preferences. As pointed out, multinationals without global trade networks may be selectively protectionist; multinationals with extensive global networks are likely to be
ardent opponents of protection. It is not simply multinationality but
the character of this foreign involvement that is crucial to understanding firms' trade preferences.

The nature of multinationals' trade relations may also affect a firm's

[14] Becker, in *Dynamics of Business-Government Relations*, attributes this weak export pressure to a serious division among U.S. exporters, which pits the large firms not desiring
any government help against smaller exporters very interested in such aid.

[15] Raymond Vernon, "International Trade Policy in the 1980s," *International Studies
Quarterly* 26 (December 1982):483-510; R. Baldwin, *Political Economy of U.S. Import Policy*,
pp. 145-51; Fong, "Export Dependence," ch. 2; Helleiner, "Transnational Enterprise and
the New Political Economy"; Lavergne, *Political Economy of U.S. Tariffs*, pp. 104-106.

[16] E.g., R. Baldwin, *Political Economy of U.S. Import Policy*, pp. 166-67.

[17] Pugel and Walter, "U.S. Corporate Interests."

trade preferences. This connection has been examined elsewhere. Réal Lavergne has tested the hypothesis that the growth of U.S. multinationals with large trade flows from abroad has altered the structure of U.S. protection. He finds little evidence for such a claim but realizes that his dependent variable may not capture their influence. Noting that multinational affiliates' exports to the United States are "of a modest proportion," or about 12 percent of all nonauto, nonpetroleum manufactured imports, he queries whether "it is legitimate to ask if such a proportion is sufficient to have an important impact in determining the *structure* of barriers to trade in the U.S.," and points out that "it is quite possible that such imports have had an impact of importance in selected sectors."[18] Our case studies support this latter point, for among Type III industries, resistance to protection was widespread.

The industries focused on in this study lend credence to others' assertions that labor intensity, high levels of concentration, export dependence, and multinationality influence firms' trade policy preferences. Our cases also imply that the influence of past policies on later demands may be quite complicated, since the industries reveal varying effects exercised by the past. The case study approach thus helps shed light on other more aggregate examinations of firms' trade preferences and can provide a more detailed understanding of how some key factors may actually affect firms' preferences.

RATIONAL BEHAVIOR AND FIRMS' PREFERENCES

The logic of the argument in this book rests on a rational actor model of firm behavior.[19] In Chapter 2, it was argued that firms highly integrated into the international economy should find protection too costly even in times of distress. But do firms appear as rational, cost-benefit calculators in the determination of their preferences? And are the key factors prompting them to resist protection the "costly" aspects

[18] Lavergne, *Political Economy of U.S. Tariffs*, p. 106. Emphasis added.

[19] This model does not postulate either: (1) perfect rationality, or (2) utility-maximizing behavior. The argument here is consistent with a bounded rationality model based on satisficing. It is claimed simply that firms, when challenged by imports and other difficulties, think about ways to alleviate these problems, including demanding protection, and attempt to evaluate the costs and benefits of their options. In particular, it is maintained that they analyze seriously the protectionist option. This implies firms act as if they were unitary actors, although the "thought process" may in fact involve much discussion and dissension within the firm. But no claim is made that firms have perfect information, infinite processing capabilities, or maximizing utility functions. See McKeown, "Firms and Tariff Regime Change."

identified? Is it fear of foreign retaliation and the other economic costs involved in disrupting a firm's international trade networks that provoke resistance to protection?

In general, the cases provide affirmative answers to these questions. Firms assessed their situations to understand the costs and benefits of different courses of action and eventually chose the course that appeared least costly. Concerns about foreign retaliation and other costs of protection were often expressed by export-oriented and multinational firms in deciding to resist protection. Other factors, however, also affected firms' decision making.

Scholars have suggested two arguments why rational behavior may not prevail. First, rationality may be outweighed by context. That is, ingrained habits, traditional ways of doing things, and standard operating procedures may exert more influence on firms than do their calculations of the costs and benefits of different courses of action.[20] This implies, for instance, a greater willingness on the part of 1920s firms to opt for protection, since historically protection had been high, than on the part of 1970s firms, many of whose recent history involved trade liberalization. But the cases challenge this claim, because industries with similar levels of international ties in the 1920s and 1970s behaved similarly. The logic of their international position transcended their particular habits and traditions.

Context is not unimportant, of course, and helps account for other behavior. For instance, since exporting behavior was new for many American firms after World War I, this may explain why these exports did not exercise as constraining an effect on protection as expected. The 1920s textile machinery industry is an example. Before the war, the firms in this industry had few exports and were dominated by British and German producers. When their exports rose after World War I, the U.S. firms lacked confidence in their ability to sustain this foreign trade when the Europeans eventually revived their industry. The U.S. firms did not become ardently protectionist. But without confidence in their export capacity, the U.S. textile machinery producers saw little to be gained from promoting exports and, as European imports surged, more to be gained from maintaining protection of the home market. In this case, the historical context of the industry influenced its trade preferences. This context, nonetheless, was not com-

---

[20] The classic piece arguing this was Robert Hall and Charles Hitch, "Price Theory and Business Behavior," *Oxford Economic Papers* 2 (May 1939):12-45. Other discussions are in Herbert Simon, "Theories of Decision-making in Economics and Behavioral Science," *American Economic Review* 49 (June 1959):253-83; Richard Cyert and James March, *A Behavioral Theory of the Firm* (Englewood Cliffs, N.J.: Prentice-Hall, 1963).

pletely determining. The industry never wanted to return to the high levels of protection accorded it before the war. The industry's new export dependence did influence its behavior and limit the effects of its historical position. Context can affect an industry's perceptions of its preferences, but it may not invalidate the influence exerted by firms' international positions.

Ideological motives, rather than rational calculations, may also be more important in understanding firms' behavior.[21] In particular, firms in the 1970s, existing after the era of the Great Depression, might have been ideologically more opposed to demanding protection, because they had imbibed the historical "lesson" that protection leads to depression.[22] If this were true, and if we controlled for import penetration levels and international ties, firms in the 1970s should have been less likely to demand protection. This does not appear to have been the case. For example, highly import-penetrated industries without international ties in both periods, such as U.S. woolens in the 1920s and U.S. footwear in the 1970s, were both ardent global protectionists. Moreover, direct evidence of such ideological behavior is lacking. Firms and industry associations rarely, if ever, pointed to the problems of the 1920s and 1930s as a reason for resisting protection. Rather, the firm's immediate trading situation and foreign operations were most cited. These findings do not invalidate arguments about ideology. They simply suggest that firms also attempt rational analyses of their situations when defining their preferences.

Ideology may actually bolster the rational behavior of firms. For instance, the experience of the Great Depression has made contemporary firms with strong international ties more able to understand the potentially devastating effects of protection on their global operations and has thus enhanced their capacity to make rational decisions about their trade preferences. The cases do not contradict an interpretation

---

[21] The term "ideology" is used loosely here. Ideology is typically defined as "a structured or closely interrelated set of beliefs." I am using it more to refer to the assumptions or underlying beliefs that decision makers in firms might have imbibed from the historical analogies or liberal economic ideas that pervade their environments. Several studies suggest firms operate in the political arena in such less than rational ways. See, e.g., Bauer, Pool, and Dexter, *American Business and Public Policy*, esp. chs. 8, 9, 12, 13; and Bruce Russett and Elizabeth Hanson, *Interest and Ideology: The Foreign Policy Beliefs of American Businessmen* (San Francisco: W. H. Freeman and Co., 1975), pp. 107-108, for this definition of ideology.

[22] Although made most often about American decision makers, this argument could also apply to U.S. businessmen; see Goldstein, "Reexamination of American Commercial Policy."

based on ideology. Historical "lessons" may in fact improve firms' rational calculations.

Finally, many of the cases confirm the observation that the high costs of protection for internationally oriented firms—involving retaliation and other economic effects—play a role in dissuading them from seeking it. But a rational actor argument implies that the higher costs of protection *relative* to other options should be determining. These other options have not been discussed systematically, although evidence of them abounds in the cases. Three options are possible: (1) do nothing, (wait and see), (2) try to adjust and improve competitiveness, and (3) demand other forms of aid from the government. The costs of these strategies, which will depend on the firm's situation, are likely to affect a firm's interest in protection as well.

Since the first option is least likely, given these firms' high levels of economic distress, let us focus on the relative costs of the last two options. First, the costs of adjusting to improve one's competitiveness appear less for large firms with international ties and other business avenues open to them. Internal adjustment was most apparent (and successful) among firms in the U.S. semiconductor, tire, and television industries and in the French tire and glass industries. In general, these firms were more willing and easily able to adapt their operations to new conditions of international competition. As large multinationals, they were better able to sell off uncompetitive businesses, move production abroad, and/or introduce more competitive production procedures in their plants.

Smaller firms, especially those without any international ties, generally found the costs of adjustment far higher and were less willing to attempt it.[23] Small, domestic firms may have only one business, and to sell it means the end of the enterprise. For them, exit may be more costly than voice. For a firm with no experience abroad, taking such a step may be extremely difficult and costly. Introducing more competitive procedures may also require large amounts of capital that small firms do not possess. The choice for small, domestic firms is often clear: protection offers the least costly option in times of distress.

The costs of protection should also be weighed against the costs of demanding other forms of government aid. Policy substitutes less

[23] This contrasts with the argument of Michael Piore and Charles Sabel in *The Second Industrial Divide: Possibilities for Prosperity* (New York: Basic Books, 1984), esp. chs. 2, 8, where they maintain that small firms with flexible production techniques may be the most adaptable to the uncertain, competitive economic environment of today. They note that large firms may develop flexible specialization, but they seem to think this is much more likely in small firms; see, e.g., pp. 28-37.

costly than outright protection may be available in some cases. The likelihood that a firm will opt for these substitutes depends generally on their availability and expected attainability. One difference between French and American firms' behavior may lie in the greater availability of such substitutes in France than in the United States. It has been maintained that the wide array of French industrial policy instruments acts as a substitute for protectionist policies.[24] Some of the cases support this. In the French footwear and watch and clock cases, firms attempted to obtain government aid as their imports and difficulties mounted. But the cases also demonstrate that industrial policy is frequently *not* an effective substitute for protection. In both of these cases, the industrial policies adopted had little effect on imports. Imports continued to surge after these policies were implemented, and the industries were driven to seek outright protection. As the French cases generally demonstrated, an industrial policy that had protectionist elements was rarely successful without actual protection. The French cases suggest demands for industrial policy may be less costly for firms initially; once they fail to address the problem, however, other options, especially protection, will be considered.

Firms thus appear to define their trade preferences rationally. Historical context and ideological atmosphere may influence them, but these factors do not outweigh cost-benefit calculations. In fact, the costs of protection, especially relative to other options, are of major importance in deterring internationally oriented firms from seeking protection in times of economic distress.

THE HISTORICAL PUZZLE

Why did the 1970s see less protection than the 1920s, despite the comparable levels of economic distress and declining hegemony that characterized both? Our answer to this puzzle can now be given. Firms more integrated into the international economy are less protectionist than domestically oriented ones under similar conditions of economic difficulty. On a macro level, this implies that in periods when such international ties are more prevalent, demands for protection throughout the economy will be less. Much higher levels of such ties, almost ten times greater, in fact, were apparent in the 1970s than in the 1920s (see table 6.3). In the 1970s, therefore, many more firms

[24] Victoria Curzon Price, *Industrial Policies in the EC* (London: St. Martin's, 1981), esp. pp. 21, 35.

TABLE 6.3 Average U.S. International Economic Ties, 1920s and 1970s

U.S. Industrial Export Dependence
1920s	2.1% (1925)
1970s	20% (1975)

U.S. Manufacturing Multinationality
1920s	2.5% (1929)
1970s	20% (1977)

SOURCES: For average U.S. industrial export dependence (the value of industrial exports as a percentage of total industrial GNP): Data for 1920s from Robert Lipsey, *Price and Quantity Trends in the Foreign Trade of the United States* (Princeton: Princeton University Press, 1963), pp. 434-35; data on the 1970s from 1985 *Economic Report of the President* (Washington, D.C.: GPO, 1986), tables B-10, B-101. For average multinationality of U.S. industry: 1920s data on value of direct foreign investment by industry from U.S. Senate, *American Branch Factories Abroad*, 71st Cong., 3rd sess., 1931, S. Doc. 258, p. 27; data on the value of industrial GNP from Lipsey, *Price and Quantity Trends*, p. 424. Data on the 1970s from U.S. Dept. of Commerce, *1977 Enterprise Statistics* (Washington, DC: GPO, 1981), for value of all foreign assets of U.S. manufacturing as a percentage of total manufacturing assets (column Q over column R).

willing to resist the temptation to demand protection in times of economic distress existed.

Although I have argued that the growth of international ties contributed to the maintenance of free trade in the 1970s and early 1980s, it must be noted that this internationalization of U.S. industry went hand in hand with trade liberalization in the postwar period. Clearly, the liberalization of trade in the 1950s and 1960s was one factor promoting the growth of these international ties. But much of this expansion occurred before the two most significant reductions in trade barriers—those negotiated in the Kennedy and Tokyo Rounds. U.S. export dependence and especially U.S. multinationality grew significantly before the phasing in of the Kennedy Round tariff cuts in the early 1970s. U.S. industrial export dependence rose 33 percent between 1960 and 1970, and the value of U.S. direct foreign investment in manufacturing increased nearly 800 percent between 1950 and 1970.[25] The growth of these international ties cannot be separated from the liberalization of trade occurring at the same time. But the

[25] The export dependence data come from Report of the President's Commission on Industrial Competitiveness, *Global Competition*, 1:36. The data on direct foreign investment come from Feldstein, ed., *The American Economy in Transition*, p. 240, table 3.30.

expansion of these ties prior to the 1970s suggests that forces for trade liberalization—e.g., industries with international ties—were in place before the 1970s and were factors in the liberalization that occurred during that decade. The growth of international ties meant that by the 1970s many more firms were more willing to resist protectionist pressures.

Demand for protection, despite higher average levels of import penetration, was less widespread than in the 1920s. This reduced demand provides a partial answer to the central puzzle. Moreover, it suggests that arguments that examine the "supply" of protection should also look closely at demand, since claims of reduced "supply" are less interesting if less protection is also initially being demanded. The 1970s were thus less protectionist than expected, given the decade's high levels of import penetration, because the demand for such protection was muted by industries' heightened international interdependence.

CHAPTER 7

Industry Politics and Policy Outcomes

RISING economic interdependence in this century has had uneven effects upon industries. It has left some firms very internationally oriented and others completely dependent on the domestic market. This has affected the politics of policy making in international trade by increasing divisions among firms on trade issues. This chapter focuses on the politics of trade among firms within an industry and examines how difficult the aggregation of firms' preferences into a unified industry position has become. The case studies will aid our consideration of why political divisions among firms have increased since World War II. These divisions have affected the politics of trade policy making and may weaken an industry's capacity to realize its preferences in the political arena. This chapter also discusses other influences on firms' abilities to realize their trade preferences. In particular, it examines how both industries' potential for influence and political decision makers' goals affect the ability of industries to get what they want.

INTRA-INDUSTRY DIVISIONS

The growth of international economic interdependence in this century has split industries in two on trade issues. Although this growth has increasingly exposed all firms to foreign competition, it has also left some firms significantly tied to the international economy and others wholly dependent on their domestic markets. This cleavage has divided industries in a particular fashion. The largest firms have tended to become the most international, while the small and medium firms have retained their domestic base, thus pitting the large multinationals against the medium- to small-sized domestic enterprises.[1]

The politics of industries concerning trade policy issues have been affected in two ways. First, as interdependence has grown and the divisions have increased, it has become harder for an industry to develop a unified position on trade policy. As the large firms in an industry have become increasingly international, their preferences have

[1] Bergsten, Horst, and Moran, *American Multinationals and American Interests*, pp. 221-43.

diverged from the rest of the industry's. These large multinationals with extensive global trade networks have come to prefer a "free trade system," one without barriers obstructing their trade and production flows. These firms have been antiprotectionist, even in times of economic distress. Smaller firms without international ties have not developed such preferences, however, and in times of mounting foreign competition have demanded closure of the home market.

As a consequence, these divergent interests often have prevented firms from developing a common industry position. When preferences have not been aggregated, individual firms, or groups of them, have presented their own positions to the government. Political decision makers have been faced with different opinions and preferences on trade issues by firms within the same industry. This proliferation of industry views has reduced an industry's influence on decision makers and allowed them more leeway to make their own choices about the issue. Divisions among social actors may therefore enhance the autonomy of political actors by splintering opposition to policy decisions.[2] Thus, not only may this uneven interdependence impede the aggregation of firms' preferences at the industry level, but it may also reduce their bargaining power with governmental actors.

A second way interdependence has reshaped the politics of trade involves its effects on the formation of industry consensus. Despite divergent interests among firms, industries have been able at times to formulate a common position. This has usually entailed much bargaining and compromise. The final position has been likely to reflect both groups' preferences to some extent; however, this compromise has often been skewed toward the preferences of the large multinationals, because they have been the biggest and potentially the most powerful actors in the industry. The agreement reached has therefore been less protectionist than the domestically oriented firms would have liked. The smaller domestic firms have not been completely without influence. Quite often, since the growth of foreign competition directly threatened their existence, these firms have organized themselves well and presented a strong case. Nevertheless, the resulting compromise on trade issues may still be less protectionist than the majority of the industry's firms would have preferred. All in all, industries that have been unevenly touched by rising interdependence have become divided in their trade policy preferences, and such divisions

[2] Peter Evans, Dieter Rueschemeyer, and Theda Skocpol, eds., *Bringing the State Back In* (Cambridge: Cambridge University Press, 1986), esp. pp. 63-64; Eric Nordlinger, *On the Autonomy of the Democratic State* (Cambridge: Harvard University Press, 1981).

have reduced their capacity for demanding closure of the home market.

INTRA-INDUSTRY DIVISIONS
AMONG THE CASE STUDIES

The importance of intra-industry divisions was apparent in the case studies. Where these divisions existed, pressures for protection were mitigated. In addition, the extent of these divisions differed between the 1920s and 1970s U.S. cases. In the 1920s, when firms' ties to the international economy were less well developed, fewer of the cases revealed these internal divisions, and those that did were the most international industries considered. In contrast, five of the six 1970s cases had such internal disagreements. The French cases displayed a pattern in between the two American ones. Divisions were less apparent in the French cases than in the U.S. cases of the 1970s, largely because the French industries had fewer firms in them. Government policy and industry's practice of fostering concentration—i.e., the development of "national champions"—in the postwar period helped reduce the number of firms in many industries and favored the preferences of large and often more international firms. Thus in the French cases, divisions were more prevalent in industries with a large number of firms and few international ties, a pattern different from that of the 1920s American cases, as we shall see.

Among the 1920s case studies, three industries, all among the most international of those studied, revealed deep internal divisions over trade issues. These divisions tended to be incipient, often the initial breach in the industry's unity as a consequence of its recent internationalization. These growing internal splits, nevertheless, affected the industry's politics on trade issues.

The textile machinery builders in the 1920s were in the aggregate a highly export-dependent industry, but these exports were concentrated among the cotton machinery builders. The makers of wool machinery, in contrast, were oriented toward the domestic market. This split affected the industry's capacity to develop a common position during the 1921 tariff revision hearings. At that time, when these exports were most important as a consequence of World War I's effect on competing European producers, the divisions within the industry were quite apparent. It did not testify at all during the hearings, largely because no common position could be developed among the firms. The builders of cotton machines had little interest in further protection, while those who made wool machinery wanted tariffs increased. This lack of consensus impeded efforts to present an industry position on the tariff to Congress. Later, in 1929, exports had fallen in significance and a mildly protectionist consensus was formulated. Even in this period, however, a compromise was necessary, and the one that resulted seemed less protectionist than many manufacturers in the industry desired. The internal cleavages promoted by uneven interdependence thus mitigated pressures for market closure in this industry.

A second case of incipient but growing intra-industry divisions involved the photographic equipment industry in the 1920s. By the end of the decade, this industry was one of the most multinational and export-oriented of our case studies, but these ties were concentrated in the hands of one firm, Eastman Kodak. As Kodak's international operations grew, its preferences increasingly diverged from the rest of the industry's. In the 1921 hearings, Kodak's position on camera and film tariffs, calling for slight increases, was close to the rest of the industry's. By 1929 Kodak's position was oriented more toward "free trade," even seeking tariff reductions on some items. This position contrasted with that of the remaining U.S. film manufacturers. In this case, rising but uneven interdependence moved the industry's preferences away from protection and fueled internal divisions, which further reduced its capacity to seek protection.

The third case of a divided industry in the 1920s involved the fertilizer producers. The extensive international ties evident in this industry were distributed in a skewed fashion. The large firms involved in the nitrate and phosphate sectors possessed most of the industry's exports and foreign production operations, while the small potash producers were largely domestic. In the 1920s, as foreign production and export of potash revived, the small U.S. producers demanded protection. These firms' demands were strongly resisted by the large multinational producers, who favored freer trade. The large firms lobbied not only against tariffs on potash but also for retention of the duty-free entry of all other fertilizer and its ingredients. Because of the global network of trade and production these firms had created in order to make fertilizer, they opposed tariff increases, which would upset these networks. In this case the large international producers, intent on preserving an open U.S. market, overwhelmed the protectionist sentiment of the small firms.

Among industries in the 1920s, intra-industry divisions were evident and did reduce protectionist influences. But they were less prevalent because interdependence had not spread widely. In the three industries where divisions appeared, these conflicts were just devel-

oping in the 1920s. At this time, moreover, *inter*industry politics may
have been more crucial in the development of industries' trade policy
positions. As the 1920s cases demonstrate, the preferences of other
industries closely connected to the industry examined often influenced its position. The woolen goods manufacturers were affected by
the wool growers and their preferences for protection. The textile machinery builders faced pressures for protection from the textile manufacturers, and the newsprint producers were pushed toward freer
trade by the newspaper publishers. Farmers backed the fertilizer industry in their advocacy of duty-free fertilizer, and motion picture
producers and distributors pressured the photographic equipment
makers to seek lower duties. Although this interindustry pressure was
not always successful, it constituted an important element in the politics of trade in the 1920s, one perhaps more important than intra-
industry divisions and one lacking in the 1970s U.S. cases.

Among the 1970s U.S. cases, *intra*-industry divisions over trade policy prevailed. Five of the six cases were marked by serious internal
divisions resulting from firms' different ties to the international economy. These divisions were deeper and more developed than those in
the 1920s and had an even greater effect on the politics of trade. In
most of the cases, intra-industry divisions mitigated protectionist pressures.

A prominent example was the semiconductor industry. It was highly
integrated into the international economy, but the largest producers
were the most international. IBM, Texas Instruments, and Western
Electric were far more multinational than were the remaining merchant producers, operating mainly in California. In the late 1970s
these California producers became interested in taking action against
Japanese semiconductor imports. These producers created the industry's political association, the SIA, and initiated action for an unfair
trading practices case against Japan. The large producers refused to
join this association and urged that this petition be dropped. IBM
even agreed to join if the trade complaint were kept quiet. This compromise was accepted, and the association's interests shifted. Instead
of seeking sanctions against Japanese imports, the producers agreed
to pressure the U.S. and Japanese governments to open negotiations
to reduce further tariff and nontariff barriers on semiconductor trade
between the two countries. In this case, pressure from the large multinationals shifted the association's interests away from market closure
to promoting market openness.

Internal divisions were also apparent among the U.S. tire manufacturers. International ties were unevenly distributed among these pro-

ducers. The largest firm, Goodyear, had the most extensive foreign trade and production operations. The other three major producers were large but without the extensive global ties of Goodyear. In the early 1970s, when imports first became a threat, the major producers, excluding Goodyear, initiated a countervailing duty case against Michelin, the main importer. These firms sought to slow down Michelin's penetration of the U.S. market. Goodyear opposed this case. Furthermore, the firm played a central role in having the duties imposed on Michelin terminated early. Goodyear thus acted as a barrier against protection for U.S. tire manufacturers. In the late 1970s Goodyear internationalized further and continued to promote open markets, while the other producers abandoned their foreign operations and trimmed their domestic ones, sometimes even exiting the industry completely. In the face of Goodyear's opposition, calls for protection were avoided.

Intra-industry conflict also affected the U.S. radio and television manufacturers. The leading firms in this industry were bifurcated into two groups. Two firms, RCA and General Electric, were very international, while the other manufacturers of importance, GTE-Sylvania, Magnavox, and Zenith, were domestic in their operations. From the late 1960s on, this latter group initiated a large number of unfair trade complaints against the Japanese. These complaints suffered various fates in the 1970s; some were dropped and others recognized. But these firms lobbied increasingly throughout the decade for relief against Japanese imports. Culminating this effort was the group's filing of an escape clause petition in 1976. This petition and others were opposed by RCA. With strong ties to the Japanese industry, RCA had no desire to see quotas placed on Japanese imports. The option that was finally taken—negotiation of an orderly marketing agreement—was less disturbing to RCA, since the OMA's quotas were generous and did not affect imports of many subassemblies or components, an important part of RCA's operations. In the end RCA did not actively oppose this measure. But it was not renewed, and little protectionist sentiment has arisen since, largely because the domestically oriented U.S. producers have either sold their operations to foreign firms or moved production abroad. Further internationalization of the industry thus reduced its divisions and its preferences for protection.

Another case of an industry riven by internal divisions over trade issues involved the U.S. manufacturers of watches and clocks. Among the firms with domestic production, two groups developed in the 1970s. The first was composed of long-standing traditional watchmakers, led by Timex. They exported little and manufactured mainly in the United States. The second group was primarily made up of semi-conductor producers who had moved into electronic watch production. These firms were more international, usually maintaining some offshore-assembly and trading operations. As electronic watches, particularly their imports, took over the U.S. market, the traditional domestic producers tried to halt the process. Pressuring both Congress and the ITC, they sought to have tariffs on electronic watches and parts increased. These efforts were opposed by the U.S. electronic watch producers. Their vocal opposition and the growing international ties of the traditional domestic manufacturers helped to ensure that protection would not be granted. Throughout the 1950s and 1960s the traditional manufacturers had been able to obtain protection, but the forceful opposition of these new producers was an important element in their failure to obtain it in the 1970s. Increased divisions within the industry thus reduced its capacity to obtain protection.

Changes in the U.S. footwear industry's internal cohesion affected its ability to demand protection. Throughout the 1960s and most of the 1970s, U.S. footwear makers had very few international ties. Until the late 1970s, the industry was unified in its trade policy preferences, which grew increasingly protectionist. After receiving some protection in the late 1970s, firms within the industry responded differently. A number of large firms began importing shoes and/or producing and assembling them abroad. Protection became less desirable for these firms, since it raised the costs of their foreign operations. They gradually came to oppose efforts of the more domestic producers and eventually allied with other importers, foreign firms, and retailers in their association. As their foreign ties developed, their opposition to further protection grew. In 1981, at the end of the first quota agreement, these firms worked to ensure that no new quota would be instituted. Their efforts evidently paid off; new protection was denied. In this case, growing divisions within the industry undermined its ability to obtain protection.

Overall, in the 1970s U.S. cases internal divisions within industries were prevalent and significant. As interdependence spread unevenly, industries became divided in two, with the large multinationals favoring open markets and the smaller domestic firms intent on protection. In the U.S. cases these divisions worked against those seeking protection. In each instance, splits either muted the smaller firms' demands for market closure or provided vocal opposition to encourage political decision makers' resistance to such demands. Unlike in the 1920s, these cleavages were deeply embedded in the industries and had a crucial effect upon the politics of trade policy making.

Fewer intra-industry divisions were apparent among the French cases, in large part because of French efforts to encourage concentration in their industries. But two cases revealed significant internal divisions. In both, international ties were only beginning to develop, and these cases may be contrasted with those in the 1920s. However, as was true of the 1920s cases, intra-industry divisions in France had less impact than they did in the United States in the 1970s, because the French divisions were less developed.

French footwear producers were seriously divided in their trade preferences. In the aggregate, these producers were neither substantial exporters nor large multinationals. But at the firm level, some large producers depended heavily on exports, foreign production operations, and imports. The rest of the industry was primarily domestic in its orientation. In the mid-1970s, as imports rose rapidly, these domestic producers began pressing for some protection of their home market. These efforts were opposed by the largest firms; and to halt them, they staged a "coup d'état" against the industry association leader organizing the protectionist movement. At this point, protection was avoided. Later, however, strong sentiment for relief against imports rose again among the majority of firms. This time the large firms were unable to stop the effort, but they were able to restrict the scope of protection to a few countries where they were not involved. Initial, successful resistance to protection was thus later overwhelmed by the vigorous effort of many smaller firms to obtain aid. Internal divisions did, nevertheless, limit this protection.

The French watch and clock producers were also an industry facing increasing divisions in the 1970s. Throughout the decade a large group of exporters resisted efforts to protect the home market. By the end of the decade, with exports falling and imports surging, a new firm, Matra, entered the industry and took over the operations of the largest and most successful exporters. This consolidation pitted Matra against the smaller, less export-oriented traditional producers. As desire for import relief increased among these firms, Matra initially resisted it. Matra's exports and ties to the Japanese worked against any interest in protection. In the early 1980s, however, the smaller firms succeeded in having quotas placed on various importers. Matra was apparently unenthusiastic about this outcome but was not actively opposed to it. Matra's initial effort, nonetheless, served to dampen protectionist pressures within the watch and clock industry.

In the French cases as well as in the U.S. cases, intra-industry divisions over trade altered the politics of trade policy making. In particular, these divisions helped reduce protectionist pressures and outcomes. After divisions arose, industries seemed less successful than they had been earlier in obtaining protection. Overall, not only did rising interdependence shift some firms' preferences away from protection, but it also created intra-industry divisions, which made the aggregation of firms' preferences more problematic and protection more difficult to realize.

POLICY OUTCOMES

Thus far this study has shown how the internationalization of an economy reduces demands for protection and the capacity to obtain it at the firm and industry level. That such demand is important in understanding the policies adopted has been assumed, but this assumption will now be examined. There is evidence to support it both in the cases here and in other works on trade policy. We focus on when industry preferences and policy outcomes are likely to be highly correlated and when they might diverge.

In general, other considerations of trade policy outcomes at the sectoral level support the claim that firms' demands have an influence on policy outcomes. Many of these studies employ aggregate regression models of industries' tariff levels and include variables expressing industry preferences.[3] The variables indicating preferences focus on those industries most adversely affected by imports, those with the most "rents" to gain from protection, and those with various ties to the international economy. Most of these works find that these preferences have some influence on the "supply" of protection, although their effects vary from one study to another.

Two of the most interesting examinations of this relationship demonstrate the importance of demand for understanding supply. Robert Baldwin tests specifically for the influence of demand for protection on its supply. He notes, "the intensity of demand for protection does play a significant role in influencing duty reductions in [certain] industries."[4] In another study, Judith Goldstein shows that "demanders" of U.S. trade law relief have a substantial success rate. Indeed, the frequency with which industries demanding relief obtained it in the 1970s ranged between 15 percent and 90 percent and averaged around 30 percent.[5] In approximately one-third of all cases, demands by firms or industries met with successful responses. Overall, these

[3] See chapter 2, note 1.
[4] R. Baldwin, *Political Economy of U.S. Import Policy*, p. 169.
[5] Goldstein, "Reexamination of American Commercial Policy," p. 329, table 59.

studies support the assumption that firms' preferences are important in the development of trade policies.

But do others corroborate the specific argument here that firms' preferences *as shaped by their export dependence and their multinationality* influence policy outcomes? These factors are less well studied, but they do appear in several recent studies. Generally, the relationship between export dependence and levels of protection among industries has been significant and robust.[6] The influence of multinationality on policy outcomes is less clear. This result is not unexpected, since the cases here show that multinationals are not equally interested in resisting protection. Only those with extensive trading networks will be resolutely antiprotectionist; others may be interested in selective protection in times of distress. This division of preferences suggests foreign operations in the aggregate, as used in most studies, may not have any clear-cut effect on policy outcomes. Indeed, few studies show it to have a significant, consistent effect on policy.[7]

We have already seen one problem with aggregate examinations of policy outcomes. As highlighted in the case studies, the distribution of international ties within an industry is important. If only one or a few firms account for the bulk of these ties, then divisions of preferences on trade among the firms will be significant and will affect the elaboration of an industry's trade policy position. That such divisions are overlooked by an industry-wide measure of multinationality explains in part this variable's poor performance in these models. The 1970s U.S. radio and television industry and watch and clock industry are two cases in point. In the aggregate both had substantial intrafirm foreign trade, but in each this activity was concentrated in the hands of a few firms. These firms—RCA in the former case and the semiconductor producers in the latter—did resist protection, although their efforts were differentially successful. The domestically oriented television manufacturers were able to obtain some selective protection; the traditional watch firms were less successful. These cases point out some of the difficulties involved in using multinationality in the aggregate to account for trade policy outcomes.

The case studies in chapters 3, 4, and 5 support the assumption that

[6] See chapter 2, notes 2, 3.

[7] R. Baldwin, *Political Economy of U.S. Import Policy*, pp. 150-72, finds outcomes little influenced by direct foreign investment, but does find outcomes effected by industry demands. Fong, in "Export Dependence," ch. 2, shows direct foreign investment to have some effect on policy, although less than other variables. Lavergne, *Political Economy of U.S. Tariffs*, pp. 153-54, shows intrafirm trade among multinationals to have only a weak effect, if any, on protectionist levels.

industry preferences influence policy outcomes. First, in none of the eighteen cases were industries accorded protection when they, or substantial parts of them, did *not* desire it. The issue of protection was usually placed on the political agenda by industries. Protection was not a political issue until industries made it one. Second, in many cases when industries demanded changes in trade barriers, they were able to obtain them. In the 1920s the six industries examined were quite successful at having tariffs raised *or lowered* to meet their preferences. Even among the divided industries—such as fertilizer and photographic equipment—the larger firms were able to have their preferences for low tariffs instituted. For the 1920s cases the translation of preferences into outcomes was apparently not a difficult process.

Among the twelve 1970s French and U.S. cases, in all but four did industry demands influence policy outcomes. Efforts by the U.S. semiconductor producers and French pharmaceutical manufacturers to further open markets at home and abroad met with success politically. A general disinterest in protection by the French glass and tire makers and by the U.S. tire makers kept protection off the political agenda for these industries. Firms desiring protection were also often successful. The U.S. tire makers' early trade petition against Michelin was acted upon favorably by the U.S. government, even though Goodyear, the industry leader, opposed it. The French watch and clock industry, once it demanded protection, was able to obtain it both in France and at the European Community. The U.S. television manufacturers had variable success. They obtained some import relief early in the decade, then were denied relief, and finally received protection through an OMA, despite the opposition of the leading firm, RCA. The U.S. watch producers were divided. In the end the traditional producers were unable to get protection from the U.S. government in the 1970s, in large part because of the ardent opposition of the U.S. electronic watch producers. In this case the preferences of electronic watch producers prevailed. Later, however, the Japanese granted temporary relief to the U.S. industry by offering to monitor their exports to the United States. In all eight of these cases, industries were able, with some effort—probably more than in the 1920s—to realize their preferences for greater market openness *and* closure.

In the four other U.S. cases of the 1970s, the industries had a more difficult time obtaining the outcomes desired. In the United States, both the footwear industry and the machine tool producers expended a great deal of effort to influence policy, with little return. In the early 1970s the footwear industry was denied all efforts at import relief. Only in 1976 did the industry get some of what it desired—quotas on imports. In the machine tool case, the industry was successful neither in obtaining aid and greater market openness for its exports early in the decade nor in receiving import relief after 1978. Although it was granted some relief in the mid-1980s, its substantial efforts for greater openness and closure in the 1970s were not that successful. In these two cases other factors influenced the policies adopted.

In two French cases the industries had little trouble gaining protection at home but more difficulty obtaining it at the EC. The French footwear industry, once it overcame its internal divisions on trade, was able to negotiate quotas on imports into France. Since it refused responsibility for negotiating them and left the task to the industry itself, the French government probably did not favor, or did not want to be seen as favoring, these arrangements. The French producers were less successful at the EC. There, their demands for protection were strongly resisted by other members' industries and governments.

For the French television manufacturers, protection at home had been willingly provided by French authorities since the industry's inception. When the industry realized that only protection at the European level would allow it to survive, the industry redirected its pressure toward the European Community. Here the French producers had difficulty in obtaining protection, because they were opposed by other states and their firms. Only after several efforts were the French able to break down resistance to their plan and obtain the protection they desired. These cases suggest that in forums where more interests are considered, the preferences of any one group may be more difficult to realize. In these cases the EC seemed much less easily swayed by protectionist demands than did the French government.

Overall, industry preferences exercised an important influence on trade policy outcomes. But the cases, as well as other studies, point out that such demands are not the only factor shaping policies. At least two other factors warrant consideration for a better understanding of trade policy making.

The political influence of an industry is obviously linked to its ability to get what it wants. Other studies, relating structural elements of industries to influence over trade policy outcomes, suggest indicators of an industry's political clout. Among these are the industry's size, its concentration, the number of workers it employs, its geographical spread, and its political organization.[8] As studies show, policy out-

[8] For a more complete list, see Daniel Esty and Richard Caves, "Market Structure and Political Influence," *Economic Inquiry* 21 (January 1983):24-38, and chapter 2, note 1, above.

comes are affected by some of these factors, especially an industry's size and work force. The larger these are, the more influence an industry appears to have.

The variable success rates of the cases also indicate that factors other than demand influence outcomes. In the cases where success was limited, one factor differentiating them from the others was the size of the industry. For instance, of the 1970s U.S. cases, the two that had limited success—footwear and machine tools—involved the smallest industries. In terms of their own size and their labor force, these two industries rank below the other cases, except for the traditional watch and clock industry, which also had limited success in obtaining its preferences.[9] Part of these industries' difficulty in obtaining their desired outcomes may have been due to their inability to amass a critical amount of public support. Other industries, such as semiconductors and tires—not to mention the textile, auto, and steel industries, which rank among the largest in the United States—had an easier time pressing their claims in part because their greater weight in the economy lent them greater political resources.

In addition to size, several other factors also condition an industry's political influence. In the French cases the importance of an industry's regional concentration was evident.[10] The French footwear, watch and clock, and tire industries were better able to get a hearing from public authorities than their size would suggest, largely due to the high concentration of each of their activities in one region. This brought them the attention of regional public officials, who in turn pressured national officials to help them. The U.S. watch and clock case was similar. The location of a number of Timex plants in Wilbur Mills's district was often cited as one reason he sponsored the bill favored by Timex

---

[9] U.S. Dept. of Commerce, Bureau of the Census, *1977 Census of Manufacturers*, Industry Series, pts. II-III (Washington, D.C.: GPO, 1980).

SIC code	labor force	value-added (*millions of $*)
3011 tires	114,000	$4347
3143 men's footwear	55,000	872
3144 women's footwear	57,000	755
3541 metal-cutting machine tools	59,400	1866
3651 radio and TV	74,600	2352
3674 semiconductors	114,000	3410
3873 watches and clocks	31,500	685

[10] Results measuring geographical concentration have been quite mixed, but these tests have usually involved only the United States. See Lavergne, *Political Economy of U.S. Tariffs*, pp. 101-104; Caves, "Economic Models of Political Choice"; Pincus, *Pressure Groups and Politics in Antebellum Tariffs*.

that would have extended protection to the industry. In these cases regional concentration may have magnified the industry's political clout beyond that expected from its size.

The 1920s cases suggest the additional importance of an industry's allies and enemies. As noted earlier, in these cases interindustry politics appeared very significant; the political influence of other, closely linked industries, combined with an industry's ability to find such allies, were important factors influencing its chances of political success. Other studies of the pre–World War II period have also noted the importance of coalitions among social actors for policy outcomes.[11] These factors—size, regional concentration, and coalitional ability— and others seem essential for a more complete understanding of trade policy.

A second feature important to understanding policy outcomes involves policy makers' goals. Although some studies have stressed the importance of policy makers' ideological frameworks, other investigations and the cases here point to the more immediate goals and concerns of policy makers as most relevant for particular policy decisions.[12] Not only who is making the decisions but also what goals and concerns these decision makers have are relevant. For example, Robert Baldwin shows that the ITC and the President are motivated by different forces in their decisions about trade complaints.[13] He suggests that presidents will be more or less receptive to protectionist pleas depending on their macroeconomic concerns; that is, whether they are primarily battling inflation or unemployment will affect their receptivity to protectionist demands.[14]

A similar argument has been made for the U.S. Congress. Though Congress is usually seen as more susceptible to industry pressure than is the chief executive, Bauer, Pool, and Dexter's study of Congress and trade policy making maintains that the particular goals and tasks members of Congress set for themselves crucially influence their re-

[11] Gourevitch, "International Trade, Domestic Coalitions, and Liberty"; Peter Gourevitch, "Breaking with Orthodoxy," *International Organization* 38 (Winter 1984):95-130; Gourevitch, *Politics in Hard Times*; Ferguson, "From Normalcy to New Deal."

[12] For arguments stressing larger ideological concerns, see Goldstein, "Reexamination of U.S. Commercial Policy"; and Goldstein, "Political Economy of Trade." On the goals of policy makers, see R. Baldwin, *Political Economy of U.S. Import Policy*, pp. 13-27; Cheh, "U.S. Concessions in Kennedy Round and Short-Run Adjustment Costs"; Lavergne, *Political Economy of U.S. Tariffs*, pp. 164-66, 186-87; Bauer, Pool, and Dexter, *American Business and Public Policy*, esp. chs. 29-34.

[13] R. Baldwin, *Political Economy of U.S. Import Policy*, ch. 3 and pp. 129-33.

[14] Ibid., pp. 132-33.

ceptivity to industry pleas.[15] From this perspective, policy outcomes often depend on who is making the decision and on what the decision maker's own goals are.

The case studies provide evidence for this argument. Industries' success rates varied, depending on who the decision maker was. For example, the 1970s American industries were more likely to be successful if the Commerce Department rather than the Treasury were in charge of a trade complaint.[16] The firms realized this and made a successful effort to have responsibility for these matters shifted to Commerce. This department was viewed as more "attuned" to industry interests, while the Treasury, especially in the 1970s, was centrally concerned with inflation and thus disinclined to protect industries. The cases also suggest that Congress was more receptive to industry pressure than the executive branch.[17] When industries did not receive, or were slow in receiving, what they desired from the President, their response was to find congressional allies to press the executive branch and/or to have Congress itself initiate a bill in the industry's interests, as the footwear, watch and clock, and radio and television manufacturers all did in the 1970s.

The importance of decision makers and their goals was also apparent in the French cases. In several instances, conflicts between the Ministry of Finance and the Ministry of Industry suggest the differential responsiveness of different decision makers to industry efforts. In these cases the Ministry of Industry, like the U.S. Commerce Department, seemed more receptive to industry desires and interested in an industry's prosperity than did the Ministry of Finance, which was consumed with budgetary matters and inflation, much like the U.S. Treasury. Overall, the case studies demonstrate the importance of political decision makers—in particular, who they are and what their central goals and concerns are. Thus though industry preferences are important for trade policy outcomes, a more complete understanding of them requires an examination of at least two other factors: the political influence of different industries as well as the identity and goals of policy makers involved in the decision.

[15] Bauer, Pool, and Dexter, *American Business and Public Policy*, chs. 29-34.

[16] Goldstein, "Political Economy of Trade," pp. 175-78, finds no real difference between the two, but she does show ITC acceptance rates to be higher than those of either Treasury or Commerce.

[17] R. Baldwin, *Political Economy of U.S. Import Policy*, chs. 3, 4, pp. 178-79, finds Congress more susceptible and able to exert pressure on the executive branch. But he notes that the President can also influence congressional votes on trade.

CONCLUSION

In sum, the uneven spread of economic interdependence—of international ties, in particular—has made the aggregation of firms' interests into a unified industry position more difficult by increasing the divergences among firms' preferences. These differences have grown in importance since the 1920s and have contributed to the reduction of protectionist pressures. This new element in the politics of trade is therefore another factor accounting for why protection was less widespread in the 1970s than in the 1920s.

In addition, industry trade policy preferences *do* affect policy outcomes, as both the cases here and other studies reveal. But other factors also influence this relationship. Industries in which firms' interests were divided, for example, provide greater autonomy for decision makers. Industries' relative political influence, as measured by their size, regional concentration, and/or coalitional ability, affect their chances for success in the political arena. The identity and goals of policy makers involved in the issue also condition whether industry demands will be met. We may say, therefore, that industry preferences are among several important factors that shape trade policy.

CHAPTER 8

Trade Politics in the United States and France

THE FRENCH CASES provide two critical contributions to this study of trade politics. First, they give the argument greater cross-national validity by helping establish that rising international economic interdependence affected industries in states other than the United States. If, as is claimed, an international-level change reshapes the domestic preferences of firms, then this change in preferences should have occurred in all advanced industrial countries experiencing new levels of foreign linkages. One test of this is to examine and compare the preferences of firms in more than one nation, in this case in the United States and France. According to the argument here, rising international interdependence in the form of exports, multinationality, and global intrafirm trade should affect firms' preferences similarly in the two countries, regardless of other differences between them. Such a finding would be unexpected by other theories, given their characterization of France and the United States as opposites in terms of their domestic political structures.[1] Comparing industries in these two nations should thus provide a good test of our hypothesis.

This chapter begins by examining how the growth of economic interdependence affected the French economy in general and its firms' preferences in particular. Have French firms' international positions shaped their trade preferences? What role have other factors played? In particular, has the "strong" French state been able to impose its preferences on firms? In some arguments about the state, it is viewed as "an autonomous entity capable of shaping societal preferences in accord with its own."[2] Has this been true for French firms' preferences?

This chapter also examines differences in the way the French and American economies experienced rising interdependence. Chapter 6 discussed the similarities between the two experiences. Indeed, this work's argument rests on such similarities, for it hypothesizes that similarly positioned firms in the two countries should have similar trade

---

[1] Katzenstein, ed., *Power and Plenty*; Zysman, *Governments, Markets, and Growth*.

[2] Nordlinger, *On the Autonomy of the Democratic State*, p. 100.

preferences. Although, as seen in chapter 6, strong similarities in the ways firms determined their preferences did exist across the countries, it is useful to focus on the differences as well.

The second contribution of the French cases is that they demonstrate how firms' preferences affect trade policy outcomes. France is a critical case. Much of the literature on economic policy making implies that France and the United States should be differentially sensitive to industry demands. The United States is depicted as a "weak" state—one very permeable to interest group pressure. France is portrayed as a "strong" state, with a "state-led" policy system highly resistant to industry pressure.[3] In this view, the preferences of French firms should have little bearing on policy because the process is so insulated from societal influence. After exploring how the policy structure in France allows firms' preferences into the process, the discussion here concludes that France is a less "strong" state than many characterizations suggest.

We will focus on four characteristics of the policy-making process to see how firms' preferences are involved in and come to exert a major influence on it. This underscores the importance of understanding what these preferences are and how they are formed. The argument, however, is not that firms' preferences alone account for trade policy outcomes or that the policy processes in the United States and France are exactly alike. Rather, firms' preferences are seen as one of the most important influences on trade policy in both countries. Examination of both firms' trade preferences and the policy making process is essential to providing an answer to the question of why the advanced industrial countries maintained relatively open economies in the 1970s despite the strong pressures for closure they faced.

RISING INTERDEPENDENCE

Growing economic interdependence has reduced some firms' preferences for protection, even in times of economic distress. Growing interdependence in France has taken a different course than in the United States (see table 8.1). Both its timing and its character have been different. For industrial products, France's integration into the international economy rose sharply only after 1958, and its most sig-

[3] Stephen Krasner, "U.S. Commercial and Monetary Policy"; John Zysman, "The French State in the International Economy"; and Peter Katzenstein, "Conclusion," all in *Power and Plenty*, ed. Katzenstein; Zysman, *Governments, Markets, and Growth*, avoids the use of the terms "strong" and "weak" but suggests much the same; see esp. chs. 3, 5, 6.

TABLE 8.1 Average U.S. and French International Economic Ties, 1970s

Industrial Export Dependence

U.S. (1970s)	20% (1975)
France (1970s)	31% (1979)

Multinationality of Industry

U.S. (1970s)	20% (1977)
France (1970s)	10% (1974)

SOURCES: For average industrial export dependence: data for the United States from 1985 *Economic Report of the President* (Washington, D.C.: GPO, 1986), tables B-10, B-101, for the value of industrial exports as a percentage of total industrial GNP. The French figure is from Ministère de l'Economie et des Finances, La DREE, *Une Décennie du Commerce Extérieur Français* (Paris: Documentation Française, November 1983), p. xiv. For average multinationality of industry: Data on United States from U.S. Dept. of Commerce, *1977 Enterprise Statistics* (Washington, D.C.: GPO, 1981), pp. 374-85, for value of all foreign assets of U.S. manufacturing as a percentage of total manufacturing assets. French value is for foreign French production as a percentage of total French production; see Julien Savary, *Les Multinationales Françaises* (Paris: Press Universitaires Françaises, 1981), p. 21.

nificant integration occurred after 1968. This was sparked by the 1958 opening of the European Common Market.[4]

In 1958, with the implementation of the Treaty of Rome, France's industrial trade accelerated and shifted geographically. From approximately 12 percent of domestic production in 1958, exports of industrial goods rose to around 20 percent in 1968 and to 33 percent by 1981.[5] Import penetration followed a similar pattern, growing from 15 percent in 1958 to over 20 percent in 1968 and finally to almost 30 percent in 1981.[6] The openness of the economy to trade grew rapidly after 1958, much more so than it had in the previous century.[7] Trade relations themselves changed. In 1958, less than 30 percent of French

[4] Prior to this market's opening, France had substantial trade relations, but these were heavily concentrated in nonindustrial goods and with former French colonies. Jean-Paul Balladur, "Les Echanges Extérieurs de la France entre 1960-70," *Economie et Société*, no. 31 (February 1972):11-13; Stoffaës, *Grande Menace Industrielle*, p. 203.

[5] CEREM, *Crise, Concurrence Internationale, et Stratégies*, table 3; Ministère de l'Economie, la DREE, *Une Décennie du Commerce Extérieur Français* (Paris: Documentation Française, November 1983), p. xiv.

[6] Ibid.

[7] Table 1 in Alain Lipietz, "The Globalization of the General Crisis of Fordism," SNID occasional paper no. 84-203, 1984, shows French export dependence peaked in 1899, declined until after World War II, and then began increasing.

trade was with its European partners. By the late 1970s close to 50 percent was with European Community countries.[8] This shift meant greater dependence on unmanaged trade and increased France's integration into the world economy. Unlike France's trade with its colonies, where relations of influence and strong barriers to other countries' products guaranteed the markets for French companies, trade within the EC was less managed and more subject to forces of market exchange. France's trade dependence thus has recently grown to sizable proportions, although it has long been greater than that of the United States.

The development of multinational enterprise among French firms has been more recent than among U.S. firms. In fact, by the interwar period the U.S. economy was already almost as multinational as French industry is today.[9] The development of French multinational ties began in the 1960s, with the greatest growth after 1974.[10] By 1974 foreign French production accounted for only 10 percent of total industrial production.[11] The creation of globally integrated firms has also been slower in France. Trade flows within French multinationals have been less well developed than among their U.S. counterparts. Despite domestic markets of similar size, re-export to the home market by all European multinationals amounted to $260 million in 1978 compared to $4.1 billion for U.S. firms.[12] Growth of both French trade dependence and multinationality thus occurred in the postwar period. French levels of interdependence were, however, much greater in trade, particularly trade within the EC, than in multinational activities, while the opposite held for the United States.

Did this mounting integration within Europe and into the international economy reduce French firms' preferences for protection, as the argument posits? Did French firms with international ties resist the urge to seek protection when the economy fell into serious difficulties in the 1970s? The French cases show that firms with extensive international ties did resist protectionist temptations in the 1970s and early 1980s. The tire, glass, and pharmaceutical industries were the most

[8] Ardagh, *France in the 1980s*, p. 37.

[9] Wilkins, *Maturing of the Multinational Corporation*, p. 201, estimates all U.S. direct foreign investment at 14 percent of GNP in 1929, while Savary, *Multinationales Françaises*, estimates French foreign industrial direct production in 1974 at 10 percent of total French production. These figures are not directly comparable, however.

[10] Savary, *Multinationales Françaises*, pp. 19-23, 26-29, 110-12; Ardagh, *France in the 1980s*, pp. 45-47; Savary, "Les Multinationales Françaises," p. 75.

[11] Savary, *Multinationales Françaises*, pp. 19-26.

[12] Grunwald and Flamm, *Global Factory*, pp. 25-27.

international of those studied. The major firms within each of these industries maintained their preferences for market openness in the face of economic distress. In the tire and glass industries, where trade barriers were low, the major firms sought to keep their home markets open and to prevent closure of foreign markets. The pharmaceutical producers, who were already protected, sought to have these nontariff barriers reduced. For these industries, sizable exports and multinational operations made protection undesirable as a solution to their difficulties.

Lack of protectionist demands may not, however, be a sure sign of preferences for freer trade among French firms. Many have claimed that the French protect their market through other means, such as industrial policy and nontariff barriers.[13] Although many countries use these practices, it has been maintained that the French use them more systematically than others, especially than the Americans. Hence examining just French firms' demands for traditional protectionist policies may miss the firms' true protectionist bent.

To avoid this problem, I surveyed all steps taken by French firms to obtain government aid, especially industrial policies. Though it could not always be ascertained whether these demands were protectionist in intent, it was assumed that most had protection in mind because the industries' key problem involved imports. Even with this restrictive assumption, the argument held. The firms with the strongest international ties made the fewest demands for government aid. The glass, tire, and pharmaceutical industries, all highly international, showed little interest in government help. They were less likely to deal with the government and more likely to rely on their own internal efforts to adjust. Only the pharmaceutical industry dealt extensively with the government, largely because of the public regulation of the industry already in place. These producers, however, were most interested in reducing, not enhancing, government intervention. Above all, they were concerned with adjusting to the new competitive conditions through their own strategies.

In the other cases, where the industries lacked international ties, efforts to restructure usually included demands for government aid. Indeed, these industries sought aid as an incentive to induce them to reorganize. In the footwear, television, and watch and clock cases, de-

---

[13] Curzon Price, *Industrial Policies in the EC*, p. 21; Zysman, "French State in the International Economy." More generally, the argument is that France and the United States have responded to rising interdependence differently, with the French developing a wide array of policy instruments, including industrial policy, to manage their interdependence.

mands for aid went hand in hand with demands for protection. In the radio and television case, protection and government support had evolved together, creating the industry in the 1950s. Protection probably predated the development of an industrial policy for this sector. In the footwear case, demands for aid were simultaneous with rising interest in protection. In the watch and clock case, industrial policy demands predated interest in protection. In all three cases, demands for protection grew alongside demands for government aid. Other aggregate studies support this. They report that the most protected sectors tended to receive the most extensive government aid.[14] Industrial policy therefore may not be a substitute for protection; rather, the two may complement each other, with protection being essential for a successful industrial policy.

In terms of the rationale firms developed to support their preferences, the French cases also showed remarkable continuity with the American ones. Protection was often opposed because of its cost to the firm's international operations, as discussed in chapter 6. Several differences in rationale are evident, however. First, for French firms the key market was often the European one more than the world one. Interest in eliminating trade barriers and resisting protection within the European market was very apparent. The relevant market for the large footwear producers, the pharmaceutical manufacturers, and later the television maker, Thomson, was clearly Europe's, not merely France's and not the world's.[15] France's international integration was more limited than that of the United States. French trade and foreign production occurred mainly within the EC, and thus the strongest resistance to protection was found in this market. This more limited integration accounts in part for the trend of decreasing French protection combined with increasing European protection, noted in the cases and elsewhere.[16]

[14] Giordano, "Analyse de la Politique Française du Commerce Extérieur," 1982; Yvonne Giordano, "Analyse de la Politique Française du Commerce Extérieur depuis le VIem Plan," *Revue d'Economie Industrielle*, no. 29 (3rd trim., 1984), esp. p. 59; Bernard Bobe, "La Politique Commerciale Française," in *Internationalisation et Autonomie de Décision*, ed. Henri Bourguinat (Paris: Economica, 1982), pp. 461-78.

[15] For the glass and tire producers, though, the European market was important but so were a number of other markets. These firms were interested in the state of the global market in large part because they exported and produced to an important extent outside of Europe.

[16] Wolfgang Hager, "Protectionism and Autonomy," *International Affairs* 58 (Summer 1982):413-28; Wolfgang Hager, "Little Europe, Wider Europe, and Western Economic Cooperation," *Journal of Common Market Studies* 21 (September-December 1982):171-97;

A second difference was that resistance to protection was often defended on the grounds that protection would hinder the industry's competitiveness. More than the Americans, the French worried about market size and scale economies. For many French industries, the French market alone was too small to generate the large production runs necessary to achieve lower costs and international competitiveness. For the French, export markets and/or a market base beyond France were crucial if an industry wanted to compete globally. The choice for many firms in France was, on the one hand, to become international competitors or, on the other, to lose competitiveness and seek protection. This choice was less severe for U.S. firms, since the size of the American market allowed them to reach scale economies without exporting. (This is becoming less true today, as optimal scale has risen.) French industries' need for a large, unhindered European market was widely appreciated. Concern for industrial competitiveness remained a central factor in guiding French firms to resist protection within Europe.

A third difference between the interdependence of the French and U.S. industries is evident in table 8.1. French ties to the international economy have focused mainly on exports, and much less and only more recently on multinationality. In contrast, U.S. industry is heavily multinational, with a more limited trade dependence. If, as the cases suggest, export dependence is a less durable bulwark against protection than well developed multinationality, French resistance to protection may be less stable than that of the United States. Declines in French exports, especially when combined with rapidly rising imports, may undermine firms' resistance to protection quickly. But the much greater level of and need for trade within Europe may enhance the importance of export dependence for the French. The country's keen interest in exports, in contrast to their general neglect in the United States, is one indication that exports play a more powerful role in French firms' preferences.

In addition to international ties, have other factors played a large role in determining French firms' preferences? Unlike U.S. trade policy, few studies of the factors influencing French trade policy exist.[17] Aggregate studies assessing the impact of factors such as firms' pref-

ERA, *EEC Protectionism*; Miles Kahler, "European Protectionism in Theory and Practice," *World Politics* 37 (July 1985):475-502.

[17] The best studies are those by Bernard Bobe and Patrick Messerlin in *Internationalisation et Autonomie*, ed. Bourguinat; Giordano, "Analyse de la Politique Française du Commerce Extérieur," 1984; Pisani, *Enjeux et Conditions des Equilibres*; François David, *Le Commerce International à la Derive* (Paris: Calmann-Lévy, 1982).

erences, industry "influence," policy-maker goals, and past policies on trade policy outcomes are not available. But the case studies here support the argument that export dependence and multinationality strongly influence firms' trade preferences. They also cast doubt on the claim that the French state exercises a central role in defining firms' preferences. Citing Andrew Shonfield, Stephen Cohen, and John Zysman, Eric Nordlinger maintains that the French state possesses this kind of autonomy. He observes "the success of the [French] higher bureaucracy in shaping societal preferences and then translating its own into public policy" and notes that "the [French] state [could] shape the preferences of even remarkably well-endowed private actors, in this instance the 'big business' community" through its many policy levers.[18] This argument is not supported by evidence here. The French state was certainly more interventionist than the American, but in none of our cases did a firm's preferences appear directly shaped by the state. More frequently, the state's activities were shaped by firms' preferences. Often the firms, and not the state, initiated policy for the sector. The French footwear, watch and clock, and television industries were central in developing and initiating the sectoral trade and industrial policies undertaken, for example. Moreover, some French industries had little need for state help. The French tire and glass producers, for instance, adjusted without seeking aid or protection.

Although perhaps not directly shaping preferences, the state, it has been claimed, may alter the context of economic activity and thereby condition firms' preferences.[19] For the French economy, the creation of the European Common Market and the building of firms into "national champions" may have had this effect. The Common Market helped create export and multinational interests, which have since become major supporters of that international market. But important support for the Common Market was evident among large, internationally oriented French firms before its inception.[20] Institutions and societal interests appear interdependent here. Societal interests in fa-

---

[18] Nordlinger, *Autonomy of the Democratic State*, pp. 104-105.

[19] Ardagh, *France in the 1980s*, pp. 30-40; Zysman, *Governments, Markets, and Growth*, ch. 3; in another context, see Gilpin, *U.S. Power*, who maintains that the rise of multinational enterprise occurred in large part because of U.S. hegemony and the conducive environment that it provided for U.S. enterprise.

[20] See Jean-François Hennart, "The Political Economy of Comparative Growth Rates: The Case of France," in *The Political Economy of Growth*, ed. Dennis Mueller (New Haven: Yale University Press, 1983), pp. 197-201; Wolfram Hanreider and Graeme Auton, *The Foreign Policies of West Germany, France, and Britain* (Englewood Cliffs, N.J.: Prentice-Hall, 1980), p. 123.

vor of the institution's goals were important for its creation. Over time, however, the institution promoted these interests, thereby establishing further support for itself. This interconnection suggests that the institutional context in which firms operate may over time influence firms' calculations of their preferences, but that firms' preferences may also affect the institutions.

The French state's creation of large, favored firms—national champions—may have also altered the economic context and thus firms' preferences. But the creation of national champions has provided equivocal support for freer trade. Despite their large size, many national champions have remained domestically oriented, often due to governmental pressure. These firms have been unwilling to see their domestic monopolies broken by foreign competition. In contrast, others have developed foreign operations, often despite the government's displeasure, and have become antiprotectionist forces. These policies to reshape the economy do not appear to have had a consistent effect on firms' trade preferences. The main point is that although firms may take numerous factors into account in developing their preferences, a critical role is played by the extent of their linkages to the international economy.

Intra-Industry Trade Politics in France

Rising interdependence has not only altered firms' preferences but also has affected the politics of industries. Interdependence has spread through industries unevenly, leaving some firms tied to the international economy and others dependent on the domestic market. This has rendered industries extremely divided in their preferences toward trade and has made developing a unified industry position on trade issues difficult. As chapter 7 argued, these intra-industry disputes have weakened protectionist pressures.

In France, trade politics have been affected by these divisions, but somewhat differently than in the United States. The internationalization of French firms was accompanied by a policy of fostering concentration within industries, which reduced the number of firms in each industry. When combined with the policy of national champions, this growing concentration left many industries controlled by a single French firm, which diminished the opportunity for intra-industry divisions to arise.

The effects of these policies are evident in the French cases. Divisions within these industries were less visible than among the 1970s U.S. cases. Only two of the six cases showed signs of strong intra-industry divisions, and these were industries with low concentration and no national champion. For instance, the footwear industry was split between the antiprotectionist preferences of its four large, internationally oriented firms and the protectionist sentiments of its smaller producers. Throughout the 1970s the large firms resisted pressures for market closure from the rest of the industry. In the manufacture of watches and clocks, the entry of Matra, a large multinational, split the industry in two. Matra initially resisted the smaller firms' protectionist attempts but then acquiesced to the imposition of selective quotas. Internal divisions thus helped alleviate pressures for protection in these industries.

In the tire, glass, and television cases, a dominant French firm controlled the industry. The primary source of competition for these firms was foreign multinationals. Industry divisions, if any existed, centered around the national champion and its foreign competitors. In general, these divisions were less apparent. Foreign firms participated in industry deliberations; however, their views were always suspect, and their opposition rarely public.[21] In three of the four cases—tires, glass, and pharmaceuticals—no divisions were evident, largely because the dominant French firms were more interested in open markets than in protection. In the radio and television case, where some divisions appeared, Thomson was pushing for protection. Its attempts to obtain protection from the EC were opposed by Philips and to some extent by its French subsidiary, Radiotechnique. Within France, these intra-industry divisions were barely evident. But at the European level they initially exercised an important brake on Thomson's demands. Divisions between domestic and foreign firms may thus be most likely to mitigate protectionist pressures when interests are brought together in an international arena, such as the EC.

As in the United States, intra-industry divisions among French firms weakened protectionist pressures. But by fostering concentration and national champions, the French state reduced possibilities for internal divisions. The relationship between firms and the state in France and the United States differed. For the U.S. government, one source of flexibility was divisions among the firms within an industry. Conflicting trade preferences within an industry either prevented formulation of any industry-wide position or compromised the position presented and allowed policy makers more room to maneuver. In contrast, the French state was often forced to deal with the national champion it had created. Resisting the appeals of such a firm was difficult because

[21] Interviews.

of the state's interests in the firm's survival and prosperity. The state's "special relationship" to these large firms reduced their conflicts of interest and made opposing these firms more difficult. Ironically, the state's creation of dominant national champions may have thus reduced its autonomy from industry.[22]

TRADE POLICY MAKING AND INDUSTRY INFLUENCE

Do firms' preferences affect trade policy outcomes? This section discusses how the structure of policy making allows business interests to play an important role in shaping policy outcomes. In particular, it examines how these interests are integrated into the policy process, suggesting the nature of U.S. and French "policy networks" linking state and society.[23]

Much of the literature on French economic policy making implies that answers to this question should differ greatly for the two countries. In these accounts, the French state is viewed as the primary determinant of policy; societal interests are seen as secondary at best. French policy is "state-led."[24] The French state is depicted as highly centralized, unified, and powerful relative to its decentralized, divided societal actors; it is a very "strong" state, "one which can exert industrial leadership."[25] The preferences of industries in this political structure are seen as much less important than they are in the United States. One scholar observes: "The [French] state is an autonomous and powerful player in the game, often able to force its will against the immediate wants and wishes of particular industries and businessmen. This does not imply that the government acts against business interests, simply that it can achieve collective outcomes not otherwise possible."[26]

In contrast, the U.S. state is viewed as a "weak" one— decentralized, divided against itself, and easily permeated by societal interests. Stephen Krasner describes it:

> Of the countries examined . . . , the United States is probably closest to the pole of [state] weakness. American policy makers have had a

---

[22] On the ironies of strong states, see G. John Ikenberry, "The Irony of State Strength: Comparative Responses to the Oil Shocks of the 1970s," *International Organization* 40 (Winter 1986):105-138.

[23] The term "policy networks" comes from Katzenstein, ed., *Power and Plenty*, p. 308.

[24] Zysman, "French State in the International Economy"; Katzenstein, "Conclusion," in *Power and Plenty*, ed. Katzenstein; Zysman, *Governments, Markets, and Growth*, chs. 1, 3, 6.

[25] Zysman, "French State in the International Economy," p. 265.

[26] Ibid.

clear objective. . . . Indeed, if the state cannot formulate a set of coherent goals, it is difficult to defend the concept of the state at all.
But implementation in the face of domestic political opposition has
been another matter. It has been very difficult for American central
decision makers to change the behavior of non-state domestic actors. Political leaders have relatively little command of material resources, such as the control of credit, that can be used to offer incentives or make threats. . . . Furthermore, the U.S. political system
offers its leaders few opportunities directly to change the structure
of the economy. . . . When [state] intervention has occurred, as in
the case of regulatory agencies or particular tax laws, the initiative
has come from the private sector more often than from the state.[27]

The closed, unified policy process in France thus is contrasted with the
open, fragmented U.S. process.

This contrast appears to be overdrawn. Evidence in this study and
others reveals that industries are deeply involved in the trade process
in both countries. The structure of policy making allows significant
industry influence in both, although the character of this involvement
differs in the two countries. Thus, knowledge of the policy making
structure, as well as the preferences of industries, is critical in both for
understanding policy outcomes.

Four characteristics of the policy process are often used to distin-
guish policy making in the United States and France: (1) the degree
of unity in the policy process (often the number of state actors involved); (2) the extent of insulation of the policy-making bureaucracy;
(3) the number of policy instruments available; and (4) the coherence
of policy makers' goals.[28] The less that each of these characterizes the
policy process, the "weaker" the state is seen to be, and the greater the
likelihood that societal influences can significantly affect the process.
The French state is seen as "strong" on each account. Its purported
differences from the United States are crucial here because, if true,
they imply that industry preferences in France, even if formed independently of the state, should have minimal effects on policy outcomes.

(1) Unity of the State Policy-Making Structure

Studies of French policy making portray it as occurring in a highly
centralized and unified state, with decision making controlled by the
executive and, within that branch, by the Ministry of Finance and the

[27] Krasner, "U.S. Commercial and Monetary Policy," p. 61.

[28] Zysman, *Governments, Markets, and Growth*, pp. 300-301, has three different criteria,
which overlap with those here.

Prime Minister.[29] Trade policy making in France, however, appears much less unified than these accounts suggest. First of all, France de jure has no independent trade policy. As many French policy makers have explained, trade policy is made by the EC, not nationally.[30] Though overstated, this point is important because most of the traditional trade policy making apparatus is located in Brussels, not Paris. The negotiation and setting of tariff rates and the use of GATT-sanctioned trade measures—such as antidumping, countervailing duty, and escape clause measures—rest in the hands of the Community. Analogues to the U.S. International Trade Commission and the Special Trade Representative are found in the European Community Commission.[31]

Within France, however, mechanisms exist to shape French positions on trade. The Direction for External Economic Relations (DREE), attached before 1975 to the Ministry of Finance and afterward to the Ministry of Foreign Trade, is the central locus for defining French positions within the EC.[32] The DREE also is responsible for French export policies and the control of imports under its old system of import restrictions. Other ministries also shape policy. The Ministry of Industry develops much sectoral policy and handles trade complaints and export aid. Industries often bring their complaints and demands first to their division of the Ministry of Industry, as both the footwear and the television producers did.[33] The Ministry of Agriculture deals with

[29] Zysman, "French State in the International Economy"; Katzenstein, "Conclusion," in *Power and Plenty*, ed. Katzenstein; Zysman, *Governments, Markets, and Growth*, chs. 1, 3, 6. For this view of trade policy making, see S. D. Cohen, *Making of U.S. International Economic Policy*, pp. 131-36. This notion of unity is similar to Michael Barzelay's idea of segmentation. He presents an argument explaining why segmentation reduces a state's control over its policy-making apparatus. See Michael Barzelay, *The Politicized Market Economy* (Berkeley: University of California Press, 1986).

[30] Milner, "Resisting the Protectionist Temptation." See also James Adams and Christian Stoffaës, eds., *French Industrial Policy* (Washington, D.C.: Brookings Institution, 1986), esp. pp. 17-20, who also note the growing fragmentation of industrial policy making in France and the increasing role of the EC in it.

[31] J.-M. Boittin and H. Valluet, *Les Importations* (Paris: Qui Est-ce Que, 1982), esp. pp. 38-121; United Nations, *Le Contrôle des Pratiques Commerciales Restrictives dans la CEE* (New York: United Nations, 1977), esp. p. 1; Alain Garcia, "Les Instruments de la Politique Française du Commerce Extérieur," *Notes et Etudes Documentaires*, nos. 4404-4405, September 2, 1977, pp. 14-19.

[32] Garcia, "Instruments," pp. 14-16; Xavier Beauchamp, *Un Etat dans l'Etat* (Paris: Bordas, 1976), pp. 117-22; Dominique Joly, "La Regime Française du Contrôle du Commerce Extérieur" (Ph.D. dissertation, Dijon, 1975).

[33] Zysman, "French State in the International Economy," p. 265, also notes this in passing.

all agricultural trade policy, while other ministries develop policies for their "clients"—for example, the Ministry of Health oversees policy affecting the pharmaceutical industry. The Ministry of Foreign Affairs watches over trade policy developments generally to ensure that they do not disturb relations with foreign governments.

Although not as directly involved with trade legislation as the U.S. Congress is, the French parliament plays a significant role in communicating its members' regional interests to the executive branch. This role was particularly evident in cases where the industry was concentrated regionally. For the footwear, watch and clock, and tire industries, firms' problems and complaints sparked regional representatives' activities, which included not only launching local initiatives but also pressing the national authorities to help the industries. All these strands of trade activity are supposedly coordinated through an interministerial committee chaired by the Prime Minister. In reality the role of this committee seems limited, and policy making often lacks centralized direction.

The fragmented French trade policy process provides many avenues for industries to voice their preferences. An industry can petition the EC or lodge its complaint with various national authorities. If the EC resists its pressure, the industry can find allies at home to increase pressure on the EC's Commission, as happened in the television case. If the Ministry of Finance or the DREE resists its appeals, it can turn to its relevant ministry or regional representatives for help, as occurred in the footwear and pharmaceutical industries. Multiple channels of access exist for industries to express their demands. These alternatives give industries the ability to play one group off against another, as they often do in the United States. For instance, in the late 1970s, the pharmaceutical industry finally succeeded in having the state lift price controls, which served to limit imports, from many of its goods by allying with the ministries of Industry and of Health in its battle against the Ministry of Finance. Regional authorities and allies in one ministry, who can countervail another's authority, enable industries to be heard. Overall, trade policy making in France exhibits a fairly fragmented character, as it does in the United States.

Scholars have frequently characterized U.S. trade policy making as highly fragmented, involving many different state actors.[34] Constitutionally, the U.S. Congress is in charge of trade policy instruments,

---

[34] Evidence of the fragmentation of U.S. trade policy making is contained in Krasner, "U.S. Commercial and Monetary Policy"; Destler, *Making Foreign Economic Policy*; Cohen, *Making of U.S. International Economic Policy*; Robert Pastor, *Politics of U.S. Foreign Economic Policy*.

such as the tariff, but since 1934 Congress has delegated much authority in this area to the executive branch. Relations between Congress and the executive over trade issues, nevertheless, tend to be conflictual, with Congress periodically remanding control. In addition, a number of independent agencies and executive departments—such as the ITC, STR, and the departments of Commerce, Treasury, State, and Defense—share in policy making. The bureaucratic politics model applies quintessentially to the trade policy area. The large number of actors and their often conflicting jurisdictions provide social actors with multiple channels of access to and possibilities for influence over the trade policy process, as in France.

(2) Insulation of the Bureaucracy

France's bureaucracy has been portrayed as highly insulated from societal influence, given the bureaucrats' similar backgrounds and strong esprit du corps.[35] Although French bureaucrats may constitute a cohesive social group because they have similar social backgrounds and educational training, this does not necessarily set them apart from other sectors of society. In fact, as Ezra Suleiman has shown, many bureaucrats and business leaders share similar backgrounds, and bureaucrats often move to business positions.[36] This has created a community among bureaucrats and business leaders. The two tend to have easy access to one another, often through close personal relations. Working groups created to develop policies for troubled industries bring business leaders and bureaucrats into extended and frequent contact, as evidence from the television industry makes clear. Indeed, some scholars have pointed out the "quiet conspiracy" between these two groups in the determination of postwar economic policy.[37] The characterization of the French bureaucracy as a socially coherent group may be accurate, but its insulation from other groups seems overstated, given its close relations with business.

Politically, the bureaucracy's independence from societal actors is also limited. The bureaucracy's access to information and development of policy expertise has not been achieved without industry help. In a number of cases, the bureaucracy's understanding of a particular

---

[35] On their common backgrounds and esprit du corps, see Ezra Suleiman, *Politics, Power, and Bureaucracy in France* (Princeton: Princeton University Press, 1974); Ezra Suleiman, *Elites in French Society* (Princeton: Princeton University Press, 1978).

[36] Suleiman, *Elites in French Society*, chs. 8, 9.

[37] The following authors all discuss the "special relationship" between big business and the state in France. Shonfield, *Modern Capitalism*; Michalet, "France," esp. pp. 124-25; Suleiman, *Politics, Power, and Bureaucracy*, esp. ch. 12.

industry's problems and the gathering of statistics on it depended on information from the industry itself. For instance, in the footwear, watch and clock, and television cases the best information on sales, imports, and exports were provided to the Ministry of Industry by the industry associations. This information was important in deciding what help the industry should be given. In these cases, moreover, the industries themselves proposed their own industrial and trade policies. Some even negotiated their own voluntary export agreements with foreign producers and their governments. The French bureaucracy does not appear independent from industry for its information collection, policy planning, or implementation.

The character of the relations between an industry and the bureaucracy in France may reduce decision makers' autonomy. As others have theorized, bureaucrats may sometimes be more willing than politicians to help industries under their auspices.[38] In particular, when bureaucracies have narrowly defined areas of jurisdiction and compete with one another, keeping one's clients happy is the key to retaining, and perhaps expanding, one's jurisdiction. Such conditions characterize the French system, especially the Ministry of Industry. It is organized into sections dealing with specific industries, and it competes with other ministries for control over these industries. In addition, the ministry's sections have extensive, long-term relations, which involve much bargaining and consensual decision making, with their industries—as the footwear, television, watch and clock, and pharmaceutical cases illustrate. In each case, the industry tended to initiate its own proposals and then negotiate with the bureaucracy to obtain what it wanted. Studies of the textile, steel, nuclear, and oil industries reveal elements of this pattern as well.[39] The French bureaucracy thus seems

[38] Messerlin, "Bureaucracies and the Political Economy of Protection"; for a contrasting view, see J. Michael Finger, H. Keith Hall, and Douglas Nelson, "The Political Economy of Administered Protection," *American Economic Review* 72 (June 1982):425-66.

[39] Messerlin, "Bureaucracies and the Political Economy of Protection," pp. 40-43; Harvey Feigenbaum, *The Politics of Public Enterprise: Oil and the French State* (Princeton: Princeton University Press, 1985); Phillipe Simonnot, *Les Nucléocrats* (Grenoble: Presses Universitaires de Grenoble, 1978). For steel, see Peter Hall, Janice McCormick, and Bruce Scott, "France Enters the 1980s," case no. 380-202, Harvard Business School, 1980; Geoffrey Shepard, François Duchêne, and Christopher Saunders, eds., *Europe's Industries: Public and Private Strategies for Change* (Ithaca: Cornell University Press, 1983), esp. pp. 66-69. For textiles, see Lynne Mytelka, "In Search of a Partner," in Stephen S. Cohen and Peter Gourevitch, eds., *France in a Troubled World Economy* (London: Butterworths, 1982); Rianne Mahon and Lynne Mytelka, "Industry, the State, and the New Protectionism," *International Organization* 37 (Autumn 1983):551-82; Shepard et al., eds., *Europe's Industries*, esp. pp. 38-40.

less insulated from industry than is often suggested. Rather, it appears engaged in an extensive negotiating relationship, which often produces mutually acceptable outcomes.

In contrast to the French, the U.S. bureaucracy is often characterized as fragmented and nonprofessional. Staffed by many political appointees and lacking any common recruitment background, this bureaucracy is open to outside pressure and "capturable" by its clients.[40] One comparative study of bureaucrats concludes:

> Across the Atlantic in the U.S., policy decisions are reached in a setting of splintered and penetrable institutions. In a country without a strong state tradition, lacking in central authority, possessed of a virile individualistic ideology, and lacking well-developed parties, decision making is highly political and depends on policy entrepreneurs. . . . American bureaucrats are required to play a more overtly political game than any of their European counterparts: in the absence of a clear and organized party will to carry out an organized agenda, . . . bureaucrats in this country often promote their own agendas, encouraged by the fluidity of the policy environment.[41]

The U.S. bureaucracy is very political in its behavior and not insulated from society, since the bureaucrats must act as "advocates, partisans, and tribunes" for different political positions.[42] These aspects of the bureaucracy and the fact that many political appointees come from business make it permeable to industry influence. In different but analogous ways, therefore, industry in both nations has important means of access to the state's bureaucracy, as the cases confirm.

(3) The Number of Policy Instruments

The French state is often seen as possessing a plethora of policy instruments, due in part to its long history of intervention in the economy.[43] Though sizable, its array of trade and industrial policy instruments is not vastly superior to those of the United States, however. In the trade area, many instruments of French policy—those involving tariff levels and unfair trade practices—have been turned over to the EC. Unlike the United States, France cannot impose its own trade law

---

[40] Krasner, "U.S. Commercial and Monetary Policy"; Katzenstein, "Conclusion," in *Power and Plenty*, ed. Katzenstein; Zysman, *Governments, Markets, and Growth*, pp. 266-81.

[41] Joel Aberbach, Robert Putnam, and Bert Rockman, *Bureaucrats and Politicians in Western Democracies* (Cambridge: Harvard University Press, 1981), p. 251.

[42] Ibid., p. 257.

[43] Zysman, "French State in the International Economy"; Katzenstein, "Conclusion," in *Power and Plenty*, ed. Katzenstein; Zysman, *Governments, Markets, and Growth*, chs. 1, 3, 6.

measures. The well-developed U.S. arsenal of legal procedures to re-
dress trade problems is not easily available to the French. Instead, they
must petition the EC, a supranational body in which French interests
are only one among those of many other countries.[44] Nor do the
French have the capacity to legislate trade assistance for particular industries, as the U.S. Congress does. Although these laws would contradict GATT provisions, they are nonetheless possible in the United
States and unheard of in France.

On the other hand, the French possess an administrative capability
for controlling imports. French trade laws developed in the 1930s
made import controls the rule and free trade the exception. Parts of
these laws still exist, allowing bureaucrats to monitor and impose quotas on imports, but much of their substance has been eliminated by
France's decision to participate in the GATT and the EC.[45] Use of these
quotas has been foresworn and control of imports has devolved to the
EC. Nonetheless, quotas and negotiated import controls have developed in both France and the United States. The proliferation of voluntary export restraints and other nontariff barriers has affected the
two countries similarly.[46] The use of import controls, then, is not restricted to France. Overall, in terms of traditional trade measures, the
French may actually be less well endowed than the Americans because
of the EC's important role in French trade policy.

The French, it has been pointed out, have numerous nontraditional
means of affecting trade. In addition to the use of standards, norms,
and government procurement, all of which are available in the United
States, the French have recourse to industrial policy and export subsidies. Many observers see industrial policy as a substitute for trade
policy.[47] The primary elements of French industrial policy have in-

[44] Boittin and Valluet, *Les Importations*, esp. pp. 94-95; David, *Le Commerce International*,
pp. 189, 192-95; Stoffaës, *Grande Menace Industrielle*, p. 426; Milner, "Resisting the Protectionist Temptation."

[45] Boittin and Valluet, *Les Importations*, esp. pp. 70-75; but these authors point out that
only 3 percent of all French imports, excluding energy products, are still under quotas.

[46] By the mid-1980s about a third of all categories of manufactured imports were subject to some form of nontariff barrier in both countries. This does not mean that imports
in all of these categories were severely restricted, however. Many nontariff barriers are
very ineffective compared to tariffs or quotas. William Cline, "Exports of Manufactures
from Developing Countries," Brookings Institution, February 1982, typescript, table 2-3;
Hine, *Political Economy of European Trade*, p. 224.

[47] Curzon Price, *Industrial Policies in the EC*, p. 21; Stoffaës, *Grande Menace Industrielle*;
Giordano, "Analyse de la Politique Française du Commerce Extérieur," 1984. But Adams
and Stoffaës, eds., *French Industrial Policy*, p. 18, also point out France's declining control
over its industrial policy tools since the EC has begun regulating the national use of instruments such as industrial subsidies.

volved two measures. The first has been to promote the restructuring of industries, usually meaning promoting concentration around the leading firm(s) in the industry. The second has been to give aid for R&D, exports, or simply as a production subsidy. For the cases examined, the two have been intertwined: industries demanded aid and the government offered it in return for the industries' agreement to restructure. Both policies seek to render the industries more competitive, but only aid has direct protectionist implications.

The amount of aid that industries receive is difficult to estimate, because it comes in numerous forms. For instance, interest-rate subsidies, whose effects are very difficult to calculate, are a frequently used device. Some estimates of this aid, however, do exist. One observer places total state aid to industry at 8 billion francs in 1972 and over 20 billion francs in 1979.[48] This accounted for roughly 3 percent of French industrial production in 1979. But of 15 billion francs in total aid in 1976, 3.5 billion or only a fifth, went to promote exports.[49] These export credits equaled 2 percent of France's total exports. In addition to these outright credits, export insurance was provided by the state's Compagnie Française d'Assurances du Commerce Extérieur (COFACE) to approximately one-third of all French exports.[50] Of this state aid, however, over 60 percent was channeled to five industrial sectors—steel, shipbuilding, computers, electronics, and aeronautics.[51] Export aid in France was thus limited both in its percentage of total aid and in its distribution among industries.

Comparison of this with U.S. activity in the same area reveals similar *levels* of expenditures in both countries. In 1975 *direct* state aid to exports totaled $27.3 million in France and $23.7 million in the United States.[52] Though the U.S. figure is obviously a much lower percentage

[48] Christian Stoffaës, "La Politique Industrielle," Cours aux Sciences Politiques, vol. 1, 1980, pp. 37-44.

[49] Pisani, *Enjeux et Conditions des Equilibres Extérieurs de la France*, pp. 170-75. This is for all state aid, both direct and indirect. See also Adams and Stoffaës, eds., *French Industrial Policy*, p. 28.

[50] *La Vie Française*, April 22-28, 1985.

[51] Giordano, "Analyse de la Politique Française du Commerce Extérieur," 1982, p. 211; Giordano, "Analyse de la Politique Française du Commerce Extérieur," 1984; Adams and Stoffaës, eds., *French Industrial Policy*, pp. 32-35.

[52] This figure is for just direct state aid to industry; see *Les Echos*, February 24, 1977. Figures on export subsidies as a percentage of total manufactured exports averaged 40-45 percent for France and around 10 percent for the United States in the late 1970s; see Cline, ed., *Trade Policy in the 1980s*, p. 32, and European Management Forum (EMF), *Report on International Industrial Competitiveness, 1984* (Geneva: EMF Foundation, 1984), p. 7, table 1.3. Data on all subsidies as a percentage of GNP place it at about 2 to 2.5 percent for France in the 1970s and about 0.5 percent for the United States; see Shailendra An-

of its total exports, the absolute figures show that export subsidies are an instrument available to either government. In addition, government funding of R&D is very important in the United States as well as in France. Public funding of industrial R&D as a percentage of total funding (public and private) in 1979 was about 29 percent for France and 32 percent for the United States.[53] These comparable figures imply that the United States also has an active industrial policy, one carried out mainly in conjunction with its defense policy.

The French state's control over credit has been cited as one primary example of its ample means of control over societal actors.[54] But the cases suggest that this instrument was rarely used as a "stick" toward industry. Rather, financial aid was the "carrot" offered for industry restructuring. The granting of aid seemed less the result of the state's autonomous decisions than the result of a process of negotiation between industry and the state. For example, the watch and clock industry association presented its own rescue plans to the government and then spent a great deal of time negotiating for the aid it had requested and arguing about how to restructure. This bargaining between the two sides was common; it appeared in every case where aid was demanded. The French state did have ample negotiating leverage in this process. In most cases, it was able to prompt restructuring, even if not desired by the industry. But this was a bargained outcome. Whether it wanted to or not, the state paid for restructuring by giving aid to the industry.

As has been noted by other observers, relations appear far more adversarial in the United States.[55] In the cases examined here, less could be done to induce industries to change their ways, but threats and denials of help were possible. The threat of antitrust action was used in several of the U.S. cases to force industries to back down from making trade complaints. For instance, by impounding all of the machine tool industry's documents in an antitrust suit, the government prevented it from filing a major trade complaint. The denial of indus-

jaria, Zubair Iqbal, Naheed Kurmani, and Lorenzo Perez, *Developments in International Trade Policy* (Washington, D.C.: IMF, Occasional Paper no. 16, November 1982), p. 56; and Lawrence Franko, in Gerald K. Helleiner, Helen Junz, and Lawrence Franko, *Protectionism or Industrial Adjustment* (Paris: Atlantic Institute, 1980), p. 39.

[53] EMF, *International Industrial Competitiveness*, p. 168.

[54] Zysman, "French State in the International Economy"; Zysman, *Governments, Markets, and Growth*, esp. chs. 2, 3, 6; and Peter Hall, *Governing the Economy: The Politics of State Intervention in Britain and France* (New York: Oxford University Press, 1986), pp. 152-53.

[55] E.g., see Steven Kelman, *Regulating America, Regulating Sweden* (Cambridge: MIT Press, 1981); David Vogel, *National Styles of Regulation* (Ithaca: Cornell University Press, 1986).

try demands was also possible through the ITC's findings or presidential decisions, as happened to the footwear industry several times. Such denial and threats were less evident in France. There, the long-standing, intimate relations between industries and the state fostered the negotiated resolution of industry problems. Overall, the French state did not appear to be significantly better equipped with trade or industrial policy instruments. Both countries had a plethora of their own, specific means for aiding industries.

(4) Coherence of State Policy Goals

French policy makers have been characterized as possessing a set of goals, distinct from much of their society's, by which they have directed the French economy in the postwar period. The central aim of French foreign policy has been the enhancement of national autonomy and influence.[56] This has involved policies to maximize French economic power combined with attempts to minimize its external dependence. Such goals have entailed promoting economic growth, creating and protecting strategic infant industries, and maintaining a rough balance of payments to uphold the franc's value through capital and import controls.

Evidence of a coherent policy following these goals is mixed for the 1970s, however, as it was for earlier periods.[57] Trade and industrial policy making in this decade have been characterized as "ad hoc, inconsistent, and short term."[58] Money was given to ailing industries in the hope that they would recover, and protection was granted to various industries at times.[59] As the cases here demonstrate, some sectors received protection and aid—e.g., footwear, watches and clocks, and televisions—while larger and more significant industries in difficulty

[56] Douglas Ashford, *Policy and Politics in France: Living with Uncertainty* (Philadelphia: Temple University Press, 1982), pp. 148-52; Ardagh, *France in the 1980s*, ch. 2; Kuisel, *Capitalism and the State in France*, ch. 10; Edward Kolodziej, *French International Policy under De Gaulle and Pompidou* (Ithaca: Cornell University Press, 1974), chs. 1, 4.

[57] Vincent Wright, "Politics and Administration under the French Fifth Republic," *Political Studies* 22 (March 1974):44-65, is one of the few to note the earlier policies' incoherence.

[58] Giordano, "Analyse de la Politique Française du Commerce Extérieur," 1982, pp. 54-57; see also Bobe, "La Politique Française Commerciale," and Patrick Messerlin, "Reconquête du Marché Intérieur ou Protectionnisme?" in *Internationalisation et Autonomie*, ed. Bourguinat.

[59] Giordano, "Analyse de la Politique Française du Commerce Extérieur," 1982; Stephen S. Cohen, "Informed Bewilderment: French Economic Strategy and the Crisis," in *France in a Troubled World Economy*, ed. Cohen and Gourevitch; Suzanne Berger, "Lame Ducks and National Champions," in *The Fifth Republic at Twenty*, ed. Andrews and Hoffmann, pp. 292-310.

went without them—e.g., pharmaceuticals, tires, and glass. In the latter cases, the industries adjusted on their own; adjustment proceeded through a "company-led" approach.[60] This haphazard "pattern" of protection and aid in France does not support a vision of policy makers unified in the pursuit of common goals, but rather one of a state making ad hoc adjustments, in part to meet its industries' demands.

Like the Americans, French policy makers in the 1970s were increasingly caught in the dilemma of how to preserve their national autonomy in the face of growing international interdependence. External economic shocks multiplied, and the French found it more and more difficult to pursue their long-standing aims. Their response did not involve a coherent plan, but rather a series of uncoordinated measures and compromises designed to revive growth and allow for some autonomy without disrupting their new interdependence. In 1981 and 1982, when the Socialists undertook a concerted effort at reflation, France's constrained ability to pursue national goals was starkly revealed.[61] In the early 1980s, greatly increased interdependence frustrated French policy makers. Rather than reduce this interdependence by closing the economy, the Socialists accepted it and instead altered their domestic policies. The management of their economy's new integration into the world marketplace thus proved a continuing and growing problem for the French from 1968 on, as it did for many other advanced industrial countries, including the United States.

In sum, the picture of the French state drawn here is one much less insulated from and imposing over its society than many characterizations suggest. This state constantly negotiates with its industries; it does not dictate policy to them. Policy making concerning trade and industrial issues seems less unified and not dominated by isolated bureaucrats. Instead it involves frequent contact between business and the state as well as dependence by bureaucrats on industries for help in collecting information and implementing policies. Moreover, the policy instruments available in these issue areas do not seem much more numerous than those available in the United States. In addition, French policy in the 1970s does not appear to have been a coherent, planned effort in pursuit of well-established goals. It was rather a series of ad hoc measures, frequently prompted and designed by industries themselves, to absorb the impact of the decade's external shocks.

[60] Zysman, *Governments, Markets, and Growth*, in contrast, claims that the United States follows a "company-led" adjustment strategy, while France follows a "state-led" one.

[61] Hall, *Governing the Economy*, ch. 8; Kahler, "European Protectionism."

The traditional view of the French state may have been more accurate for the period before the 1970s. But the success of the state in transforming its society and increasing its integration into the world economy has altered the state and its relationship with its society. As theorists concerned with the state have concluded:

Although strong, effective state interventions in economic processes may grow out of coherent bureaucracies relatively autonomous from dominant social classes, those very interventions are likely in time to lead to diminished state autonomy and capacities for further intervention, because affected groups will mobilize to pressure state authorities or to penetrate relevant parts of the state apparatus.[62]

This phenomenon, which reduced state autonomy, affected France by the 1970s for a number of reasons. According to one study, it was

the evolution of French planning [that] began to erode the "etatism" of the French state. To drive the French economy to new levels [of growth], the state forged an alliance with advanced sectors of capital that radically narrowed the distance between itself and society. Although planning institutions greatly enhanced the capacity of the French state for strategic thinking, they did not ultimately improve its cohesion. Moreover, planning eroded the traditional bases on which the state's claim to authority rested and forced policy-makers to seek new ways to legitimate their actions.[63]

Others maintain that the roots of the French state's problem lay in opening its economy.[64] This opening made planning exceedingly difficult, forced the state to ally with industry to promote competition, and fostered the growth of large, dynamic multinational French firms that were less dependent on the state. For these reasons and others, the autonomy, insulation, and coherence of the French state eroded in the 1970s, and the state that emerged was one more in contact with and dependent upon its major societal actors, especially business.

What does the picture here of the French policy process imply about the French state, its relationship with business, and its "capacity" for controlling political outcomes? First, as others have pointed out, this question has no general answer. These relations and the state's capacity vary over time, by issue, and by sector. As John Zysman notes, "a

[62] Evans, Rueschemeyer, and Skocpol, eds., *Bringing the State Back In*, p. 42.

[63] Hall, *Governing the Economy*, p. 180.

[64] Michalet, "France," pp. 115-22. Zysman, *Governments, Markets, and Growth*, pp. 150-51, sees a reduction in firms' dependence on the state but not a loss of state independence.

government's ability to act in one policy arena will be very different from its ability to act in another."[65] Confining ourselves to the trade policy area, can anything be said about the French state and its capacity to act, especially relative to the United States? It is clear that the distinction between the United States as a "weak" state and France as a "strong" one in the trade, and perhaps industrial, policy arena is not accurate. What seems most important is the recognition that the French and American states, as advanced industrial democracies, are constrained in similar ways. Other observers have pointed out:

> In a complex industrial society like that of France, any government is faced with a number of problems: it is constrained by the past, since yesterday's commitments and policies invariably provide today's basic priorities; it is faced with all the inherent problems of managing an "intermediate economy" in an interdependent world; it is inhibited by powerful interests entrenched in the various "policy communities"; . . . it has at its disposal a vast but unwieldy, fragmented and divided state apparatus. And it has to win elections.[66]

All elements in this but one apply equally well to the United States. Only America's predominant economic role seems different. The economic hegemony it has wielded has freed it from many of the external constraints that the French have faced, but not from the internal ones. Although it is arguable that as a hegemon, the U.S. state was able to pursue an "ideological foreign policy" divorced from societal interests, it is clearer that the loss of U.S. competitiveness in many sectors, a manifestation of its hegemonic decline, has intensified societal pressures on the state.[67]

As for the French state, it too faces the same constraints that force it to respond to societal interests, especially business ones. In advanced industrial democracies, as Charles Lindblom argues, business has a "privileged position" with the state because its economic performance affects the electoral prospects of politicians, who therefore listen closely to business demands. He characterizes the relation between the

[65] Zysman, *Governments, Markets, and Growth*, p. 297; Howard Machin and Vincent Wright, eds., *Economic Policy and Policy-Making under the Mitterrand Presidency, 1981-84* (New York: St. Martin's Press, 1985), p. 21.

[66] Machin and Wright, *Economic Policy under Mitterrand*, p. 34.

[67] The argument about ideology is in Stephen Krasner, *Defending the National Interest* (Princeton: Princeton University Press, 1978), ch. 9. Later he discusses the consequences of declining hegemony; see Stephen Krasner, "The Tokyo Round: Particularistic Interests and Prospects for Stability in the Global Trading System," *International Studies Quarterly* 23 (December 1979):491-531.

French state and industry as "an explicit exchange of favors: industry offers performance—expansion, relocation, technological innovation, and the like—in exchange for governmental favors like tax rebates, subsidies, or credit advances."[68] This pattern was evident in our cases, when industries offered better performance through restructuring in exchange for state aid. Lindblom also notes the limits on this exchange:

> Obviously in no system do businessmen get all they ask for. The task of government is to find responses to the demands of businessmen sufficient to motivate them to perform the tasks delegated to them, but without simply turning policy-making over to them lock, stock, and barrel. It is a task that requires great skill if it is to be done well enough to maintain economic stability and growth.[69]

Again, the cases here support this. Industries did not always get what they wanted. The relationship between industry and the state in both countries seems set within certain constraints that force the state to include business demands in its policy deliberations. Within these constraints, however, the state has the capacity to act independently, especially under certain circumstances, such as when firms in an industry are severely divided in their preferences.

Conclusion

Rising international economic interdependence has been experienced similarly in the United States and France. In both economies, firms' growing ties to the world economy have altered their trade preferences, shifting them away from protectionism even in times of economic distress. As in the United States, firms in France with sizable international ties were less protectionist than more domestically oriented industries. The costs of protection motivated these firms to seek other solutions to their problems. These costs, especially the loss of competitiveness associated with a small home market, were often even more imposing for the French. However, French interdependence was less well established and more geographically limited than that of the United States. France's international ties developed most after 1958, and its multinationals remain small in comparison to those of the United States. In addition, France's ties were strongest within Europe. Resistance to protectionism in France thus depended more on

---

[68] Charles Lindblom, *Politics and Markets* (New York: Basic Books, 1977), chs. 12, 13, esp. p. 183.
[69] Ibid., p. 183.

its export-oriented firms and was most powerful when involving the European market.

The change in firms' preferences due to increased interdependence has helped to divide industries on matters of trade policy. Intra-industry disputes over trade have weakened pressures for protection. But these divisions were less apparent in France than in the United States. The government's policy of fostering concentration and national champions reduced some industries to one major firm. These policies have limited intra-industry divisions in France and thus undercut another source of resistance to protection.

Finally, the French policy process has shown that firms' preferences helped shape trade policy outcomes. The traditional view of the French state as a "strong" one—operating in isolation from its society through a centralized structure run by professional bureaucrats, possessing clear and autonomous goals and all the instruments needed to forward them—is challenged by our cases and other recent studies, which point to a state in constant negotiation with its industries. This state in the 1970s and early 1980s at least was less centralized and less well endowed with policy instruments than other accounts suggest. Its policy makers did not appear so isolated or independent, and its policy was less coherent and long-term oriented. As in all advanced industrial democracies, the preferences of its firms and industries were able to influence trade and industrial policy outcomes because these groups played an important role in the policy process.

CHAPTER 9

Conclusions

WE MAY now review the answer given to the puzzle motivating this study and examine several of its broader ramifications, which include (1) the relationship of the argument here about rising international interdependence to other arguments about interdependence; (2) the light the comparison of the French and U.S. cases may shed on various aspects of comparative politics; (3) the relationship of this study's conclusions to key theories in international political economy about the sources of free trade and cooperation; and (4) its policy implications.

THE PUZZLE AND RISING INTERDEPENDENCE

This work has asked why the 1970s were less protectionist than the 1920s, when economic and political pressures for protection were similar in both. Serious economic distress and declining British hegemony led, in the eyes of many scholars, to widespread protectionism in the 1920s. Similar conditions characterized the 1970s, but markets remained relatively open then. What was different about the two periods that might have created such different trade policy outcomes?

I have argued that the increased economic integration of advanced industrial states into the world economy in the 1970s altered the domestic politics of trade. Firms and industries that had become dependent on exports, imports, multinational production, and global intra-firm trade were now opponents of protectionism, for such policies had become extremely costly for them. As the cases revealed, when threatened by import competition, internationally oriented firms in both the 1920s and 1970s opposed protectionism, while domestically oriented ones sought it. More firms with more international ties existed in the 1970s, and thus resistance to protection was stronger than in the 1920s. Because fewer demands for protection were made by firms in trouble in the 1970s, states could more easily resist the temptation to close their markets.

This argument touches on one of the key disputes in international political economy—the problem of rising interdependence and its effects. We have examined how the greater integration of domestic and international economies elevated the costs of limiting trade. As their integration rose, protectionism became a more costly option for advanced industrial democracies, since it would hurt many of their most competitive industries, usually the most internationally oriented ones. These greater international ties raised the costs of severing trade relations via protection for certain industries in all the countries involved. This increased interdependence, then, meant an increase in the mutual costs of foregoing economic relations.[1]

In this sense, the argument is that in the 1970s the advanced industrial countries were more interdependent than in the 1920s. But in both periods interdependence made protectionism a costly strategy. It was avoided by internationally oriented firms in each decade. Nevertheless, the increased economic integration of the 1970s does not rule out protectionist responses by these states. Indeed, rising international trade and production may generate other pressures for market closure, for they may increase the costs of continuing trade relations as usual. For instance, surging imports may threaten sectors once untouched by foreign competition, thereby turning domestically oriented firms into advocates of protection. The growth of economic integration among states may thus generate new pressures both for and against protection. Heightened interdependence need not lead to greater market openness, although one of its effects—as identified here—surely is to do this.

In this study, interdependence has two distinct features. First, interdependence manifests itself *within* the state. Most examinations of interdependence locate it at the level of the state.[2] Here, however, it involves the international economic ties of firms within states. Domestic social actors, not states, are the agents of interdependence. Looking within the "black box" of the state, the analysis has focused on how international economic integration affects domestic social actors. Second, this study has a different view of the effects of interdependence. Traditionally, rising interdependence has been described as affecting states by rendering their individual policy instruments ineffective and thus reducing their autonomy.[3] Here the effect demonstrated was to reshape firms' trade preferences and thus influence states' policy

[1] This definition is from Albert Hirschman, *National Power and the Structure of Foreign Trade* (Berkeley: University of California, 1945); see also David Baldwin, "Interdependence and Power: A Conceptual Analysis," *International Organization* 34 (Autumn 1980):471-506.

[2] Richard Cooper, *The Economics of Interdependence* (New York: McGraw-Hill, 1968); Keohane and Nye, *Power and Interdependence*; Edward Morse, *Modernization and the Transformation of International Relations* (New York: Free Press, 1976).

[3] Ibid.

choices. The consequences of interdependence are internal to states; they affect domestic social actors' policy preferences, not states' policy instruments. In addition, the effects of growing interdependence are mixed. Rising trade and production among states not only increase the costs of severing these relations but also elevate the costs of maintaining these flows for import-competing firms. Growing interdependence is unlikely to prevent protectionism in sectors where domestically oriented firms are dominant. Only further internationalization of these firms' operations may prevent recourse to protection.

This brings us to the question of why the international integration of advanced industrial economies grew in the postwar period. Why did firms increasingly choose to export and invest abroad? Why did many of them become ever more dependent on the international economy? Economists and political scientists have proposed various answers to this question.[4] For many economists, trade and direct foreign investment (DFI) are the products of firms' comparative advantages. Trade occurs when firms can produce and sell abroad at a relatively lower cost than can the firms in that market. Likewise, DFI occurs when "[s]uperior knowledge or technology gives American firms a competitive edge in overseas markets that more than compensates for the costly disadvantages of operating in a foreign country."[5] In addition, observers have noted that DFI often acts as a substitute for exports, since this investment provides entry to markets where trade barriers are high.[6] Economists thus focus on the specific assets—tangible and intangible—of firms that give them competitive advantages globally to explain the internationalization of firms. But have these assets gained importance since World War II in a way that induced the secular increase in firms' international ties? The growing significance of high technology industries might account for this. In the postwar period, knowledge and technology—both intangible assets—have become more important for firms, at least in the United States, as skill levels and R&D requirements for industries have risen.[7] These economic changes may account in part for the growing internationalization of firms since 1945.

Others have focused more on the political determinants of trade

<hr/>

[4] See, e.g., Raymond Vernon, *Sovereignty at Bay* (New York: Basic Books, 1971); Gilpin, *U.S. Power*; Caves, *Multinational Enterprise and Economic Analysis*.

[5] Kenneth Flamm, *Targeting the Computer* (Washington, D.C.: Brookings Institution, 1987), p. 1.

[6] Caves, *Multinational Enterprise*, pp. 36-45.

[7] Feldstein, ed., *The American Economy in Transition*, pp. 359, 392, 533-36.

and DFI.[8] One prominent theory maintains that the growth of trade and DFI were dependent upon U.S. hegemony, which established a stable regime conducive to such flows. Robert Gilpin claims:

> Just as the *Pax Britannica* provided the security and political order for the expansion of transnational economic activity in the nineteenth century, so the *Pax Americana* has fulfilled a similar function in the mid-twentieth century. Under American leadership, the various rounds of GATT negotiations have enabled trade to expand at an unprecedented rate. . . . Finally, the multinational corporations found the global political environment a highly congenial one. As a consequence, they were able to integrate production across national boundaries.[10]

In this view hegemony was necessary for the internationalization of firms.

This theory fails to consider explicitly why a hegemon wants an open international system. Why do hegemonic states, or at least the United States, prefer openness? Answering this necessitates looking at the hegemon's "national interest" and its definition. By examining the domestic bases of support for an open system, the argument here can help fill this gap in hegemonic stability theory. U.S. interest in the creation of an open system in the 1940s and 1950s was probably encouraged by domestic social actors' interests in such openness. Gilpin himself notes that "corporate interest and the 'national interest' . . . have coincided. . . . Corporate and political elites have shared the American vision of a liberal world economic order."[11] In the immediate postwar period, large multinationals and exporters were likely supporters of such a policy, while the lack of foreign competition quieted traditional opponents of liberalization.[12] Policy makers' understanding of the rising importance of the country's international ties may thus have been one factor propelling them to act "as a hegemon should." Although hegemonic stability theory helps explain the growing internationalization of firms, this study points out the domestic political sources of support underlying the United States' initial decisions to create a system promoting such internationalization.

[8] E.g., Gilpin, *U.S. Power.*

[9] See the literature on hegemonic stability theory in chapter 1, note 2.

[10] Gilpin, *U.S. Power*, pp. 111-12.

[11] Ibid., p. 142.

[12] While U.S. DFI at the time was low, U.S. export dependence in the late 1940s was quite high. See the 1985 *Economic Report of the President* (Washington, D.C.: GPO, 1986), tables B-10, B-96, B-98 on export dependence.

COMPARATIVE POLITICS
AND DOMESTIC ACTORS

A second argument in this book has been that French and U.S. firms responded similarly to the growth of their international ties in the 1970s and early 1980s. For both, strong dependence on the international economy mitigated preferences for protection even when the firms were besieged by imports. A common international event evoked a similar domestic response in the two countries. This finding contrasts with many in comparative politics that tend to stress the differences in states' responses. Studies often emphasize how particular national characteristics shape states' policies and neglect similarities across the countries.[13] However, as others have argued, the character of the international system may generate similar pressures and responses among states.[14] As Realists in international relations see the condition of international anarchy leading all states to adopt similar balancing behavior, I have argued that rising interdependence prompts the growth of domestic preferences for free trade among certain actors in all developed industrial countries. The compelling logic of these international pressures promotes similar responses in widely differing states. These similarities, as well as differences, deserve recognition.

Responses to international conditions may differ not only among states but also over time. This study, however, found similarities across time in domestic groups' responses to heightened interdependence. In both the 1920s and the 1970s, internationally oriented firms resisted protectionism despite foreign competition. But between these two periods, one change is evident. In the 1920s industries had little trouble translating their trade preferences into policy, as long as they were not too divided. By the 1970s the process was less simple. Industries had more difficulty in realizing their preferences, as discussed in chapter 7. Often firms within industries were seriously divided in their preferences. Other times policy makers resisted their demands. Domestic political institutions had become more important in the determination of policy. Peter Gourevitch notes this change, stating that over time

the machinery that links state and societal actors has grown in importance, and the variance of countries on that point has also

[13] E.g., Peter Katzenstein, ed., *Power and Plenty*; Zysman, *Governments, Markets, and Growth*.

[14] Gourevitch, *Politics in Hard Times*. Realist balance of power theory also suggests this; for an extreme version, see Kenneth Waltz, *Theory of World Politics* (Reading, Mass.: Addison-Wesley, 1979).

grown. At the onset of the first crisis, in the last third of the nineteenth century, organizations were relatively weak. Functional interests worked directly on politics and policy debate in a relatively un-
mediated way, and outcomes could be inferred fairly directly from
the struggles of societal actors. . . . [Later s]ocietal actors had to act
through parties and associations that had their own agendas, goals,
and categories. . . . With the growing importance of associations in
shaping the behaviors of societal actors and participating in actual
making and implementation of policy, differences among associations have come to play a greater role in accounting for choice of
policy.[15]

This change has important implications, because it suggests that in
the 1970s policy structures in France and the United States should
have greater influence over outcomes and their differences should be
reflected more in policy choices. How important are differences in the
French and U.S. responses to rising interdependence? As argued in
chapter 8, these states' behavior is constrained in similar ways. As advanced industrial democracies, these governments need the support
of their societies, and this support often depends on the economic situation. Since this situation is affected to a large extent by business decisions—e.g., regarding investment and hiring—the government is dependent on business decisions and is responsible for creating an
environment conducive to economic growth.

Since the 1940s, both states have taken on increasing responsibility
for their economies, intervening more and more. The forms of these
interventions have differed. The French developed a planning system
and promoted selected industries, all the while creating a "special relationship" with big business. The American government kept a more
distant relationship with business, but still aided and created markets
for selected industries through large military and space programs.
These differences are apparent in the 1970s cases. The U.S. government still has a more adversarial, arms length relationship with industry, although it has been willing to help, especially when "national security" concerns have been raised. The French state, especially the
Ministry of Industry, has a much closer relationship with industry.
This relationship involves much negotiation and mutual accommoda-
tion; the government exchanges aid in return for the restructuring of
industries, so they can perform better.

The balance of influence in this relationship has shifted over time.
In the years following World War II, the French state held the upper

[15] Gourevitch, *Politics in Hard Times*, pp. 230-32.

hand, as industry was discredited and devastated. State control began to wane by the late 1960s. The reconstruction and internationalization of French industry gave it more resources of its own. As we have seen in the cases, in the 1970s this allowed many French industries to design their own policies and pursue their own business strategies. At times, when facing serious foreign competition and economic problems, certain industries looked to the state for help, as they did in the United States. In neither country was there a clear preference among industries for seeking state aid or adjusting on their own. The evolution of French industry in the 1970s was not predominantly "state-led"; nor was that of U.S. industry solely "company-led."[16] Rather, a mix of state action and corporate strategy prevailed in both.

In each country, large international firms preferred to pursue their own adjustment strategies, largely independent of the state, while smaller domestically oriented firms were more likely to seek state aid. Larger firms in both seemed to possess greater resources and flexibility for adapting, especially when success depended on further internationalization of their operations. Contrary to arguments touting the adaptive powers of small, specialized firms, the cases here show that when facing strong foreign competition small firms, if they lacked international ties, had trouble adjusting and often turned to the state for help.[17] In numerous cases, the market had become international, and only by expanding to a global scale could these firms survive and prosper.

In many ways the internationalization of markets since 1945 has produced similar pressures in advanced industrial democracies. This expansion of the market has forced industries to compete internationally. Increasingly, domestic markets, even in the United States, are not large enough to support firms; rather, firms must become global players. This makes firms at once more and less dependent on their governments. If they are successful internationally, the home market is less important. But often to be successful on a global scale, they need their government's help. To ensure the safety of their foreign investments, to open markets abroad, or to maintain convertibility of currencies, firms must rely on the actions of their, and other, states. Creating the conditions necessary for a stable, open international market therefore requires the active participation of states and often their international cooperation. Even those firms that operate globally depend upon their governments. Furthermore, if interstate cooperation and the creation of international regimes are necessary for maintain-

---

[16] This contrasts with the argument of Zysman in *Governments, Markets, and Growth.*

[17] This contrasts with the claims of Piore and Sabel in *The Second Industrial Divide.*

ing open markets, then these internationally oriented firms may provide the support and impetus domestically for policies promoting such cooperation.[18]

Firms and their governments are bound in an interdependent relationship. If, as I am arguing, industries are becoming more international, this may lead to new relations between them and the state in advanced industrial countries. The two may become even more interdependent, as the state must come to the aid of its firms in international markets so they can produce prosperous conditions at home, and firms must rely ever more on their state to ensure a stable, open international system. Governments' foreign economic policies will be of increasing concern to their industries and to their own electoral prospects. Advanced industrial democracies will face similar pressures, and, if this argument is correct, many will be forced by the logic of the market to react in similar ways. Differences in their domestic political structures, ideologies, and governing coalitions will shape the exact way they react, but all will be pressured to act closely with their industries to ensure their international competitiveness.

THE INTERNATIONAL POLITICAL ECONOMY AND DOMESTIC PREFERENCES

Many observers in the 1970s claimed that the decline of U.S. hegemony would lead to the closure of the international trading system. The

---

[18] A less optimistic view of business–state relations is evident in the strategic trade policy literature. The argument there is that as industries become more oligopolistic and international in scale, optimal trade policy changes. In such industries, state intervention is critical. A state can capture additional national rents if it protects or subsidizes its firms. More defensively, the claim is that a state must retaliate by protecting or subsidizing its firms if other states are doing this, or else its firms will not survive. In such oligopolistic, international industries, firms must get their governments to aid them in either retaliating or persuading other countries to stop protecting their industries. In this case, firms may be proponents of either cooperative or discordant international trade policies. See James Brander and Barbara Spencer, "Tariffs and the Extraction of Rents under Potential Entry," *Canadian Journal of Economics* 14 (1981):371-89; Avinash Dixit, "International Trade Policies for Oligopolistic Industries," *Economic Journal* 94 (supplement, 1984):1-16; Barbara Spencer and James Brander, "International R&D Rivalry and Industrial Strategy," *Review of Economic Studies* 50 (1983):707-722; Antoine Auquier and Richard Caves, "Monopolistic Export Industries, Trade, Taxes, and Optimal Competition Policy," *Economic Journal* 89 (September 1979):559-81; Jonathan Eaton and Gene Grossman, "Optimal Trade and Industrial Policy under Oligopoly," *Quarterly Journal of Economics* 101 (May 1986):383-406; David De Meza, "Commercial Policy toward Multinational Monopolies," *Oxford Economic Papers* 31 (July 1979):334-37; Paul Krugman, ed., *Strategic Trade Policy and the New International Economics* (Cambridge: MIT Press, 1986); Henry Kierzkowski, ed., *Monopolistic Competition and International Trade* (Oxford: Oxford University Press, 1984).

argument here challenges this. Closure of the system through wide-spread protectionism depends less on declining U.S. power than on reductions in an economy's integration into the world economy. As the cases indicate, despite the loss of U.S. influence, extensive inter-dependence helped prevent spiraling protectionism like that of the 1920s from recurring in the face of serious economic distress. Protec-tionism, nevertheless, did increase in the late 1970s and early 1980s. Certain troubled sectors—e.g., textiles, apparel, footwear, and steel—were given protection in most advanced industrial countries. But this sectoral pattern of trade policy cannot be explained by focusing on the loss of hegemony.[19] The argument here is more helpful in explaining this pattern. The most internationally oriented sectors should be the most open, and those whose international ties are weak or declining should be the most protected. As noted, U.S. hegemony may have been partly responsible for the creation of a stable international econ-omy, which allowed the expansion of interdependence in the postwar period. But the decline of such hegemony need not cause the collapse of the free trade system. Rather, the persistence of interdependence, itself a legacy of U.S. hegemony, may promote the maintenance of an open trading system, even after hegemony has passed. Pessimism over the imminent decline of the liberal trading system may thus be over-stated.

This is not to claim that in the future protectionist outbreaks like that of the late 1920s and early 1930s cannot or will not occur. Con-ditions in the international and domestic political economies are con-stantly changing. In fact, changes in the economics of industries, com-bined with new forms of state intervention in the economy, may be leading to the growth of new, strategic trade preferences and policies. As increasing numbers of industries have become global in scope, their trade preferences have come to depend more on the trade prac-tices of other countries. When industries, as their scale economies, R&D requirements, and learning effects all multiply, require access to foreign markets to remain profitable, they are pushed to adopt stra-tegic trade preferences in the face of foreign governments' activities aimed at protecting their markets. These preferences entail a shift from demands for freer trade at home and abroad by large exporters and multinationals, to increasing demands by these firms for closure of the home market *if* foreign markets are kept closed. These strategic

[19] Aggarwal, *Liberal Protectionism*, has a sectoral argument about the effects of heg-emonic decline. But some of the cases here appear to be in "hegemonic decline" in his terms (that is, facing declining oligopsony power), and not all of them turn protectionist.

demands link access to the home market to access to foreign markets; this is not old-fashioned protectionism. If, as is argued elsewhere, these changes in industry economics and foreign-government intervention are increasing, then the future international trading system may be a more strategic and closed one than that predicted by simply extrapolating from the argument here about the 1970s and early 1980s.[20]

Other explanations for the persistence of international cooperation in trade in the 1970s in the absence of U.S. hegemony focus on elements of the international system. In these analyses, the sources of pressures against a revival of widespread protection lie either in the structure of the trading system—i.e., its payoffs, iterativeness, or number of players—or in the functions of the international trade regime.[21] These accounts overlook what states' preferences regarding trade are and how they are formed. Instead, large, often implicit assumptions about these preferences are made. For example, in arguing that states will maintain a liberal trade regime because of the transaction costs they save in doing so, it is being implicitly assumed that those costs are more significant for the state than the costs of not protecting their economies.[22] Game theoretic models of cooperation also provide little discussion of how each country's payoff from cooperation or defection are determined. For example, Duncan Snidal constructs states' payoffs by assuming that "all states benefit from provision of the good ... [;] the benefits received by the state are proportional to its size: larger states benefit more ... [; and] there are declining marginal payoffs, ... while its unit cost is constant."[23] Whether these assumptions hold for cooperation in trade is unclear. It is debatable, for instance, whether large states gain more from liberal trade than small states.[24]

The costs and benefits of different actions by states in the trade area

[20] Helen Milner and David Yoffie, "Between Free Trade and Protectionism: Strategic Trade Policy and a Theory of Corporate Trade Preferences," APSA paper, August 1987.

[21] Stephen Krasner, ed., "International Regimes," *International Organization* 36 (Spring 1982); Keohane, *After Hegemony*; Robert Axelrod, *The Evolution of Cooperation* (New York: Basic Books, 1984); Kenneth Oye, "Cooperation under Anarchy," *World Politics* 38 (October 1985); Duncan Snidal, "The Limits of Hegemonic Stability Theory," *International Organization* 39 (Autumn 1985):579-614; Duncan Snidal, "Coordination versus Prisoners' Dilemma," *American Political Science Review* 79 (December 1985):923-42.

[22] Keohane, *After Hegemony*, ch. 6.

[23] Snidal, "Limits of Hegemonic Stability Theory," p. 604.

[24] William Cline, Noboru Kawanabe, T.O.M. Kronsjo, and Thomas Williams, *Trade Negotiations in the Tokyo Round: A Quantitative Assessment* (Washington, D.C.: Brookings Institution, 1978), show empirically that smaller states often gain more from liberalization of trade; see esp. pp. 187-88, 220-27.

need more exploration. The argument in this book contributes to this inquiry. To understand the structure of the international trading game, the extent of each economy's international integration might be examined, since this affects the payoffs states anticipate from liberalizing or protecting. In times of stiff foreign competition, a state whose economy is dominated by domestically oriented firms may find continued cooperation in a liberal system very costly. The payoff a firm receives from defecting may be high. On the other hand, a state with an internationally oriented economy may find protection at home or abroad—i.e., defection by itself or others—costly. Its payoff is maximized, *ceteris paribus*, if cooperation with a liberal trade regime is maintained globally. Overall, this suggests that an international economy with high levels of interdependence may promote continued international cooperation in trade.

SOME POLICY IMPLICATIONS

This study suggests that protectionism will be most likely in sectors menaced by foreign competition and lacking strong international economic ties. Actions that reduce these ties but leave import competition intact will engender new protectionist pressures. For example, macro-economic policies that reduce international ties will promote widespread protectionist sentiment throughout the economy. Indeed, this may be one of the lessons of the early 1980s. The growth of protectionist pressure in the United States between 1981 and 1985 was partly attributable to sharp reductions in U.S. export dependence (by almost one-third) and in the profitability of foreign operations, both due to a large extent to the serious and persistent overvaluation of the dollar.[25]

Mismanagement of the macroeconomy can have damaging effects on a country's trade and its trade preferences. Policies eroding an economy's international linkages—i.e., its exports, multinational production, and global intrafirm trade—may undercut its domestic bases of support for free trade. In this way domestic policies, even those unrelated to trade, may affect the state of the international trading

[25] Destler, *American Trade Politics*, ch. 3, makes a similar argument. Destler also in a talk at Harvard University on February 18, 1986, cited figures showing that U.S. industrial export dependence (exports as a percent of national production) grew from 9 percent in 1970 to 14.2 percent in 1980 and then fell sharply to 10 percent in 1984. This was, he noted, the same percentage decline experienced in the Great Depression, between 1929 and 1933.

system. Policy makers thus should be conscious of the indirect effects of macroeconomic policies on domestic political preferences. They should appreciate these indirect costs when choosing macroeconomic policies, so that domestic support for a liberal trade system is not inadvertently undermined.

Aberbach, Joel; Putnam, Robert; and Rockman, Bert. *Bureaucrats and Politicians in Western Democracies*. Cambridge: Harvard University Press, 1981.

Ackerman, Carl. *George Eastman*. Boston: Houghton Mifflin, 1930. Reissued 1973.

Adams, James, and Stoffaës, Christian, eds. *French Industrial Policy*. Washington, D.C.: Brookings Institution, 1986.

Aggarwal, Vinod. *Liberal Protectionism: The International Politics of Organized Textile Trade*. Berkeley: University of California Press, 1985.

Aggarwal, Vinod; Keohane, Robert; and Yoffie, David. "The Dynamics of Negotiated Protectionism." *American Political Science Review* 81 (June 1987):345-66.

Aldcroft, Derek. *From Versailles to Wall Street, 1919-1929*. Berkeley: University of California Press, 1981.

American Footwear Industry Association (AFIA). "Petition for Relief from Imports of Nonrubber Footwear under Section 201 of the Trade Act of 1974." Washington, D.C.: AFIA, 1984.

Andrews, William. *Presidential Government in Gaullist France*. Albany: SUNY Press, 1982.

Andrews, William, and Hoffmann, Stanley, eds. *The Fifth Republic at Twenty*. Albany: SUNY Press, 1981.

Anjaria, Shailendra; Iqbal, Zubair; Kurmani, Naheed; and Perez, Lorenzo. *Developments in International Trade Policy*. Washington, D.C.: IMF, Occasional Paper no. 16, November 1982.

Ardagh, John. *France in the 1980s*. New York: Penguin, 1982.

Arthur D. Little (ADL). *Analyse des Marchés et des Grandes Tendances Technologiques dans le Domaine de l'Electronique Grand Public*. Paris: Ministère de l'Industrie, 1979.

Ashford, Douglas. *Policy and Politics in France: Living with Uncertainty*. Philadelphia: Temple University Press, 1982.

Auquier, Antoine, and Caves, Richard. "Monopolistic Export Industries, Trade, Taxes, and Optimal Competition Policy." *Economic Journal* 89 (September 1979):559-81.

Axelrod, Robert. *The Evolution of Cooperation*. New York: Basic Books, 1984.

Baldwin, David. "Interdependence and Power: A Conceptual Analysis." *International Organization* 34 (Autumn 1980):471-506.

———. "Power Analysis and World Politics." *World Politics* 31 (January 1979):161-94.

Baldwin, Robert. "The Political Economy of Protectionism." In *Import Competition and Response*, pp. 263-92. *See* Bhagwati 1982.

———. *The Political Economy of U.S. Import Policy*. Cambridge: MIT Press, 1986.

Baldwin, Robert, and Anderson, Kim. "The Political Market for Protection in Industrial Countries: Empirical Evidence." *World Bank Staff Working Paper*, no. 492 (October 1981).

Baldwin, Robert, and Richardson, J. David. *International Trade and Finance*. 3rd ed. Boston: Little, Brown, 1986.

Balladur, Jean-Paul. "Les Echanges Extérieurs de la France entre 1960-70." *Economie et Société*, no. 31 (February 1972):11-13.

Banque de France. *L'Industrie de l'Horlogerie*. Paris: Banque de France, 1974.

Barzelay, Michael. *The Politicized Market Economy*. Berkeley: University of California Press, 1986.

Bauer, Raymond; Pool, Ithiel de Sola; and Dexter, Lewis. *American Business and Public Policy*. Chicago: Aldine-Atherton, 1972.

Beauchamp, Xavier. *Un Etat dans l'Etat*. Paris: Bordas, 1976.

Becker, William. *The Dynamics of Business-Government Relations*. Chicago: University of Chicago Press, 1982.

Berger, Suzanne. "Lame Ducks and National Champions." In *The Fifth Republic at Twenty*, pp. 292-310. *See* Andrews and Hoffmann 1981.

Bergsten, C. Fred. "The Crisis in U.S. Trade Policy." *Foreign Affairs* 49 (July 1971):619-35.

Bergsten, C. Fred; Horst, Thomas; and Moran, Theodore. *American Multinationals and American Interests*. Washington, D.C.: Brookings Institution, 1978.

Bhagwati, Jagdish, ed. *Import Competition and Response*. Chicago: University of Chicago Press, 1982.

Bobe, Bernard. "Les Importations des Biens de Consommation en Provenance de Tiers Monde." *Revue d'Economie Industrielle*, no. 14 (4th trim., 1980).

————. "La Politique Commerciale Française." In *Internationalisation et Autonomie de Décision*, pp. 457-79. *See* Bourguinat 1982.

Boittin, J.-M., and Valluet, H. *Les Importations*. Paris: Qui Est-ce Que, 1982.

Boorstin, Daniel. *The Americans: The Democratic Experience*. New York: Vintage Books, 1973.

Borkin, Joseph. *The Crime and Punishment of I. G. Farben*. New York: Free Press, 1978.

Borrus, Michael; Millstein, James; and Zysman, John. "Trade and Development in the U.S. Semiconductor Industry." In *American Industry in International Competition*, pp. 142-248. *See* Zysman and Tyson 1983.

Bourguinat, Henri, ed. *Internationalisation et Autonomie de Décision*. Paris: Economica, 1982.

Brander, James, and Spencer, Barbara. "Tariffs and the Extraction of Rents under Potential Entry." *Canadian Journal of Economics* 14 (1981):371-89.

Brock, William, and Magee, Stephen. "The Economics of Special Interest Politics: Case of the Tariff." *American Economic Review Papers and Proceedings* 68 (May 1978):246-50.

Broder, David. "The Case of The Missing Shoe-Import Option." *Washington Post*, July 23, 1977, p. 16.

Caves, Richard. "Economic Models of Political Choice: Canada's Tariff Structure." *Canadian Journal of Economics* 9 (May 1976):278-300.

―――. *Multinational Enterprise and Economic Analysis.* Cambridge: Cambridge University Press, 1982.

Centre pour le Développement Horlogére (CPDH). *Bilan des Activités du CPDH depuis 1982 et Propositions pour un Nouveau Program à Moyen Terme.* Paris: CPDH, 1985.

―――. *Rapport sur l'Horlogerie Française.* Paris: CPDH, 1986.

Centre d'Etudes et de Recherche sur les Entreprises Multinationales (CEREM). *Crise, Concurrence Internationale, et Stratégies des Multinationales Françaises.* Paris: CEREM, 1981.

Chambre de Commerce. *La Concurrence Etrangère et les Importations Sauvages.* Paris: Chambre de Commerce, 1977.

Chang, Y. S. *The Transfer of Technology: The Economics of Offshore Assembly, Semiconductors.* UNITAR report no. 11. New York: United Nations, 1971.

Cheh, John. "U.S. Concessions in the Kennedy Round and Short-Run Adjustment Costs." *Journal of International Economics* 4 (1974):323-40.

Clark, Victor. *History of the Manufactures of the United States, 1893-1928.* Vol. 3. New York: McGraw-Hill, 1929.

Cline, William. "Exports of Manufactures from Developing Countries." Brookings Institution, February 1982. Typescript.

―――, ed. *Trade Policy in the 1980's.* Washington, D.C.: Institute for International Economics, 1983.

Cline, William; Kawanabe, Noboru; Kronsjo, T.O.M.; and Williams, Thomas. *Trade Negotiations in the Tokyo Round: A Quantitative Assessment.* Washington, D.C.: Brookings Institution, 1978.

Cohen, Stephen D. *The Making of U.S. International Economic Policy.* New York: Praeger, 1977.

Cohen, Stephen S. "Informed Bewilderment: French Economic Strategy and the Crisis." In *France in a Troubled World Economy*, pp. 21-48. *See* Cohen and Gourevitch 1982.

―――. *Modern Capitalist Planning.* Berkeley: University of California Press, 1977.

Cohen, Stephen S., and Gourevitch, Peter, eds. *France in a Troubled World Economy.* London: Butterworths, 1982.

Committee to Preserve the American Color TV Industry (COMPACT). *Petition to the U.S. ITC for Import Relief.* Washington, D.C.: COMPACT, September 1976.

The Competitive Status of the U.S. Machine Tool Industry. Washington, D.C.: National Academy Press, 1983.

Cooper, Richard. *The Economics of Interdependence.* New York: McGraw-Hill, 1968.

Corden, W. M. "The Costs and Consequences of Protection: A Survey of Empirical Work." In *International Trade and Finance: Frontiers in Research*, ed. Peter Kenen. Cambridge: Cambridge University Press, 1975.

Corden, W. M. *The Theory of Protection.* Oxford: Oxford University Press, 1971.

Crane, Rhonda. *The Politics of International Standards.* Norwood, N.J.: ABLEX Co., 1979.

CREI. *L'Industrie en France.* Paris: CREI, 1983.

Crozier, Michel. *The Bureaucratic Phenomenon.* Chicago: University of Chicago Press, 1964.

Curzon Price, Victoria. *Industrial Policies in the EC.* London: St. Martin's, 1981.

Cyert, Richard, and March, James. *A Behavioral Theory of the Firm.* Englewood Cliffs, N.J.: Prentice-Hall, 1963.

DAFSA. *Electronique Grand Public.* Paris: DAFSA, 1983.

———. *L'Industrie de la Chaussure en Europe.* Paris: DAFSA, March 1979.

———. *L'Industrie de la Chaussure en France.* Paris: DAFSA, 1976.

———. *L'Industrie Horlogère.* Paris: DAFSA, 1978.

———. *L'Industrie Mondiale des Appareil de Radio, Télévision, et Electroacoustique.* Paris: DAFSA, 1978.

———. *L'Industrie Mondiale des Pneumatiques.* Paris: DAFSA, 1980.

———. *L'Industrie Mondiale de la Pharmacie: Structure et Stratégies.* Paris: DAFSA, 1981.

———. *L'Industrie des Téléviseurs en Europe.* Paris: DAFSA, 1975.

———. *L'Industrie du Verre dans le Monde.* Paris: DAFSA, 1976.

———. *L'Industrie du Verre dans le Monde.* Paris: DAFSA, 1981.

David, François. *Le Commerce International à la Derive.* Paris: Calmann-Lévy, 1982.

De Meza, David. "Commercial Policy toward Multinational Monopolies." *Oxford Economic Papers* 31 (July 1979):334-37.

De Rosa, Dean; Finger, J. Michael; Golub, Stephen; and Nye, William. "What the 'Zenith Case' Might Have Meant." *Journal of World Trade Law* 13 (January-February 1979):47-54.

de Tocqueville, Alexis. *Democracy in America.* Trans. J. P. Mayer. New York: Doubleday, 1969.

Destler, I. M. *American Trade Politics: System under Stress.* Washington, D.C.: Institute for International Economics, 1986.

———. *Making Foreign Economic Policy.* Washington, D.C.: Brookings Institution, 1980.

Destler, I. M., and Odell, John. *Anti-Protection: Changing Forces in United States Trade Politics.* Washington, D.C.: Institute for International Economics, 1987.

Dixit, Avinash. "International Trade Policies for Oligopolistic Industries." *Economic Journal* 94 (supplement 1984):1-16.

Dunn, Robert. *American Foreign Investments.* New York: Viking Press, 1926.

Dunning, John. *American Investments in British Manufacturing Industry.* London: Allen, Unwin, 1958.

Eastman Kodak. *29th Annual Report.* New York: Kodak, 1929.

Eaton, Jonathan, and Grossman, Gene. "Optimal Trade and Industrial Policy under Oligopoly." *Quarterly Journal of Economics* 101 (May 1986):383-406.

Electronic Industries Association (EIA). *Electronics and International Competition.* Washington, D.C.: EIA, 1978.

Esty, Daniel, and Caves, Richard. "Market Structure and Political Influence." *Economic Inquiry* 21 (January 1983):24-38.

European Community (EC). *The Community's Pharmaceutical Industry.* Brussels: EC, 1985.

————. *The Consumer Electronics Industry.* Brussels: EC, 1985.

————. *Etude sur l'Industrie de l'Electronique Grand Public en Europe.* Brussels: EC, 1978.

————. *Investigation by the Commission of the EC of Imports of Quartz Watches.* Brussels: EC, February 9, 1984.

————. "Official List of Anti-Dumping and Anti-Subsidy Complaints." Brussels: EC, 1981.

————. *Rapport de la Commission de la CE sur les Négociations Multilaterales, Bilan par Secteur.* Brussels: EC, 1979.

————. Commission. *Etude sur l'Evolution de la Concentration dans l'Industrie des Pneus en France.* Brussels: EC, August 1977.

————. Commission. *1st Annual Report of the Commission of the EC on the EC's Anti-Dumping and Anti-Subsidy Activities.* Brussels: EC, 1983.

————. Commission. *2nd Annual Report of the Commission of the EC on the EC's Anti-Dumping and Anti-Subsidy Activities.* Brussels: EC, 1984.

European Confederation of Footwear Industries (ECFI). *Sectoral Study of the European Footwear Industry.* Brussels: ECFI, November 13, 1978.

————. *The Situation of the European Footwear Industry.* Brussels: ECFI, 1983.

European Management Forum (EMF). *Report on International Industrial Competitiveness, 1984.* Geneva: EMF Foundation, 1984.

European Research Associates (ERA). *EEC Protectionism.* Brussels: ERA, 1982.

Evans, Peter; Rueschemeyer, Dieter; and Skocpol, Theda, eds. *Bringing the State Back In.* Cambridge: Cambridge University Press, 1986.

Federal Trade Commission (FTC). *A Report on the Fertilizer Industry.* Washington, D.C.: GPO, 1916.

————. *A Report of the FTC on the Fertilizer Industry.* Washington, D.C.: GPO, 1950.

Fédération Nationale de l'Industrie Chaussure Française (FNICF). *Chaussures de France.* Paris: FNICF, September 1984.

Feigenbaum, Harvey. *The Politics of Public Enterprise: Oil and the French State.* Princeton: Princeton University Press, 1985.

Feldstein, Martin, ed. *The American Economy in Transition.* Chicago: NBER, 1980.

Ferguson, Thomas. "From Normalcy to New Deal." *International Organization* 38 (Winter 1984):40-94.

Finger, J. Michael; Hall, H. Keith; and Nelson, Douglas. "The Political Economy of Administered Protection." *American Economic Review* 72 (June 1982):425-66.

Flamm, Kenneth. *Targeting the Computer.* Washington, D.C.: Brookings Institution, 1987.

Fong, Glenn. "Export Dependence and the New Protectionism." Ph.D. dissertation, Cornell University, 1982.

Footwear Industries of America (FIA). *Petition for Relief from Imports of Nonrubber Footwear under Section 201 of the Trade Act of 1974.* Washington, D.C.: FIA, January 23, 1984.

Fourier, Jean-Marie. "Développement d'une Entreprise à Vocation Internationale." *Humanité et Entreprise*, no. 106 (December 1977):41-52.

Frost and Sullivan. *The U.S. Watch Market.* New York: Frost and Sullivan, 1978.

Gallarotti, Giulio. "Toward a Business Cycle Model of Tariffs." *International Organization* 39 (Winter 1985):155-87.

Garcia, Alain. "Les Instruments de la Politique Française du Commerce Extérieur." *Notes et Etudes Documentaires*, nos. 4404-4405, September 2, 1977, pp. 14-19.

George, Alexander L. "Case Studies and Theory Development: The Method of Structured, Focused Comparison." In *Diplomacy: New Approaches in History, Theory, and Policy*, ed. Paul G. Gordon. New York: Free Press, 1979.

Gibb, George. *The Saco-Lowell Shops.* New York: Russell & Russell, 1950.

Giersch, Herbert, ed. *On the Economics of Intra-firm Trade.* Tubingen: Mohr, 1979.

Gilpin, Robert. *U.S. Power and the Multinational Corporation.* New York: Basic Books, 1975.

————. *War and Change in World Politics.* Cambridge: Cambridge University Press, 1981.

Giordano, Yvonne. "Analyse de la Politique Française du Commerce Extérieur depuis le VIem Plan." Ph.D. dissertation, University of Nice, 1982.

Giordano, Yvonne. "Analyse de la Politique Française du Commerce Extérieur depuis le VIem Plan." *Revue d'Economie Industrielle*, no. 29 (3rd trim., 1984).

Glover, John, and Cornell, William, eds. *The Development of American Industries.* New York: Prentice-Hall, 1932.

Goldstein, Judith. "The Political Economy of Trade." *American Political Science Review* 80 (March 1986):161-84.

————. "A Reexamination of American Commercial Policy." Ph.D. dissertation, University of California, Los Angeles, 1983.

Gourevitch, Peter. "Breaking with Orthodoxy." *International Organization* 38 (Winter 1984):95-130.

————. "International Trade, Domestic Coalitions, and Liberty." *Journal of Interdisciplinary History* 8 (Autumn 1977):281-313.

————. *Politics in Hard Times.* Ithaca: Cornell University Press, 1986.

Groupe Ecole Supérieure de Commerce de Paris (ESCP). "Le Développement International des Groupes Français." *Cahiers d'Etudes et de Recherche*, no. 82-30 (October 1982).

Grubel, Herbert. *International Economics.* Homewood, Ill.: Irwin, 1977.

Grunwald, Joseph, and Flamm, Kenneth. *The Global Factory: Foreign Assembly in International Trade.* Washington, D.C.: Brookings Institution, 1985.

Guido, Robert, and Morrone, Michael. "The Michelin Decision." *Law and Policy in International Business* 6 (Winter 1974):237-266.

Gutfleich, Ronald. "Why Protection? U.S. Corporate and State Responses to a Changing World Economy." Ph.D. dissertation, University of California, Berkeley, 1987.

Guthrie, John. *The Newprint Paper Industry.* Cambridge: Harvard University Press, 1941.

Hager, Wolfgang. "Little Europe, Wider Europe, and Western Economic Cooperation." *Journal of Common Market Studies* 21 (September-December 1982):171-97.

——. "Protectionism and Autonomy." *International Affairs* 58 (Summer 1982):413-28.

Haggard, Stephan. "The Institutional Foundations of Hegemony: Explaining the RTAA of 1934." *International Organization* 42 (Winter 1988):91-120.

Haight, Frank. *The History of French Commercial Policies.* New York: Macmillan, 1941.

Hall, Peter. *Governing the Economy: The Politics of State Intervention in Britain and France.* New York: Oxford University Press, 1986.

Hall, Peter; McCormick, Janice; and Scott, Bruce. "France Enters the 1980s." Case no. 380-202, Harvard Business School, 1980.

Hall, Robert, and Hitch, Charles. "Price Theory and Business Behavior." *Oxford Economic Papers* 2 (May 1939):12-45.

Hanreider, Wolfram, and Auton, Graeme. *The Foreign Policies of West Germany, France, and Britain.* Englewood Cliffs, N.J.: Prentice-Hall, 1980.

Hawkins, Robert, and Walter, Ingo, eds. *The U.S. and International Markets: Commercial Policy Options in an Age of Controls.* Lexington, Mass.: Heath, 1972.

Haynes, William. *The American Chemical Industry: A History.* Vols. 4, 5, 6. New York: Van Nostrand, 1948, 1949, 1954.

Helleiner, Gerald K. "The Political Economy of Canada's Tariff Structure: An Alternative Model." *Canadian Journal of Economics* 4 (May 1977):318-26.

——. "Transnational Corporations and Trade Structure." In *On the Economics of Intra-Firm Trade. See* Giersch 1979.

——. "Transnational Enterprise and the New Political Economy of U.S. Trade Policy." *Oxford Economic Papers* 29 (March 1977):102-116.

Helleiner, Gerald K.; Junz, Helen; and Franko, Lawrence. *Protectionism or Industrial Adjustment.* Paris: Atlantic Institute, 1980.

Helleiner, Gerald K., and Lavergne, Réal. "Intra-firm Trade and Industrial Exports to the U.S." *Oxford Bulletin of Economics and Statistics* 41 (November 1979):297-312.

Henahan, John. *200 Years of American Chemicals.* New York: McGraw-Hill, 1976.

Hennart, Jean-François. "The Political Economy of Comparative Growth Rates: The Case of France." In *The Political Economy of Growth*, ed. Dennis Mueller, pp. 197-201. New Haven: Yale University Press, 1983.

Hine, Robert. *The Political Economy of European Trade*. Brighton, U.K.: Wheat-sheaf, 1985.

Hirschman, Albert. *National Power and the Structure of Foreign Trade*. Berkeley: University of California Press, 1945.

Hoffmann, Stanley, ed. *In Search of France*. Cambridge: Harvard University Press, 1963.

Houdaille Industries. "Petition to the President of the United States through the Office of the U.S. Trade Representative for the Exercise of Presidential Discretion Authorized by Section 103 of the Revenue Act of 1971." May 1982.

Hughes, Katherine. *Corporate Responses to Declining Rates of Growth*. Lexington, Mass.: Lexington Books, 1982.

Hughes, Kent. *Trade, Taxes, and Transnationals*. New York: Praeger, 1979.

Ikenberry, G. John. "The Irony of State Strength: Comparative Responses to the Oil Shocks of the 1970s." *International Organization* 40 (Winter 1986):105-138.

Institut Nationale de Statistiques et d'Etudes Economiques (INSEE). *Annuaire Statistique de la France*. Paris: Documentation Française, 1983.

——. *Les Comptes de l'Industrie: Situation en 1979*. Paris: Documentation Française, 1980.

Institut de Recherche et d'Information Socio-économique (IRIS). *Restructuration de l'Appareil Productif Français*. Paris: Documentation Française, 1976.

Isaacs, Asher. *International Trade: Tariff and Commercial Policies*. Chicago: Irwin, 1948.

Jemain, Alain. *Michelin: Un Siècle des Sécrets*. Paris: Calmann-Lévy, 1982.

Jenkins, Reese. *Images and Enterprise*. Baltimore: Johns Hopkins University Press, 1975.

——. "Technology and the Market: Eastman and the Origins of Mass Amateur Photography." *Technology and Culture* 16 (January 1975):1-19.

Jeremy, David. "Innovation in American Textile Technology during the Early Nineteenth Century." *Technology and Culture* 14 (January 1973):40-76.

Joly, Dominique. "La Régime Française du Contrôle du Commerce Extérieur." Ph.D. dissertation, Dijon, 1975.

Jones, Joseph. *Tariff Retaliation: Repercussions of the Smoot-Hawley Bill*. Philadelphia: University of Pennsylvania Press, 1934.

Kahler, Miles. "European Protectionism in Theory and Practice." *World Politics* 37 (July 1985):475-502.

Katzenstein, Peter, ed. *Between Power and Plenty: Foreign Economic Politics of Advanced Industrial States*. Madison: University of Wisconsin Press, 1978.

Kelly, William, ed. *Studies in U.S. Commercial Policy*. Chapel Hill: University of North Carolina Press, 1963.

Kelman, Steven. *Regulating America, Regulating Sweden*. Cambridge: MIT Press, 1981.

Keohane, Robert. *After Hegemony: Cooperation and Discord in the World Political Economy*. Princeton: Princeton University Press, 1984.

————. "The Theory of Hegemonic Stability and Changes in International Economic Regimes." In *Change in the International System*, ed. Ole R. Holsti, Randolph M. Siverson, and Alexander L. George, pp. 131-62. Boulder, Colo.: Westview, 1980.

Keohane, Robert, and Nye, Joseph. *Power and Interdependence: World Politics in Transition*. Boston: Little, Brown, 1977.

Kierzkowski, Henry, ed. *Monopolistic Competition and International Trade*. Oxford: Oxford University Press, 1984.

Kindleberger, Charles. "Dominance and Leadership in the International Economy." *International Studies Quarterly* 25 (June 1981):242-54.

————. *The World in Depression, 1929-39*. Berkeley: University of California Press, 1973.

Kindleberger, Charles, and Lindert, Peter. *International Economics*. 6th ed. Homewood, Ill.: Irwin, 1978.

Kolodziej, Edward A. *French International Policy under De Gaulle and Pompidou*. Ithaca: Cornell University Press, 1974.

Krasner, Stephen. *Defending the National Interest*. Princeton: Princeton University Press, 1978.

————. "State Power and the Structure of International Trade." *World Politics* 28 (April 1976):317-47.

————. "The Tokyo Round: Particularistic Interests and Prospects for Stability in the Global Trading System." *International Studies Quarterly* 23 (December 1979):491-531.

————. "U.S. Commercial and Monetary Policy." In *Between Power and Plenty*. *See* Katzenstein 1978.

————, ed. "International Regimes." *International Organization* 36 (Spring 1982).

Kronholz, June. "Trade and Currency Wars Deepen the Depression." *Wall Street Journal*, October 23, 1979, p. 1.

Krueger, Anne. "Political Economy of the Rent-Seeking Society." *American Economic Review* 64 (1974):291-303.

Krugman, Paul, ed. *Strategic Trade Policy and the New International Economics*. Cambridge: MIT Press, 1986.

Kuisel, Richard. *Capitalism and the State in Modern France*. Cambridge: Cambridge University Press, 1981.

Lake, David. "Beneath the Commerce of Nations." *International Studies Quarterly* 28 (June 1984):143-70.

————. "International Economic Structures and American Foreign Economic Policy." *World Politics* 35 (July 1983):517-43.

————. "Structure and Strategy: The International Sources of American Trade Policy, 1887-1939." Ph.D. dissertation, Cornell University, 1983.

Landes, David. *Revolution in Time*. Cambridge: Harvard University Press, 1984.

Lavergne, Réal. *The Political Economy of U.S. Tariffs: An Empirical Analysis*. Toronto: Academic Press, 1983.

League of Nations. *Economic Fluctuations in the U.S. and U.K., 1918-1942*. Geneva: League of Nations, 1942.

Lenway, Stephanie. *The Politics of U.S. International Trade*. Boston: Pitman, 1985.

Lewis, Cleona. *America's Stake in International Investments*. Washington, D.C.: Brookings Institution, 1938.

Lewis, W. Arthur. *Economic Survey, 1919-1939*. London: Allen, Unwin, 1949.

Liepmann, H. *Tariff Levels and the Economic Unity of Europe*. New York: Macmillan, 1938.

Lindblom, Charles. *Politics and Markets*. New York: Basic Books, 1977.

Lipietz, Alain. "The Globalization of the General Crisis of Fordism." SNID Occasional Paper no. 84-203, 1984.

Lipsey, Robert. *Price and Quantity Trends in the Foreign Trade of the United States*. Princeton: Princeton University Press, 1963.

Lipson, Charles. "The Transformation of Trade." *International Organization* 36 (Spring 1982):417-56.

Machin, Howard, and Wright, Vincent, eds. *Economic Policy and Policy-Making under the Mitterrand Presidency, 1981-84*. New York: St. Martin's Press, 1985.

Madison, Christopher. "The Troubled U.S. Footwear Industry Is Kicking for Relief from Imports." *National Journal*, February 5, 1983, pp. 283-85.

Mahon, Rianne, and Mytelka, Lynne. "Industry, the State, and the New Protectionism." *International Organization* 37 (Autumn 1983):551-82.

Malmgren, Harald. "Coming Trade Wars?" *Foreign Policy*, no. 1 (Winter 1970):115-43.

Markham, Jesse. *The Fertilizer Industry: Study of an Imperfect Market*. 1958. Reprint. New York: Greenwood Press, 1969.

Marshall, Herbert; Southard, Frank; and Taylor, Kenneth. *Canadian-American Industry*. New Haven: Yale University Press, 1936.

McKeown, Timothy. "Firms and Tariff Regime Change: Explaining the Demand for Protection." *World Politics* 36 (January 1984):215-33.

Messerlin, Patrick. "Bureaucracies and the Political Economy of Protection: Reflections of a Continental European." *World Bank Staff Working Paper*, no. 568, 1983.

Michalet, Charles-Albert. "France." In *Big Business and the State. See* Vernon 1974.

———, ed. *L'Intégration de l'Economie Française dans l'Economie Mondiale*. Paris: Economica, 1984.

Mille, Christian. "Evolution de la Branche Verre Plat en France et en Europe." Ph.D. dissertation, Université de Paris I, 1981.

Millstein, James. "Decline in an Expanding Industry: Japanese Competition in Color TV's." In *American Industry in International Competition*, pp. 106-141. *See* Zysman and Tyson 1983.

Milner, Helen. "Resisting the Protectionist Temptation: Industry and Trade

Politics in the U.S. and France in the 1920s and the 1970s." Ph.D. dissertation, Harvard University, 1986.

Milner, Helen, and Yoffie, David. "Between Free Trade and Protectionism: Strategic Trade Policy and a Theory of Corporate Preferences," APSA paper, August 1987.

Ministère de l'Economie, la DREE. *Une Décennie du Commerce Extérieur Français.* Paris: Documentation Française, November 1983.

Ministère de l'Industrie. *Les Chiffres Clés de l'Industrie, 1984.* Paris: Documentation Française, 1985.

——. *Note d'Information*, no. 66. Paris: Ministère de l'Industrie, September 13, 1977.

Moody's. *Moody's Manual of Industrial Securities: 1927.* New York: Moody's, 1927.

——. *Moody's Manual of Industrial Securities: 1975.* New York: Moody's, 1975.

Moore, Charles. *Timing a Century: History of Waltham Watch Company.* Cambridge: Harvard University Press, 1945.

Moretti, Christian. "Les Restructurations Industrielles en Europe: Le Cas de l'Electronique Grand Public." ESCP research series, *Cahiers d'Etudes et de Recherche*, no. 81-16, 1981.

Morici, Peter, and Megna, Laura. *U.S. Economic Policies Affecting Industrial Trade: A Quantitative Assessment.* Washington, D.C.: National Planning Association, 1983.

Morse, Edward. *Modernization and the Transformation of International Relations.* New York: Free Press, 1976.

"Les Multinationales." *Cahiers Français*, no. 190. Paris: Documentation Française, March-April 1979.

Murphy, John. "Entrepreneurship in the Establishment of the American Clock Industry." *Journal of Economic History* 26 (June 1966):169-86.

Mutti, John, and Bale, Malcolm. "Output and Employment in a 'Trade Sensitive' Sector: Adjustment in the U.S. Footwear Industry." *Weltwirtschaftliches Archivs* 117 (1981):352-66.

Mytelka, Lynne. "In Search of a Partner." In *France in a Troubled World Economy.* *See* Cohen and Gourevitch 1982.

National Archives (N.A.). Bureau of Foreign and Domestic Commerce (BFDC) files. Record Group 151. "Trade Representatives," memos of BFDC on Trade Representatives—E. Kodak, 1929.

——. U.S. Tariff Commission (USTC) files. "Docket Files of Investigations under Section 315, 316, 317," "Investigation of Phosphates and Superphosphates," 1932.

——. USTC files. Record Group 81. "Applications and Investigations," Investigation of Cameras, 1922.

——. USTC files. Record Group 81. "Applications and Investigations," Investigations of Clocks and Parts, 1922.

——. USTC files. Record Group 81. "Applications and Investigations," Investigation of Hosiery Machinery, no. 446, 1925.

National Archives (N.A.). USTC files. Record Group 81. "Applications and Investigations," Investigation of Motion-Picture Film, no. 347, 1924.

———. USTC files. Record Group 81. "Applications and Investigations," "Investigations of Para. 80—potash," application nos. 539 and 542-A, 1927.

———. USTC files. Record Group 81. "Applications and Investigations," Investigation of Woolen Cards, no. 388, 1924.

———. USTC files. Record Group 81. "Applications and Investigations," Investigation of Wool Goods, 1923.

———. USTC files. Record Group 81. "Applications and Investigations," 3 investigations: Worsted Yarns, Wool Wearing Apparel, nos. 392 and 464, 1925.

———. USTC files. Record Group 81. "Tariff Information Surveys," Survey of Knitting Machinery, 1920.

———. USTC files. Record Group 81. "Tariff Information Survey," Survey of Watches and Clocks, 1920.

———. USTC files. Record Group 81. "Tariff Information Surveys," 3 surveys: Wool/Yarns, Wool Cloths, Wool Wearing Apparel, 1920.

———. USTC files. Record Group 81. "Tariff Information Surveys," "Tariff Info Catalog: Photographic Goods," 1920.

National Bureau of Economic Research (NBER). *Industrial Profits in the U.S.* By Ralph Epstein. New York: NBER, 1934.

National Industrial Conference Board (NICB). *Trends in the Foreign Trade of the U.S.* New York: NICB, 1930.

National Institute of Economic and Social Research (NIESR). *Trade Regulations and Commercial Policy in the U.K.* Cambridge: Cambridge University Press, 1943.

National Machine Tool Builders' Association (NMTBA). *Economic Handbook of the Machine Tool Industry.* Washington, D.C.: NMTBA, 1982.

Navin, Thomas. *The Whitin Machine Works since 1931.* New York: Russell & Russell, 1950.

Nordlinger, Eric. *On the Autonomy of the Democratic State.* Cambridge: Harvard University Press, 1981.

O'Connor, Harvey. *The Guggenheims.* New York: Covici Friede, 1937.

Odell, John. *U.S. International Monetary Policy: Markets, Power, and Ideas as Sources of Change.* Princeton: Princeton University Press, 1982.

Office of Technology Assessment (OTA). *International Competitiveness in Electronics.* Washington, D.C.: GPO, November 1983.

Oman, Ralph. "The Clandestine Negotiations of Voluntary Restraints on Shoes from Italy." *Cornell International Law Journal* 6, no. 7 (1974):6-19.

Organization for Economic Cooperation and Development (OECD). *The Footwear Industry.* Paris: OECD, 1976.

———. *Selected Industrial Policy Instruments.* Paris: OECD, 1978.

———. *Technical Change and Economic Policy: The Machine Tool Industry.* Paris: OECD, 1980.

Oye, Kenneth. "Cooperation under Anarchy." *World Politics* 38 (October 1985).

Parlement Européen. *Rapport du Parlement Européen.* By E. Romagnoli. Strasbourg: Parlement Européen, November 1981.

Pastor, Robert. *Congress and the Politics of U.S. Foreign Economic Policy.* Berkeley: University of California Press, 1980.

Phelps, Dudley. *The Migration of U.S. Industry to South America.* New York: McGraw-Hill, 1936.

Pincus, Jonathan. *Pressure Groups and Politics in Antebellum Tariffs.* New York: Columbia University Press, 1977.

Piore, Michael, and Sabel, Charles. *The Second Industrial Divide: Prospects for Prosperity.* New York: Basic Books, 1984.

Pisani, Edgar. *Enjeux et Conditions des Equilibres Extérieurs de la France.* French Senate Report 31, part 2. 1978.

Pollard, Robert. *Economic Security and the Origins of the Cold War.* New York: Columbia University Press, 1985.

Porter, Roger. *Presidential Decision-Making: The Economic Policy Board.* Cambridge: Cambridge University Press, 1980.

Pugel, Thomas, and Walter, Ingo. "U.S. Corporate Interests and the Political Economy of Trade Policy." *Review of Economics and Statistics* 67 (1985):465-73.

Rapport de la Commission Industrie. 7th Plan, 1976. Paris: Documentation Française, 1976.

Ratner, Sidney. *The Tariff in American History.* New York: Van Nostrand, 1972.

Ratner, Sidney; Soltow, James; and Sylla, Richard. *The Evolution of the American Economy.* New York: Basic Books, 1979.

Ray, Edward. "The Determinants of Tariff and Nontariff Trade Restrictions in the U.S." *Journal of Political Economy* 91 (February 1981):105-121.

————. "Tariff and Nontariff Barriers to Trade in the United States and Abroad." *Review of Economics and Statistics* 63 (May 1981):161-68.

Reich, Robert. "Beyond Free Trade." *Foreign Affairs* 61 (Spring 1983).

Report of the President's Commission on Industrial Competitiveness. *Global Competition: The New Reality.* Washington, D.C.: GPO, 1985.

Riedel, James. "Tariff Concessions in the Kennedy Round and Structure of Protection in West Germany." *Journal of International Economics* 7 (1977):133-43.

Ruggie, John. "International Regimes, Transactions, and Change." *International Organization* 36 (Spring 1982):379-415.

Russett, Bruce. "The Mysterious Case of Vanishing Hegemony." *International Organization* 39 (Spring 1985):207-231.

Russett, Bruce, and Hanson, Elizabeth. *Interest and Ideology: The Foreign Policy Beliefs of American Businessmen.* San Francisco: W. H. Freeman and Company, 1975.

Safarian, A. E. *Foreign Ownership of Canadian Industry.* Toronto: McGraw-Hill, 1966.

St. Gobain-Pont-à-Mousson. *Annual Report, 1984.* Paris: St. Gobain, 1984.

Savary, Julien. "Les Multinationales Françaises." *Economie et Humanisme,* no. 257 (January-February 1981):69-84.

———. *Les Multinationales Françaises.* Paris: Presses Universitaires Françaises, 1981.

Schattschneider, E. E. *Politics, Pressures and the Tariff.* Englewood Cliffs, N.J.: Prentice-Hall, 1935.

Semiconductor Industry Association (SIA). *The Effect of Government Targeting on the World Semiconductor Competition.* Cupertino, Calif.: SIA, 1983.

———. *The International Microelectronics Challenge.* Cupertino, Calif.: SIA, 1981.

Sergent, Patrick. "L'Industrie Verriére Française de 1962 à 1971." Thesis, Fondation Nationale des Sciences Politiques, Paris, October 1973.

Shepard, Geoffrey; Duchêne, François; and Saunders, Christopher, eds. *Europe's Industries: Public and Private Strategies for Change.* Ithaca: Cornell University Press, 1983.

Shonfield, Andrew. *Modern Capitalism.* New York: Oxford University Press, 1965.

Sigvard, Jacqueline. *L'Industrie du Médicament.* Paris: Calmann-Lévy, 1975.

SIMAVELEC. *L'Electronique Grand Public Français en 1983-84.* Paris: SIMAVELEC, 1985.

Simon, Herbert. "Theories of Decision-making in Economics and Behavioral Science." *American Economic Review* 49 (June 1959):253-83.

Simonnot, Phillipe. *Les Nucléocrats.* Grenoble: Presses Universitaires de Grenoble, 1978.

Singh, Rana. *Transnational Corporations in the International Semiconductor Industry.* New York: United Nations, 1983.

Snidal, Duncan. "Coordination versus Prisoners' Dilemma." *American Political Science Review* 79 (December 1985):923-42.

———. "The Limits of Hegemonic Stability Theory." *International Organization* 39 (Autumn 1985):579-614.

Southard, Frank. *American Industry in Europe.* Boston: Houghton Mifflin, 1931.

Southworth, Constant. "The Newsprint Paper Industry and the Tariff." *Journal of Political Economy* 30 (1922):681-97.

Spencer, Barbara, and Brander, James. "International R&D Rivalry and Industrial Strategy." *Review of Economic Studies* 50 (1983):707-722.

Stevenson, Louis. *The Background and Economics of American Paper Making.* New York: Harper & Bros., 1940.

STISI. *Les Entreprises Moyennes dans l'Industrie.* Paris: Documentation Française, 1976.

Stoffaës, Christian. *La Grande Menace Industrielle.* Paris: Calmann-Lévy, 1978.

———. "La Politique Industrielle." Vol. 1, Cours aux Sciences Politiques. Paris: Fondation Nationale des Sciences Politiques, 1980.

Stoleru, Lionel. *L'Impératif Industriel.* Paris: Seuil, 1969.

Strange, Susan. "Protectionism and World Politics." *International Organization* 39 (Spring 1985):233-60.

———. "Still an Extraordinary Power." In *Political Economy of International and Domestic Monetary Relations*, ed. Raymond Lombra and Willard Witte. Ames: Iowa State University, 1982.

Strange, Susan, and Tooze, Roger, eds. *The International Politics of Surplus Capacity*. London: Butterworths, 1980.

Suleiman, Ezra. *Elites in French Society*. Princeton: Princeton University Press, 1978.

———. *Politics, Power, and Bureaucracy in France*. Princeton: Princeton University Press, 1974.

Syndicat National de l'Industrie Pharmaceutique (SNIP). *Dossier Economique*. Paris: SNIP, 1985.

———. *L'Industrie Pharmaceutique et Ses Réalités*. Paris: SNIP, 1982.

Szenberg, Michael; Lombardi, John; and Lee, Eric. *The Welfare Effects of Trade Restrictions: A Case Study of the U.S. Footwear Industry*. New York: Academic Press, 1977.

Takacs, Wendy. "Pressures for Protection: An Empirical Study." *Economic Inquiry* 19 (1981):687-93.

Taussig, Frank. *The Tariff History of the U.S.* 8th ed. New York: Putnam & Sons, 1931.

Tilton, John. *The International Diffusion of Technology: The Case of Semiconductors*. Washington, D.C.: Brookings Institution, 1971.

United Nations. *Le Contrôle des Pratiques Commerciales Restrictives dans la CEE*. New York: United Nations, 1977.

U.S. Bureau of the Census. *See* U.S. Department of Commerce. Bureau of the Census.

U.S. Bureau of Foreign and Domestic Commerce (BFDC). *The American Chemical Industry*. Trade Promotion Series no. 78. Washington, D.C.: GPO, 1929.

———. *American Direct Investments in Foreign Countries*. Trade Info Bulletin no. 731. Washington, D.C.: GPO, 1930.

———. *Fertilizers: Some New Factors in Fertilizer Production and Trade*. Trade Info Bulletin no. 372. Washington, D.C.: GPO, 1925.

———. *Foreign Commerce and Navigation of the United States*, various issues. Washington, D.C.: GPO, 1920s.

U.S. Congress. House. *Effects of Agricultural Depressions on the Fertilizer Industry*. 67th Cong., 1st sess., 1922. H. Doc. no. 195.

———. Judiciary Committee. *Study of Monopoly Power: Newsprint Paper Industry*. 81st Cong., 2nd sess., 1950. Serial 14.

———. Judiciary Committee. *Study of Monopoly Power: Newsprint Paper Industry*. 82nd Cong., 1st sess., 1951. H. Rept. 505, pt. 1.

———. Ways and Means Committee. *Comparison of Tariff Acts of 1913, 1922, 1930*. Washington, D.C.: GPO, 1930.

———. Ways and Means Committee. *Competitive Factors Influencing World Trade in Semiconductors*. Hearings, 96th Cong., 1st sess., November 30, 1979.

U.S. Congress. Ways and Means Committee. *General Tariff Revision of 1921.* Hearings, 67th Cong., 1st sess., 1921.

———. Ways and Means Committee. *Tariff Readjustment—1929.* Hearings, 70th Cong., 2nd sess., 1929.

———. Ways and Means Committee. *Trade Reform.* Hearings, 93rd Cong., 1st sess., 1973.

———. Ways and Means Committee. Subcommittee on Trade. *Causes and Consequences of the U.S. Trade Deficit and Developing Problems in U.S. Exports.* Hearings, 95th Cong., 1st sess., 1977.

U.S. Congress. Senate. *American Branch Factories Abroad.* 71st Cong., 3rd sess., 1931. S. Doc. 258.

———. *American Branch Factories Abroad.* 73rd Cong., 2nd sess., 1933. S. Doc. 120.

———. *FTC Report on the Fertilizer Industry.* 67th Cong., 4th sess., 1923, S. Doc. 347.

———. *FTC Report on the Newsprint Paper Industry.* 71st Cong., spec. sess., 1930. S. Doc. 214.

———. Finance Committee. *Emergency Tariff.* Hearings, 66th Cong., 3rd sess., 1921.

———. Finance Committee. *Tariff Act of 1921.* Hearings, 67th Cong., 2nd sess., 1921.

———. Finance Committee. *Tariff Act of 1929.* Hearings, 71st Cong., 1st sess., 1929.

———. Finance Committee. Subcommittee on International Trade. *Multinational Corporations.* 93rd Cong., 1st sess., February 1973.

———. Finance Committee. Subcommittee on International Trade. *Private Advisory Committee Reports on the Tokyo Round of the MTN.* Hearings, 96th Cong., 1st sess., August 1979.

———. Finance Committee. Subcommittee on International Trade. *The Use of 'Low Labor' Components in the Insular Possessions' Watch Industry,* 95th Cong., 2nd sess., August 21, 1978.

U.S. Department of Commerce. *American Direct Investments in Foreign Countries.* Trade Info Bulletin no. 731. Washington, D.C.: GPO, 1930.

———. *Concentration Ratios in Manufacturing.* Washington, D.C.: GPO, 1977.

———. *1972 Enterprise Statistics.* Washington, D.C.: GPO, 1977.

———. *1977 Enterprise Statistics.* Washington, D.C.: GPO, 1981.

———. *A Report on the U.S. Semiconductor Industry.* Washington, D.C.: Commerce Department, 1979.

———. *Survey of Current Business,* various issues. Washington, D.C.: GPO, 1919-1930.

———. *U.S. Commodity Exports and Imports as Related to Output, 1976/75.* Washington, D.C.: GPO, 1979.

———. *U.S. Commodity Exports and Imports as Related to Output, 1977/76.* Washington, D.C.: GPO, 1982.

———. *U.S. Direct Investment Abroad.* Washington, D.C.: GPO, various years.

———. Bureau of the Census. *Annual Survey of Manufactures*. Washington, D.C.: GPO, 1970s, various years.

———. Bureau of the Census. *Census of Manufactures*. Washington, D.C.: GPO, 1970s, various issues.

———. Bureau of the Census. *Census of Manufactures, 1929*. Washington, D.C.: GPO, 1930.

———. Bureau of the Census. *Historical Statistics of the U.S., Colonial Times to the Present*. Washington, D.C.: GPO, 1975.

———. Internal Revenue Service (IRS). *Statistics of Income—1974-78, International Income and Taxes, U.S. Corporations and Their Controlled Foreign Corporations*. Washington, D.C.: GPO, 1981.

———. International Trade Administration (ITA). *An Assessment of the Competitiveness in U.S. High Technology Industries*. Washington, D.C.: GPO, February 1983.

U.S. International Trade Commission (ITC). *Bicycle Tires and Tubes*. Investigation no. TA-201-33, pub. no. 910. September 1978.

———. *Color TV Receivers and Parts*. Pub. no. 1067. May 1980.

———. *Color TV Receivers and Parts*. Pub. no. 1068. May 1980.

———. *Competitive Assessment of the Metal-Working Machine Tool Industry*. Investigation no. 332-149, pub. no. 1428. September 1983.

———. *Competitive Factors Influencing World Trade in Integrated Circuits*. Investigation no. 332-102, pub. no. 1013. November 1979.

———. *Economic Factors Affecting the Use of Items 807.00 and 806.30 of the Tariff Schedules of the U.S.* Pub. no. 339. September 1970.

———. *The Effectiveness of Escape Clause Relief in Promoting Adjustment to Import Competition*. Pub. no. 1229. March 1982.

———. *Footwear Investigation*. Investigation no. TA-201-7, pub. no. 758. February 1976.

———. *Footwear Investigation*. Investigation no. TA-201-18, pub. no. 799. February 1977.

———. *Import Trends in TSUS Items 806.30 and 807.00*. Pub. no. 1029. January 1980.

———. *Investigation of Televisions*. Investigation no. 337-TA-23. January 1976.

———. *Protection in Major Trading Countries*. Pub. no. 737. August 1975.

———. *Report on Watches and Parts*. Investigation no. 332-80. May 1977. *In* U.S. Congress, House, Ways and Means Committee, *Report on Watches and Parts* (H.R. 14600), May 30, 1977, print.

———. *A Summary of Trade and Tariff Information: Semiconductors*. Pub. no. 841. July 1982.

———. *Tariff Items 806.30 and 807.00, U.S. Imports for Consumption, Specified Years, 1966-79*. Misc. pub. June 1980.

———. *Television Receivers, Color and Monochrome*. Pub. no. 808. March 1977.

U.S. Tariff Commission (USTC). *5th Annual Report of the U.S. Tariff Commission*. Washington, D.C.: GPO, 1921.

U.S. Tariff Commission (USTC). *14th Annual Report of the U.S. Tariff Commission*. Washington, D.C.: GPO, 1930.

————. *Trade Barriers: An Overview*. Pub. no. 665. Washington, D.C.: GPO, 1974.

————. *12th Annual Report of the U.S. Tariff Commission, 1928*. Washington, D.C.: GPO, 1928.

Vernon, Raymond. "International Trade Policy in the 1980s." *International Studies Quarterly* 26 (December 1982):483-510.

————. *Sovereignty at Bay*. New York: Basic Books, 1971.

————, ed. *Big Business and the State*. Cambridge: Harvard University Press, 1974.

Vogel, David. *National Styles of Regulation*. Ithaca: Cornell University Press, 1986.

Wagoner, Harless. *The U.S. Machine Tool Industry from 1900 to 1950*. Cambridge: MIT Press, 1968.

Waltz, Kenneth. *Theory of World Politics*. Reading, Mass.: Addison-Wesley, 1979.

Warshow, Herman T., ed. *Representative Industries in the U.S.* New York: Holt & Co., 1928.

Webbink, Douglas. *The Semiconductor Industry: A Survey of Structure, Conduct, and Performance*. Washington, D.C.: FTC, 1977.

Weeks, Lyman. *A History of Paper Making in the U.S., 1690-1916*. New York: Lockwood Trade Journal Co., 1916.

Wilkins, Mira. *The Emergence of Multinational Enterprise*. Cambridge: Harvard University Press, 1970.

————. *The Maturing of Multinational Enterprise*. Cambridge: Harvard University Press, 1974.

Wilson, Joan H. *American Business and Foreign Policy, 1920-33*. Boston: Beacon, 1971.

Wilson, Robert; Ashton, P.; and Egan, T. *Innovation, Competition, and Government Policy in the Semiconductor Industry*. Charles River Associates' study. Lexington, Mass.: Lexington Books, 1980.

Winham, Gilbert. "Robert Strauss, the MTN, and the Control of Faction." *Journal of World Trade Law* 14 (September-October 1980):377-97.

Winkler, Max. *Investments of U.S. Capital in Latin America*. Boston: World Peace Foundation, 1928.

Wright, Chester. *Wool-Growing and the Tariff*. Cambridge: Harvard University Press, 1910.

Wright, Vincent. "Politics and Administration under the French Fifth Republic." *Political Studies* 22 (March 1974):44-65.

Yoffie, David. "Adjustment in the Footwear Industry." In *American Industry in International Competition. See* Zysman and Tyson 1983.

————. *Power and Protectionism*. New York: Columbia University Press, 1983.

————. "Zenith Radio Corporation vs. the U.S." Case no. 0-383-070, Harvard Business School, 1982, pp. 1-23.

Zysman, John. "The French State in the International Economy." In *Between Power and Plenty*, pp. 255-94. *See* Katzenstein 1978.

———. *Governments, Markets, and Growth*. Ithaca: Cornell University Press, 1983.

Zysman, John, and Tyson, Laura, eds. *American Industry in International Competition*. Ithaca: Cornell University Press, 1983.